14,50

THE MIDDLE EAST ON THE EVE OF MODERNITY
Aleppo in the Eighteenth Century

A STUDY OF THE MIDDLE EAST INSTITUTE

A view of Aleppo in the mid-eighteenth century.

From A. Drummond, *Travels Through Different Cities . . . and Several Parts of Asia.* London, 1754. Courtesy of the Harry Ransom Humanities Research Center, the University of Texas at Austin.

The Middle East
on the Eve of Modernity

ALEPPO IN THE EIGHTEENTH CENTURY

ABRAHAM MARCUS

COLUMBIA UNIVERSITY PRESS
NEW YORK

Columbia University Press
New York   Oxford
Copyright © 1989 Columbia University Press
All rights reserved

Library of Congress Cataloging-in-Publication Data

Marcus, Abraham.
The Middle East on the eve of modernity: Aleppo in
the eighteenth century / Abraham Marcus.
p.   cm.
"A Study of the Middle East Institute."
Bibliography: p.
Includes index.
ISBN 0-231-06594-9
1. Aleppo (Syria)—Civilization.
I. Columbia University. Middle East Institute.
II. Title.
DS99.A56M37   1989
956.91'3—dc19
88-36599
CIP

Book design by Jennifer Dossin
Printed in the United States of America

c 10 9 8 7 6 5 4 3 2

To my parents and parents-in-law

Contents

Illustrations

Illustrations

FIGURES

TABLES

Preface

THIS BOOK IS the fruit of several years of research and reflection on one Middle Eastern community and on the nature of premodern society in the region as a whole. It represents an attempt, by way of a case study, to address systematically a set of important yet inadequately explored issues in Middle Eastern history, and to move scholarship in the field closer to an informed composite portrait of that society often identified as "premodern," "Islamic," and "traditional," as it was during the last century before the onset of modernization. Using a broad conceptual framework and fresh information drawn largely from local archives, the work undertakes an in-depth exploration of a complex world whose social history is still in its infancy.

I wrote the book in the hope of contributing to the scholarship in the fields of Middle Eastern, Arab, and Ottoman studies, and of helping to integrate the region into the mainstream of historical research by addressing questions of interest to scholars working in more advanced areas of history as well as to those engaged in cross-cultural comparative studies of past societies. I was also guided by the desire to make available a work which would prove useful as a classroom introduction to the society and culture of the region on the eve of modernization. Those of us who teach courses on the modern Middle East still lack a text in English which gives beginning students a vivid sense of the "traditional" society, without which it is all the more difficult to appreciate the meaning of the great changes and dislocations experienced by the region in the course of the last two centuries. The standard textbooks in the field seldom go beyond some brief and often inaccurate generalities about social and economic life in the period before modernization. A detailed historical sketch focused on one eighteenth-century society can, I believe, serve as a useful supplement to more general texts in courses on the modern as well as premodern periods. In its presentation the work is attentive to the needs of students lacking a close familiarity with the field. It assumes no prior knowledge of Aleppo and the region, and attempts to provide a readable narration uncluttered by foreign terms and technical usages more readily accessible to the specialist.

In the course of writing this book I received invaluable help and encouragement from friends, colleagues, and family. I owe a special debt of gratitude to Richard Bulliet, who inspired my enthusiasm for social history, helped me launch this study, and gave me guidance and support over the years. I am grateful to him for countless generosities, among them the grant toward the publication of this book made by the Middle East Institute at Columbia University. The former director of the Institute, J. C. Hurewitz, was helpful in various ways, and has my appreciation.

At the University of Texas my colleague Richard Graham took an interest in my work, made useful comments on an early draft of the manuscript, and helped me on many occasions with an unfailing friendship; he, and Sandra Lauderdale-Graham, have my deepest gratitude. Dean Robert King provided me with helpful support, for which I am most grateful. I would also like to express my appreciation to Standish Meacham, who as my departmental chairman gave me his useful support on various occasions. Abazar Sepehri, the Middle East librarian at the university, acquired numerous Arabic and Turkish works at my request and made his services available to me with unflagging good cheer; I thank him for his assistance. A grant from the National Endowment for the Humanities helped to finance some of my research.

Helpful comments were made on an early draft of the manuscript by a reader whose anonymity it is a convention to maintain, and who has my appreciation. I am also grateful to Kate Wittenberg of Columbia University Press for her help and patience, and to the editorial staff for its professional assistance.

Finally, I would like to thank my wife, Rina, who helped me immeasurably with her love, patience, and good advice. She as well as our children, Leon and Julia, bore stoically Aleppo's extended invasion of their family life.

THE MIDDLE EAST ON THE EVE OF MODERNITY
Aleppo in the Eighteenth Century

Introduction

THE MODERN AGE in the Middle East began, as the history books
tell us, at the turn of the nineteenth century. It was then that
the region, with its venerable civilization, started to move on a
different course, adopting new ways and institutions while shedding off
long-held practices and beliefs. An unprecedented movement of reform,
led by government, expanded in the course of the century into more
and more areas of life. This process of change, which is commonly
known as modernization or Westernization, did not grow organically
from within the Middle East. The stimulus came from outside, from
the pressures posed by the encounter with the more powerful and
aggressive Europe. Disastrous Ottoman defeats on the European front
in the late eighteenth century shook the leadership in Istanbul into the
painful realization that the balance of power had tipped definitely in
favor of Europe. The lesson sank in deeper when Napoleon's army
easily captured the province of Egypt in 1798. Alarmed by the mounting European threat, rulers in the region moved to shore up their
defenses by reorganizing their armies, administrations, and societies
along Western models, now seen as the proven paths to success. With
their sponsorship, and independently of it, Europe penetrated the region as never before. European ideas, manners, advisers, investors,
goods, capital, armies, and diplomatic intervention now shaped increasingly the world of Middle Easterners.

The dual processes of modernization and European penetration dominate the historiography of the nineteenth century. Indeed, they have

practically come to define the very essence of the era, assuming an
exaggerated presence which overshadows other realities of the time.
The search for the new, and the explanation of its origins and effects,
stand at the forefront of most inquiries. That which is in the process of
becoming takes center stage while that which is tends to recede into the
background, a dim reality representing more mass than energy. In
intellectual history, for instance, a handful of thinkers influenced by
Western ideas have attracted the bulk of attention, leaving the wrong
impression that traditional thought, still pervasive, was either gone or
no longer worthy of study. This orientation toward the new, replicated
in other areas as well, tends in turn to inflate the role ascribed to Europe
in Middle Eastern life. Directly or indirectly, it is Europe that figures in
the historiography as the moving force behind developments in the
region, serving as a kind of master key to which explanation and interpretation often lead almost instinctively. European ideas, economic interests, political pressures, and military force appear as the immediate
or underlying causes of the important events in a region now perceived
as revolving in Europe's orbit and being acted upon by outside forces
beyond its control.

Set against this backdrop of an era of change in the shadow of
Europe, the Middle East of the eighteenth century must appear of
necessity as a different world. Europe was absent as a force of real
moment in its life, and so also were the modernizing changes it set in
motion in the nineteenth century. Images of a contrast between the two
periods spring to mind easily. Lying across from nineteenth-century
society, on the other side of the historical divide marking the beginning
of modernity, appears a society commonly labeled "premodern," "traditional," and "Islamic," whose basic realities seem quite unlike those
associated with its modern counterpart. If one society was opening up,
the one which preceded it was still closed and intact; if one was seeking
to rejuvenate itself, the other was sunk in weakness and decline; if one
was acquiring the complex and advanced institutions of the modern
world, the other was still simple and unsophisticated in its structures; if
one was undergoing major change which undermined its past heritage,
the other was static and traditional; if one was taking on a familiar
facade by adopting Western ways, the other was culturally alien and
different.

These images of eighteenth-century society as a closed, alien, backward, static, and simple world must be questioned if they are based
merely on an impressionistic glance backwards guided by the assump-

tion of a necessary polarity. Such an approach evaluates the premodern society from the perspectives and experiences associated with another age rather than on its own terms. It also draws too sharp and artificial a contrast between two centuries which shared much in common, glossing over the fact that the nineteenth century saw much continuity and that even at its close some geographical areas, aspects of life, and social groups were still largely untouched by the currents of modernization. And it yields broad generalities which, even if they were accurate, would tell us little in themselves about the actual workings and realities of eighteenth-century society.

A more informed understanding of that world must be pursued in other ways. The search for it forms the broad purpose of this book. The historical literature into which such an inquiry leads promises no easy answers. There is no comprehensive synthesis of the period, nor does the range of studies needed for such a synthesis exist. The coverage of the different localities and themes is highly uneven. Many aspects of social, economic, and cultural history remain unstudied and obscure. The basic groundwork needs to be done even on the great urban centers, let alone the rural world. A city like Aleppo illustrates well this rudimentary state of knowledge. A major Arab metropolis whose sizable population of over 100,000 people ranked it as the third largest settlement in the region after Istanbul and Cairo, the administrative capital of an important Ottoman province extending over most of northern Syria, and a renowned center of textile manufacturing and East-West trade, Aleppo has figured more prominently in historical writing than most other places. Yet the overall research on its society in the eighteenth century (and in most other periods as well) adds up to a limited output highly uneven in its coverage. Many spheres of life remain poorly known. One is hard pressed, for instance, to find much or any detailed empirical work on family life, health conditions, medicine, death, pastimes, popular culture, literacy, education, women, children, the trade guilds, market organization, charity, poor relief, subsistence crises, social stratification, the legal system, crime, judicial practice, neighborhood life, or the workings of communal institutions. Even those areas which have attracted research, notably politics, administration, the European trade, aspects of the economy, the religious minorities, and urban issues, still contain many gaps.

With so much in the dark it is difficult not only to answer many specific questions about Aleppo's society, but also to arrive at a more comprehensive historical vision of the place from which larger conclusions can be drawn. Making informed generalizations about larger issues like the culture, economy, stratification, power, Islam, conflict, social relations, and change would require a better grasp of realities in various areas of behavior and thought than that which exists presently. A similar state of affairs appears in one community after another, indicating just how far we are from an integrated social history of the Middle East grounded in systematic research and sensitive to the variations between places and the changes over time. Terms like "traditional," "premodern," and "Islamic," commonly applied to Middle Eastern communities in different periods of history, are clearly not self-explanatory. They have to be filled with precise meaning according to time and place.

This is the historical problem with which the present study is concerned. Using eighteenth-century Aleppo as a specimen, the book reconstructs the world of a Middle Eastern society on the eve of modernization. It seeks to fill in the main gaps in the city's history, to capture its way of life and experiences, and to illuminate the forces which shaped its realities and dynamics in the course of an eventful century. The study is confined to one Middle Eastern community, but underlying it is a concern with substantive and methodological issues central to our understanding of society in the region as a whole. The questions it addresses, the conceptual framework and methodology it proposes, the assumptions it challenges, and the sources it uses all have a relevance to the history of other communities in the area, which shared much in common with Aleppo.

At the outset Aleppo presents a society which resembled in its basic features contemporary urban communities in other parts of the world. Its social landscape was composed of a highly differentiated population dominated by a thin elite of wealth and status. An authoritarian government with a rudimentary bureaucracy and few social responsibilities ruled over it, upholding the elaborate body of laws and institutions which guided behavior in many areas of life. Political life revolved largely around the pursuit of material benefits by factions and power figures whose competition spilled occasionally into violence. Trade and small-scale artisanal manufacturing subject to detailed market regulation formed the mainstay of the urban economy, with various types of investment and property offering additional sources of income. Periodic slumps, famines, and epidemics as well as an unyielding condition of high mortality were normal features of the times. The culture combined a tradition of high learning and the orally transmitted mental baggage of the illiterate majority, with religion occupying a central place in the local world of thought and belief. A functional physical environment and a network of communal institutions served the daily needs of a population proud of its hometown and convinced of the superiority of urban life. Intense face-to-face contacts and limited personal privacy, evident especially at the level of neighborhood life, placed their distinct mark on the texture of social relations.

This bare and static outline gives little sense of how Aleppo's society actually worked, and of the particular dramas and experiences which shaped the lives of its residents in the eighteenth century. Using a thematic rather than a chronological approach, the study sets out to fill the skeleton with life by exploring systematically the larger setting of the community, its social structure, political and legal systems, economic life, culture, health conditions, and urban environment. Each of these presents a context or slice of life which tells something important about Aleppo's world. Our aim is to scrutinize them with an eye to drawing out and explaining several levels of thought and experience: the ideals, values, beliefs, norms, attitudes, and tastes of the townspeople; how their institutions worked in practice; their processes of decision making and control; the material conditions in which they lived; their characteristic patterns of relations and social conflict; and the changes they experienced in the course of the century. The focus is not confined to the rich and powerful, who tend to attract the bulk of attention. Ordinary people, women, and non-Muslims figure prominently in the story. Differences of class, sex, and religious affiliation mattered in this society, and accounted for marked differences in behavior and experience which ought to be integrated into our understanding of the times.

By undertaking an inquiry of this broad scope the book attempts to arrive at a fuller understanding of many specific aspects of Aleppo's society, to establish a more vivid sense of the meaning for the residents of work, fun, money, government, family, health, politics, charity, status, taxes, education, neighborhood, ethnicity, marriage, religion, hometown, poverty, death, morals, investment, authority, revolt, urban space, famine, justice, sex, slavery, architecture, property, law, plague, patronage, medicine, homeownership, security, travel, food, clothes, privacy, and order. The broad context also helps to see the intricate links among these particulars, which in a sense formed a single web of meaning.

Through this story runs a concern with the issue of stability and change. Both processes figured in Aleppo's history, their interplay appearing in configurations which differed with the sphere of life and the period. The city was certainly not a calm and sleepy place. Its residents lived through periodic plagues, subsistence crises, economic fluctuations, and turnovers of provincial administrations. These developments, built into the routine rhythms of their society, subjected them to uncertainties, social tensions, misery, and other unsettling effects. In addition to this cyclical pattern, the community experienced a marked change in conditions between the first and second half of the century. In the last three or four decades of the century it sank into a long period of crisis, experiencing a decline of economic prosperity, a sharp rise in the cost of living, a deterioration of public order, factional violence in the streets, large-scale extortion, revolts against governors, and the waning of Ottoman authority. This unusual combination of troubles, which brought to the surface aspects of the community not readily visible in the earlier period, originated at least partly in external developments, including the Ottoman preoccupation with exhausting wars, unfavorable shifts in European trade patterns, and problems in the agricultural countryside. Independently of this unhappy conjuncture, Aleppo also witnessed various long-term changes of a less dramatic although not negligible sort, such as an increase in personal precaution against the plague and the spread of Catholicism among the Christians.

A closer examination of this process of change—its pace, direction, causes, and effects—as it appeared in different areas can help to answer questions about the dynamics of premodern society. So also can a corresponding attention to the striking continuity which governed many basic aspects of the community despite the upheavals. Change did not penetrate or alter radically the fundamental values and beliefs, the basic social institutions, the premises of the political system, the social stratification, the structure of the economy, the demographic regime, or the appearance of the urban landscape. This stability ought not to be taken for granted; it too calls for explanation. We cannot simply assume that behind it lay inertia, or universal satisfaction with everything, or society's blind march to the drumbeat of tradition. Continuity in many areas was maintained by active effort and investment on the part of those with a stake in the existing arrangements, and hence involved a historical process which deserves to be examined alongside the process of change.

The clues about stability, change, and the general patterns of Aleppo's history lead very often outside the confines of the city. Aleppo was in several essential respects part of a larger world and sensitive to its rhythms. As an Ottoman territory, it was subject to the system of rule, policies, and fortunes of an empire dominated from the sultan's seat in Istanbul. It participated in the regional and European economies through various types of exchange and appropriation, drawing food, raw materials, tax revenues, and profits from these external associations. The currents of migration in the region shaped the size and social makeup of its population, and elaborate social ties linked the residents to people in other places. Culturally too, Aleppo was part of a wider zone with shared ways, and open to the ideas flowing within it. More exposed to European contacts than most other places in the Middle East, it was affected in the eighteenth century by Western consuls and missionaries who cultivated local followings among the non-Muslims.

The book examines the conditions and developments in the city with this larger context in mind. It assesses the role of the Ottoman, regional, and European connections in local history, and explores several issues of interest in the study of the Middle East in general: the nature of Ottoman rule as experienced by a provincial population; the meaning and effects of Ottoman "decline"; the complex of urban-rural relations and the geographical scope of the city's functional hinterland; the integration of the city into the European economic system; the extent of Western penetration and influence before the onset of modernization; and the world beyond the city as it figured at the level of local knowledge and consciousness.

The road to the larger generalizations and insights about Aleppo's society leads through a lot of historical spadework. With so much still unexplored, the inquiry into many topics must start from scratch. An inordinate amount of effort and space must be devoted to establishing the basic facts and laying out fresh evidence unavailable in the secondary literature before working up to the larger arguments. In approaching the tasks of establishing, explaining and interpreting the historical facts, the book follows a set of methodological guidelines aimed at enriching the inquiry while avoiding certain flawed approaches current in the literature.

A strictly empirical orientation appears as the first imperative, especially in a field in which the absence of a large pool of evidence often allows untested assumptions to substitute for documented fact. Two questionable ways of arriving at facts have been particularly common: using ideals and formal laws, which are usually easier to establish, to infer the actual realities; and applying the conditions observed in one segment of the population, especially the better known upper class, to society as a whole. From this kind of approach various generalizations appear to have emerged about the premodern society, including the notions that polygamy was widespread, that households were extended in form, that economic competition was stifled by the guild system, and that families lived in conditions of protected domestic privacy. One also reads often that the residential neighborhoods in the premodern cities were inhabited by members of the same social group, an observation usually inferred from the names of the quarters rather than a survey of their composition. All these generalizations can be made about Aleppo by using the same types of historical reasoning; yet they prove inaccurate when examined empirically. Poverty and other constraints deprived many people of access to cherished ideals; laws were abused; and old names often lost their original relevance. The discrepancies between ideals and realities, and the variations in the realities of different groups, need to be pursued rather than ignored if a more accurate and dynamic sense of society is to be reached.

The book's concern with an empirical approach is coupled with an attentiveness to the intricacies of explanation. What lay behind certain conditions and why people behaved as they did are questions which run through the study, and often suggest more than a simple line of causation. Many of the clues can be found in the culture of the community. Its norms, attitudes, ideals, and understanding of nature help to explain behavior and conditions, and deserve close attention. At play, however, were also political, economic, demographic, and climatic factors, acts of violence and accidents, all of which had a hand in shaping historical events. The task of explanation needs to be approached with an eye to the role of these various possible forces, especially in a field with a long tradition of seeking explanations in the culture, or more precisely, in Islam.

The cliché that "Islam is a total way of life," heard even in descriptions of the present-day Middle East, encapsulates a prevailing perception of the Islamic religious-cultural system as the chief force molding conditions and behavior in all areas. Taking this construct literally as the key to explanation is problematic and misleading. It ascribes to Islam an all-encompassing power it did not really exercise; many rules, desires, attitudes, and practices developed outside the Islamic fold, in areas ranging from the economy and administration to material culture and social relations. The cultural determinism it promotes narrows the field of explanation to exclude relevant factors. Far from being a settled matter, the role of Islam in premodern society still needs to be defined accurately. The study examines it empirically in every sphere to arrive at a fuller sense of its relative weight. Since we commonly refer to the premodern Middle East as an "Islamic society," we ought to know what was Islamic about it rather than allow the term to take on maximal or speculative meanings.

The methodological route to a clearer view of Islam's role and other important questions lies in broadening the conceptual framework within which various issues in Middle Eastern history have conventionally been examined and interpreted. The discussion of culture in the region, for instance, focuses most commonly on the world of high learning and on the related sphere of Islamic thought and tradition. This approach opens up rich areas which are central to our understanding of the culture, but which cannot be taken as the sum total of the cultural scene without doing injustice to the contemporary mind. It ignores, for example, the pursuit of fun, entertainment, music, company, and fashion which absorbed people, and the store of superstitions and oral wisdom they carried in their heads and used routinely in order to make sense of their world and guide their conduct. Without these and other layers of popular culture we are apt to cast the mindset of individuals in oversimplified terms, and to miss the richness and inner dissonances of the premodern culture.

The book treats the popular and nonreligious elements as parts of Aleppo's culture, in the interest of a fuller appreciation of the cultural scene, of the place of Islam in it, and of the mental world of the townspeople. On similar grounds, it broadens the discussion of other topics commonly given to partial treatment. The examination of the law extends beyond the Islamic code to include the large body of non-Islamic legislation. In the discussion of spiritual life, popular religion figures alongside the orthodox practices, which by themselves tell only part of the story. The examination of medicine deals with the popular healers as well as the learned physicians; both are essential to illuminating the medical scene. In all these areas the non-Islamic and popular elements enrich our understanding of the scene in ways which argue against treating them prejudicially as something marginal, entirely distinct or just unworthy of scholarly attention.

The bulk of the material needed to address the issues raised in the book had to be drawn from primary sources. The body of contemporary writings and records on the city is voluminous, although somewhat uneven in its coverage. Some types of useful information are scarce or entirely unavailable. One must work without any compiled serial figures on incomes, prices, interest rates, unemployment, charitable contribu-

tions, school attendance, literacy, crime, births, deaths, marriages, population, household sizes, immigration or emigration, and without any
systematic records from which precise quantitative data in these areas
can be obtained. The premodern Ottoman state simply did not concern
itself with this kind of record keeping. The absence of printing and the
widespread illiteracy also set limits on the written output of the period.
Songs, music, stories, plays, and jokes were passed on orally without
being committed to paper, as were also professional skills and practical
knowledge in various areas from cooking and childrearing to investment
and etiquette. The writing of social studies or commentaries on contemporary conditions did not attract local authors, and newspapers were
unknown. Missing too are diaries, memoirs, autobiographies, personal
correspondence, and other writings which reveal more intimate feelings
and experiences. These gaps limit our ability to penetrate certain arenas,
to establish precise orders of magnitude, and to detect the more subtle
changes in attitudes, sensibilities, and social conditions. The personal
relations between husbands and wives, or between parents and children,
for example, remain hidden, and even the size of the city's population,
let alone the demographic trends over the century, cannot be determined with certainty.

The problems posed by missing or poor data are offset in good
measure by the mass and variety of information that does exist. Official
documents, chronicles, biographies of distinguished figures, poetry,
popular lore, Christian church records, Jewish rabbinical writings, the
archives of the European consulates and merchant communities, and
accounts by foreign travelers and residents are all available, and provide
between them a good body of material on different groups and spheres
of life. The backbone of information for this study, however, comes
from one particular indigenous source: the records of the city's *shari'a*
(Islamic law) court (Sijill al-mahkama al-shar'iyya). Large parts of the
book would have been impossible to write without this source; some
sections, as the notes indicate, rely almost entirely on material drawn
from it. These records make up an incomparable repository of information covering no single subject or group. The institution which produced them was at once the main court for adjudicating civil and
criminal disputes, a notarial office in which the townspeople drew up
deeds and contracts, and a busy administrative agency which handled
all sorts of official business in the city and province. Thousands of men
and women from all walks of life visited it every year to register business
and settle litigation touching on various matters, including loans and

credit, sales of houses and other real estate, property rights, commercial dealings, marriage payments, divorce, child custody and support, inheritance, family trusts, market and guild regulations, water supply, appointments to public office, charitable endowments, business partnerships, conversion to Islam, communal institutions, official abuses, taxation, construction, crime, and public morals. Scribes of the court entered a formal description of each case, written in Arabic or Turkish, in the official court registers.

The material in the Sijill appears initially like a hodgepodge of unrelated matters thrown together chronologically without regard to any topical order, each usually dealing with some minor concern of no apparent significance in the grand scheme of things. But it is precisely the raw and individualized quality of the information, coupled with its abundance and view from the inside, which makes the court records unusually valuable as a historical source. Through concrete stories and events recorded contemporaneously by locals, the material gives a vivid sense of how society actually worked, of the pursuits, practices, strategies, conflicts and accidents which wove the texture of daily life. Women and ordinary people, who barely figure in most other sources, appear on virtually every page of the records. With a sufficiently large body of cases in hand it is possible to draw larger patterns out of the bits and pieces of detail. The book draws on the records for a quarter of a century (1746–1771), which include over 50,000 cases, using them in a variety of ways for quantitative analysis and historical reconstruction. The potential of the Sijill is of relevance to research in the field in general. The development of Middle Eastern social history will depend in good measure on the creative use of this source, which is available for many parts of the Ottoman Empire.

Steeping ourselves in these writings of the period and striving to get a feel for the place and time can achieve a closer understanding of the history, but not a wholly faithful and final account of it. It bears remembering that the source material on eighteenth-century Aleppo recounts in its totality no more than a tiny fraction of what took place. As in other past societies, most of the historical information was never recorded at all. The surviving residues open to view only parts of the city's past. Sometimes they reveal just enough to set us guessing and wondering, but without allowing us to know things for sure.

Our ability to recapture that bygone age fully is limited still further by its remoteness in time and ways. We cannot visit it, experience its events, or use empirical observation and experiment to verify the contemporary accounts, which are surely not free of error and bias. Eighteenth-century Aleppo is a world now vanished and unknowable at first hand. Its past exists only in the form of the surviving evidence. What we see when looking at this evidence is inevitably filtered through present-day mental lenses. However immersed in it, we cannot divest ourselves of the knowledge and assumptions we carry, or avoid the biases these create in the impressions we absorb and the understanding we reach. The explanations and interpretations we pursue are framed in current modes of thought and discourse. These can provide much insight into the past, but that past remains in some ways contingent on our own perspective and present.

This portrait of Aleppo is therefore a historical approximation, a rough interpretive sketch seeking to capture as closely and faithfully as possible the world of an important eighteenth-century community. The place and time in which the account is set have a broader relevance. As part of a larger society and culture, Aleppo shared much in common with other Syrian, Arab, and Middle Eastern cities. Although certainly not identical with them in every detail and experience, it offers a model representative of their structure and way of life in the eighteenth century. That time period, lying on the edge of the great divide between the premodern and modern eras, carries particular importance in Middle Eastern history. It presents a final snapshot of that world before it was set on a new course and steadily overtaken by the irreversible sweep of modernization. A good sense of that premodern scene, important in its own right, helps also to render the subsequent history more intelligible. What the new pressures and changes have meant for Middle Easterners can be appreciated best when viewed against the kind of society in which they appeared. The world of the premodern era has not lost its relevance for the present. Throughout the region old ways survive alongside the new, undissolved by modernization. There is, indeed, an active yearning by many for an ideal society associated with the premodern era. Most clearly visible in the movements of Islamic fundamentalism, it expresses the persisting weight of the past and its power to stir nostalgic visions and social action.

CHAPTER I

The Place: Setting and Local Consciousness

S OME SEVENTY MILES from the northern Syrian shores of the Mediterranean, in a spot neither lush nor barren, stood the city of Halab, or Aleppo, as it was most commonly known on the maps and tongues of Europeans. Viewed against the shabby villages, small towns, and tribal encampments that dotted the surrounding landscape in the eighteenth century, the place presented a splendid prospect. It lay perched among the hills, a massive and closely packed multitude of stone buildings. The ancient citadel, situated a hundred-odd feet above its surroundings on top of a steep mound, dominated the skyline. Around this symbol of Ottoman imperial authority the city stretched out on every side, its uniformly low structures interrupted occasionally by slender minarets which highlighted the Islamic character of the place. The entire stone facade radiated that dull, aged hue which caused Aleppo to be known as the Gray City (al-Shahba').

A large body of Arabic-speaking people, numbering perhaps one hundred to one hundred and twenty thousand, inhabited the city in the eighteenth century.[1] Most of them were Muslims, who shared the place with some twenty thousand Christians and three to four thousand Jews. The size of its population alone distinguished Aleppo as one of the great urban centers of the Middle East. A prominent metropolis, it was a center of business and learning, a renowned station of regional and East-West trade, and, since its incorporation into the Ottoman Empire in 1516, the administrative capital of a sizable province extending over much of northern Syria.

Syrian, Arab, Middle Eastern, Islamic, Ottoman—Aleppo of the eighteenth century was all of these. The labels capture facets of its character and point to those larger territorial units and groupings of which it was part. Two contexts within this setting figured most prominently in the life of the community: the Ottoman Empire, and the surrounding region, including both the immediate hinterland and the larger Middle Eastern area. The realities of the city were affected by the institutional arrangements of the empire, the policies of its leaders, and the level of internal stability and safety from external threats; by the fortunes of agriculture in the countryside and the patterns of regional trade; by the security of the roads; by the currents of migration into the city and out of it; and by the larger cultural and social trends. The annals of the empire and the region in the eighteenth century are filled with stories of fierce power struggles in the provinces, bloody wars on the frontiers, severe shortages of food, business slumps, the desertion of villages, tribal defiance, and pillage on the roads. These distant dramas reverberated in Aleppo.

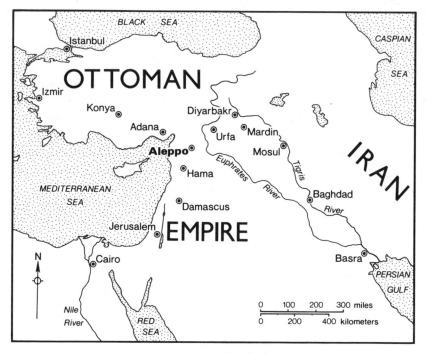

FIGURE 1.1. *Aleppo in its Middle Eastern setting*

For the townspeople many of the developments of the period followed patterns familiar from earlier times. Their city was part of a state and society that remained very much set in their ways. The same Ottoman regime, now into its fifth century of rule, continued to govern. A profoundly conservative state now past its heyday, it continued to uphold its traditional vision of order. In the Middle Eastern region no major transformations altered the pattern of settlement, the social makeup of the population, the modes of livelihood, the technology, or the world of thought and belief. The diversity of religions, ethnic groups, languages, dialects, customs, and local particularisms remained a feature of the social landscape. This was not a conquering, expanding world of warriors and pioneers. The land and society were old, chastened, and full of solemn memories. And yet the generations of the eighteenth century did not live through a mere replica of the preceding period. The state and region experienced some long-term shifts which left a distinct imprint on the times. Among the most profound changes was the weakening of Ottoman power domestically and internationally; this alone set in motion various internal changes that by the beginning of the nineteenth century steered the Middle East into a new era.

For better or worse, Aleppo participated in the life of this larger milieu, responded to its rhythms, and had much in common with it. In some respects, however, it remained distinct, with local particularisms and experiences that set it apart from other places. The residents, not unlike their counterparts in other urban centers in the region, tended to stress and exaggerate the uniqueness of their town. They insisted on its distinctness and superiority, expressed pride in its accomplishments, and felt certain attachments to it. In their minds the city possessed an existence of its own, separate in both real and imagined ways from the world around it. Facts, ideals, and prejudices reinforced in them a local consciousness that colored their perceptions of the city's place in the world.

The sense of distinctness formed yet another level on which the urban community related to its larger mileu. The kind of world and age in which Aleppo of the eighteenth century was set, seen through a tour of its imperial and regional contexts, helps to understand not only these elements of local identity, but also the larger realities and developments that shaped the city's history and are essential to explaining its dynamics during an eventful century.

CITY AND EMPIRE

O N THE MAP of Ottoman territories Aleppo appeared as a mere speck. The Ottoman Empire of the eighteenth century, widely acknowledged as an attenuated image of its former self, could still claim the status of an imposing world power. Its territorial possessions, stretching across three continents, included the Balkans, Anatolia, and the Arab lands from the border of Morocco in the west to the Iranian frontier in the east. This vast and diverse world boasted a large population, a variety of abundant resources, and important international routes and waterways. The great capital of Istanbul, a bottomless pit of consumption, still displayed the pomp of an imperial nerve center which set trends in fashion and refinement and made the momentous decisions of peace and war.[2]

Aleppo, and the Arab lands in general, became part of this empire at a relatively late phase of its territorial expansion. The rise of the Ottomans from a small Turkish principality in Anatolia to a world power began as early as the thirteenth century. In the course of endless wars and conquests the Turkish warriors subjugated Anatolia, crossed over into Europe, and conquered extensive Christian territories which now came for the first time under Muslim rule. In 1453 they took Constantinople and so wiped off the world scene the venerable Byzantine Empire, which had resisted Islam since the rise of the new faith in the Middle East. The Ottoman state swallowed the imperial domains of the Byzantines and adopted their capital, emerging in a sense as a Muslim successor to Byzantium. The bulk of Ottoman territory remained European, and most of the subjects Christian, until the Ottomans turned southward in the sixteenth century and absorbed the Arab lands. The character of the empire then changed. By incorporating the old Islamic lands, the two holy cities of Islam, and millions of Muslims, the Ottomans established themselves as the foremost Islamic state in the world and the heirs to the great empires that had ruled the region since the Arab conquests. This prestigious status suited the Ottoman leadership, which liked to stress its Islamic credentials by pointing to its long and heroic struggle against the infidel.

In this far-flung and multiethnic empire internal conditions varied widely. In every territory they conquered the Ottomans encountered a settled population with its particular culture and institutions. Guided by a pragmatic approach favoring control at minimal cost, they tended to leave existing local arrangements undisturbed unless they conflicted with official interests. Ottoman rule gave the various areas a shared system of government and some common institutions, but inevitably left in place an unstandardized, eclectic mix of past legacies.

Like other localities, Aleppo came into the empire with its own historical baggage. It had been under a host of Muslim regimes since the Arab armies first appeared at its gates in A.D. 636. Hittites, Arameans, Assyrians, Persians, Greeks, and Romans had ruled it successively before that. The city's first mention under the name Halab, or some variation of it, actually went back to the twentieth century B.C., at which time the place had already had a long past behind it. The towns-people were aware that theirs was a city of very ancient origins: popular legend associated its name with the patriarch Abraham, who was re-puted to have milked (Ar. *halab*) his flocks there. The local Jews habitu-ally referred to it in their Hebrew writings by the biblical name Aram Soba, and proudly traced the origins of their community to the days of King David. The marks of the past were everywhere. Most of the mosques, monuments, and public buildings that dotted the city in the eighteenth century dated back to the pre-Ottoman period. The hundreds of inscriptions carved on them reminded the residents of their city's presence on the stage of history well before the Ottomans set foot there in 1516.[3]

From the outset the Ottomans recognized Aleppo as the foremost settlement in northern Syria and stationed in it the government of a province. This province, one of the several dozen such administrative units that made up the imperial domains, extended in the eighteenth century roughly from the Mediterranean in the west to the Euphrates river in the east, and from Ma'arrat al-Nu'man in the south to 'Ayntab in the north.[4] The formal line of authority led through the provincial administration to the central bureaucracy in Istanbul and the person of the ruler at the top. The sultans who headed the empire all came from the house of Osman, the Turkish family that led the state from its inception to its final days in the aftermath of World War I. The actual grip of the ruler over his lands varied widely among provinces and fluctuated over time, depending on the give-and-take of politics. In some areas central control was loose and tenuous, especially during the second part of the eighteenth century. For people in Aleppo the link to the center remained quite real. Delegates of the sultan, notably the pro-vincial governor, the judge, and some subordinate officials, occupied the key positions of authority in the city. They were almost invariably

Turks or Turkish-speaking members of the official class, not natives of the city.

People in Aleppo saw the Ottoman sultan as their ruler and the Ottoman Empire as their state, but they were not accustomed to speaking of themselves as Ottomans. In the political community to which they belonged the label "Ottoman" *(osmanlı)* was applied only to the officials in the service of the ruling house. The mass of subjects were not encouraged to develop a strong sense of affiliation with the state or powerful bonds of common Ottoman citizenship. The state did not expect intense demonstrations of patriotism: it did not call upon them to serve in its armies or to die for their country.

Nor did the state seek to encourage the participation of its subjects in political life and decision making. The official conception of governance, which echoed a long tradition familiar to people in Aleppo from preceding regimes, rested on a set of despotic notions: that the sultan was the

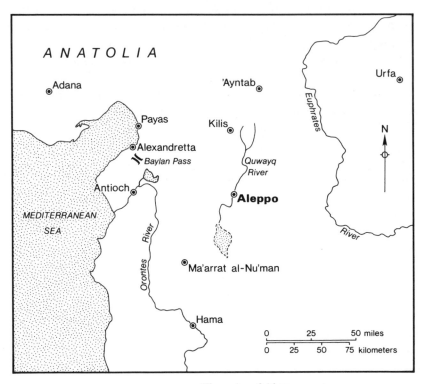

FIGURE 1.2. *The region of Aleppo*

absolute master of the realm; that the governmental apparatus was his private instrument rather than an agency for serving the public; that the subjects were entitled to security and justice in return for their obedience, but had no formal share in the exercise of power; and that the tasks of government were to remain in the exclusive hands of a ruling class clearly differentiated from the ruled. This political ideology applied a symbolically appropriate term for the ruled: *ra'aya* (flocks). Ideally, the loyalty of the subjects was to be expressed by obedience, and in more active form by devotion to the person of the ruler, not attachment to the state as a political abstraction.

The great ethnic diversity within this political community affected further the meaning of collective bonds as well as the social experiences of the population. Aleppo's townspeople counted among their fellow subjects Arabs, Turks, Greeks, Serbs, Bulgarians, Kurds, Albanians, Romanians, and a host of other peoples. With large segments of this population they had little in common, either in language, identity, custom, or historical memory. But while they belonged ethnically with the Arabic-speaking people of the region, their Arab identity was strikingly muted. Indeed, they did not speak of themselves as Arabs. The term *'arab* (or *'urban*) referred at the time only to the bedouin tribesmen, and hence carried derogatory connotations from which the settled Arabic-speaking population distanced itself.

This attenuated ethnic consciousness mirrored the work of an old cultural disposition to stress the primacy of religious identity and belittle the meaning of ethnic distinctions. For centuries Islam and Middle Eastern states had promoted the notion that religious bonds must transcend ethnic differences and link all believers in the higher community of faith. This outlook denied to ethnicity any primacy in the organization of society and effectively stripped it of political importance. That groups such as Arabs and Turks formed distinct nations and that by virtue of shared culture, language, and history each were entitled to an independent collective existence and to self-rule were ideas alien to people in Aleppo and the wider region. The fact that a non-Arab dynasty and elite ruled over an Arab population therefore excited in the townspeople no opposition to the Ottoman regime; domination by non-Arabs ruling in the name of Islam had been part of local experience even before the Ottoman conquest. The Muslim affiliation and commitments of the ruler, not his ethnic identity, determined the legitimacy of government. Only in the late nineteenth century, in the wake of European penetration and social change in the region, did Arabs in Aleppo and the wider region begin to speak with pride about an Arab nation, to criticize Turkish rule, and to demand political rights as Arabs.

As subjects of this multiethnic Ottoman state, people in Aleppo accepted pluralism and diversity as normal features of the political community. In practice, their cultural and personal contacts with non-Arabs revolved most intimately around Turks and Turkish-speaking people, and not only because of the fact of Turkish rule. Their city sat on the frontier between Arab and Turkish lands. Just a few miles to the north one began to encounter an ethnically mixed population which extended well into southern Anatolia, including cities like Kilis, 'Ayntab, Diyarbakr, Urfa, and Mardin. Turkish-speaking residents from these areas, as well as some Turkman tribesmen, were among the immigrants who settled in Aleppo during the century. The city also carried on extensive trade with Anatolia; local merchants traveled routinely to Turkish lands while Turkish businessmen visited Aleppo frequently.

These interactions took place at a time when differences between the two ethnic groups had been diluted by centuries of contact and common experiences. Islam and Ottoman rule fostered a shared world of thought and belief as well as common institutions and loyalties. The music, food, fashions, and other aspects of Aleppo's culture showed the effects of Turkish influences. Many residents, among them local merchants and government employees, acquired a knowledge of Turkish for a variety of practical reasons, and many Turkish words and expressions made their way into the local Arabic. The linguistic acculturation was mutual; the contemporary Turkish was a language heavily loaded with Arabic words and written in the Arabic script.

While the townspeople were not subject to any official pressure to adopt the Turkish language and culture, the facts of power certainly colored the cultural orientation of some local groups. The city's Muslim elite came closest to an active participation in the dual heritage of the region. More intimately allied with the state than other groups, the local men of wealth, learning, and influence were drawn into the social circles and cultural affectations of the Ottoman elite. They adopted the trappings of the high Ottoman life-style as passports to advancement. Learning the Turkish language was a natural part of their education. Their names rang proudly with Turkish titles of honor and rank—agha, effendi, chalabi. Their familial patronyms, borne like pedigrees, were sounded with the Turkish-Persian extension *Zadeh* (son) in keeping with Ottoman practice. Istanbul, the seat of power and opportunity, drew them into a non-Arab milieu.

For all this shared heritage, however, ethnic distinctions remained real in people's minds, and prejudices and stereotypic notions reinforced attention to real differences. Some sense of their force can be glimpsed from the experiences of Mahmud Effendi al-Antaki, who found himself thrust in the midst of ethnic frictions. An immigrant from the ethnically mixed city of Antioch (Antakya), he could have been of Arab or Turkish descent; his biographers were typically inattentive to this point. During the 1730s and 1740s he ranked among Aleppo's most popular professors of Muslim religious studies. To his classes flocked Arabs as well as Turkish students from Anatolia, who sat together at his feet as he delivered his material in Arabic and then repeated it in Turkish. The relations between the students were hardly harmonious, and not for difficulties of communication. The Turks looked down on the Arabs as an inferior lot with whom they would not fraternize. Distressed by their conduct, Mahmud Effendi preached incessantly for brotherhood and tolerance, evoking for the Turkish students historical and religious traditions of praise for the Arabs.[5]

More central in shaping the experiences of the townspeople in the eighteenth century and the times in which they lived were several realities of greater drama and public concern than the ethnic pluralism. This was a century in which central control was loose in many parts of the empire, especially during the last decades. It was also a period of almost constant war between the empire and its external enemies, fought with particularly heavy Ottoman losses in the last three decades. Europe became a force of increasing influence on the fortunes of the empire.

These long-term developments, visible already in earlier periods, had a profound bearing on the fortunes of state power domestically and on the international scene, which in turn affected a host of conditions in the provinces: the level of public order, the efficiency of administration, the assertiveness of local power figures, the burden of taxation, the security of the roads, the prosperity of agriculture, the patterns of trade, and the fortunes of different social groups.

The Ottoman government itself had limited success at best in dealing with internal challenges to its authority, the attacks by enemies, and the looming threat of European power. Its weaknesses only confirmed for the leadership the painful realization that the empire was past its heyday, that it had fallen from its glorious stature in the age of Süleyman the Magnificent in the mid-sixteenth century. The sense of weakness at the top, muted in times when things went relatively well, turned to outright alarm in the last three decades of the century. The empire sank to one of its lowest points, prompting the leadership to break with the past and begin the process of modernization that was to alter the face of Middle Eastern society in subsequent years. While modernization was not part of the experience of the Ottoman population in the eighteenth century, the long-term developments that led up to it certainly affected life. These developments and their rhythms reveal the major historical changes of the period, but also the remarkable durability of the Ottoman imperial structure.

The internal politics of the empire certainly put that durability to the test. Stories of uprisings, sieges, conspiracies, military expeditions, and executions fill the annals of government relations with the provinces in the eighteenth century. Istanbul was involved in a constant tug-of-war with ambitious figures and groups in the various localities. While conditions shifted, the general picture was one of widespread challenge to central authority. Almost everywhere power figures succeeded in wresting varying degrees of control from a state that appeared unable to assert its authority vigorously. Much of Anatolia was in the hands of local chieftains. In the European provinces notables built their own armies, administrations, and treasuries, establishing virtual autonomy. The North African territories followed an autonomous course as well. In Egypt the Mamluk military caste took over the country; Ottoman governors continued to be dispatched by Istanbul, only to be placed in polite imprisonment in the Cairo citadel for the duration of their tenure. Large parts of Iraq, Palestine, and Syria were ruled intermittently or continuously by vigorous dynasties and leaders resting on power bases of their own. In the last three decades of the century, when surviving the difficult wars on the front preoccupied Istanbul, central authority deteriorated at an unprecedented rate.

The Ottoman Empire of the eighteenth century was clearly not so much a centralized structure as a conglomerate of loosely held districts in which political realities were often shaped to a great extent by the will of local forces. Yet the instances of assertiveness did not represent a revolution against the Ottoman system; no territory seceded from the empire. Many of the powerful local potentates were actually men loyal to the sultan, from convenience if not from conviction. They did not stand for a new ideology or political system; indeed, they often introduced a degree of order and prosperity that won them the tacit approval of the Ottoman sultan. Their competition with the government revolved very much around access to taxes and other material resources in their localities. Through it all the state remained an important actor on the local scenes, exerting its influence on events through bribery, patronage, military pressure, and political intrigue.

The almost constant warfare on the fronts, like the internal power play, also affected the setting and circumstances in which the townspeople lived. Except for an extraordinarily long interval of peace between 1747 and 1768 the state did not enjoy even a decade free of major military encounters with enemies, and seldom saw more than five years of uninterrupted quiet between wars. The line of foes extended along the empire's European borders all the way to its Asian frontiers with Russia and Iran. The seventeenth century closed with a series of disastrous Ottoman defeats in Europe and the loss of considerable territories, including Hungary. In the first half of the eighteenth century the Ottomans succeeded by and large in meeting the military challenge of Europe. Except for a setback in 1718, they won back the Morea (1709), defeated Peter the Great (1711) and the Venetians (1715), and won concessions from the Russians and Austrians (1739). Between 1723 and 1746 they were also engaged in a series of bloody wars with Iran in which they could claim only mixed success. What vigor the Ottomans were able to display in the first part of the century seemed utterly spent when the long interlude of tranquility ended in 1768. In the succeeding three decades they fought several disastrous wars with Russia in which they suffered strategic losses of unprecedented proportions. On top of this they watched the province of Egypt in the very heart of the empire fall easily to Napoleon's army in 1798.

Aleppo was too removed from any of the battle zones to suffer direct damage; the indirect toll of the wars was nonetheless heavy. The immense defense expenditures drained the state treasury and in turn subjected the population to onerous tax demands, which excited much public resentment and protest. In addition, the long succession of wars with Iran, fought along the Iraqi front, played havoc with Aleppo's long-distance trade, which was oriented toward the lands to the east. The hostilities and the resort to economic warfare by both sides stopped the shipment of Iranian silk to the city, bringing to an end a commercial activity that had enriched the city's merchants for several centuries. The Iranian wars also exposed Aleppo to the dreaded visits of unruly Ottoman troops moving to and from the front. In December 1743, when the city was seized with anxiety at rumors of a possible march on it by the Iranian army, the French consul could pointedly note that "the people seem even more distressed by the announced arrival of the Grand Vizir and his army, which will cause the entire ruin of this land."[6]

The challenges of war were hardly unique to the eighteenth century; they had accompanied the Ottoman state without cease from its early days. Now, however, the terms of confrontation and prospects for success were shifting increasingly in favor of the empire's European adversaries. Militarily, the Ottomans did hold their own as late as the second part of the century. Their successes, however, reinforced what proved to be a false feeling of strength and assurance, and their severe losses on the battlefield in the last decades of the century exposed their military inferiority and brought home to the leadership a painful reality made increasingly evident in other spheres as well: that the balance of power had tipped definitely in favor of Europe. Although eighteenth-century European influence on Ottoman society remained limited in comparison with the scale of Western penetration in the following century, it already projected a threatening superiority.

In the diplomatic arena the Ottomans lost the global stature and initiative that had impressed and daunted the European powers in earlier centuries. They became increasingly dependent for survival on Europe's system of international relations; no longer could they act unilaterally or without reference to the attitudes of the major European powers. European representatives in Istanbul exerted growing influence on the sultan's policy, and extracted concessions and privileges for their subjects. In the major cities of the empire English, French, and other European consuls cultivated hundreds of protegés among the non-Muslims by extending to them consular protection and a privileged status— in a flagrant abuse of their diplomatic agreements with the Ottoman government. From the seventeenth century European missionaries worked zealously in Ottoman territories to bring the Eastern Christians into the Catholic fold. Their work, backed by French diplomats, was crowned with success; by the end of the eighteenth century the Maronite church had accepted papal authority, while thousands of Melkites, Armenians, and Jacobites accepted Catholicism and set up new churches affiliated with Rome. These European inroads into Middle Eastern society, although confined mostly to the Christian population, brought into existence a group of Ottoman subjects motivated by new affinities with the West.

The Europeans were also on the ascendant in their commercial relations with the empire. They continued to maintain the trade they had established several centuries earlier with Ottoman territories, selling their products and taking back to Europe regional and Eastern goods. In the course of the seventeenth and eighteenth centuries, however, they won considerable competitive advantages in this exchange. New colonies and markets gave them access to silk, coffee, sugar, and other products at prices that the traditional Middle Eastern suppliers were hard pressed to match. Much of the shipping on the seas passed into European hands. Within Europe itself the industrial revolution was opening up the capacity to produce goods on a massive and efficient scale that could overwhelm the manufacturers in Ottoman territories. These European advantages did not come into full play until the nineteenth century, when Europeans dumped their cheaper industrial goods in Middle Eastern markets, increased considerably their importation of raw materials from the region, and increasingly dictated the terms of trade. In the eighteenth century Middle Eastern commerce with Europe was still limited in comparison with the intraregional and Eastern exchange, and the area was not as deeply integrated into the European economic system as it was to become after the Napoleonic Wars. The effects of fluctuations in demand and prices originating in Europe tended to touch mainly those places that were more intimately involved in the trade with Europe.

Aleppo was among the Ottoman localities that felt the European influence. England, France, Holland, Austria, and Italian city-states maintained consulates in the city. Merchants from European countries had, centuries earlier, selected the place as a favorite station for their trade with the East, and set up permanent living quarters in its central business district. Situated on the crossroads of the important trade routes of the region and in convenient proximity to the Mediterranean, Aleppo offered European businessmen advantages matched by only a few other urban centers. As the home of a formidable Christian population the city also attracted Catholic missionaries, who found in it fertile ground for their religious work.

Yet even in Aleppo the eighteenth-century European penetration affected only a small portion of the city's economic activities and touched in restricted ways the fortunes of some local non-Muslims. No genuinely Westernized group emerged at the time in Aleppo or the Middle East in general, not even among those Christians closely associated with the Europeans through business and religious activities. The region was isolated from Western culture and unfamiliar with its ways, and the Muslims, up to the Ottoman elite, took pride in their cultural heritage and looked down upon the infidel world. At the end of the eighteenth century they were still unstirred by the great changes that had transformed the West since the Reformation. Biased against Christian Europe by hostile memories, they tended to dismiss it as the source of anything of cultural worth. Very few of them visited Europe or had any knowledge of a Western language. The European world of thought and ideas remained unfamiliar and the source of little curiosity even to scholars.

This cultural isolation extended to the Ottoman political leadership. Even at the highest official levels, firsthand knowledge of developments in Europe was limited. Only in the 1790s did the empire first station permanent diplomatic representatives in the European capitals. The early reports of these men showed a poor understanding of what they observed. The government did borrow European ideas that could be useful for military purposes, but there its interest ended. It failed to keep up with the range of revolutionary advances in thought, science, technology, government organization, and economic behavior on which Europe's superiority ultimately rested. In all of these areas Ottoman society had been surpassed, in some instances three centuries earlier.

Once the implications of the changed balance began to sink in, the leadership felt compelled to embark upon a belated and costly race to catch up. In the 1790s Sultan Selim III proceeded to implement the New Order, a daring reform project designed to reorganize the army and the administration along models copied from Europe, in an effort to shore up Ottoman power. With this move, launched in the dark days of defeat and internal disarray, was born the process of Westernizing reform that was to introduce foreign ways into every sphere of life. It took the external threats, not an organic development from within, to bring about this historic shift in the empire's direction. A disaffection with various traditional institutions; a receptivity to European ideas; the emergence of the state as a leading agent of change; and the evolution of a Westernized class committed to reform were some of the new conditions to emerge in the nineteenth century. The virtual absence of such forces in the eighteenth century helps to explain the continuity of the traditional imperial structure.

Throughout the eighteenth century the Ottoman leadership remained firmly committed to preserving the traditional order. Its profound conservatism was rooted in conviction as well as vested interest; with the full weight of government thrown on the side of continuity the odds against change were overwhelming. Reformers did see various ills and advise their correction; however, they came almost invariably from within the bureaucracy and advocated piecemeal schemes confined to the improvement of administrative and military institutions. Even these restricted efforts at change had their enemies. Conservative circles in the ruling class successfully blocked various reforms, including aspects of the New Order; indeed, they were sufficiently opposed to certain reforms to have Sultan Selim removed in 1807.

The reformers ultimately prevailed, opening the gates of the empire to revolutionary changes and imported ways. For better or worse, Ottoman subjects of the eighteenth century were spared the experiences of this internal modernization. Even when the century drew to a close people in Aleppo, cushioned within the stable albeit declined imperial regime, had no premonition of what was coming nor the sense that they lived in an age of transition.

REGIONAL SETTING AND LOCAL IDENTITY

THE REGION SURROUNDING Aleppo also imposed on the city certain routines and crises. While the sultan appeared remote to the townspeople and developments such as the international shifts in power were of little interest to them, the immediate environment represented a concrete presence in their lives. Social ties, economic interests, and cultural affinities linked them to the outside. Their city's role in the area exposed them to external developments but also fostered sentiments of local identity.

A metropolis set in a largely rural world—that fact more than any other determined Aleppo's place in the region. Cities of its stature formed a select group in the Middle East of the eighteenth century. Large portions of the region—most of Arabia and Egypt as well as large parts of the Fertile Crescent—were desert. In this land, too dry and barren to allow continuous agriculture and permanent settlement, nomadic tribes established their domain. Settled life concentrated in several limited areas of adequate rainfall and easy irrigation: the fertile valleys of the Nile, Tigris, and Euphrates; a belt of land along the eastern Mediterranean; and much of Anatolia. Most of the settled population led a rural existence, living in small and scattered agricultural villages which extended to the fringes of the desert. Even in Syria, more urbanized than the other parts, not more than 20 percent of the population resided in the bigger towns. By the standards of the day urban settlements of ten or twenty thousand souls qualified as places of considerable magnitude. Few regional towns actually exceeded that order.

In its immediate region Aleppo was by far the predominant settlement. "The road from every village leads to Aleppo," boasted a local saying.[7] The cities that approached its size were far off: Damascus more than a week's caravan journey away, Baghdad and Izmir both about a month away. Only Cairo (with about 260,000 people) and the imperial capital of Istanbul (with some 450,000) clearly outmatched it in magnitude; both were more distant still.[8] For miles around Aleppo stretched a region largely rural in character. Small villages and towns dotted the landscape; at close view they gave little appearance of prosperity. The more pleasing parts of the hinterland lay in the relatively fertile areas west and north of the city. The plain of Antioch, rich in water and vegetation and backed by a rugged mountain range rising just off the Mediterranean, ranked among the prettiest spots in the country. Quite different was the landscape that extended to the east and south of the city: an arid plateau that merged into the Syrian desert and in the hot summers was hardly distinguishable from it. Settled life was sparse and precarious, not only from the natural harshness of the area. Many villages and fields lay deserted, the victims of decades of depopulation.

Set against this backdrop Aleppo appeared particularly impressive. The built-up area did not exceed 365 hectares (about 1.5 square miles), but may have appeared more extensive because some neighborhoods spread out into the agricultural gardens and largely undeveloped land on the outskirts. Estimates by residents as well as foreign visitors placed the population at two and even three times its actual size. In the absence of any reliable head count, local pride and personal impressions were left to manufacture highly inflated figures.

In any case, it was not only its size that set Aleppo apart from most other localities in the region. The city was the administrative capital for an extensive area, a seat of culture and learning, a large center of industrial production, and a major station of regional and international commerce. This was the natural habitat of powerful, wealthy, and learned men, the sort of place where luxury and pretension thrived. People from lands as distant as England and India came there to trade, study, visit, and settle. The place certainly appeared impressive to contemporaries, even when compared with other great urban centers. European visitors, many of them seasoned travelers in the East, commented on its agreeable appearance, the abundance in its markets, the civility of its inhabitants, and its salubrious climate. Overall they deemed it one of the most elegant and pleasant cities in the Ottoman Empire.[9]

Extensive ties, primarily economic, connected Aleppo to other parts of the Middle East. The major cities in the region were the principal links in the network of commercial exchange within the area and with lands further afield. They exported their locally manufactured products, and also served as the places of assembly for goods from the hinterland and foreign countries, which they in turn redistributed. Aleppo participated heavily in this trade, a busy caravan traffic connecting it with other centers. Alexandretta (Iskandarun), a shabby, humid port town on the Mediterranean, was Aleppo's outlet to Europe; on the road between it and the city traveled pack animals laden with products arrived from the West and with regional as well as Eastern goods destined for shipment to Europe. In the opposite direction extended the roads to Baghdad, Mosul, and Basra; Aleppo maintained an extensive exchange with these cities, which conveniently assembled Iranian, Arabian, and Indian goods. Busy too were the main routes connecting the city with some Anatolian trading centers to the north, notably ʿAyntab, Urfa, and Diyarbakr. Southward the main road led to Damascus, the chief Syrian link with Palestine, Egypt, and Arabia.

The city also had ties with the more immediate region around it which served as its functional hinterland. From this region, which had a radius of about seventy miles, the townspeople drew most of the food on which their sustenance depended and most of the raw materials needed for their various artisanal manufactures. The city also routinely syphoned off considerable wealth from it in the form of rents, interest, taxes, and exactions. Aleppo was the base of operations for officials and state agents entrusted with administering the affairs of the large provincial population; for tax farmers and landlords who controlled vast rural lands and resources; for moneylenders with financial claims on countless rural folk; and for traders who tapped the markets in the countryside.

This regional setting, so essential to the fortunes of Aleppo, was a world with a life of its own rather than a ready instrument in urban hands. To produce a successful crop the peasants depended on the whims of the annual rainfall as well as on security from attack and exploitation. Commercial interests in other localities and in world markets determined the movement of goods and the prosperity of business. The safety of the roads and the peasantry, so important for the city, depended ultimately on the will of the government to provide protection. In the course of the century the city's vulnerability to regional forces was frequently shown. Crops failed numerous times. Bandits and tribesmen lurked on the roads and robbed travelers. Wars, epidemics, and market cycles disrupted trade or altered its patterns. Peasants burdened by insecurity and oppression deserted their fields in large numbers. The city felt the effects of these periodic developments in the form of food shortages, loss of merchandise, reduced revenues, and various other inconveniences.

In this complex rural world surrounding the city tribes were an inseparable part of the landscape. They added much more than exotic color and variety to the scene; their behavior shaped rural conditions and affected urbanites in Aleppo. The bedouin Arabs, who led a life of pastoral nomadism in the Syrian desert and lands on its fringes, were a formidable presence in the eighteenth century, their numbers swelled by large-scale migrations from Arabia. They established virtual mastery over their territories of migration and seasonal settlement, collecting tolls from travelers, pillaging caravans, and subjecting villages to extortion and robbery. Similar forms of leverage were exercised by the sedentary Kurdish tribesmen inhabiting the rugged Amanus mountain range to the north of Aleppo. From their autonomous strongholds they dominated the strategic routes in their areas, especially the coastal road from Syria into Anatolia, and cast a threatening shadow over the neighboring settlements.

Many of Aleppo's residents had come to it from the surrounding region, and many others left to settle in various parts of it. This migration, part of a regional pattern of mobility, affirmed in a tangible way the porous character of the city. In the sixteenth and seventeenth centuries immigrants, attracted by prosperous times, added many new neighborhoods to the urban landscape; but the city's physical growth came to a near halt from at least the early eighteenth century.[10] Yet even in this period the community continued to absorb immigrants. Recurrent visitations of plague and famine carried off multitudes of victims. At the same time several thousand residents left for good to seek their fortunes elsewhere. Without drawing on the reservoir of manpower outside, primarily in the hinterland, the city could not have made up these losses. While no one at the time counted the numbers of people moving into the city or out of it, the flow in both directions was constant. Throughout the region restless men and women too ambitious or disadvantaged to be held back by local attachments took to the road in search of escape, adventure, or a new future. Some of them thronged the highways leading to Aleppo.

The immigrants came by and large from the Arab lands of the Middle East and from Anatolia. Their status spanned the entire gamut of the city's social hierarchy. Lowly and poor persons arrived alongside scholars, high officials, and wealthy businessmen. Immigrant women, some of them from as far away as Urfa and Diyarbakr, swelled the ranks of Aleppo's prostitutes.[11] A good number of rural people were among the newcomers: Arab bedouin and Turkman and Kurdish tribesmen as well as peasants from villages in the hinterland. These were all familiar types, members of groups already encountered in Aleppo. Their arrival renewed the social diversity in the city without altering the makeup of the population.

The established natives had their gaze cast outward. During the eighteenth century a sizable number left their hometown for good, partly in response to certain unhappy circumstances that plagued the city during the period: religious persecution within the Christian communities, periodic economic slumps, and official oppression.[12] Among them, however, were also people driven by ambitions that could not be satisfied at home and for whom relocation was an acceptable price for success. The prospect of seeing a son go abroad never to return was real enough to worry some local mothers, who sought to get their children settled in marriage early as a way of securing their stay in the city.[13]

Business opportunities dispersed Aleppines throughout the Middle East and beyond. They figured among the cosmopolitan merchant communities active in the capital and the major cities of Egypt, Iraq, Syria, and Anatolia. A particularly sizable and prosperous Aleppine diaspora thrived in Egypt, to which a large number of Christian families made their way from the 1730s onward. Together with immigrants from Damascus they rose to economic prominence by seizing control over lucrative areas of trade and finance.[14] A few set out to explore new frontiers of business that opened up outside the Middle East. Some Christians and Jews from Aleppo established themselves in Livorno, a center of exchange between Europe and the Middle East. In the late eighteenth century, when India began to beckon as a new sphere of commercial opportunity, Jews from Aleppo, along with coreligionists from Baghdad, moved to the subcontinent. The first Jew to settle in Calcutta, Shalom ha-Kohen of Aleppo, was followed by a wave of newcomers from his native town who founded a successful business community.[15] Educated men and members of the Muslim religious establishment also responded to opportunities abroad. Patronage and employment opportunities in other cities, especially the imperial capital, attracted them. Some of them succeeded in obtaining good teaching appointments in colleges, generous stipends, and middle-echelon positions in the central Ottoman bureaucracy.[16]

Many residents could count among their relatives, friends, colleagues, business associates, patrons, and clients people living elsewhere in the region. Migration alone manufactured many such links. Branches of the same family were sometimes scattered in several localities. ʿUthman ibn Yahya, a religious scholar, moved from Mecca to Aleppo, and there married his cousin who had immigrated from Istanbul.[17] Some of the notable families in Alexandretta, Idlib, and other towns in the hinterland originated in Aleppo or had branches there.[18] The heirs of deceased people occasionally included relatives living abroad; Aleppines traveled or sent agents to other cities to collect their shares in estates, and outsiders came to the city to settle similar claims.[19] Some residents owned and inherited property, usually houses, in Baghdad, Mosul, Antioch, Diyarbakr, Urfa, and other cities in the region.[20]

People from the larger region who visited Aleppo recognized it as a cosmopolitan place of considerable stature in their part of the world. Yet they also found it a familiar type of community. In its culture, social arrangements, and general way of life Aleppo was a typical Arab city of the period. Even its appearance and physical layout—the narrow winding alleyways, the tightly built clusters of courtyard houses, the city center surrounded by residential quarters, the walls, the gates, the architectural styles—replicated the characteristic features of urban set- tlements in the region.[21]

Alongside the general similarities that people took for granted were local peculiarities that caught the attention of contemporaries. Within the Syrian provinces alone there were confusing local variations in weights, measures, prices, wage rates, land tenure systems, taxes, diets, and social customs. Communities everywhere developed arrangements adapted to their particular conditions and held on to them because they were functional or simply familiar. Restricted literacy and slow com- munications allowed these local differences to thrive, especially in a period when the authorities did little to standardize conditions. Even the spoken Arabic varied from district to district. Aleppo's colloquial language had peculiarities of idiom and intonation that were quite dis- tinct to the ears of contemporaries. In Maʿarrat al-Nuʿman, a small town some fifty miles south of Aleppo, a local historian could note sadly how wives brought from Aleppo, Damascus, and Hama had introduced the linguistic particularisms of these cities into the local Arabic and cor- rupted its purity. "The townspeople have become like the strings of the lute, each one sounding a different note."[22]

Such keen attention to the dissimilarities among neighboring places came naturally to contemporaries. People tended to exaggerate their differences and to single out unique qualities; they seized on small variations and stressed them. Their perceptions reflected the strong sentiments of localism current in the culture of the region.

Aleppo's townspeople, like the residents of other places, accepted that their locality had a separate history and a set of characteristics peculiar to itself. Their sentiments of pride and superiority were sometimes given forthright expression: "Aleppo is the choicest of places on earth; no other locality matches it in the excellence of its climate, people and food."[23] The residents took pride in the comforts of civilized urban living that their city offered. Construction of fine local stone gave their city a pleasing solid look; its streets were paved, its courtyard houses comfortable and well designed. On the outskirts flowed a sleepy river surrounded by gardens and orchards—a perfect setting for peaceful retreat away from the humdrum of the daily routine. The climate added to the comforts: the air was dry and salubrious, the sky serenely blue for most of the year. Natural springs nearby supplied excellent water which on summer days could be drawn deliciously cool from the domestic reservoirs. And the local culinary tradition boasted exquisite dishes and specialties by the dozens. "Aleppo's cuisine is superior to any other."[24]

The inhabitants saw in themselves the graces and accomplishments of a cultured community. They produced noted scholars and fine institutions of learning. Etiquette and good manners marked their conduct. The saying "Halabi chalabi"—"the Aleppine is a gentleman"—expressed an essential aspect of their self-image; they prided themselves on being tolerant, sober, and composed. "The Egyptian and Damascene always respond impetuously, the Aleppine only after consulting his mother."[25] For the superiority of the local women over outsiders they had unequivocal praise: "Better Aleppo rye than imported wheat."[26] They looked on the rural world with particular scorn and contempt. Ignorance, crudeness, dishonesty, and violence separated the peasant and nomad from the refinements of urban living.

Such sentiments were articulated partly in a rich lore of popular sayings and stories transmitted orally from generation to generation. They carried a direct and confident message, garnished with occasional fun poked at outsiders. Similar feelings were also echoed, if in more refined form, in the literary expression of educated men. Local writers composed poems of praise for the city, and proudly assembled the many verses of tribute to it penned by renowned visitors since the early medieval period.[27] They treated Aleppo as a natural and self-contained subject, worthy of study and reflection in its own right. They compiled biographical dictionaries of distinguished scholars and pious men who were associated with the city over the years, drew detailed sketches of the urban landscape and its monuments, and wrote histories chronicling local events and dramas. Colored by a somewhat antiquarian concern with local detail, these works were intended to depict the city's glory. They advertised Aleppo's credentials as a place of historical importance, and above all as a center of Islamic learning and piety.

One concrete expression of the strength of such sentiments of localism can be seen in the place the residents gave to the city as the most natural focus for their territorial loyalties. They referred to it as their *watan*, the place from which they hailed or that they considered their home. The concept lacked the connotation of national homeland which was to be attached to it in the nineteenth century in the wake of contact with European ideas. People spoke of territorial home in the narrow terms of specific localities. In 1752 one ʿAbd al-Razzaq ibn Hasan obtained a court order preventing his daughter-in-law from moving to Damascus with his grandson. The judge was sympathetic to his contention that she ought to stay and raise her son in Aleppo, "her original hometown" *(watanuha al-asli)*.[28]

Affection for one's hometown was seen as a natural sentiment. Yaʿqub Arutin, a Christian priest who headed a monastery in Mount Lebanon, returned in 1714 to visit his native town of Aleppo, having manufactured pretexts and ignored the objections of his superior. An eighteenth-century church chronicler, himself an Aleppine in origin, did not find Arutin's irregular conduct entirely odd. "Love of family and hometown [*watan*] had overcome his dedication to obedience," he explained.[29] The culture of the day did not reject local attachments as parochial and negative. The local community had its recognized place in a larger scheme of collective affiliations and loyalties. Like Aleppo, other towns also displayed strong claims to distinctness and excellence, expressed in their literature and folklore. That such local attachments thrived had much to do with the weakness of the larger territorial loyalties. The Muslim world, the Arab lands, even the Ottoman Empire could not excite in the residents quite the same concrete sentiments associated with the locality. In an age predating nationalism and patriotism these territorial units appeared all too vast and diverse to stir focused feelings of identity. Nor were the more immediate geographical units closer to home more meaningful. Aleppines did not consider themselves Syrians; the term *Syria*, common on the tongues and maps of Europeans, was seldom used by locals.[30] The Aleppo province, for its part, was no more than an administrative entity; it defined the boundaries of certain official jurisdictions, not of collective loyalties.

While they saw the city as the natural unit of geographical provenance and identity, residents made some fine distinctions about their levels of association with it. "Damascus is my place of birth and up-bringing, Aleppo my place of origin [*asl*] and my hometown [*watan*]," wrote ʿAbd al-Rahman ibn ʿAbdallah in an autobiographical sketch written in 1776. His family's roots were in Aleppo, from whence his ancestors had at some point emigrated and to which he had himself come to settle. His grandfather had proudly considered himself to be Aleppine in origin, even though he was born in Baʾalbek and had made Damascus his *watan*.[31] Birth in Aleppo was clearly not a prerequisite for considering the city one's home; it could become one's *watan* by adoption as well. Nor did generations of residence elsewhere render ancestral links to the city irrelevant; these ties could remain alive in familial memory and be evoked at appropriate moments.

If ʿAbd al-Rahman went to some lengths to establish the details of his geographical provenance he did so for a society attentive to such matters. Writing at the age of seventy-eight, many years after settling in Aleppo, he could note that the residents still identified him as "al-Shami" (the Damascene). They were not thereby denying him full inclusion in their community—he was after all a respected religious scholar—but merely attaching to him a convenient label of identification of a sort routinely applied to people of external origin.

To be Aleppine meant also to be urban, a fact that figured as a prominent component in the sentiments of local identity and pride. City dwellers nurtured a sense of their superiority over the peasant and the nomad. Scorn for rural life was characteristic of urban culture through-out the region.[32] No nostalgia for nature or association of the country with pastoral innocence burdened the outlook of the townspeople. If anything, the experiences of the period only strengthened in them an image of the countryside as a raw, unfriendly world to be feared and avoided. They heard many stories of robbed travelers, pillaged cara-vans, overrun villages, and other types of rural mischief. On this and other counts they perceived basic distinctions between urban and rural.

The sense of urban identity was not anchored in legal privileges or a tradition of urban autonomy. Residents could boast no special juridical status by virtue of dwelling in a city; the law made no formal differentia-tion between their rights and those of peasants and nomads. Nor was the city possessed of a recognized corporate status or a separate munici-pal authority representative of urban interests; for the Ottoman admin-istration based in Aleppo the city was but part of the extensive province under its jurisdiction. The distinction that the townspeople drew between themselves and the rural world rested essentially on differences in way of life. From the urban vantage point the countryside was inferior in material conditions, crude in cultural expression, and even wayward in religious orthodoxy. In a large and sophisticated metropolis the perceptions of contrasting life-styles were apt to take particularly sharp forms.

These notions of urban superiority, as also the claims to local distinctness and excellence, were clearly a blend of fact and exaggeration, of real experiences and ideal images. They papered over the various material discomforts suffered by the masses of poor and insecure residents in the city: chronic shortages of water, stale and insufficient bread, mean and crowded housing, and the fierce cold of winters. They also concealed the uncivil and impious aspects of city life. In practice, the sense of belonging to the place was not nearly universal or absolute. Local attachments were apparently not strong enough to weigh down the many Aleppines who left the city to settle elsewhere, and the immigrants did not see their new home in quite the same manner as the long-established natives; their lives had been shaped in some measure by other places and ways. Many of them were tribesmen and peasants who for years maintained an identity not fully urban or Aleppine. The distinctions between Aleppines and outsiders, between urban and rural, actually cut across the community itself.

Yet on a plane distinct from the actual conditions the repertoire of local sentiments and attitudes mirrored the sort of collective self-images that could stir in the residents of a place a sense of community and local pride. It elevated Aleppo above a mere aggregate of insignificant people who happened to share a common space. The city stood for a set of worthy ideals, primarily civility, urbanity, culture, and piety. Superiority in ethics and aesthetics, in the spiritual and the material, defined its essence and goals as a community. In a society divided along many lines the shared local loyalties and sentiments added an important ingredient to the bases of social cohesion.

CHAPTER 2

The People: Groups, Classes, and Social Contrasts

"WHOEVER CLAIMS THAT all people are equal must be hopelessly mad."[1] So jotted an eighteenth-century resident of the city in his private handbook, among other sayings and bits of useful information. The social world in which he lived was indeed a place unlikely to occasion delusions of equality. A mixed and colorful lot crowded into his metropolis: Muslims, Christians, and Jews; Ottoman subjects and foreign nationals; households fabulously wealthy and miserably poor; rural immigrants and long-established urbanites; pious believers and underworld criminals; learned scholars and illiterates; families of noble lineage and of humble origins; skilled professionals and menial laborers; men of power and abject slaves. There were differences of dress, life-style, speech, and manners; ceremony and refinement thrived, but alongside unconcealed wretchedness.

Aleppo's townspeople took the human diversity for granted, but without neglecting to attach social importance to the distinctions around them. Theirs was a world keenly attentive to status and to the differences between men. The relevance of social distinctions was especially evident in the meaning given to religious affiliation, sex, and level of wealth, three attributes which accounted for differences in opportunity, status, circles of social relations, cultural traits, and social identity. Religious distinctions had their basis in strong communal attachments as well as in the law, which imposed on the non-Muslims various disabilities placing them in a subordinate social position. Yet the religious parochialism and the formal discriminatory rules, both characteristic of Middle Eastern societies in other places and times, tell only part of the story; an image of differences, segregation, and persecution would distort the actual conditions in the city. Likewise, the vision of a male-dominated society, which Aleppo certainly was in many respects, captures only partially the meaning of sexual distinctions and the actual position of women.

Not less complex were the economic distinctions. The highly uneven distribution of wealth fostered vast differences in material and social circumstances. Wealth, indeed, was a key ingredient determining one's place in the social hierarchy. Aleppo's was a stratified society dominated by a small elite whose members were distinguished by great personal wealth, although not by wealth alone. They also boasted prestigious lineages and held high positions in the religious establishment, the administration, and the military. These were among the sources of social esteem and political influence which, in addition to wealth, helped them reach the top, where they stood in sharp contrast to the mass of residents at the bottom of the ladder who could claim little or no wealth, prestige or influence. Between the two poles were a substantial number who possessed property, a comfortable life-style, learning, good occupations, and other attributes considered desirable by their community. These three levels suggest the rough outlines of Aleppo's class structure, a structure which was not rigid, nor defined exclusively by economic criteria, nor limited to the division into elite and commoners often associated with premodern urban societies in the region. The inequalities appeared not only between groups; they also cut across them. Women, Christians, carpenters, men of religion, and even slaves formed each a socially differentiated group whose members belonged to more than one single class.

Many of the distinctions and inequalities in Aleppo's society were institutionalized: Islamic law defined unequal rights for various groups, while the Ottoman state conferred ranks, titles, tax exemptions, dress privileges, and various advantages which added other formal marks of inequality. Various forms of differentiation had their basis in rules of etiquette, social prejudices, and notions of status embedded in the culture. In the course of the eighteenth century the institutional arrangements and ideological schemata underlying the social structure underwent no major changes, and the social composition of the population remained fairly stable. Wealth, power, and prestige continued to be drawn from roughly the same sources, and their benefits remained distributed in roughly the same fashion. There was no revolution from below or shift in direction at the top which restructured the existing social arrangements, and no ideological movement emerged to challenge the premises of the hierarchy. Yet even in this stable social scene competition and mobility were normal. People crossed group lines and moved up and down the social scale, although various barriers set limits on the opportunities for advancement.

A profile of the complex of groups, classes, and social contrasts in Aleppo is the first essential step toward making sense of the great diversity of circumstances and experiences within the community, its social conceptions and attitudes, and the dynamics of its daily relations.

RELIGIOUS IDENTITY

W HEN THEY THOUGHT of their society in terms of religious affiliations, the townspeople of Aleppo saw a world irreparably divided. Members of other faiths were their neighbors, business associates, and professional colleagues; they usually spoke their language, lived in similar homes, enjoyed similar food, and were absorbed by like pursuits and pleasures. Yet confessional differences set them apart. Muslims, Christians, and Jews saw themselves as members of distinct communities organized around different beliefs. They were brought up to feel a moral superiority to the adherents of other creeds and a loyalty to their faith and coreligionists. These divisive effects of religious differences occasioned no public debate or remorse; no one expected things to be otherwise. Religion was woven into the institutional fabric of society and its relevance affirmed at every turn. Every child was deemed to be born into a religious community. Education, laws, learning, rites of passage, beliefs, and practices bore heavy marks of religious influence. In this milieu religious identity was not a private matter left to individual choice. Each person carried it as a social stamp, irrespective of personal piety and observance. Nonbelief was not a recognized option.

The religious distinctions appear on the face of it quite clear-cut. Townspeople of all creeds viewed religious affiliation as the central component of personal identity and accepted the logic of differentiating between individuals on the basis of their faith. The law itself affirmed the importance of religious distinctions, most notably between Muslims and non-Muslims: it assigned rights and restrictions unequally to members of different communities. The formal status of the various confessional groups, the parochial aspects of religious life, and the general outlook on religion tell much about the meaning of religious distinctions in Aleppo. But one must also go beyond them and observe the actual relations and behavior at different levels; corporate life, formal rules, and religious differences appear to have been meaningful in some areas but not in others.

The city's Sunni Muslim population, some eighty to ninety thousand strong at midcentury, lived alongside a substantial minority of some twenty thousand Christians and three or four thousand Jews. The religious pluralism extended beyond this tripartite division. The Christians were divided among four distinct churches—Melkite (Greek), Armenian, Jacobite (or Syrian), and Maronite—each with its own house of worship, liturgy, traditions, and clergy. The first three actually split in the course of the century, with new Catholic versions emerging alongside the mother churches. The Melkites, the most formidable congregation in geographical Syria, constituted about half of Aleppo's Christians.[2] The Jews too were a motley group, composed of native Middle Easterners and descendants of the Spanish emigrés (Sephardim). The two elements, still conscious of their different origins and traditions, were joined from the late seventeenth century by some Sephardic merchant families from Italy, who added yet another social element to the community.

In this scene of religious pluralism one formal distinction overrode all others—that between Muslims and non-Muslims. When Yusuf ibn ʿAbdallah declared in court in 1753 that he had transferred his affiliation from the Armenian religious community *(milla)* to the Maronite, and asked for permission to pay his taxes as a member of his adopted group, the qadi saw no hindrance. "Infidelity constitutes one religious community [*milla*]," he stated, repeating yet again a traditional Muslim view that seemed to lump all non-Muslims into one undifferentiated mass.[3] The judge was not naively blind to the finer religious distinctions in the city. His scribes always took care to note in the court documents the particular church affiliation of Christian litigants and witnesses. But they were even more meticulous about distinguishing Muslims from non-Muslims. When listing the names of a mixed group of neighbors or craftsmen, they separated them by religion, recording the Muslims first. The names of non-Muslims they presented and spelled in ways that clearly differentiated them from Muslims.[4]

The Christians and Jews were defined by law as a distinct category, to be barred from a share in power, subjected to special taxation, prohibited from proselytizing or worshiping publicly, and set apart from Muslims by restrictions on clothing and other social disabilities. This discriminatory scheme rested on a reasoned vision of society, one that allocated social and political status according to religious affiliation.

In an Islamic society and state, Muslims were the politically dominant group. They enjoyed the prerogatives of enforcing their own law and doctrine and of promoting Muslim causes. Non-Muslims could choose to live in this society, but as *dhimmis*, tolerated subjects of subordinate status.

This formal scheme remained in effect throughout the eighteenth century as the guiding framework for ordering the place of non-Muslims in society. It upheld a principle of inequality that the non-Muslims disliked but were in no position to undo. The specific restrictions were not themselves enforced uniformly and consistently. Non-Muslims remained effectively excluded from participation in political power; high positions were closed to them. The special poll tax *(jizya)* that was demanded from every adult Christian and Jewish male also remained a permanent feature of the period. The exaction was enough of a financial burden on the poor to warrant special communal instruments of charity to assist in its payment.[5] The legal prohibition on the construction of new churches and synagogues was enforced without significant relaxation. In 1686 the Maronites succeeded in adding an adjoining room to their church only after appeals to Istanbul backed by the French ambassador.[6] Even the repair of the existing houses of worship was closely supervised by the authorities to safeguard against unauthorized additions.[7] The freedom of worship itself was respected.

The non-Muslims succeeded in winning more concessions in the enforcement of restrictions on their public appearance. At least during part of the eighteenth century they were able to take the liberty of riding on horseback without meeting with more than verbal abuse from Muslims offended by the violation of a traditional rule.[8] Restrictions on dress proved the most chronic irritant. For the explicit purpose of differentiating them visually from members of the dominant faith, Christians and Jews were required to limit their clothes, shoes, and headgear to particular colors and styles. The better-off among them had to satisfy their fancy for forbidden dress in the privacy of their homes.[9] Periodically governors issued clothing regulations imposing new restrictions on permissible colors. In 1775, when Muhammad Pasha announced his reform of dhimmi dress, the non-Muslims stayed indoors for eleven days in protest. The Christian leaders, who approached the authorities to negotiate a settlement, were thrown in prison for their uncooperative spirit. Finally, after some bargaining between the parties, the pasha agreed to withdraw his order in return for a large payment. These maneuverings recurred time and again, with the periodic clothing restrictions serving as little more than pretexts for officials to exact money.[10] The differentiation in clothing was maintained even in the public bath houses, where non-Muslim men were provided with robes bearing particular markings. Muslim women were required to have separate use of the baths. According to the judge who reaffirmed this segregation in 1762, for a Muslim woman to expose herself before a dhimmi female was as sinful as baring herself before a man.[11] Enforcement of these rules tended to degenerate with time, however, especially since the bath house operators found the restrictions harmful to their business.

While they resented the official restrictions, the non-Muslims had no interest in becoming indistinguishable from the majority. Indeed, they worked hard to foster a strong identity and to discourage conversion to Islam or marriage outside the faith. Equipped with its own leaders, laws, legislation, social control, education, indoctrination, and instruments of mutual aid, each community was able to assert a certain autonomy which reinforced its sense of separateness. In matters intimately related to their religious ideals, notably in the area of personal status, the Christians and Jews were permitted to follow and enforce their own laws. Communal leaders also legislated regulations that were binding on members: limits on the size of dowries, the prohibition of ostentatious clothing and jewelry, the restriction of overnight visits among friends, the prohibition of premarital meetings of engaged couples, restrictions on the outdoor movement of women, and so on. Fines and even communal bans awaited offenders.[12] Each community also maintained an array of funds and endowments for the support of schools, the clergy, welfare payments, and other causes. All families paid dues and contributed their share during fund raisers, with the well-to-do shouldering much of the financial burden.

Life in this parochial setting bred a strong religious identity which found expression also in solidarity with coreligionists abroad. Each community saw itself as part of a larger ecumenical body extending beyond the confines of Aleppo. Various links with fellow believers reinforced religious identity. The Christians, whose patriarchs resided in Istanbul and Lebanon, were accustomed to decisions and ecclesiastical appointments originating from without. Correspondence and travel kept their leaders and members in touch with communities in other localities.[13] Pious Christians performed pilgrimages to Jerusalem, and many donated money and property for the support of monasteries and churches abroad, especially in Lebanon and Palestine. At the turn of the eighteenth century three young Aleppines founded a new monastic order in Lebanon which continued for years after to draw its recruits and financial support from Aleppo.[14] The Jews raised funds annually to help support coreligionists in the Holy Land; these were delivered to emissaries from Palestine.[15] The community also provided lodging to Jewish travelers passing through the city.[16] The rabbis maintained contact with their counterparts in the Middle East and even in Europe on Jewish affairs; the Iraqi Jews often turned to them for legal advice. In 1743 the Jews of Baghdad recruited an Aleppine rabbi, Sedaqa Husayn, to lead their community. Under his guidance their Babylonian liturgical tradition came to be replaced with the Syrian.[17]

The state added further to the sense of separate corporate existence in the minority communities by treating them as units with collective administrative responsibilities. It imposed various taxes as lump sums on entire communities, to be collected from individuals by the group itself. The four Christian groups came to blows periodicallly over the allocation of the tax burden among them.[18] Each community appointed from its ranks an agent *(wakil)* to represent it before the authorities and to oversee the fulfillment of official demands.[19] The authorities also held each community collectively responsible for the conduct of its members. The leaders were expected to make misdeeds known and find the offenders. The entire community suffered a heavy fine for crimes that it failed to report or discover. The Melkite Jirjis ibn Bashur was not alone to suffer when his illicit affair with an unmarried cousin became known to the authorities in 1752. His communal leaders, held responsible for cover-up and negligence, faced harsh reprimands from the authorities, very likely in addition to a collective fine.[20]

The religious differences, stressed and exaggerated in so many ways, did not separate the communities into segregated social worlds of their own. Their divisive effects were limited by the great similarities between Aleppines of different religious persuasions, and by the pragmatism that guided daily behavior. The confessional boundaries were so clearly drawn and religious beliefs so little open to debate that people could associate freely in various spheres without compromise. Sharing a common cultural heritage, Muslims, Christians, and Jews were hardly strangers to each other. Their religions, based as they were on many of the same traditions, instilled in them similar moral visions and social ideals. They also shared much of the same repertoire of attitudes, tastes, superstitions, and prejudices that made up the contemporary urban culture. "Three Jews from Aleppo, expert musicians in command of the finest repertoire, are in Damascus these days," noted a Damascene chronicler in his account of the events of 1744. "They performed in the coffeehouses of Damascus, and entertained both the high and the low."[21] Such participation by non-Muslims in the general musical culture of the time was replicated in other spheres as well.

Practical activities in the sphere of work and business were little affected by religious differences. Non-Muslims practiced most professions and trades; they were doctors and merchants, porters and domestics. They belonged to the craft and trade guilds in which much of the labor force was organized, often occupying privileged positions as masters and guild officers, and participating in the making of policy in their particular trades.[22] Members of different communities often worked together under one roof, with Muslims as employees of dhimmis.[23] Transfers of property, the ownership of houses and other real estate, all manner of credit and commercial dealings, and even business partnerships cut across confessional lines.[24] So also did patterns of residence. The Christians and Jews lived in particular parts of town, but in neighborhoods that were religiously mixed. There was no neighborhood exclusively Jewish or Christian in its composition. This residential proximity and the open business association helped to narrow the social distance between members of different religious groups.

Yet the truly intimate circles of relatives and friends, as distinct from those of neighbors and business associates, appear to have revolved almost exclusively around coreligionists. It is here that the formal differentiation and the prejudices alive in all groups displayed their effective hold. Intermarriage was uncommon. Popular sayings current in Aleppo and the Middle East as a whole advised against it: to marry or associate closely with members of other religious groups was to court trouble.[25] Christians married members of other churches, but seldom outside the faith.[26] The Jews were more clannish still. The few mixed marriages that broke this social rule developed most often from the conversion to Islam of an already married dhimmi, with the spouse refusing to follow suit.[27] Conversions, which were quite rare and usually involved lower-class people, created rather anomalous and uncomfortable situations in which relatives were scattered across two sides of a religious divide.[28] Although the number of people affected was too small to dilute the social distance between religious groups in the community at large, one is still left wondering about the familial relations and social image of someone like Muhammad Effendi al-Mansuri, a Christian convert to Islam who attained high rank in the scribal service. His son remained a Christian and married within the faith.[29]

Interconfessional friendships were more common than marriages, although the evidence is limited to the writings left by a handful of educated Muslims and Christians, which point to ties of companionship, or at least mutual respect. As was common among the literate, these men exchanged poems expressing cordiality, congratulations, and condolences. Christians like Ibrahim al-Hakim, a pious physician, and Ni'ma ibn Tuma, who served as personal secretary to two Melkite archbishops, used their poetic talents at once to praise the Virgin Mary and to express care for Muslim friends and neighbors.[30] A relatively new fascination with classical Arabic and its elaborate poetic styles drew some Christians into closer association with learned Muslims. From the late seventeenth century a few young clergymen educated in Latin mission schools began to translate religious works into Arabic and to try their hand at Arabic poetry. They sat at the feet of the Muslim religious scholar Sulayman al-Nahawi to learn the intricacies of Arabic grammar and style. Among them was Germanos Farhat, who was to become Maronite archbishop of Aleppo in 1725.[31]

Such contacts heralded no major break in the traditional patterns of religious identity and intercommunal relations. Of far greater moment were the contacts of the Christians with Europe, which produced something quite novel on the social scene. Two new groups emerged in Christian ranks during the eighteenth century: Catholics and protegés of European powers. Both possessed new sorts of affinities with the West on which they hoped to build possible escape routes from dhimmi status. Their rise grew out of the ever-closer Christian links with several types of Europeans who had stationed themselves in the city: Catholic missionaries zealously engaged in bringing the Eastern Christians into communion with Rome, European merchants involved in the lucrative East-West trade, and Western consular representatives who offered new forms of patronage and privilege attractive to locals.

The resident community of European merchants and commercial agents, whose presence in Aleppo went back several centuries, was hardly formidable or conspicuous. In the eighteenth century its size at no time exceeded one hundred persons, mostly Frenchmen and Englishmen supplemented by a few Italians and Dutch. They lived in Aleppo as foreign nationals protected by extraterritorial privileges guaranteed in agreements between their governments and the sultan. Their respective consuls in Aleppo represented their collective interests and individual affairs before the authorities. Although some of them stayed for many years they remained outsiders to Aleppo's community. The city was for them but a temporary business station, an alien place where they lived

comfortably but constantly sighed for home. Only an odd few brought
wives with them or married local women.[32] They lived in several caravanserais in the heart of the business district, away from the residential
areas of the local population. Few of them bothered to learn Arabic;
Christian and Jewish intermediaries in their employ guided them through
the intricacies of local business life.[33]

Around this small foreign presence grew a considerable body of
protegés. A multitude of local non-Muslims, most of them Christians,
established associations with the European consulates and traders, from
whom they obtained useful privileges. Originally each consul was permitted to employ one or two interpreters or dragomans *(turjmans)* from
among the non-Muslim subjects. These men enjoyed consular protection and the enviable privilege of exemption from taxes. In the course of
the eighteenth century hundreds of people came to obtain these rights.
The consuls, especially the French and English, dispensed them with
abandon to the employees and relatives of their dragomans, to the host
of clerks, agents, and salesmen employed by their merchants, and to
numerous wealthy non-Muslims willing to buy a diploma *(berat)* of
protection which would exempt them from taxation.[34]

The Jews, somewhat less conspicuous than the Christians in this
pursuit of European patronage, found a particularly useful source of
privileges in their Italian coreligionists. Known locally as the Francos,
these merchant families arrived in Aleppo as protected foreign nationals,
not as dhimmis. They established thriving commercial businesses, and
took many local Jews into their employment and protection. The opportunities improved still further when Raphael Picciotto, a member of the
most prominent of these Italian families, became Austrian consul in the
city in 1784.[35]

From the abuse of consular powers was born a group of privileged
Christians and Jews, estimated by the local authorities to number some
fifteen hundred at the end of the century.[36] Its members sought eagerly
to dissociate themselves from the common dhimmi and to win recognition as a separate social category. A pretentious fur cap symbolized their
distinct status. Secure in their privileges, they defied the demands for
taxes and contributions made by their communities, even to the point of
openly withdrawing recognition of the official communal agents as their
representatives.[37] The communal leaders, alarmed by the steady defec-
tion of taxpayers, put pressures on them to fulfill their duties, even
threatening excommunication.[38] The leading rabbi lashed out at the
protected Jews, whose refusal to contribute their allotted share multi-

plied the tax burden on their poor brethren.[39] As the ranks of protegés swelled in Aleppo and other localities Ottoman officials too began to turn against them, primarily because their tax exemptions ate into state revenues. At the end of the century the authorities launched a belated and unsuccessful campaign to do away with them. An official order issued in 1806 abolished their privileges, fur cap and all.[40]

The other social group to emerge in the wake of early European penetration, the Catholics, was more formidable in size and more disruptive in its effects on Christian life. The Catholic missionaries, at work from the 1620s, had by the late eighteenth century won over the majority of native Christians in Aleppo and other parts of Syria. With unrelenting zeal they provided education, rendered material and moral help in times of plague and famine, and obtained subsidies from Rome for the support of local causes. Their success would not have been quite so remarkable were it not for the powerful backing they received from the French government, which not only defended them against local and official obstacles but used its patronage to buy local souls. In return for submission to papal authority, French consuls offered native Christian merchants insurance against attacks on their ships by Maltese corsairs in the Mediterranean, and diplomatic protection in general. Many local businessmen hesitated little in the face of an arrangement that greatly improved their economic prospects in the competitive world of commerce.

While the shift to Catholicism entailed no marked change in the familiar rites, customs, and beliefs of the converts, it did modify their outlook and identity in some significant ways. Rome became their spiritual center, Western Catholics their coreligionists, and Catholic powers their protectors and benefactors. They withdrew from their churches in a bitter break which unsettled the Eastern Christian world. Only the Maronites accepted papal authority as a collective. The hierarchy of the other three churches fought tooth and nail against the missionary effort, but failed to stem the tide. The Catholics who broke off established new Uniate versions of their parent churches, led by their own clergy. Seven churches emerged where once there were four. Until 1839, when the Ottoman authorities officially recognized these novel ecclesiastical creations, Catholic and Orthodox fought for control of their churches. Each party invited the authorities to intervene against its rivals, setting in motion an endless cycle of arrests, deportations, and exactions. Hundreds of Catholics tired of the oppressive climate and emigrated, mostly to Egypt and Lebanon.[41] In violence and intensity the religious intolerance among Christians far outweighed the frictions between Muslims and non-Muslims.

In 1740, 8,120 Christians paid the poll tax in Aleppo; the number fell to 7,213 in 1754, and in 1793 stood at 5,200.[42] The sharp decline—by one-third in the span of half a century—mirrored the dramatic effects of large-scale emigration and tax exemption. Behind these developments was the impact of European penetration. At this early stage it touched only the Christian and Jewish populations; the mainstream of society and its basic social arrangements were as yet unaffected.

SOCIAL DISTINCTIONS AND INEQUALITIES

THERE WERE SEVERAL attributes besides religious affiliation that determined one's circumstances, opportunities, and social identity in Aleppo. Of these, one's level of wealth was perhaps the most important in a society which harbored great material contrasts. A thin crust of very wealthy families attained what stood at the time for the good life, with all its known comforts and pleasures: handsome mansions, servants, slaves, harems, exquisite clothes, abundant food, horses, amusements, and luxuries of various sorts. They owned real estate and land, speculated in commodities and money, and invested in tax farms and venal offices.

The enormous fortunes and luxurious life-styles of the wealthy few dazzled when set against the circumstances of the mass of residents. A vast gulf separated the uppermost layer from those at the very bottom. In between these extremes, a sizable number of Aleppines lived comfortably, enjoying varying degrees of ease and financial security. They formed a middle group of people neither affluent nor needy who thrived on the opportunities made available by a great city. From them the economic ladder descended into the increasingly precarious material world inhabited by most of the townspeople. Here were the multitudes of residents who lived at bare subsistence levels, surviving from hand to mouth in wretched conditions: families crowded into congested dwellings often shared with other households; parents reduced by poverty to putting their children in the custody of others; debtors who languished in prison for months for the inability to pay back petty sums; the victims of hunger and starvation in periods of high bread prices; and the host of those dependent on charity.

In the middle years of the century employees at the lowest income

level—servants, doormen, watchmen, and laborers in various trades—
earned wages of 1 to 6 piastres *(ghurush)* a month.[43] With a monthly
income of 4.5 piastres one Muhammad Amin ibn Ahmad was reckoned
by the court to be poor, and hence released of his legal obligation to
support his siblings.[44] Although no figures exist for the incomes of the
self-employed, business transactions by the well-to-do indicate financial
means of an entirely different order. In 1766 seven villages acknowledged a combined debt of 138,691 piastres to one wealthy man. The
assets of another person of means included over 30,000 piastres just in
cash loaned out.[45]

Still more telling are the figures on contemporary housing. Computed
from thousands of sales deeds, they provide the best available indicator
of relative material conditions in all levels of society. Not only the vast
economic inequalities but also the predominant size of the poorer groups
appear in striking form. Dwellings ranged in price from as little as 8 to
as much as 11,500 piastres. They varied widely in size and amenities.
In the 1750s about 60 percent of houses sold annually were priced at
less than 200 piastres. Two-thirds of the houses sold were small and
short on domestic amenities; 31 percent were larger and more comfortable homes; and less than 4 percent were the luxurious residences of the
most wealthy. Those mansionlike houses cost on the average four times
more than the middle-sized dwellings and fourteen times more than the
small ones.[46]

The townspeople took for granted these great economic differences.
They spoke routinely of the poor *(fuqara')* as a natural part of society.
Religious communities, neighborhoods, and trade guilds all acknowledged the presence of a layer of poor; they funded charities and made
special arrangements to accommodate those considered needy.[47] Various government taxes were assessed according to three brackets (high,
middle, and low); in practice the lowest bracket came to be divided into
several subcategories, a recognition of the fine economic gradations that
existed even at the lowest levels.[48] Although contemporaries left no
precise definitions of those they considered to be poor, it is likely that
they thought not of all of those unblessed with the comforts of a good
life, but more specifically of those who could not provide for their most
basic needs without outside support. A multitude of widows, orphans,
elderly, and disabled people fell into that category. Their demands for
charity, welfare, and shelter from their relatives and communities were
heard frequently in the city's courts. Although certain types of poor
remained a chronic aspect of the social scene, the overall numbers

fluctuated sharply. The recurring economic slumps and famines of the eighteenth century always thrust some of the self-supporting poor into the ranks of the destitute.

Aleppo's residents held the pursuit of material comforts and property to be perfectly legitimate. Driven by the practical dictates of survival they worked since childhood or early adolescence, and their economic aptitude and competitive urges were thus sharpened at a young age. The religious leaders sought to temper the intensity of material pursuit by stressing the virtues of charity and modesty, but even they did not advocate anything like a rejection of the material world. Indeed, Muslim men of religion from the most respected and learned families ranked among the great property owners and entrepreneurs of the time. The poor shared the aspirations of their better-off neighbors; theirs was not a distinct subculture unmindful of the material standards and values of the larger community. Poverty was nothing to boast about or even overlook in their society. "Be known for wealth, not poverty," was the unequivocal recommendation of a popular saying.[49]

With wealth came status and influence; this linkage the residents clearly saw. "Power on earth rests on wealth, in the hereafter on good deeds," declared a local saying.[50] Popular lore, drawn from the world of experience, commented abundantly on the advantages of wealth: "The piastre equips its owner with seven languages"; "the well-to-do person owns a firm back"; "he who has wealth will win the hand of the sultan's daughter."[51] Aleppo's wealthy boasted honorary titles, prestigious positions, useful connections, networks of clients, and a voice in local affairs; their circumstances confirmed the generally accepted notion that money and social advantages are correlated, each reinforcing the other.

People often took care to impress others through conspicuous consumption and public display, and Aleppines learned to estimate the material worth of a person from various indicators, including his address, his dwelling, his life-style, and even the fabrics, style, and colors of his clothes. Occupation provided one of the most important clues to wealth and status. The working population, which included many women and children, filled a broad range of trades and professions varying widely in income and prestige. Most people were employed in manufacturing or the retail trade, largely in the areas of food, clothing, and construction, in which the bulk of demand was concentrated. The services, which formed a relatively limited sector, added numerous other trades, ranging from physicians to prostitutes, with domestics making up perhaps the largest group.

Society attached different degrees of respectability to these occupations. Prostitutes, entertainers, and servants fell into the category of lowly and denigrated professions. On the other hand, members of certain crafts and trades bore the honorific title of chalabi (Turk. *çelebi*, meaning "gentleman") that was enjoyed at the time by men of some social standing. They included doctors, master builders, moneychangers, goldsmiths, coppersmiths, and carpenters; men who produced and sold textiles and clothing; and dealers in drugs, spices, coffee, paper, and butter.[52] The respectability attached to these professions was clearly not unrelated to the fact that they were relatively lucrative. High income mattered irrespective of the ranking of a given profession in any ideal hierarchy of trades. It made it possible to attain a desirable life-style and so to improve the status of one's family. It was therefore not accidental that in the business world of the day no other group attained the prestige accorded to the great export-import merchants *(tujjar)*, who happened to be engaged in the most lucrative of all pursuits. Unlike the craftsmen and bazaar shopkeepers, these prosperous merchants boasted great fortunes, and were the only element in the business world to penetrate the city's elite. Although they varied in wealth and success, as a group they ranked among the most prestigious social elements in Aleppo. In correspondence and court documents the merchant was identified, as no artisan or shopkeeper was, as a member of a distinguished group: he ranked as "the pride of the noble merchants" and "the pillar of the honorable traders."[53] The Muslim merchants bore the titles of chalabi and agha along with other men of social distinction; their Christian and Jewish colleagues were addressed respectfully as *khawajas*.[54]

The differences in prestige among certain trades were not very clear-cut or subject to general agreement. In public processions, when the members of each trade marched as a unit, arguments over precedence erupted which at some point brought an end to the parades.[55] Clearly, the labor force did not share a consensus about the hierarchy of trades; those relegated to the lower scales felt unduly slighted and refused to accept judgments on their inferiority.

Besides the distinctions *among* trades, substantial differences in income and position actually cut *across* trades. The master craftsman who owned a workshop and equipment was distinguished from the wage laborers and apprentices working under him, although they all shared the same line of trade. Self-employment in an established business indicated a certain economic security which thousands of skilled and unskilled employees aspired to attain. Social recognition and titles of honor went selectively to the better-off, professionally established members of the more respectable trades—not to all members. Unlike their subordinates, men of high professional reputation enjoyed the title of master *(ustadh* or *muᶜallim).*[56]

Many of the inequalities in position and income within professions had a formal basis in the collective arrangements of the guilds in which the various crafts and trades were organized. Among other things, guild regulations set up different rates of taxation and quotas for the distribution of raw materials and jobs among members.[57] The guild codes also regulated entry into the profession and promotion within its ranks. In the craft guilds, a professional hierarchy usually distinguished between the master, the journeyman *(saniᶜ),* the wage employee *(ajir),* and the young apprentice *(ghulam* or *ajir).*[58] Seniority within this structure brought with it prestige as well as material advantages. The elder members *(ikhtiyariyya)* of each guild were recognized as an informal policymaking body; this privilege, and the access to the office of shaykh, placed them in a position to shape the rules in ways favorable to their rank. While some guilds provided for the equal distribution of raw materials, jobs, and financial burdens, many others upheld arrangements decidedly advantageous to their senior members.[59]

The city's labor force also included several hundred slaves, who ranked juridically as the most disadvantaged category in society. Their fellow human beings literally owned them and could dispose of them at will. The possession of slaves was a symbol of status, a common feature of well-to-do households. Families bought slaves on the market, for prices ranging from 20 to 250 piastres,[60] or received them as gifts. Like other groups in the city, they too were highly differentiated, the actual status and fortunes of individual slaves varying considerably. Some of them, usually those of black skin, were domestics relegated to the most menial household chores. Some of the more highly esteemed white slaves served as concubines and pages. A select few were privileged with a trust and training that converted them into loyal agents of their masters. These men grew up within the intimate family circle like adopted children, enjoying care and education. Their masters trusted them with the most important and confidential affairs, even dispatching them on business trips abroad.[61]

Aleppo's privileged slaves were the product of an ideal of ultimate loyalty that had a venerable regional tradition behind it. Their status corresponded more to that of respected protegés and aides than lowly minions. A close relationship tied them to their adoptive families even after their manumission; some of them even took their masters' daughters in marriage. Men and women who endowed property for the support of their kin occasionally included freed slaves (*ʿutaqaʾ*) of the family among the designated beneficiaries.[62] The social and economic fortunes of these slaves reflected the rewards of loyalty: some bore the title of agha,[63] and when manumitted walked into the world of free men carrying business skills, political experience, valuable connections, and substantial property. Sulayman Agha ibn ʿAbdallah, the former slave of a prominent man, endowed for his children's benefit an orchard as well as several houses and shops. Another freed slave was able to purchase from his master nine houses, two workshop complexes, a dye shop, and two stores.[64] The merchant Musa Agha al-Amiri ran his far-flung commercial ventures with the aid of loyal slaves, on whom he showered wealth and benefits. A comfortable life-style, titles, literacy, and acts of philanthropy all brought them social esteem as freed men.[65] Such was one odd route into Aleppo's respectable society.

Far more basic and important than the distinction between slave and freeman was that between male and female. Society held it as axiomatic that men and women were different in nature and capacity and so ought to play distinct social roles. The notion of male superiority enjoyed unchallenged currency in the culture of the city and the wider region. Women did not figure among government officials, clergy, soldiers, or heads of guilds and neighborhoods; positions of authority and public office belonged to men only. Contemporary chroniclers, preoccupied largely with the drama of politics, found little occasion to mention women. Islamic law drew distinctions between the rights of men and women. For instance, the testimony of two female witnesses in court was equivalent to that of one male, and a female was entitled to half the inheritance of her male equal; a popular saying had it that "a woman is endowed with half a brain, half a religious faith, and half an inheritance."[66]

The consciousness of social differences between the sexes was particularly keen in a society that took extraordinary care to segregate males from females. The strict veiling of women, official restrictions on their outdoor excursions, the segregation of the sexes in familial celebrations and public places of assembly, the unlawfulness of sexual relations outside marriage and concubinage, the prohibition of dating by couples, the arrangement of marriages by the family, the provision of secluded female quarters in houses—these were among the routine measures that people of all levels took to prevent undesirable contact between the sexes. Even Christians and Jews shared these practices and enforced them.[67] The community took all necessary precautions to uphold its ideals of modesty and sexual morality, with women bearing the larger share of restrictions; female chastity, and thus family honor, were at stake. The barriers did not preclude business and other legitimate associations between the sexes—or even prevent violation of the norms. Court documents record illicit affairs, illegitimate pregnancies, seductions, the discovery of foundlings, and the confessions of women of loose morals.[68] On the whole, however, the segregation did work effectively to enforce a pattern of relations in which friendships tended to revolve around members of one's own sex.

Women were not, however, entirely relegated to a closed world of their own. Judicial records show the remarkable degree to which they participated in the general life of the community in various recognized capacities. Like men, women worked in the marketplace, invested in property, engaged in moneylending, founded and administered charitable endowments, negotiated marriage arrangements, and organized familial celebrations. In the 1750s, women constituted some 40 percent of the buyers and sellers of houses in the city.[69] They sued and were sued in court on a host of matters. Many successfully obtained divorces from their husbands despite their legal disdavantages. Women formed part of the fabric of the family, the neighborhood, the economy, and the general social scene. They even participated actively in the popular protests against oppressive officials and bread shortages which rocked the city periodically.[70]

The wealthier women of Aleppo were easily distinguishable by their clothing, jewelry, manners, and, above all, their freedom from the indignities of employment in the marketplace. They attained the female ideal of a life of leisurely seclusion, unburdened by employment and the compromises of promiscuous mixing with the public. Servants ran their errands and did their daily shopping. Court documents referred to these wealthy models of righteous female life as "the most eminent of secluded women" *(fakhr al-mukhaddarat)*. Many women at the lower levels of society, on the other hand, had from practical necessity to work out of the home. They filled a whole range of undistinguished occupations: maids, midwives, wet nurses, matchmakers, bonesetters, hairdressers, professional mourners, bath house attendants, tutors for girls, textile workers, peddlers, singers, dancers, and prostitutes. Some also worked in the production or sale of various commodities such as bread, wool, wine, and wheat. And, many of these working women made their living by catering to the needs and whims of better-off females.

Some of Aleppo's men and women were distinguished from the rest of the population by their rural origin. The immigrants who settled in the city during the eighteenth century included a good number of Arab, Kurdish, and Turkman tribesmen whose language, dress, customs, and life-style set them apart from the urban population and from urban immigrants. They joined previously established groups of fellow tribesmen who had preserved their traditions and ways. A rural air hung over their poor residential districts outside the city's eastern walls. To an English visitor that part of town looked "like a country Arab town fifty miles off."[71] The tribesmen brought with them no wealth, learning, or distinction; they found employment in lowly occupations, as camel drivers and guides in the caravan service, manual laborers in industry and agriculture, and domestics. They married within their respective groups and mixed little with outsiders.[72] Arab tribesmen from the caravan station of Sukhna in the Syrian desert inhabited a quarter of their own (al-Sakhkhana). They maintained a clannish behavior even into the twentieth century, when the urban community still saw them as outsiders. The bedouin who came to do business in the city entrusted their affairs to these fellow tribesmen to ensure that they were not outwitted by the local merchants.[73]

Local rejection by the urban population, who disdained their lifestyle and feared them as a troublesome lot defiant of authority and order,[74] only reinforced the tribesmen's clannishness. These prejudices had more to do with the fact that the tribesmen were different in their ways than with their outside origin or ethnic background. Nontribesmen were less likely to remain outsiders for long. They joined urban groups and gained acceptance. The community did not harbor xenophobic prejudices against all immigrants. Indeed, some climbed to the highest social circles. Of the 137 distinguished Muslim scholars and teachers of the eighteenth century who were deemed worthy of biographical notices, as many as 37 were immigrants. The majority of the newcomers (27 men) originated in settlements in northern Syria; the rest, with the exception of one Afghan scholar, came from the larger urban centers of the Arab Middle East. An additional 9 prominent scholars born locally were also known to be of families who had migrated to Aleppo in a previous generation.[75] Among the distinguished families of the day were the Tarabulsis, Misris, Hamawis, Arihawis, Taftanazis, and others whose very names betrayed their external origins.

When the residents distinguished between urban and rural, as also between people of different economic levels and occupations, they were reacting partly to real differences and partly to stereotypes and prejudices current in their cultural milieu. Religious opinion frowned upon some of these divisive attitudes, which ran against the ideals of communal fraternity and equality. Some of the distinctions, however, were anchored in law and Islamic doctrine, which defined the status of women and slaves as well as non-Muslims. Social practice fostered categories and relations not explained entirely by the formal rules—a situation most dramatically evident in the peculiar status of the privileged slaves. The varied collective notions held by different groups added still more to the complexity of the scene. The dhimmis rejected society's judgments on their social inferiority. The immigrant tribesmen measured their own worth by standards different from those applied to them by urbanites. Those who practiced various trades and crafts quarreled with the status attributed to them by general opinion. Women countered some of the denigrating attitudes expressed toward them by males and asserted positive self-images. The local folklore, to which females as well as males contributed, stresses the importance of women, their indispensable role, and their ability to get their way.[76]

Despite the dissonant voices, however, the basic distinctions remained stable throughout the eighteenth century. The townspeople, who inherited the ideological framework of earlier generations, continued to recognize essentially the same social categories and to determine identity and standing by the same criteria. The laws were not modified, and popular attitudes appear to have perpetuated themselves without major alteration. That none of the existing social categories disappeared from the scene and no new groups emerged during the period sheltered the existing cultural conceptions from the need to accommodate new realities.

THE SOURCES OF HIGH STATUS

THE BASIC SOCIAL distinctions suggest some of the inequalities in Aleppo's society, but one must go beyond them to see more fully those particular attributes which singled out certain segments of the population and gave them high status. Those residents who enjoyed high standing in the eighteenth century possessed one or more of the following as the basis of their elevated position: wealth, official position, command of military force, religious vocation, learning, or prestigious lineage. These were usually correlated assets, the most promising routes to which were by way of affiliation with what constituted the city's high-status groups: the government, the military, the religious establishment, the merchants *(tujjar)*, and the *ashraf* (lineal descendants of the Prophet Muhammad). Members of these groups—not all but rather the leading figures—formed the urban elite. Although the groups were made up of individuals who varied in their social standing and influence they enjoyed general recognition as privileged categories. The government itself promoted their special status; it held them up for their honorable associations with the state and Islam, and graced them with patronage in the form of honors, titles, appointments, tax privileges, and revenue farms. Official documents identified them as prestigious; a prominent member of such a group was always rated, depending on his particular affiliation, as "the pillar of eminent scholars," "the model of noble teachers," "the cream of the illustrious," "the pride of the noble merchants," or "the glory of the eminent ashraf."[77]

Government service was one established route to high standing in the city. Some of the key posts in the provincial administration were inaccessible to locals: the governor and the qadi, the top figures in the city-based provincial government, were both outsiders appointed from Istanbul. They brought with them a staff of aides and attendants who accompanied them on their routine moves from province to province. Various other positions, however, were open to locals. The government staffed the courts and administrative offices with a host of accountants, clerks, and bureaucrats of different ranks. Many posts and venal offices were sold locally by the government. The Muslim jurisconsult *(mufti)*, the deputy judges in the shari'a courts, the water and building inspectors, and other appointees invested considerable sums in their posts in the expectation of using their official status to enrich themselves, cultivate useful connections, and improve their social standing. Among the social rewards of state service were officially conferred titles of rank: effendi for the top scribes and legal functionaries, agha for a variety of administrative posts.

The most lucrative and influential government positions involved tax collection. The state "farmed out" the right to collect the revenues in the city and countryside. Well-to-do merchants, officials, army officers, and men of religion invested capital in tax farms, competing in the auctions for one-year farms *(iltizams)* or acquiring the life tenure farms *(malikânes)* which became increasingly available from the early eighteenth century. There were good profits to be made, in both legal and irregular ways, from this form of government service. In addition, the tax farmer acquired the title of agha and had an opportunity to establish good government connections.

While some of the tax farmers were small investors who acquired a share in a village or in urban market dues, others distinguished themselves by large-scale involvement in the tasks of revenue collection, notably in the provincial countryside where the greatest opportunities lay. The great tax farmers established hereditary rights over dozens of villages, in which they acted as virtual landlords and patrons. In addition to collecting taxes from the peasants they took care of various administrative tasks, mediated local disputes, and lent money on a large scale. Large stocks of food came into their possession as tax payments, giving them a highly profitable control over the grain supply to the city. Their operations rested on the services of hundreds of employees and dependents. In wealth and influence the great tax farmers ranked among the most prominent families in the city. By virtue of their command of the administrative and fiscal machinery of the province they became indispensable to the state. The authorities recognized them collectively as the *aᶜyan*, a notable class distinguished by its special alliance with government.[78]

Service in the city's Janissary garrison opened other means of social advancement. The corps, which carried out police duties in the city and province as well as contributing troops to the sultan's armies in times of war, formed a sizable body numbering normally around four thousand men recruited locally.[79] While it showed little of the celebrated discipline and valor of earlier centuries the force still offered social and material advantages to its members, and exercised an influence on local affairs out of proportion to its numbers. As members of the military (*ᶜaskari*) class the Janissaries enjoyed exemption from various taxes—a great advantage, since many of them were engaged in business, a practice established in the sixteenth century.[80] Some craftsmen and merchants acquired membership in the force for this reason alone. Regulations in various guilds distinguished between the benefits of the *ᶜaskari* members and those of the *raᶜaya*, or common subjects, creating inequalities that occasionally led to frictions within trades.[81]

The real rewards of membership in the Janissary corps went not to the rank and file of lowly troops and small businessmen, but to the chief commander (*serdar*) and his staff of high officers, or aghas. These were men of considerable power and wealth whose activities went well beyond their formal roles. Like other entrepreneurs of the time, they held tax farms in the city and countryside, engaged in moneylending, and traded in grain. Their advantage over others lay in the command of a military force that they were more than willing to use to promote their political and economic interests. Through a combination of violence and patronage they exercised control over some guilds and neighborhoods; by the early nineteenth century they had won practically all of the city's key offices and resources. The corps that they commanded was in many respects more like an armed power group than a dutiful imperial unit.[82]

A different path to social standing and influence was made available by affiliation with the Muslim religious establishment, which figured as a recognized branch in the official structure of authority. The several hundred men who staffed its ranks, known collectively as the *ulama* (sing. *alim*), filled a whole range of occupations: leaders of prayer; preachers; chanters of the Koran; teachers of the Islamic religious sciences; scholars; and judges, court clerks, and jurists. They guided the faithful in their worship and ritual, enforced the law, adjudicated disputes, transmitted knowledge and tradition, and contributed to the body of scholarship. In a society that wove religion into its law, education, and social institutions, the professional men of religion enjoyed great prestige. They were deemed the living repositories of high values and morals—the models of the kind of conduct that was held to be most worthy by the community. The state graced them with honors and privileges, not least of them an exemption from taxes.

The ulama possessed something of a self-conscious identity as a group. Their learning and professional outlook fostered a collective self-image and an expectation of public respect. Writing around 1780, the scholar Khalil al-Muradi articulated in detail the social role and responsibilities of the alim. He was above all the custodian of his community's knowledge, a sacred trust he could never forget or abuse. His command of knowledge distinguished him from the uneducated but did not diminish his obligation to respect all men, however low and ignorant. His lofty calling demanded that he live up to the highest standards of modesty, piety, compassion, and integrity. An air of dignity should surround him at all times; an excess of frivolity, jest, and informality could only compromise his image. Fellow men owed him deference, and form dictated that they avoid all informal language or rude gestures in his presence.[83]

But to describe a man merely as a member of the ulama left much unknown about his precise status. Wide differences in learning, piety, position, wealth, and lineage cut across the group. Some of Aleppo's ulama boasted a rigorous education under the great masters of their day, a creative inclination to scholarly work, and a regional reputation for expertise that attracted aspiring students; others had but limited training and no intellectual renown. Some ulama led a life of modesty and self-denial, shunning worldly pleasures and exhorting their disciples to a spiritual existence; theirs was an extraordinary level of piety which contemporaries were quick to note.[84] The ulama who held positions in the courts and in the great colleges and mosques were in a league apart from the minor functionaries in neighborhood mosques; they held the title of effendi and enjoyed a good income, generous patronage, and great prestige. Some ulama lived in comfortable circumstances, a few boasting great wealth and a luxurious life-style. Many, however, were men of modest means who could not support themselves on the meager stipends and wages of their religious vocations; they worked in the marketplace as shopkeepers and artisans.[85] Some ulama came from poor and humble origins; while education elevated their standing considerably, their colleagues from families with a long tradition of learning commanded the social advantage of reputable lineage.

That the ulama were not men of religion and learning to the exclusion of all else is illustrated well by the careers of four of their leading members in the second half of the eighteenth century. Muhammad Effendi Taha Zadeh, Ahmad Effendi Kawakibi Zadeh, Muhammad Effendi Tarabulsi Zadeh, and Muhammad Sharif Effendi 'Imadi Zadeh all held teaching positions in the city's major colleges. The first three held the office of jurisconsult (mufti), the most prestigious position in the city's religious establishment. They were also leading ashraf; in fact, all four officially headed this influential corps by appointment from Istanbul. All four boasted considerable wealth. They invested in tax farms, and, like the a'yan, involved themselves on a large scale in moneylending and speculation in grains; Taha Zadeh came to control dozens of villages. They also figured among the greatest landlords in the city, investing heavily in homes, commercial real estate, and agricultural properties. Their influence won them the administration of the most important charitable foundations, including that of the Great Umayyad Mosque with its hundreds of endowed properties.[86] They enjoyed considerable influence in local affairs through their close connections with government and their control over resources and extensive networks of clients. They were in fact political figures no less than religious and economic figures. Their influence and ambitions involved them in the city's politics at the highest level; Taha Zadeh and Kawakibi Zadeh suffered periods of banishment from the city when they lost official favor.

Even for the more ordinary ulama membership in the religious establishment was socially advantageous. Acquiring an education and entering a religious vocation were at the time among the surest paths to upward mobility. Many men of modest background with an inclination to learn improved their standing considerably by joining the ranks of the ulama, whose social standing rested in part on the fact that they formed the core of the educated and literate public in a society with very high illiteracy. Few townspeople could read or write; even fewer had a broad formal education. Illiteracy, being so normal and widespread, carried no social stigma; even some provincial governors and high officials were illiterate.[87] Nor did it represent, in the absence of newspapers and books of broad interest, a socially debilitating handicap. But while they were denied the luxury of a good education, the larger public respected learning and those who possessed it, and all ranks of the ulama basked in popular admiration for their knowledge of texts and command of the pen.

Another source of high standing in society was a prestigious lineage. Descent from the Prophet's family formed at the time the only institutionalized lineage. Those who claimed this noble ancestry, the ashraf, enjoyed hereditary privileges and high status. The government granted them exemption from various taxes, honored them with the privilege of distinct clothing in the form of a green turban, and exhorted the public to show them due respect and deference. It placed jurisdiction over the affairs of the ashraf in the imperial domains in the hands of the *naqib al-ashraf* in Istanbul, a high dignitary selected from among the top Ottoman ulama. This official appointed a deputy *naqib* in Aleppo, usually a high-ranking alim, to oversee all matters affecting members of the group in the city and province. His formal authority included the power to certify new members, to adjudicate certain legal matters in his court, and to imprison offenders in his jail.[88]

The ashraf in Aleppo numbered in the thousands. Observers were impressed with their formidable presence. Their ranks swelled considerably in the eighteenth century as ambitious men bribed their way into membership with the aid of fraudulent genealogies; the *naqib* received periodic orders from Istanbul to stop these rampant abuses of admission.[89] The attraction of membership lay not only in the honor accorded to noble descent but also in the considerable material advantages offered. The ashraf did not pay certain property taxes and exactions imposed on the neighborhoods, nor did they share equally in the fiscal obligations of their guilds. Collective arrangements in the trades often differentiated them from the "commoners" (*'awamm*).[90]

Like the other high-status groups, the ashraf were differentiated in wealth and standing. They included porters and butchers, dealers in pastries and wheat, rope makers and textile artisans. But they also included many of the city's most prominent ulama, merchants, and aʿyan. Descent from the Prophet's family was clearly not sufficient in itself to determine one's standing; it was a potential social asset that buttressed the status of those equipped with other useful attributes. The benefits of affiliation with the ashraf improved in the second part of the eighteenth century, when the group emerged on the scene as an organized political faction with its own militia. Like the Janissaries, and in direct competition with them, the leading ashraf used patronage and violence to seize positions and resources in the city. Some of their benefits trickled down to their clients.

The ashraf were the only group in Aleppo to approach anything resembling a nobility of blood. It was common, however, for individual families, such as those with a reputation for scholarship, to cultivate pride of familial lineage by stressing their descent from certain distinguished ancestors and conveying the impression of continuing accomplishment. Saying of someone that he was a Kawakibi or a Jabiri, for instance, placed him immediately in a renowned line of learned men. Wealth and high office also supported claims to fine lineage.

To stress their lineage, the families of high standing identified themselves by patronyms which they carried like pedigrees. In this respect they differed from most other residents, who usually had no family name or, if they did, were not so inseparably identified with it as to bear it as a fixed part of their personal names on all occasions. In contemporary writings, including even careful legal documents, men and women were most commonly identified only by their patrifiliative name chain (for example, Ahmad ibn Ibrahim, or Fatima bint Mustafa ibn Sulayman). However, the personal names of members of the most prominent merchant, ulama, and aʿyan families appeared almost invariably with a patronym, one based most commonly on the profession, high office, place of origin, or personal name of an ancestor. Among these socially conscious families the patronymic affiliation was often expressed with the Turkish extension *Zadeh* (son) in keeping with Ottoman practice (Taha Zadeh, Misri Zadeh, Naqib Zadeh). In the third quarter of the century only some one hundred and twenty families were dignified with this usage in the judicial records. To contemporaries many of these were household names.

Lineage passed in the male line. Men and women of upper-class background born of concubines or manumitted slave girls suffered therefore no loss of status; their father's high lineage defined their social identity. A woman of high lineage, however, could not pass her name to her husband or children. One Husayn Effendi ibn Ahmad, a scholar of modest background, did the unusual when he adopted his wife's notable patronym. Living in his father-in-law's household, he became inseparably associated with the family. He and his descendants signed their name al-Dadikhi.[91]

A good familial lineage was a social asset, but one not sufficient in itself. Individuals had to live up to the family's reputation in order to benefit fully from its rewards. Aleppo's society made no room for an entrenched aristocracy sitting on the laurels of its ancestors. For reaching high standing and maintaining it, live social connections were in many respects more essential than ancestral ties. In a society in which relations of patronage were accepted as perfectly normal types of association, people of all ranks routinely entered the service of those above them and cultivated their good will in the hope of advancing themselves. With the helping hand of their patrons many of them skillfully worked their way up and overtook their less-protected peers. The biographies of the more distinguished ulama tell time and again the story of the able scholar or teacher taken under the wing of a generous patron who, depending on the circumstances, secures him a good appointment, a stipend, a home, and even a wife.[92] Ibrahim Agha Qattar Aghasi, an illiterate servant in the household of Muhammad Effendi Taha Zadeh, rose with his master's favor to prominence as a tax farmer, and by the turn of the nineteenth century became governor of the province.

One's ties of patronage were open and even a source of prestige in themselves. In court people occasionally identified themselves as the dependents (sing. *tabi*) of this or that prominent figure; some were slaves or former slaves, others free-born Muslims.[93] For the patrons, their queues of clients were tangible symbols of status and influence. The networks of patronage led inevitably to government, which dispensed the tax farms, appointments, tax exemptions, titles, honors, and privileges so essential to achieving status, wealth, and influence in Aleppo. Access to these prized official favors depended on good connections. Even the most influential and wealthy local men relied on patrons, some of them at the highest levels of government in Istanbul. Like their clients they too knew at first hand the meaning of dependence.

STRATIFICATION AND SOCIAL MOBILITY

IN THEIR PRIVILEGES and social expectations the groups of high status displayed something of the keen attention paid to hierarchy in Aleppo's community. Consciousness of inequalities was woven into the outlook and behavior of the townspeople. They were brought up to accept them as part of the natural scheme of things, to know their place in society, and to show deference to their superiors. The concern with upholding social differences was especially evident in the many formalities which governed relations. In addition to the titles, ranks, and dress codes there were elaborate rules of etiquette and ceremony which dictated proper behavior in different social situations. People kissed the hands of elders, rose in respect when superiors appeared, and paid attention to the sitting order in meetings and the marching order in processions. There were even special modes of written address appropriate for individuals in different stations and positions. Polite men assembled in private handbooks many samples of these long and flowery formulas to help them open their letters with the right greetings and respects.[94]

While contemporary thought recognized the hierarchical nature of society, several stratification schemes tended to enjoy currency, each of them based on a particular axis of social division. Official ideology spoke of a society of rulers and the ruled. A distinct ruling class of officials and soldiers exercised authority in the name of the despotic sultan; it enjoyed a privileged status that set it apart from the mass of subjects, who were appropriately termed the "flocks" *(ra'aya)*. Religion, like power, was also seen as dividing society into two classes: the dominant Muslim population whose law and ethics set the tone of public life, and the subordinate non-Muslim communities it suffered to live in its midst. Yet another prevalent notion saw the community as a dual hierarchy of notables and commoners, in which influence, wealth, and social esteem differentiated a patrician class from the mass of plebs. "The notability and the common people" ("al-khass wa 'l-'amm") was a phrase that the residents used idiomatically to mean the community at large. They spoke habitually of grandees and notables *(akabir, a'yan, wujuh)*, and of the rank and file of commoners *('amma, 'awamm,* sing. *'ammi)*.[95]

These schemata, which echoed venerable political and social notions, captured what were perceived to be the meaningful and enduring divisions in society. As ideological constructs they served to legitimize certain inequalities rather than to describe precise social realities. Taking them at face value risks attributing to the urban community a degree of order and harmony that it did not necessarily possess. Aleppo's was not a society stratified according to one or another grand divide: it appears landscaped more nearly in a slope than in two sharply defined tiers. The actual distribution of wealth, power, and status reveals the presence of a thin group of Muslim elite families distinguished by their command of the key social and economic advantages as well as by recognized political leadership; of a formidable mass of residents who could claim little or no wealth, influence, or status; and of, between the two poles, a significant body of people who possessed, in varying degrees, some wealth, prestige, and power. These three levels in the city's social hierarchy may be identified, for lack of better terms, as the lower, middle, and upper classes, but without thereby attributing to them a necessarily homogeneous, rigid, or self-conscious character. They were not strata defined by wealth alone; other measures of status also determined one's class. Each was a rough category composed of people of different backgrounds and occupations, and containing some inner variations of status. However, the members of each class shared a set of comparable social circumstances and opportunities that distinguished them from others outside their level.

This element of coherence was due in large part to the tendency of wealth, status, and influence to be highly correlated with each other. Access to one often opened the way to the others. Ulama of modest means were able to marry into well-to-do families precisely because their prestigious vocation and academic reputation promoted them above their economic peers. Such matches traded wealth for prestige. High status opened up opportunities for the increase of wealth; and wealth made it possible to acquire the trappings of social standing and political influence. Positions of influence led, even if by devious paths, to riches and esteem. Although people did move up and down the social scale as their circumstances changed, mobility was sufficiently limited by all sorts of barriers to keep large segments of the population within the class into which they were born, giving the social divisions of the hierarchy a certain stability.

The proposed three-class structure could no doubt be refined were better evidence available on the distribution of wealth and the other sources of social inequality. Yet even in this rough form it provides a useful working scheme with which to approach the complex social scene and make sense of its arrangements. A broad profile of each of the three

classes helps to visualize more realistically the circumstances of various
segments of the population, and to see why lumping everyone outside
the thin elite into an undifferentiated mass of "common people" misrep-
resents the social hierarchy.

The lower class illuminates the world of the unprivileged and the
have-nots, to which perhaps between two-thirds and three-quarters of
the population may have belonged. The core of what contemporaries
defined loosely as the ʿamma, or commoners, people in this rank pursued
lowly, relatively unspecialized, and poorly paid occupations. They ranged
from petty artisans and shopkeepers to unskilled laborers, peddlers, and
servants, and, lower yet, to prostitutes, thieves, and beggars. They
survived on low incomes and had little or no property. Some owned all
or part of their small homes, while others rented mean dwellings and
rooms. Cold, disease, famine, and economic depression hit them the
hardest. Many depended on charity for survival, turning to the mercy
of public welfare and private almsgivers.

The members of the lower class lived in all parts of the city, with the
heaviest concentration in the solidly poor districts outside the eastern,
southern, and western walls. They included many unassimilated rural
immigrants as well as established urbanites. Largely illiterate and lacking titles, privileges, or reputable lineage, they could lay little claim to
social prestige. Some of them were considered respectable while others
lay beyond the pale of decency, part of an underworld of vice and
crime. At the mercy of employers, landlords, creditors, the literate, and
the charitable, the lower-class families displayed a pervasive subservi-
ence. "The low wall is sat on by everyone," observed a local saying of
the lot of the socially weak.[96]

There were many in Aleppo, perhaps one-quarter to one-third of the
population, who belonged to that middle range of society blessed with
more fortunate circumstances. They occupied the more respectable
professions and the more lucrative trades. They included merchants,
businessmen, master craftsmen, skilled professionals, ulama, officials,
and tax farmers. Most members of the city's high-status groups fell into
this category. In levels of wealth they ranged from the moderately
comfortable to the affluent, although they included some poorer men
who were respected for their learning and piety. Theirs were houses
equipped with domestic amenities and servants. They owned their
homes and often their shops, and enjoyed surplus capital which they
invested in real estate, in shares of urban and rural tax farms, in public
offices, in moneylending, in trade, and in gold. They were often tax

exempt or benefited from other economic privileges. Along with the upper-class families they contributed substantially to charity and the support of communal institutions. Most of them resided in the better neighborhoods located in the intramural city and the districts outside the northern walls. A relatively high measure of literacy and learning prevailed in their ranks. Titles of honor abounded as well, and close attention was paid to social graces and familial reputation. The positions and pursuits of men and women in this class gave them some authority over others below them, whether as landlords, employers, creditors, tax collectors, heads and senior members of guilds, religious leaders, army officers, or government officials.

The upper reaches of this middle class blended into the urban elite. At any one time during the century only some four or five dozen families occupied this tip of the social pyramid, but between them they exercised an influence vastly out of proportion to their numbers on the administrative, political, military, religious, judicial, educational, cultural, financial, fiscal, and commercial affairs of the city. The members of the elite were familiar public figures; their names and exploits fill the pages of contemporary chronicles and biographical sketches. They impressed the public with their lavish life-styles, their handsome homes, their large households, their big property holdings and financial operations, their high offices and connections, and their extensive networks of dependents and hangers-on. In the eighteenth century they were all Muslim men who came from the ranks of the ulama, aʿyan, government officials, merchants, Janissaries, and ashraf—that is, from the groups that at the time provided the best access to the forms of wealth, status, and influence that mattered. The authorities recognized them as the local power brokers and incorporated them into the decision-making process. The governor's consultative council included the highest-ranking ulama and aʿyan, the leader of the ashraf, and the commander of the Janissary corps, a composition that formally acknowledged the realities of the local hierarchy.

This striking mix of elements—civilian and military, religious and lay—reflected the eclectic social makeup of the elite. The members differed in their social background, government connections, power base, and network of clients. They spoke for certain local interests and segments of opinion, and commanded particular resources that helped them make their voices heard and their arms felt. Yet for all their seeming diversity they were not unlike each other in the resources on which they founded their social and political fortunes; formal labels tend to obscure the many overlaps in their group affiliations, interests, and pursuits. Men formally identified as ulama, like Muhammad Effendi Taha Zadeh and Ahmad Effendi Kawakibi Zadeh, were also leading ashraf, holders of official posts, prominent tax farmers, landlords, and businessmen. At the same time a lay notable like ʿAbd al-Wahhab Agha Shurayyif Zadeh, usually identified as one of the leading aʿyan, was a merchant, a landlord, and a leading member of the ashraf, in addition to being a large tax farmer. Close familial connections tied him with the ulama: he was married to the daughter of Muhammad Sharif Effendi ʿImadi Zadeh, a leading member of the ulama and ashraf, and one of his sons joined the religious establishment.[97] All such attributes contributed in one way or another to placing these prominent figures at the summit of their society.

It was a mix of attributes that helped one to reach the top; nothing helped, however, if one was not a Muslim. The elite remained throughout the century an exclusively Muslim club. Potential non-Muslim candidates equipped with the proper wealth, education, and life-style found the top reaches permanently sealed off by the religious barrier. As dhimmis they were unable to attain a social standing in the city commensurate with their attributes. They sought and obtained in their own communities that full social recognition denied to them and to the other non-Muslims by the larger society. Their religious groups had their own social hierarchies, in which the members applied to each other the same standards of judgment current in the Muslim population, but without the social discount for religious affiliation. Each minority community recognized a leading elite composed, not unlike the Muslim one, of lay leaders and the clergy, who were distinguished from the common people.[98] For the non-Muslim, whose social life revolved largely around members of his community, the opinion of his coreligionists mattered most in any case. In this circle he could establish a more positive social identity and so compensate somewhat for his disabilities in the larger Muslim milieu. Such mini-hierarchies helped to ease social tensions without threatening the arrangements of the dominant hierarchy.

The wrong religious affiliation posed only one of several barriers to social mobility. Although the community developed no castes, estates, or hereditary aristocracies that locked individuals in place, and a good number of Aleppines experienced a change of status, the opportunity for upward mobility appears nonetheless to have been limited by formidable social and institutional barriers. Indeed, there was a real danger of falling in the social scale. The famines, economic slumps, and epidemics that struck the city periodically left behind them broken homes, dispersed children, collapsed businesses, and widespread destitution. The high mortality rate of the time claimed many young fathers and mothers; their absence often dimmed the prospects of their children. In the face of these unpredictable strikes of nature and market forces, simply maintaining one's existing standing was an accomplishment in itself. Even the elite families had to contend with the hazards of decline. In the rough-and-tumble of high-level politics some fell victim to loss of favor with the authorities, or to dismissal, banishment, confiscation of property, and even execution.

Upward mobility occurred more commonly within groups than across them. A dyer, a merchant, an alim, or a government official had substantial room for personal advancement in his profession. The social standing of some individuals rose when the relative standing of their group improved. Affiliation with the ashraf and the Janissaries, for instance, gained in social importance as the two groups proved able to deliver more to their members and to impress the public with their increasing influence. Some, however, did cross group lines and thereby changed their identities dramatically. Those who converted to Islam or Catholicism, or obtained manumission from slavery, or infiltrated the ranks of the ashraf, or acquired European protection, or entered the religious establishment, or joined government service or enlisted in the military all altered their formal status in society. Education, a good marriage, and skill in the games of patronage, favor, and protection clearly helped some win entry into higher circles. Individual luck, health, and ambition also made a difference in terms of the potential for advancement; longevity, a scarce commodity, in itself guaranteed an opportunity for overtaking others.

A certain unknown proportion of the population benefited from the possible avenues and opportunities for moving up. But the odds were stacked against making a big leap forward. Rags-to-riches stories were probably highly unusual. There were powerful built-in tendencies for the rich to sustain their wealth and the poor their poverty. "Just let a poor man marry a poor woman," predicted a local saying, "and before long they will produce poor children."[99] While success depended in great measure on personal achievement, the advantages of good birth weighed heavily in one's favor. The children of the better families received from their parents not only property but also skills, privileges, social contacts, lineage, and reputation. All of these were convertible into social and economic capital. In the middle and upper levels of society families paid attention to their reputations and life-styles, and strove to ensure the proper conduct of their children. They selected marriage partners for their sons and daughters with an eye to the implications for familial status. The absence of random mating tended to reinforce interclass inequalities and to limit the opportunities for dramatic self-advancement through a good marriage.

Hereditary privileges and nepotism oiled the path into desirable positions and offices, in government as well as the private sector. They essentially sealed off large segments of the job market to people without the backing of patrons or familial rights. The trade guilds limited entry into their respective professions, often reserving first priority for the masters' sons. In some guilds the senior craftsmen were privileged with a guaranteed quota of the business in their trade, a monopolistic asset that they passed on to their heirs.[100] Some families succeeded in staking out for themselves the leadership of certain guilds. One man held the office of shaykh in three guilds, inherited from his father and grandfather before him. In the weavers' guild the top office passed in the 1760s to the hands of a minor child, for whom a trustee had to be appointed.[101] Many of the brokers, weighers, tax farmers, and other officers in the city's markets held lucrative monopolies over certain fees and revenues which they often passed on within the family for generations.[102]

The shari'a court, the principal clearinghouse for appointments to public offices, consistently gave first priority to the relatives of deceased or retiring officeholders. Appointments to positions in the court itself, whether for doorman or chief scribe, went regularly to the sons, and in some cases even to the fathers of the previous occupants of the offices concerned.[103] The same principle applied in the replacement of administrators of public institutions, teachers, readers of the Koran, preachers, leaders of prayer, muezzins, and various mosque functionaries. Their positions went most often to their sons, and less frequently to their brothers, nephews, and grandchildren.[104] When Husayn ibn 'Abdallah died, the qadi transferred his two positions in a mosque to an unrelated person because, the deed of appointment notes, "the deceased had no son to replace him."[105] Some of the more enterprising ulama assembled a host of part-time positions which they eventually passed to their children. On his death in 1755 'Abd al-Rahman Effendi ibn Muhammad Effendi held the posts of hospital physician, preacher and reader of the Koran in the Great Mosque, leader of prayer in another mosque, and muezzin in yet another. His two sons divided the spoils between them.[106]

Families clung to their appointments and professional privileges as valuable sources of income and prestige. With such legacies children were in a better position to maintain and improve their standing. Building on their established advantages, people passed on to their offspring their skills and secrets, their tools and privileges, their connections and customers. Such familial continuity pervaded all professions. Among the fifty-seven tanners who appeared in court in 1754 to settle a professional matter there were four father-son pairs, six sets of two brothers, one set of three brothers, and one set of four brothers.[107] Many of Aleppo's prominent ulama were born to families with a tradition of learning; from their fathers they received their early education and a useful introduction into the network of teachers and patrons on which their careers depended.[108] Some elite families like the Kawakibis and Shurayyifs were able to keep members at the top over several generations.

Not all sons entered their fathers' trades, but many families appear to have successfully maintained their general social standing over several generations. The titles of rank and honor, characteristic symbols of respectability in the middle and upper classes, often perpetuated themselves in the family line. The social distribution of these titles and their transmission over generations, which can be reconstructed from the vast repository of names in the judicial records, offer the best available evidence on the dynamics of mobility over time. Of the three important titles, chalabi was the most widely prevalent, while agha and effendi were restricted to smaller numbers of men. In themselves the titles did not indicate the precise status of individuals but rather identified them as men of some recognized social standing. A remarkably mixed group of people of different occupations shared each of them. An effendi could be a higher member of the ulama or a ranking scribe in government employ; the aghas included military officers, government officials, tax farmers, and merchants; among the numerous chalabis could be found lower-level members of the religious establishment, merchants, craftsmen, and scribes in government service.

The thousands of recorded names show a decided tendency for the sons of people without a title to have no title themselves, and for the sons of title bearers to hold titles as well. In the notable families even teenage sons held the titles of chalabi and agha; property and tax farms registered in their names, academic preparation under prominent scholars, and the family's favorable standing obtained for them early the rewards of good background.[109] Sons often held the same title as their fathers; such continuity extended in some cases over three or four generations, especially when the sons of prominent ulama, tax farmers, and men of business pursued their fathers' professions.[110]

Variations in title between fathers and sons as well as among brothers were also quite common. A man like ʿUmar Chalabi ibn Muhammad Agha ibn ʿUthman Effendi illustrates by his very name the possible extent of intergenerational changes in title. Of the eight sons who survived the wealthy ʿAbd al-Wahhab Agha Shurayyif when he died around 1767 one was an effendi, one a chalabi, one without title (he was mentally retarded), and five were aghas, one of them at fourteen years old.[111] Such variations mirrored the complex dynamics of social advancement. Members of the same family occasionally pursued different occupations, or advanced at an unequal pace. The sons of some effendis went into lay professions, while the sons of businessmen occasionally entered the religious establishment and rose to obtain the high rank of effendi. Many in the middle and upper classes started out as chalabis, but eventually acquired the title of effendi or agha through official appointments.[112] If in many cases these people ended up in roughly the same standing as their fathers, even when they followed different pursuits, some clearly fell behind. Social differences cut even across families. The less able and less fortunate children failed to live up to the family's reputation and formed less distinguished branches. Some of the descendants of ʿAbd al-Wahhab Agha Shurayyif stayed at the top, attaining even the office of governor, while others fell into relative obscurity.

All groups, including the elite, experienced some turnover over time. New names appeared on the scene while established lineages faded away. This fluidity helped to prevent the different social levels identifiable in the community from hardening into a rigid class structure. Of profound importance in weakening class barriers were also the patron-client relations. These ties linked in bonds of common interest persons of different social levels. Dependent on their patrons for protection, material advantages, and advancement, clients linked their destinies with those above them. Their loyalties militated against class solidarity and adversarial class relations. Group solidarities of the sort promoted by the religious communities also helped to dull the sharpness of class divisions.

Despite the periodic upheavals and conflicts, Aleppo's history in the eighteenth century shows no evidence of developed class antagonisms. Nor does it reveal major changes in the social structure. The stories of power, politics, the law, the economy and the culture, told in the following chapters, help to clarify the processes by which the social order was maintained and perpetuated.

CHAPTER 3

Order and Disorder: Power, Politics, and the Law

"ALL AUTHORITY HAS ceased to exist. There is no longer a leading figure in Aleppo capable of imposing his will."[1] In these grim words the local chronicler Yusuf al-Halabi summed up the situation in the city as he observed it in the spring of 1788. Government authority and the rule of law, accepted by his society as the basis of order, appeared shaky. The Janissaries, the sultan's garrison in the city, were going on a rampage, robbing shopkeepers in broad daylight, breaking into homes and extorting money at gunpoint as they prepared for their departure to join the imperial army on the European front. Their power in local affairs had been on the rise in the past fifteen years or so. Their officers controlled various neighborhoods and trade guilds, operated a system of extortion, and manipulated the city's food supply. In the famine of the previous year they had compounded the misery by their large-scale profiteering and black market activities. Popular riots broke out to protest against the high bread prices and government inaction. Many of the hungry turned in desperation to theft, driving crime and insecurity to high levels. In the midst of this crisis the Janissaries organized armed resistance to the governor's entry into the city. Three years earlier, and on another occasion nine years before that, they had led violent uprisings against oppressive governors, expelling them in the name of justice under Islamic law.

This defiance, without precedent in the first three quarters of the century, reflected a new reality: that Ottoman authority, the key force in the local system of rule, had grown decidedly weaker. The preoccupation with the wars on the European front, which had raged with little respite since 1768, had eroded Istanbul's attention to internal control and encouraged local power figures to increase their influence. The turmoil in the spring of 1788 was hardly the last episode in this process. Local leaders and groups, primarily the Janissaries, continued to exercise an inordinate amount of power for the next twenty-five years. During this time the townspeople experienced revolts, factional strife, high food prices, heavy tax demands, and large-scale extortion by the powerful.

In the annals of the city in the eighteenth century the realignment of power at the top stands as the foremost political development, primarily because of the larger changes it set in motion. Contemporary observers like al-Halabi recognized the changes, but drawn as they were to the dramatic and unusual episodes in what were unusual times, their accounts often give the misleading impression of a society without a real government, without the rule of law, and without orderly political mechanisms for accommodating conflicting interests. Such were not the realities of the century as a whole, or even of the years of political instability. The townspeople were subject to an organized government with its officials, procedures, and effective methods of administration and control; an organ of the Ottoman state, it was the single most influential institution in their society even in times of relative weakness. Violations of the law and even serious crimes did occur, but on the whole this was a law-abiding community equipped with a vast body of laws, and with mechanisms of legislation, courts, police, and other law enforcement institutions. There was also an established political system which provided the local population with mechanisms for articulating interests and influencing government decisions. Members of the local elite dominated politics, but larger segments of the public, including even non-Muslims and women, also took part in the process.

Yet the institutions and processes of power, politics, and the law in Aleppo were far from simple. They took peculiar forms and often worked in elusive ways. One must fathom the role of a state that was authoritarian and administratively corrupt, but at the same time had few social concerns and intruded little into the lives of its subjects in comparison with the modern state. One must penetrate a political game that played itself out largely in informal and personal networks rather than formal bodies like councils and parties; that revolved around a set of narrow, nonideological issues; and that employed a variety of instruments, from negotiation and bribery to extortion and violence. The "politics of notables"—the term describing an observed regional pattern of political interplay among the government, local leaders, and the governed population in which the local leaders, or "notables," acted as intermediaries and power brokers—cannot be reduced to a simple model of three elements.[2] The number of actors, the range of interests, and the web of relations in Aleppo's politics were more complex. And in the areas of law and law enforcement one encounters courts operating without lawyers, much adjudication in informal settings, police tasks shared by the public, and a large body of laws closed off to change.

A close view of the political and legal systems—one that goes beyond political chronology and the formal institutions—helps to clarify several important aspects of the city's public life and historical experiences: the role of government in society and the pattern of relations between government and people; the local participation in decision making, and the ways in which local leaders acquired and exercised their influence; the issues, interests, style, and relevance of contemporary politics; the meaning of the power shift and instability of the late eighteenth century; the realities of crime, violation, judicial practice, and law enforcement; and in a more general way, the meaning of order in an eventful time period.[3]

GOVERNMENT AND LOCAL POWER

WHEN A SULTAN acceded to the throne or had a child born, Aleppo, like other cities in the empire, celebrated the event. Decorative lights appeared on public buildings, the governor's band played airs and marches, and the cannon on the citadel blasted in salute. For a week or so the residents spent their evenings about town delighting in the entertainments and festive atmosphere. The celebrations were not spontaneous outbursts of joy; they were traditionally sponsored by the government, as a way of fostering popular bonds to the ruling house. The townspeople, generally unaccustomed to intense shows of loyalty to the state, welcomed the festivities as breaks from the daily routine. They did wish for the ruler to thrive and the realm to prosper, if only because they themselves stood to benefit from it. But beneath this abstract hope, reaffirmed on the special royal occasions, lay a mixture of attitudes toward the state.

No institution excited quite the same range of sentiments and attitudes as did the state. For better or worse, it was the single most important presence in the political and social order. Power, according to the official view, was in the hands of the ruler; the state was his patrimony, the people his obedient subjects. Government institutions displayed the current pretensions of Ottoman power. The seven sultans who ruled the empire during the eighteenth century sat in high pomp in the magnificent palace, surrounded by hundreds of courtiers, advisers, attendants, and concubines. A large bureaucracy, with its elaborate hierarchy of ranks, titles, and rewards, administered the domestic and international business of the government. It handled the correspondence, managed the revenues, disbursed funds, carried out policies, issued orders, appointed and dismissed officials, and negotiated with other countries. A military machine whose size and destructive power were matched by only a few armies in the world stood at the sultan's command.

With its vast resources in wealth, manpower, and despotic powers, the government was equipped to interfere in the lives of the subjects, to affect their welfare, and to shape the political and social climate of their society. All this it did, but on a limited and uneven scale. Although its powers were potentially enormous, the government conceived of its role in society in rather narrow terms. Defending the territories from external attack, maintaining law and order, and collecting taxes—these figured among its chief concerns and responsibilities. There were a great many matters with which it was largely or entirely unconcerned, and others which it handled with the help of locals and their participation in the tasks of administration. Generalities and abstractions about state power cannot convey fully what this government actually meant for Aleppo's residents, how much they participated in it, and what local politics was all about. The answers lie in the actual performance and structure of government in the city, in the local networks of power, and in the political behavior and concerns of the public.

Government concerns were most strikingly weak in the sphere of social policy. The modern notion of the welfare state was alien to the traditional Ottoman conception of rule. Aleppo had institutions designed to provide the public with education, health care, social welfare, and urban services, but these functioned without much government direction or financial support. The local schools were set up and funded by private philanthropists, not by government. The state did not require people to attend them, nor did it promote mass literacy. In the area of health, the townspeople relied on the medical services of private doctors and healers. The government regulated in a rudimentary way some aspects of public health, but provided no public facilities or financing of medical care or research.

There was also no government system of social welfare. The needy, the disabled, the aged, the homeless, and the unemployed depended on several nongovernmental sources of support: family members, group charities, pious foundations, and private almsgivers. People did not turn to the government for welfare even in times of famine, when hunger, epidemics, and unemployment created large-scale misery. The government was expected to assist them by importing food and lowering market prices, not by subsidizing bread or aiding the victims of dislocation. In the provision of urban services the government played a similarly minimal role. Aleppo had no distinct municipality that planned, financed, and directed urban needs through a centralized administrative machinery. Water, sanitation, physical maintenance, and other needs were handled by a host of public charities, neighborhoods, and private entrepreneurs, without financial assistance by government or management by government employees. The authorities provided only a limited measure of oversight to the running of municipal affairs.

For many services touching on their quality of life and personal welfare the townspeople relied on self-help or on public institutions that functioned independently of government programs and budgets. Lobbying by various groups for shares in government allocations for health care, public works, education, or welfare was hence not part of contemporary politics. The limited scope of government interest in these areas is shown in the vast gaps in official record keeping. The authorities maintained no systematic medical or educational records; no registration of births, deaths, marriages, and divorces; no data on incomes or employment; and no cadastral surveys or construction records. Such information was not deemed essential to the tasks of governance. State power was measured not by the quality of life of the masses, but by the effectiveness of government institutions in defending the realm, maintaining order, and appropriating wealth. These concerns more than any others absorbed official energies.

The Ottoman art of keeping law and order rested on an unabashed use of both enticement and force. Without requiring the population to display intense shows of patriotism the government expected loyalty and obedience to authority. In the event of revolts and large-scale violations of order it granted its officials and army commanders very broad powers to restore order and punish troublemakers. Intimidation, military force, and summary executions figured among their normal instruments of pacification.

But if the state knew how to wave a stick it was not less adept at

dangling attractive favors with which it bought a base of popular support. It sold offices and tax farms, awarded titles and tax exemptions,
and granted monopolies and various other privileges. These, not allocations for social programs, were the real instruments of state patronage
and objects of political competition. The government used them openly
to manipulate politics to its advantage and to cultivate vested interests
in the system.

The state took responsibility for order in a still broader sense. It saw
as essential not only obedience to authority but also a general respect for
the law in the relations between people. Islamic law, the orders of the
sultan, and other established rules were binding on society. The authorities, committed in principle to protecting the life, property, and honor
of the subjects, ran a law enforcement machinery that provided courts
for the settlement of legal conflicts as well as police to deal with crimes
and violations of public morals. The law enforcement officers enjoyed
wide powers to search, arrest, investigate, prosecute, and punish.

Even with its limited scope the business of government was a costly
affair. The administration of vast territories, the constant wars, and the
luxurious life-style of the court and high officialdom demanded enormous sums. Tax revenues kept the system going; the appropriation of
part of society's wealth was accepted as one of the chief prerogatives and
rewards of power. And indeed to no other task was the government so
consumingly devoted. Inasmuch as it determined the kinds of taxes,
their amounts, their rates, their timing, and their victims, the state was
in a position to affect the material welfare of individuals, the distribution
of wealth, and the economic institutions of society. Fiscal considerations
prompted it to regulate certain economic activities in ways that would
facilitate the monitoring of transactions and increase state revenues. The
official practice of farming out the collection of taxes alone had far-
reaching economic and social consequences.

The state did involve itself in economic matters, although rather
unevenly. It did not own commercial, industrial, or agricultural enterprises in Aleppo or the province. Nor did it engage in centralized
planning of the economy, or promote long-term programs of economic
development, or invest much in infrastructure. Nonetheless, it shaped
in a general way the framework within which economic activities took
place in the private sector. Guilds of tradesmen and craftsmen devised
numerous detailed rules to regulate production, quality, prices, wages,
and entry into professions. Although initiated from below, such arrangements could hold only if they conformed to official preferences
and interests.

If the eighteenth-century Ottoman state appears rather lackadaisical and unintrusive by modern standards, these features do not minimize its relevance for the welfare of the population. It affected society as much by what it did not do as by what it did: in not concerning itself with many matters, it let various institutions evolve and take particular forms; in not working to promote change, it helped to preserve the bases of the existing order.

This state ruled Aleppo through a system in which outside officials appointed by the central government controlled the key positions, backed by the extensive assistance of local leaders. The officials worked within a small but formally organized administration which relied on set procedures, formal meetings, and written decrees. Through the instruments of the bureaucracy and army Ottoman officialdom dominated the structure of power in the city, but without monopolizing it entirely. There were local leaders who exercised an influence independent of government, who spoke on behalf of segments of the population and could mobilize opinion and even armed militias. They took part in the decision-making process through informal channels as well as through formal authority parcelled out to them by government.

The tip of the power pyramid was occupied by two Ottoman officials: the governor, or pasha, and the qadi. Between them they carried out the main functions of government. Both were outsiders, not Aleppines; the townspeople had no say in their appointment. They bought their posts for considerable sums, and usually held office only for a one-year term, after which they were reassigned to another locality. Their territorial jurisdiction extended well beyond Aleppo; they headed the provincial administration, which concerned itself with the city as well as the numerous settlements and tribal groups around it. Their roles in the life of the community defy easy definition. Viewing the governor and qadi as the heads of the executive and judicial branches respectively is to describe their roles too neatly. They both took part in the processes of administration, justice, policymaking, and local politics.

The governors, who headed the provincial administration, oversaw the maintenance of order and the collection of taxes. They kept an eye on the overall political and economic climate, intervened in crises that threatened public order, and maintained communications with their superiors in Istanbul. No other figure in the city wielded the wide range of powers at their disposal. The pashas imprisoned, executed summarily, exacted fines, ordered curfews, fixed food prices, supervised the markets, and even imposed taxes. Troops under their command policed the population and quelled disturbances. The governors kept their own mercenary soldiers, whom they hired and discharged according to their needs and financial means. They also brought with them a supporting staff that included the deputy governor, the commander of their troops, and some administrators, accountants, scribes, and personal attendants. Raghib Pasha, recalled from Aleppo to Istanbul in 1756 to assume the post of grand vizier, hired as many as two hundred and twenty pack animals to transport his effects and retinue.[4]

The pashas came from a pool of hardened administrators and military officers who led troops in battle and confronted much political intrigue and violence in the course of their official careers. In background and training they differed from the qadis, who were ulama with years of study in Islamic colleges as well as service in various religious and scribal posts. Appointment to the office of qadi in a province of Aleppo's stature carried considerable prestige. Qadis arrived in the city with the staff of aides and attendants characteristic of high Ottoman officialdom. Sixty-two animals of burden accompanied by thirty drivers transported the qadi Ibrahim Effendi and his entourage to Aleppo in 1769.[5]

The principal task of the qadi in the provincial government was to run the shari'a court, an odd office that did much more than just adjudicate legal disputes and sentence offenders. In a sense the court substituted for a host of specialized agencies that the government never set up: it issued marriage permits and deeds of sale, offered the services of a notary public, supervised the activities of charitable foundations, and appointed legal guardians for orphaned children and incompetents. It also handled the execution of estates; when people died, a court official put a seal on their possessions, drew up an inventory, and determined the distribution of shares among the legal heirs. Official decrees and letters of appointment issued to individuals by the central government became valid after they were certified and read aloud in the court. The qadi issued regulations touching on public morals, oversaw the periodic reassessments of tax rates, and participated in decision making in provincial affairs.

Both the qadis and governors possessed a striking range of powers; but none of those who occupied these offices in Aleppo during the eighteenth century were given the opportunity to exercise their responsibilities there for very long. The townspeople saw ninety-nine qadis and one hundred appointees to the office of pasha in the course of the century. The rotation of governors, unlike that of the qadis, was given to occasional deviations from the regular annual cycle. A few governors returned to the province for a second or third one-year term, while a few governed only a few months, their full term cut short by death or transfer to another post. In 1752 three governors were appointed in the span of six months; one was dismissed and the other two died in office.[6]

The appointment of governors from outside the province and their frequent rotation conformed to a deliberate pattern set by Istanbul from the early days of its rule in the area. In the eighteenth century it had ceased to function with any regularity in the other Arab provinces, where local power figures and even governors often held office for many years at a time. In Aleppo it was only in August 1799 that a native of the city, Ibrahim Agha Qattar Aghasi, won an appointment to the governorship of the province. A leading member of the local a'yan, or tax-farming elite, he remained in office for an extraordinary stretch of five years. His son succeeded him, but was soon expelled by a revolt that put an end to this short-lived deviation from the traditional pattern.

The official preference for appointing outsiders as provincial governors and keeping them on the move had its political logic. Such an arrangement subjected the officials to close control by the central government and aborted any opportunity for them to develop an autonomous power base in any locality. For Aleppo's population, however, the constant rotation of top officials was far from advantageous; the appearance of a new team every year or so occasioned frequent uncertainty and disruption. Pashas differed in their personalities, honesty, and style of government. While they were not in a position to make any lasting changes in the span of one year their conduct certainly affected the general political and economic climate. More serious was the fact that the governors cared little about their local popularity. Since they paid considerable sums for their appointments they were more concerned with recouping their investments and possibly enriching themselves before their year-long term was over. This preoccupation showed itself most clearly in the resort to excessive exactions from the population, which was almost a routine feature of governors' conduct.

From the pattern of rotation of outsiders followed yet another characteristic of Ottoman rule in the city: it depended on local assistance. The top administrators lacked the opportunity to become well acquainted with the place and its circumstances, and had to rely heavily on local leaders and groups. Some of the townspeople thus came to participate in government and to exercise an influence on the process of decision making.

Part of this local involvement in government was institutionalized in formal arrangements. The heads of the city's neighborhoods, trade

guilds, and religious minorities helped the authorities with various administrative tasks. While not in a strict sense government officials, they
were responsible to the authorities for the collection of taxes from their
respective groups, for enforcing official regulations, and for reporting on
problems, and were involved in many of the routine interactions between the people and the government.

The government also employed locals to fill various posts in the
administration. The deputy judges in the shariʿa courts, the water and
building inspectors, the commanding officers of the Janissary corps, the
Muslim jurisconsult (mufti), and the farmer general of taxes *(muhassil)* in
the province all came from local ranks, as did a host of minor clerks and
accountants. The tax farmers who ran the revenue collection system on
behalf of the government were also local men. With the aid of their large
staffs of personal employees they kept the books, monitored economic
activities in the city and countryside, and did business with the authorities and the taxpayers. The great tax farmers, or aʿyan, were so fully
integrated into the top administrative level that a member of their group
was often entrusted with the office of interim governor *(mutasallim)*
when the pasha was away.

In addition to delegating authority to locals, the government consulted routinely with the leading men in the community. The governor's
council or *divan* provided the most important formal setting for local
participation in policymaking. In addition to the pasha and qadi the
council included several local figures with official positions and close
associations with government: the farmer general of taxes and leading
aʿyan; the jurisconsult and leading ulama; the head of the ashraf; and
the commander of the Janissaries. It met regularly to discuss and make
decisions on local and provincial issues, such as insecurity in the countryside, food supply to the city, fiscal and budgetary problems, local
appointments, and popular unrest and complaints. The local leaders,
who had only an advisory function, brought various matters to the
attention of the governor and made recommendations to him. In turn he
instructed them to carry out official policies and help with the resolution
of problems.

How the local leaders conducted themselves in the governor's council
remains a mystery; the authorities kept no minutes of the deliberations.
The leverage of the local members probably varied with their personal
stature, with the governor in office, and with the problems at hand.
That government sought their counsel and aid, however, was itself an
acknowledgement of their importance. And indeed they were powerful

men, figures whose voice in local affairs was not confined to the pasha's council. Together with a small number of other influential men they formed the city's political elite. It is this select club that dominated the local structure of power and participated most prominently in the workings of government. Its members held high positions, controlled resources, distributed favors, commanded loyalties, extended protection, exacted payments, shaped opinion, and even mobilized armed militias.

Those who exercised such influence in the eighteenth century came from the same privileged Muslim groups represented on the governor's council: the a'yan, the ulama, the ashraf, and the Janissaries. Some of them hailed from great families, such as the Kawakibis, with decades of prominence on the local scene, although such prestigious background was not a prerequisite to political influence. Ibrahim Agha Qattar Aghasi, who emerged at the turn of the nineteenth century as the most powerful figure in the city, was an illiterate from a family of no known reputation. He entered the service of powerful patrons, and eventually became a great tax farmer, the farmer general of revenues for the province, and the governor.

The power of the elite figures is explained more readily by several other resources at their disposal. They held high official positions, from which they derived formal authority, titles, connections, prestige, and wealth. They all sat on great fortunes, which helped them to acquire their offices and to develop and maintain their base of power in the community. In a world in which familiarity and pull counted for much they enjoyed alliances with influential men in the city and connections with high-placed patrons in Istanbul. They also commanded extensive networks of clients, whose members included leading men in the trade guilds, neighborhood strongmen, mosque preachers, ulama, and other middle-echelon leaders who had influence over segments of the population. These men formed part of the informal political machinery which the power figures used in order to control and direct behavior in the lower levels of society—sometimes through intimidation and extortion. The leaders of the Janissaries and the ashraf had the added advantage of command over organized armed groups which they mobilized to their advantage in political contests.

How far local leaders could carry their influence in the city is perhaps best illustrated by the career of Muhammad Effendi Taha Zadeh (d. 1786), or Chalabi Effendi as he was commonly known. A master politician, he attained a hold over the community unmatched by any other local leader of the eighteenth century. "The entire city, from the elite to the most lowly, is in his hands," commented a local resident.[7] The French consul described him as "the master of Aleppo."[8]

This standing, not much exaggerated by contemporary observers, came to Chalabi Effendi by skillful use of all sources of power available at the time. He was an extremely wealthy man, an alim, a member of the ashraf, and the son of a qadi who founded the city's Ahmadiyya College. In the course of his career he held a variety of high offices: jurisconsult, head of the ashraf, tax farmer, and, in the last year of his life, farmer general of revenues. A tough politician and able administrator, he mastered the art of cultivating allies and clients. Although a miserly person in general, he spent lavishly on governors as well as high officials in Istanbul. His word counted in government circles; many official decisions were altered after his intervention. The Christian communities used his services to win release from financial exactions. He himself, however, extorted on a large scale. Many paid him protection money without daring to protest. In 1768, when he was away in exile, the sellers of dairy products gathered courage to complain in court about a burdensome tribute they had been paying him annually. Shortly afterward, a Jew came in to describe how some years earlier Chalabi Effendi had extorted from him 750 piastres that he had collected in market dues.[9] A whole network of aides and dependents did his bidding. The ashraf, under his command for many years, gave him a political tool and armed force which he used to advantage. He helped to promote their interests while mobilizing them at will to further his own ends.[10]

The government needed the cooperation of Chalabi Effendi and the other local leaders to rule effectively. Their skills and capital helped it to run the administration. Unlike the transient Ottoman officials, the local leaders had roots and followings in the city, and were familiar with the inner workings of the community. Their local networks of control gave them the means to assist the government or to undermine it.

While they participated in the Ottoman system of rule as loyal auxiliaries accountable to higher authority, the local leaders were not submissive creatures given to total control from above. Their interests did not always coincide with those of the government, which had to work constantly to keep their influence within acceptable bounds and to prevent the competition among them from degenerating into public disorder. The local rivalries themselves helped it to maintain control; the competing leaders set limits on each other's influence. They also tended to seek official backing for their particular causes in their squabbles with rivals, which presented the government with welcome opportunities to play off one party against another and to mediate settlements favorable to its own interests.

More directly, the government used its powers of patronage and coercion to control the local power figures. Even the most influential leaders were reminded periodically of their dependence on the whims of a higher authority. What positions and benefits government awarded to them it also took away at pleasure. Most of the power figures experienced dismissal from office and loss of favor, often more than once. A few who fell out with the authorities suffered more severe penalties, including sequestration of their property, banishment, and execution. Mustafa Agha Shahbandar Zadeh, a leading member of the aʿyan, alienated government officials while serving as interim governor in 1779; by orders from above he was banished to Jerusalem after his property was confiscated. A year later, an unusually tough governor exiled a prominent local leader who served as interim governor on his behalf, after squeezing out of him every piastre he owned. Soon afterward he imprisoned the next interim governor, and had the man's father, the influential Ahmad Agha Khunkarı Zadeh, executed and his head sent to Istanbul. Even Chalabi Effendi and his distinguished rival Ahmad Effendi al-Kawakibi spent some years in forced exile.[11]

The loss of patrons, the appearance of excessive influence, the flagrant abuse of office, intrigue by enemies—these were the common sources of such falling out with government. One needed luck, nerves, and sharp instincts to remain at the political summit. Personal setbacks often spelled temporary eclipse rather than political doom; wounded leaders lay low for a while, reemerging when their circumstances brightened. Chalabi Effendi reestablished his extensive power in the city almost immediately upon his return in 1782 from six years of exile.[12]

The local leaders did not exercise their influence with government or the people to promote changes in the basic structures of society, nor did they stand for distinct ideological platforms. Their competition focused on positions and benefits for themselves and their constituents. For this reason, politics at the top was fairly fluid. The narrow scope of the elite's political activity reflected a feature characteristic of the city's politics in general. Larger or smaller segments of the public did become actively involved in efforts to shape or change government behavior in ways favorable to their interests. They lobbied, complained, bargained, bribed, pulled strings, resisted, protested and, on rare occasions, even revolted. Yet their actions to influence decisions were driven by a narrow set of concerns revolving chiefly around the burdens of taxation and the access to food. And the ends of these actions were limited as well: to redress specific grievances rather than to achieve major structural changes.

Aleppo's politics, both at the level of the elite and of the larger public, thus appear especially striking for what they were *not* about. They were not about who the government should appoint to administer the city; these decisions lay with the central authorities in the capital. They were not about issues of foreign policy, deemed an exclusive government concern in which the population of a provincial city had no recognized say. They were not about public programs in the areas of health, education, housing, welfare, or employment, with which government did not concern itself. They were not about the rights of women, the legal status of non-Muslims, the rules of marriage and inheritance, or any of a host of other established social institutions; governed by Islamic law, which society accepted as divinely ordained and immutable, these arrangements remained essentially closed to debate and change. And they were not about Arab national aspirations, the liberalization of despotic rule, or Westernization, which did not become political issues before the nineteenth century.

The unchallenged acceptance of many essentials, the limited social responsibilities of the state, and the authoritarian premises of political life combined to narrow the scope of local politics. Yet the political scene was not entirely dull. Politics excited emotions and even provoked violence precisely because they revolved so much around elemental concerns and raw ambitions.

THE ROUGH-AND-TUMBLE OF POLITICS

D URING MUCH OF the eighteenth century, or more precisely until the 1770s, the government maintained its authority fairly effectively in Aleppo. Pashas arrived and departed according to Istanbul's will, and during their tenure could rightfully claim to be the most powerful and feared men in the city. Although official conduct and economic grievances excited occasional tensions between people and government there were no revolts against authority. Power politics too were generally subdued and constrained. Some years passed without much political drama for local chroniclers to record: the townspeople went about their pursuits and pleasures peacefully, and routine seemed to rule public life.

From the 1770s, however, government steadily lost its control, and the local leaders and power groups increasingly decided the course of events. Their political competition heated up, assuming an intensity and violence not witnessed before in the city. Governors were expelled by armed uprisings or forced to accept local terms limiting their authority. The Ottoman government, its energies absorbed by the renewed warfare on the European front, failed to check the local defiance and encroachments on its authority, especially by the powerful Janissary corps. By the early nineteenth century the Janissaries came to dominate the city temporarily, while the governors were reduced almost to nominal figures.

This dramatic shift in the balance of power was by far the most important long-term development in local politics in the eighteenth century. It came about not in one single coup, but rather in the course of a protracted succession of crises extending over some four decades. In this restless and uneasy period the traditional political constraints loosened, the rules of the game changed, and ambitions ran wild. Street battles, revolts, and disorder became standard. Exploitation intensified, economic conditions worsened, and social tensions surfaced in acute forms. An array of developments that affected society as a whole thus accompanied the realignment of power at the top.

The first major drama in the shifting balance between the government and local groups occurred in the fall of 1775, when for the first time in the eighteenth century the townspeople forced their governor out of the city. It was actually the Janissaries, driven by a grievance of their own, who set the revolt against 'Ali Pasha in motion, although disgust with the governor was widespread, and there was general enthusiasm for their move. The governor, who came on the heels of an extortionate pasha and held office in a time of exorbitant food prices, added to existing material hardships by subjecting the population to unusually heavy exactions, not sparing even the leading men in the city. Chalabi Effendi, Ahmad Effendi al-Kawakibi, the farmer general of revenues, and several other prominent figures were forced to pay some 20,000 piastres each, after being arrested and threatened. Many of the well-to-do fled from the city, and trade languished.

Yet no sign of open resistance against the pasha appeared until he called on the Janissaries, who were not under his direct command, to join his military expeditions in the countryside. The officers of the corps resolved to refuse the order, and proceeded to obtain a legal opinion from the jurisconsult supporting their case. The qadi confronted the governor, who agreed to back down. Encouraged by this turn of events, the Janissaries decided to press for the removal of the pasha from office. They asked the qadi to authorize his expulsion on the grounds of gross abuses. The judge collected a large dossier of testimonies against the governor and his oppressive subordinates. When the pasha refused to leave the city voluntarily the qadi authorized a revolt. The Janissaries besieged the palace, and excited crowds came out to support them. After several days of stand-off, with sporadic exchanges of fire, the governor agreed to withdraw. Several of the a'yan negotiated safe passage for him and his staff. As the expelled pasha rode toward the outskirts thousands of triumphant residents, including many women, stood in the streets, jeering and spitting in contempt. Until news arrived that he had been reassigned to another province the Janissaries remained on the alert. At the same time the local leaders sent a formal report to Istanbul explaining the unusual developments.[13]

Politics were not quite the same after this revolt. While the public euphoria soon died down, the power groups now knew how far their armed force could go in shaping events to their advantage. The Janissaries and ashraf resorted to large-scale extortions from the public. In 1778 the two groups fought it out in the streets, until the ever-cautious a'yan intervened to negotiate a reconciliation. At the end of the year an interim governor dispatched from Istanbul decided to crack down on the assertive groups by executing their leaders. Getting wind of the plan, the two factions joined forces to attack the palace, forcing the interim governor to accept a restriction on the number of troops he could maintain in the city.[14]

This extraordinary achievement set another attractive precedent for the local groups. Free of close official control, they indulged in financial exploitation of the public with impunity until 1780, when a strong governor backed by a large army curbed their power. Many of the ashraf were thrown in prison or fled from the city, and the Janissaries suffered heavy exactions. Their local power, however, was hardly crushed. In 1784 the Janissaries engineered another expulsion of a governor, replaying the revolt of nine years earlier. They acted in order to unburden themselves of a pasha who subjected them to arrests and harassments, but used his unusually oppressive extortions from the population as convenient grounds for his removal. The qadi and leading ulama gave their blessing to a revolt against 'Abdi Pasha for his injustices and gross violations of the shariʿa. The markets closed down and multitudes of rebellious residents poured into the streets as the Janissaries mounted a fierce attack on the governor's troops, inflicting heavy losses on them. With his forces outmatched, the pasha accepted an offer of safe passage negotiated by the aʿyan, and left the city—to everyone's relief.

A delegation of five residents carried to Istanbul a report on the affair drawn up by the qadi and local leaders. For three months, until the governor was reassigned to another province, the population lived under fear of his possible return. The Janissaries organized a citywide defense effort, taking control of the neighborhoods, setting up local patrols of volunteers, and collecting contributions and arms. During this state of alert the leaders of the Janissaries and ashraf exercised firm control of their members to prevent financial exploitation of the population. Order and respect for the law prevailed despite the absence of a governor.[15]

But it was an illusory order. The power groups, especially the Janissaries, had climbed further up the ladder of power and were not about to stop. In 1786 the Janissary officers imposed on the governor a deal, worked out in the house of Chalabi Effendi, by which he would keep his troops out of the city. In the following year they and the leaders of the ashraf refused entry to the next governor after he sought to impose heavy taxes to finance his military expeditions in the province and rebuffed their demand that he trim down his forces to a token number. As grounds for their defiance they used the economic hardships in the city caused by a severe food shortage, which they had themselves worsened by manipulating the supplies and running a black market in grains. The leaders of both groups obtained the qadi's permission to resist the governor. Under their direction the city organized itself for armed defense against a siege by the pasha. Eventually a large force of Janissaries and ashraf went out to confront his troops. After weighing the odds, the governor chose to withdraw rather than suffer defeat.[16]

These events established the erosion of Ottoman control and the dominance of the Janissaries in Aleppo's politics. The Janissary officers assumed a pompous air, riding their fine horses in the streets surrounded by numerous subordinates. Immense economic power was now in their hands. They acquired a monopoly over the import and sale of sheep, and controlled the food supply as well as land, orchards, and various trade guilds. A host of new recruits swelled the size of the corps and strengthened its presence in the city. In the spring of 1788, when they were ordered to the war against Russia and Austria, the Janissaries went on a rampage, extorting huge sums of money from the population and helping themselves to commodities in the shops. They laid every quarter under tribute and even robbed homes. There was no authority in the city to check their abuses.[17]

The deterioration of Ottoman control became still more evident in the following decade. In 1790 the Janissaries forced the governor to keep his troops outside the city. In the following year the power groups expelled his successor and organized the city's defense against a siege. The population suffered massive extortions, and many hid in their homes for fear of being robbed in broad daylight. The conservative-minded aʿyan found the breakdown of authority intolerable, and left the city. A new governor, ʿUthman Pasha, arrived in 1792 with a token force incapable of restoring official control at a time when the townspeople needed it most. A severe shortage of food developed in the fall, and both Janissaries and ashraf exploited the situation to enrich themselves. They hoarded wheat to push the prices up and bought up grain imported to the city, selling it on the black market at double the price. They even monopolized the sale of bread in the bakeries, imposing a surcharge on every loaf. Complaints to the governor proved useless; he too was reduced to buying wheat on the black market. In this climate of loose authority extortion of all kinds by the two groups reached new heights. Jewish families were even forced to pay for the right to bury their dead.[18]

An informal but pervasive structure of control dominated by the two power groups had thus established itself in the city as government authority waned. By intimidation and the manipulation of economic resources the leaders essentially superimposed on society their own system of taxation and networks of control. The Janissaries scored the greatest successes in this political game, steadily increasing their wealth and hold on the city in the 1790s. The main threat to their pursuits came from the ashraf, who wanted access to the same benefits. In April 1798, after some minor clashes provoked largely by the resentful ashraf, the two factions met in an all-out battle in the streets. For two weeks the population lived in terror as shells flew overhead, property was pillaged, and buildings burned. Numerous residents fled from their homes, carrying their valuables or leaving their servants behind to watch their belongings. Business came to a standstill. When the dust settled the Janissaries emerged still the dominant party, having held their own.[19]

A more formidable threat to Janissary power in the city came from Ibrahim Agha Qattar Aghasi, the local tax farmer who emerged in the 1790s as a key power broker. During his term as pasha from 1799 to

1804 he restored real power to the governorship, establishing an iron rule which the townspeople had not experienced for almost two decades. A large army of over five thousand men helped him to control and tax at will. He turned with a vengeance against the Janissaries with the intent of breaking their power once and for all. In 1802 he obtained from the grand vizier an authorization to have thirty-six of their chief officers executed. News of the plot leaked out, however, and the targeted men fled from the city. But the pasha sequestered their property holdings, captured many members of the corps, and imposed heavy fines on people associated with them. The leaders were permitted to return two years later after pledging submission to the governor.[20]

The power of the Janissaries was hardly crushed by this setback. Within a year they turned matters around, defeating all their rivals and winning unchallenged mastery of the city. Their fortunes brightened considerably when the pasha was transferred to Damascus and his son Muhammad took over in May 1804. The arrogance of the young governor and his unbridled exactions in a time of severe famine played into their hands. They had no difficulty in interesting the ashraf in a rebellion and in obtaining permission from the qadi and ulama to take action against him. In June the two groups launched a joint attack on the pasha's troops, and defeated them. They expelled the pasha from the city, permitting him to return two months later with only a token force and a shred of authority. The Janissaries and the ashraf held virtually all of the key offices in the administration. Then, in June 1805, the ashraf, in conspiracy with the pasha, launched a massive attack on the Janissaries with the intent of crushing them. After eight days of ferocious fighting in the streets the Janissaries emerged victorious, having defeated both the ashraf and the pasha's troops. The governor left the city while the ashraf lay vanquished as a political force. Many of their leaders died or went into hiding; a few switched sides and joined the Janissary corps.[21]

With this victory the Janissaries won virtual domination of the city. They continued to admit Ottoman pashas appointed to the province and to remit the taxes due to the sultan. But the main responsibilities and benefits of power were now in the hands of several Janissary officers and their subordinates. Backed by the control of armed force, positions of authority, property, tax farms, food supply, and, above all, a machinery of appropriation, they were able to impose their will on the population and syphon off wealth to themselves and their dependents. They imposed their system of protection on the entire population: every resident had to submit to a Janissary agha who acted as his protector in return for payment. Extortion and the manipulation of the food supply reached new heights while the population suffered untold material hardships.[22]

The Janissaries were not to enjoy these rewards for too long; the tide in the capital was beginning to turn. The sultan and his advisors, determined to reconsolidate central control of the loosely held provinces, launched a vigorous policy of assault on local power figures everywhere. Aleppo's turn came in 1813, when a pasha driven by the new resolve massacred the Janissary leaders and reestablished Ottoman hold on the province.

So ended an extraordinary period in the city's political life in which the weakness of central authority, evident throughout the region, had encouraged the defiance of local elements, who were able to have their day while Istanbul's attentions and resources were absorbed by external threats. For all its drama, though, this shift in power represented less than a major break with the traditional order. It was not a revolt against the sultan or a movement for local autonomy; nor was it accompanied by any overtones of Arab nationalist sentiment. The Janissaries and ashraf encroached on the state while remaining within its fold and professing loyalty to it. When rebelling against governors sent by the sultan they took care to obtain the blessings of religious opinion. Their defiance was an adaptation to their temporarily more favorable position in the traditional power play of provincial Ottoman politics. Their goals were not ideological; they were the less lofty ones of raw power and material gain. Their rise brought a change of cast rather than of regime, a realignment of power at the top rather than a restructuring of society.

The rough-and-tumble of Aleppo's politics in the late eighteenth century tested and affirmed the underlying stability of the city's social and political order. But it also brought into the open the interactions and conflicts of interest between government, local leaders and the larger public. The elite, whose members set in motion so many of the political dramas of the period, was itself a divided group with conflicting orientations. The initiatives for the revolts and other pressures for change came from the Janissaries and ashraf; the aʿyan, on the other hand, took a dim view of the factional strife and the unstable climate it created. In political crises they took a conservative approach, acting to calm aggressive spirits, to mediate between governors and rebels, and to restore public order. When Qattar Aghasi, one of their number, became governor, he applied himself vigorously to the containment of the factions.

The governors and the a'yan were able to put temporary checks on the power struggles of the rival groups, but not to crush them. The Janissaries especially held their own and prevailed in spite of the obstacles; and although their esprit de corps, effective leadership, and networks of control contributed in large measure to their success, it was ultimately military superiority that tipped the balance in their favor. The governors lacked the troops needed to match the strength of the factions. Because of this military inferiority, five of them were expelled or kept out of the city by force, and several others submitted to severe limits on their authority. Only one governor, Ibrahim Pasha Qattar Aghasi, broke with the pattern of weakness. His rule demonstrated that with adequate troops a pasha could keep the ambitious groups in check. As a native, he did start off with what the other pashas of the eighteenth century lacked: an insider's close familiarity with local realities, an established power base in the community, and ambitions of extended rule for himself and his family. But it was his reliance on a combination of large armies and heavy taxation, with the two elements necessarily supporting each other, that allowed him to overcome the weaknesses that had plagued his predecessors for some fifteen years. But his son, who was not nearly as shrewd, failed to keep the same control of the situation when he succeeded to the governorship. He lost out on the battlefield to a rebellion by the two factions.

This revolt and the four preceding expulsions of governors were the most extreme actions taken by the townspeople in the eighteenth century to change official behavior. They were a feature specific to the period of instability; nothing of the sort had occurred until 1775. The striking feature of these revolts is that they were not popular uprisings provoked by grievances of the people and set in motion by angry mobs. All five insurrections were engineered by the power groups, primarily the Janissaries, and for reasons connected with their own fortunes and ambitions in the city's power politics. Although the leaders were able to cast their acts of defiance as legitimate struggles of the people for justice and to obtain the precious approval of the qadi and leading ulama as insurance against official reprisals, they clearly decided on rebellion in each case after they failed to obtain concessions from a pasha who seriously threatened their group interests rather than the community at large. The organized militias, primarily the Janissaries, did the fighting and took charge of defense against a forced comeback by expelled governors, erecting barricades, organizing neighborhood patrols, collecting contributions, and fostering in the population a sense of common purpose. The larger public did become involved in some fashion once the revolts got under way. In 1775 and again in 1784, crowds surrounded the governor's palace and gave open support to the fighters. The people were happy to see these two pashas, and at least two of the other three as well, removed from the scene, primarily because of their oppressive tax demands. They also cooperated in the defense efforts from interest, not only from necessity. Their grievances, in short, drew them into participation in acts of resistance but not into the initiation of revolts; they had endured other years of oppressive taxation without rising in rebellion against governors.

The convergence of interests of power groups and people during the revolts was a temporary occurrence. As the record of late eighteenth-century politics illustrates, the power groups distinguished themselves on the whole more by their exploitation of the general populace than by the promotion of its causes. Both the Janissaries and ashraf offered their members material privileges and protections, but often at the expense of other segments of the population. They resorted to intimidation and extortion, even in broad daylight: the Janissaries turned their departures for imperial campaigns into nightmarish occasions of theft and abuse; the ashraf were no better when a force of their volunteers left in 1800 to participate in the campaign against the French occupation of Egypt.[23] The increase in the power of the two groups was actually disadvantageous to most of their fellow Aleppines, who in some respects suffered greater abuse than in the preceding period of effective Ottoman control. Unlike government officials, the local power figures worked from a permanent base in the community and an intimate knowledge of its inner workings. They saw in their increased power a license to exploit the public rather than a civic responsibility to serve it.

The political instability and abuses of power in the late eighteenth century affected the townspeople primarily on the economic level. Government officials made heavy tax demands on them, to which local leaders and groups added their system of appropriation. The official tax figures record only a fraction of these massive involuntary transfers, which can be subsumed for convenience under the general category of taxes. In addition, food was unusually scarce and expensive, in part due to the manipulation of the market by the powerful. Taxes and food were the objects of competition at the top and, because of their abuse, also common sources of popular grievance and political conflict. Not only in the period of instability, but throughout the century, they figured as central issues in the political interplay between government, local leaders, and the general public.

The taxes current in the eighteenth century included a patchwork of impositions paid on a regular basis to the imperial treasury, as well as extraordinary levies ordered by the sultan from time to time.[24] The legitimacy and rates of these tax demands remained outside public debate, although the townspeople approached the payment of virtually all taxes without any sense of civic spirit, accustomed as they were to seeing few tangible benefits from these outlays. More touchy politically were the taxes that the governors and other officials imposed at their discretion, very often for personal gain. The pasha had the authority to collect taxes for the purpose of financing provincial projects, such as campaigns to subdue tribesmen in the countryside. As the chief law enforcement officer he also exacted fines from groups and individuals who violated order and administrative rules; these sums went to him and his subordinates. The officials had a familiar repertoire of income extension devices to serve their ends: subjecting groups to exactions on contrived pretexts, a practice commonly known as ʿawan (or avania, as the Europeans in the region called it); issuing intolerable orders with the purpose of obtaining payments for rescinding them; and making various services and benefits dependent on bribes and exorbitant fees.

The circumstances by which the governors acquired their positions practically ensured that they would resort to such practices. They paid considerable sums and bribes for their appointments; in the early nineteenth century the office cost from 200,000 to 240,000 piastres. In return for this enormous investment they acquired a position whose official income from various taxes and dues was manifestly inadequate to defray their expenses and allow for any profit. In the 1770s it was commonly believed that the officially allotted revenue, which amounted to about 100,000 piastres, could cover barely two-thirds of the expenses of the pashas for the administration of the province and the cultivation of patrons in the capital.[25] Supplementing their income and recouping their investment hence figured inevitably as central preoccupations of their office. The official milieu in which they operated encouraged them to use their post for personal gain. The venality rampant in all levels of government, and not least among their superiors in the highest echelons, set a compelling example. Their wide discretionary powers as well as their short term of office in a place to which they did not expect to return made abuse all the more simple and attractive.

The abusive forms of taxation involved considerable sums. In the span of eight months in 1740–1741 the Christians made payments of over 50,000 piastres just in collective fines, bribes, and fees for settling business with the authorities. A dozen or so officials and power figures shared this sum.[26] When 'Abd al-Rahman Pasha died in 1752 just three months into his term, the court oversaw an inspection of his outstanding accounts which exposed the entrepreneurial spirit of contemporary administrative office. After reviewing dozens of taxes and fines imposed by the deceased governor, the court summed up its findings: of a total of 125,432 piastres in recorded debts and payments, some two-thirds (79,259 piastres) were illegal exactions demanded under threat or without the sultan's authorization.[27] Were it not for his untimely death the governor would have departed from Aleppo with a booty of still larger proportions. Some of his colleagues carried off impressive spoils. 'Ali Pasha, who was expelled in 1775, amassed 700,000 piastres in four and a half months of rule, while Ibrahim Pasha Qattar Aghasi was reported to have collected as much as two million piastres a year during his term in the early nineteenth century.[28]

The townspeople took for granted a certain amount of abusive taxation. "The hunger of Ottoman officials for money is insatiable," sighed a Christian exasperated with the seemingly endless government exactions.[29] When the governor cracked down on subordinate officials who extorted money from the Christians in 1767, an Armenian was prompted to exclaim in wonderment: "He did all this without it costing the Christian community even one piastre!"[30] Actually, the level of exaction varied widely among administrations, causing sharp swings in circumstances. It depended largely on the rapacity of the pasha, his hold over his subordinates, and the size of his staff. As a rule, the potential for abusive taxation rose with the number of aides and troops serving the governor; a larger personnel increased both the need for revenues and the number of people in a position to make demands of the population. There were just pashas who refrained from abusive taxation and thereby won the heart of the townspeople. Others went on a rampage, dragging down the local economy and the public mood.

The extortionate 'Ali Pasha who was expelled in 1775 was succeeded by Ahmad 'Izzat Pasha, a mild man of good intentions who restored a sense of security in the public. He employed a small body of troops and avoided abusive exactions. However, he failed to take forceful action against the ashraf, who engaged in large-scale extortions during his second term in 1779.[31] In the following year the residents experienced a reign of terror under 'Abdi Pasha. His troops, reinforced by many local recruits, extorted money from shopkeepers and had hundreds of people arrested and fined on false charges. The troops also quartered themselves with the residents, forcing many to vacate their homes. The guilds suffered heavy collective fines, and even the prominent merchants and tax farmers were laid under tribute. Fear reigned everywhere, and business stagnated. "Consequently, in the month of Ramadan you found all the markets closed and the men of trade gone, some to Hama, some to Damascus, some to Urfa, and some to Baghdad. . . . Damascus is full of Aleppines, so many indeed that the rent on a house has soared to fifty piastres a month."[32]

The population breathed a sigh of relief when 'Abdi Pasha's term ended. His successor, 'Uthman Pasha, ordered everyone to return to work normally, and called on the merchants who had fled to return. He went so far as to execute one of his top officials who had extorted large sums of money. Ibrahim Pasha, who assumed the governorship in 1782, renewed the *avanias* and extortions, although al-Halabi found him to be "somewhat gentler than his predecessors in his exactions."[33] The next appointee, 'Ali Pasha, seemed a positive blessing. He put a stop to the extortions and restored security while maintaining only a small body of troops and administrative aides. "We have not seen a governor like him in fifteen years," observed al-Halabi happily.[34] But six months later, under Mustafa Pasha, *avanias* and vexatious suits reappeared as standard practices. Following public complaints, the qadi and Chalabi Effendi intervened, and the pasha curbed the zeal of his subordinates.[35]

Conditions reached a new low under the next governor, Keki 'Abdi Pasha. Guilds, neighborhoods, and multitudes of individuals suffered heavy exactions. Many residents fled the city, and many others stayed indoors from fear of the unbridled extortions. The excesses drove the populace to join the revolt that forced the governor out. Mustafa Pasha restored peace with assurances of justice. "His arrival occasioned great joy among the people."[36]

These several cycles of joy and despair in the short span of ten years reflected the potent force of taxation as a public concern. The townspeople did not feel consistently oppressed by unjust tax demands; benevolent feelings toward pashas were not unknown.[37] But they certainly faced many bad years in which official exactions weighed on their pockets and peace of mind. Long experience fostered in them a high threshold of tolerance for abusive taxation. In difficult times the hope of improvement under the succeeding administration fortified them. Overall, they complied and paid, but not without maneuvering and some actual resistance; taxation had its politics.

The strategies for dealing with extortionate taxes were geared more commonly to the softening of financial demands by peaceful give-and-take than to aggressive resistance. Rebellion, the most drastic of possible public responses, was clearly rare; most years of oppressive taxation passed without provoking a violent uprising. Uncommon too was another confrontational albeit nonviolent approach: sending a collective petition to Istanbul detailing the governor's abuses and pleading for his removal. A formal appeal of this sort carried weight only when sponsored by the local leaders and ranking ulama, who risked such confrontation with the government only on the rare occasions when their own interests had been seriously hurt by the governor in question. Of the several petitions sent by the elite in the course of the eighteenth century, only one is known to have succeeded in removing a governor before the end of his term.[38]

Nor could the residents rely on the central government to discipline its officials. They watched many governors violate their rights with impunity; even those expelled by the populace or removed by the authorities for gross abuses were casually reassigned to the governorship of other provinces. Under these circumstances people tended to rely for their defense on local leaders and self-help. The well-to-do, who were tempting targets for extortion, often fled from the city in times of oppressive taxation, making their return when the administration changed; but for the mass of ordinary people escape was not a practical option. Since most of the exactions they faced were lump sum demands imposed on groups—neighborhoods, trade guilds, or religious minorities—it was the group leaders or representatives who actually handled the contacts with the authorities and oversaw the collection of taxes from members. The process was seldom a simple one of immediate group compliance with official demands; politics came into play and ultimately determined the final sum and schedules of payment.

Group leaders often turned to powerful figures with government connections to help reduce the burden. They also negotiated with officials to bargain down the original demands. In these bazaarlike exchanges they usually won some concessions. Even the Christians took to such politicking when faced with collective exactions. In 1766–1767 their communal representatives went into hiding and the congregations locked the four churches for seventy-two days in a battle of wits with extortionate officials. The passive resistance finally paid off when the pasha took action against his oppressive subordinates. In 1802, 1806, and 1808 the Christian leaders employed the same tactics, closing the churches and going into hiding until the governor agreed to a reduction of his original demands.[39] When governors announced new dress regulations for non-Muslims—a practice understood by all as no more than a veiled means of exacting money in return for a repeal of the orders— the Christians negotiated hard over the price of an official reprieve. In 1775 they stayed indoors for eleven days in protest against new clothing restrictions, while their representatives engaged in tough bargaining, in the course of which they suffered threats and temporary imprisonment. When the dust finally settled, they paid only one-third of the original sum demanded. Five years later, in similar circumstances, the Christians managed to lower their collective payment from twenty-five to fifteen thousand piastres.[40]

The burden of taxation weighed heavily on the non-Muslim communities, which presented particularly tempting targets. In the late eighteenth century both Christians and Jews were reduced to selling silver artifacts belonging to their respective houses of worship in order to meet the tax demands.[41] The Muslim population suffered heavily too; even the prominent families had no immunity. While they all employed various defenses to deal with abusive taxation, their measures proved too weak to defeat the system. They were able to win occasional relief, but without removing the root causes of the exploitation. The level of abuse actually rose in the latter part of the century. The increase in the power of local leaders worked, ironically, to worsen the tax burden on the population. The Janissaries and ashraf established a pervasive system of protection and racketeering, and under the native Aleppines Ibrahim Pasha Qattar Aghasi and his son Muhammad Pasha, the level of taxation exceeded anything attempted by previous governors in the eighteenth century. Even a seasoned observer of official exploits like al-Halabi was impressed by the systematic vigor with which these two rapacious men tapped every possible source of wealth; their abuses and exploitation were, in his words, "unheard of": "people could not earn enough to pay their taxes."[42]

The political struggles and the rise of local leaders worsened also the problems of subsistence in the city. Like taxes, food was a highly prized asset in the competition over resources and power. At least from the mid-1780s much of the food supply came under the control of several Janissary and ashraf leaders, who essentially determined the availability of bread, its quality, and its price. Especially in years when crops failed they manipulated the market to make immense profits. Their activities, largely free of any effective control by the authorities, pushed food prices sharply higher in the late eighteenth and early nineteenth centuries. For the masses of poor families, who lived at bare subsistence levels even in the best of times, the inflated prices of basic foodstuffs spelled untold hardships.

These problems were an acute version of a condition that accompanied the population throughout the century. The crop in the countryside failed many times. Profiteers, who included tax farmers, power figures, and even governors, invariably appeared on the scene to make a bad situation worse. Measures taken by administrations to alleviate the shortages were usually inadequate. In years of particularly severe scarcities there followed widespread hunger, epidemics, unemployment, economic slumps, and increases in crime.

Set against these social and economic dislocations the political repercussions of subsistence crises appear strikingly subdued. Feelings of anger and injustice brewed among the poor as they faced the realities of unaffordable food, adulterated bread, black markets, profiteering, and inadequate government measures. But only infrequently did the resentments break out in open political protest, and then mostly in the form of small outbursts of despair rather than massive and organized action. A group of women occupied the minaret of the Great Mosque in 1751, disrupted the prayers, and hurled loud abuse at the governor for doing too little to relieve the famine. In 1778 a crowd dragged the qadi to the governor's palace with demands that he be executed for not helping to alleviate the severe food shortage. Nine years later, during one of the worst famines of the century, a crowd of protesters advanced on the shariʿa court, but was turned back by troops. A number of women gathered in the courthouse some days later and cursed the aʿyan, while the qadi took refuge in the citadel.[43]

These were the poor's hunger spasms, spontaneous cries for help backed by no organization or force. At no time during the century did subsistence crises excite revolts or major upheavals that threatened the political stability in the city. The local leaders, while ready periodically to protest against abusive taxation, especially when they became its victims, had no interest in lending their support to disturbances over the issue of food: they usually profited from the shortages, and in general saw no advantage in popular unrest, especially when it was directed partly at them. Without political backing from above the multitudes of poor victimized by the shortages had no effective means of forcing changes in the behavior of government or the local elite.

The politics surrounding food demonstrated yet again the differences of interest between the local leaders and the public. It would clearly be simplistic to think of the leaders as spokesmen or agents of the community at large, as if they espoused the causes of the populace and acted on its behalf with the authorities. Such a view, expressed often in descriptions of urban politics in the region and the intermediary role of the "notables," papers over the complexities of political relations. The local leaders represented certain groups and clienteles, not the public in general. In exercising their influence, they also exploited various segments of the population. They practiced the politics of hierarchy and subordination, not of consensus.

THE LAW AND LEGAL INSTITUTIONS

THE STORY OF power and politics in Aleppo paints a rather unflattering picture of local respect for the rule of law. The abusive taxes, the extortion, and the violent destruction of life and property involved gross violations of rights which compromised the current conceptions of justice. The very officials and communal leaders charged with upholding the law participated actively in breaking it. The political milieu in which they functioned appeared ridden with self-perpetuating corruption.

This pattern of violation, although serious, made up only one layer in the complex realities of the law in Aleppo. The abusive practices of the powerful did not represent the general behavior in the community, nor did the deteriorated conditions of its last decades represent the realities of the eighteenth century as a whole. Aleppo's was generally a society that believed in the rule of law, invested in efforts to enforce it, and achieved a good measure of success in upholding its legal norms.

Upbringing and education exposed the townspeople from an early age to notions of right and wrong, of lawful and unlawful. They learned that they had legal recourse if their rights were violated, and that they risked prosecution if they broke the law. Violations did occur nonetheless, but they remained within acceptable bounds—a normal condition rather than a symptom of the breakdown of order. Most legal conflicts at the time revolved around matters of civil law: co-owners arguing about their shares in a house; heirs disputing their respective portions of an estate; couples quarreling about marriage obligations, divorce payments, and child support; business partners at loggerheads over their respective dues from a joint venture; creditors demanding debts owed to them; and guild members suing over violations of their collective rules. The community viewed these conflicts as perfectly normal; even the most respectable residents were apt to fall out with others on matters of disputed obligations, and to take their cases to court.

Crimes against life and property, regarded as much more serious, were relatively rare. Every year a few fell victim to physical assaults and even murders. Money and belongings were stolen from some homes and shops.[44] In 1754 a mosque was the target of a thief, who escaped with three prayer rugs.[45] Some residents lost their donkeys, mules, and horses, which were tempting targets when left unattended in public places.[46] For a large metropolis, however, the overall number of such crimes was low indeed. Only a dozen or so complaints reached the shari'a court every month; although not inclusive of all incidents, they attested to the generally low crime rate. In years of subsistence crises and economic hardship, when widespread hunger and unemployment turned the desperate to theft, the level of crime shot up. The precise trends over the century are otherwise impossible to reconstruct. On the whole, serious crimes against life and property appear to have been less numerous than violations of public morals, such as drinking, gambling, the production of wine, and illicit sexual relations. Usually discreet and victimless, many of the moral offenses never reached official attention or found their way into the records.

Aleppo's society was equipped with a complex body of laws, processes of legislation, courts, notarial services, informal arbitration, police, neighborhood watches, prisons, and gallows. Thousands of people became involved in their processes every year: offenders, victims, litigants, witnesses, legal proxies, judges, notarial scribes, mediators, policemen, government officials, neighborhoods, and interest groups. The institutional arrangements and the actual behavior of the townspeople tell how society approached the tasks of protecting rights, preventing violations, resolving conflicts, and punishing criminals. They show the current notions of justice, the degree of local commitment to the rule of law, and the abusive sides of law enforcement. That the residents remained subject throughout the century to the same system of laws as well as the same institutions for making and enforcing the laws reflects not only cultural stability, but also the weight of power, which was inextricably tied to the law.

The laws that directed the daily activities of the residents were a mix of Islamic law, state legislation, and local custom. They were a curious blend of religious and secular, formal and informal, written and unwritten, changing and immutable. At the center stood the elaborate written code of the shari'a, or Islamic law, whose wide-ranging rules regulated criminal and civil matters as well as personal conduct. When a resident inherited property, or bought a house, or divorced a spouse, or made a business partnership, or endowed property, or defaulted on a debt, or suffered injury in an assault, Islamic law defined his rights and obligations. The code was in effect throughout the Middle East and in Muslim lands around it. Religious thought held it to be a corpus of heavenly commands designed to guide the faithful to moral perfection on earth and prepare their path to the hereafter. As a divinely ordained law, it was essentially immune to change. Aleppo's residents inherited its rules as they had been developed and codified in the medieval period, and saw no reform in them during the eighteenth century.

A substantial body of manuals, commentaries, collections of legal opinions, and classical texts on jurisprudence conveniently provided students and practitioners of shari'a law with answers to almost every conceivable question. The religious colleges in the city and the wider region taught Islamic law as a core subject of their curriculum. The law in the Hanafi version—one of the four schools of legal interpretation recognized in Islam—was the official choice of the Ottoman Empire. The qadis appointed by Istanbul, all of them Hanafis, applied this version in the shari'a court. One of the four local courthouses, however, adjudicated the shari'a according to the Shafi'i interpretation for the benefit of the adherents of that school. The differences between the two versions were usually limited to detail rather than principle, but they did widen the range of legal options available to the residents in some matters. For instance, women who wanted a judicial release from marriage after their husbands had disappeared went invariably to the Shafi'i court, which accepted the presumption that men absent for a considerable period were most probably dead. The Hanafi law in the matter, which required an abandoned woman to wait patiently until her missing husband had reached the mature age of ninety before applying for an annulment, was hardly of use.

The Ottoman government upheld the shari'a as the supreme law of the land. While not free to tamper with the religious code, it did exercise the prerogative to legislate in matters of state and public order not addressed adequately by the shari'a. In keeping with a practice established by previous regimes in the region the Ottoman sultans manufactured a large body of nonshari'a laws known as *qanun* or *'urf*. Unlike the immutable shari'a, these were open to change; the government added and altered as it saw expedient. They included regulations and decrees in matters of taxation, public appointments, administrative jurisdictions, and personal privileges. These formed the operative core of public law, defining the relationship of individuals to the state. The amount of taxes a resident paid on his house, the authority of governors and tax farmers, the tax privileges of Janissaries—these were matters regulated by official rules. A tax register authorized by the sultan was a binding document; the residents were obligated to pay the rates specified for them, and those who were mistakenly omitted enjoyed freedom from them until the books were corrected. Multitudes of people in the city carried official papers certifying certain rights, powers, or tax exemptions. To those who on occasion protested in court that the issuing of such privileges harmed them the qadi had one invariable answer: such are the sultan's orders and they must be obeyed.[47] The ruler's will was law; its fairness was not subject to debate in the court.

Also part of state law were criminal codes that supplemented the shariʿa's provisions and went beyond them to widen the prerogatives of the authorities in enforcing public order. The codes defined precise punishments for the many criminal offenses for which the shariʿa designated no specified penalties. In the interest of maintaining order they gave the authorities wide powers, and also elaborated on the legal responsibilities of individuals and groups to conduct themselves properly and assist in the tasks of law enforcement.[48] These rules, which shaped in some fundamental ways the status of individuals vis-à-vis the authorities, were also enforced by the qadis.

To this legal corpus which evolved outside the shariʿa the community added what amounted to customary law. Many arrangements and practices that guided water distribution, construction, and market activities in the city developed by formal agreement within groups or through informal communal consensus. Being largely unwritten, their validity was usually confirmed by the testimony of expert witnesses. To the extent that they were proven to be "established custom" *(al-muʿtad al-qadim, al-ʿada al-qadima)* the court enforced them as law. When some bakers began to produce a new kind of bread in 1768, a group of their colleagues who were threatened by the success of this innovation were able to block it by proving in court that it violated the local custom, established by the bakers' guild, of producing only four specific types of bread.[49] The qadi declared that "the old custom must stand undisturbed"—a dictum that was echoed time and again in judicial verdicts.[50]

Despite the language used to identify them these "old customs" included rules that were neither frozen, nor old, nor universally approved. They were made and unmade daily. Power, not age, shaped them and secured their hold. The process is displayed most vividly in the trade guilds, which manufactured a large body of customary rules regarding entry into occupations and promotion within them; access to raw material and jobs; shop licenses; wages; product quality; and prices. The prominent interests in the profession shaped these "customs" and maintained them while they proved useful, defending them against members who challenged or violated them. When economic conditions changed or the weight of interest and influence within guilds shifted, members appeared in court to pronounce modified rules, which were soon conveniently known as the "old customs."[51] Small groups were the usual participants in this process of shaping "customs," but the legal effects touched the entire community. The aggregate of guild rules, for instance, determined the structure of the city's commodity and job markets.

With the shari'a immune to change and state law subject to forces largely beyond local control, customary law figured as the main channel through which the townspeople could shape the legal norms of their community. It gave some legislative expression to local interests. The adaptable nature of customary and state laws lent flexibility to the legal system, allowing it to respond to shifting conditions in those areas most sensitive to change: the economy, administration, and public policy. The shari'a, for all its centrality as the hallmark of Islamic society, thus left considerable room for legal adaptation and discretion in areas not governed directly by its rules. Outside it thrived a whole body of secular laws, regulations, and customs which possessed a life of their own and were recognized as perfectly valid legal norms binding on the public.

Alongside its complex of laws Aleppo had also a network of institutions for their enforcement, in the form of both a police apparatus to prevent and handle crime and a system of courts to adjudicate disputes and protect legal rights. The official police machinery was unimpressive in size, but the law equipped it with formidable powers to impose security regulations on the public and to arrest, investigate, fine, imprison, and execute. Guided by a law-and-order approach to issues of public security, the state gave its delegates extensive authority and discretion. It even recognized the pasha as an "administrative judge" (*hakim al-'urf* or *hakim al-siyasa*) with the power to pass sentence on criminals independently of the shari'a court. While the authorities were prohibited from abusing the rights of individuals, the very scope of these rights was considerably diminished at the outset by the latitude granted to officials by the system.

Of the judicial courts that enforced the law in the city none approached the qadi's in importance. Although commonly known at the time as the shari'a court *(al-mahkama al-shar'iyya* or *majlis al-shar')*, it enforced state and customary laws as well as Islamic law. With its comprehensive jurisdiction, plurality of public functions, and official standing as the chief court of the land, it dominated the legal scene. In it was centered the mainstream of legal business. The court opened its chambers to complaints by members of all classes and groups. The non-Muslims resorted to it, as also did women, who figure prominently in the registers. The court admitted all matters, including the most petty. Its staff handled on the average some four thousand legal cases a year. Only a portion of this business passed through the hands of the qadi himself. From his seat in the Great Courthouse (al-Mahkama al-Kubra) he supervised four court offices, each run by a deputy judge *(na'ib)* appointed from among the local ulama. The qadi delegated court business to his deputies in return for a sum, making sure to reserve for himself the more lucrative cases.[52]

Court fees and dues were among the chief sources of income of the qadis, who recouped the cost of purchasing their appointment and covered their expenses from the proceeds of their office rather than from a fixed salary. They collected a fee on every legal document issued. In addition, they claimed 10 percent of the sum contested in legal suits, and certain shares of all estates executed as well as of the income of pious foundations and orphans audited by the court. On some suits they charged as much as 1,000 and even 7,500 piastres in court expenses.[53] Opinion in the city held the fees to be exorbitant; in 1770 the ashraf demanded that they be reduced considerably.[54]

The qadis came to preside over a well-established system functioning comfortably with a steady staff and venerable routines. The deputy judges as well as the interpreters *(turjmans)*, bailiffs *(muhdirs)*, scribes *(katibs* and *muqayyids)*, dividers of estates *(qassams)*, and investigators *(kashshafs)* came from local ranks and often held office for many years. They provided the court with a stable cadre of professionals well versed in local ways and judicial practice. Many of the scribes were the sons of scribes; they absorbed their notarial skills at home from fathers who prepared them early for clerical careers.[55] In periods of transition when a new qadi was not yet arrived, the court continued to operate normally under a local alim who served as substitute judge *(mawlakhilafa)*. Ahmad Effendi al-Kawakibi ran the court as a substitute for a whole month in 1768.[56]

The importance of the shari'a court in enforcing the law rested in good measure on its function as a notarial office rather than merely a forum for settling disputes. Residents went there routinely to register loans, divorce settlements, business partnerships, purchases of real estate, and various other transactions and contracts. The court issued to them officially notarized deeds *(hujjas)* written in Arabic or Turkish, and kept copies in its registers for future reference. This protective practice helped to order contractual relations, to discourage violations, and in general to add an element of security and trust to agreements. The resort to written title deeds smoothed the web of transactions in the real estate market and diminished the potential for mischief. Although oral contracts did hold in court, experience taught the townspeople the wisdom of recording rights and obligations on paper. Many of their agreements they drew up without the court's assistance. They hired the services of trained scribes to write legal documents, and sought advice from ulama about legal questions. The community had no professional lawyers to provide legal services and represent litigants in court. Those who pressed suit in the shari'a court or were summoned there to answer charges pleaded their own cases before the judge or appointed a proxy *(wakil)*, usually a relative or associate, to speak on their behalf.

The court's notarial business actually far outweighed its judicial load. As the breakdown of cases demonstrates, the townspeople resorted to the court more often to obtain useful or officially required legal papers than to press suit. Out of 363 cases registered in one sample month (Rabi' II, 1164/February–March 1751), the number of legal suits amounted only to 52 (14 percent). Most of them involved claims of property and debts, with only a handful of criminal charges of theft and assault. Registrations of the sale of houses and other real property accounted for almost half of the total (176 cases). Another 39 cases recorded the endowment of property, the transfer of offices and tax farms, business partnerships, and guild arrangements, while the remaining 96 cases set down the terms of divorce between couples, arrangements for child support, division of estates, repayment of debts, and renouncement of claims to certain pieces of property.

Conflict was actually more common and the population more litigious than the court records indicate. People had some of their disputes settled in the other available formal and informal forums. The shari'a court ranked as the foremost judicial institution in the city, but without being the sole body for settling legal business. As administrative judges the pashas were authorized to try offenders who violated public order and

security. Their actual judicial practice extended well beyond such matters, at least during the second part of the century. Residents took to
them a variety of complaints, including strictly civil ones governed by
shariᶜa law. Theft, assault, fraud, violations of public morals, cursing,
and disputes over inheritance, debts, and property rights all reached the
governor's court. Some individuals who lost in the shariᶜa court took
their cases to the governor. That this entailed an encroachment on the
jurisdiction of the shariᶜa court was acknowledged by qadis, who considered it out of line with the law to take a complaint within the shariᶜa's
competence to the administrative judge while a qadi was present in the
city.[57] Considerations of financial gain, however, encouraged governors
to accept cases that belonged in the shariᶜa court—the standard penalty
on the party found guilty was a monetary fine, which ranged usually
between one hundred and one thousand piastres.[58]

Specialized judges with jurisdiction over certain limited matters or
groups also participated in the adjudication of legal disputes. The formal
head of the ashraf sat as a judge in some cases involving members of his
corps, and maintained his own prison. The commander of the Janissaries also adjudicated disputes between his subordinate soldiers; only he
could imprison and inflict corporal punishment on them. The farmer
general of taxes exercised a limited judicial power in revenue matters,
and had his own prison. The *shahbandar*, officially appointed as representative of the merchants, settled commercial disputes between members of his professional group. The European consuls enjoyed some
extraterritorial jurisdiction over their resident nationals.[59]

The non-Muslim minorities also exercised a measure of legal autonomy. The Christian archbishops adjudicated property and other disputes brought before them by members of their respective communities.
The Jews, especially jealous of their comprehensive religious law, maintained a rabbinical court (Heb. *bet din*) headed by a single judge. It
settled questions of marriage, divorce, and inheritance, notarized business transactions, and adjudicated property disputes. A communal notary (Heb. *sofer*) drew up deeds and marriage contracts in accordance
with Jewish legal norms. In many matters, including even intracom-
munal disputes, the Jews did resort to the shariᶜa court. The rabbis
conceded to the need to abide by state law, but encouraged their flock
to follow Jewish law whenever possible, even if it proved less favorable
to their case than the shariᶜa.[60] Out of respect for this religious obligation some Muslim businessmen had property disputes with Jews settled
before the Jewish court in accordance with Jewish law. The Jewish

judge in the late eighteenth century, Ephraim Laniado, described this as a fairly common occurrence during his time on the bench.[61]

In addition to this array of formal institutions, informal mediation also figured in the judicial process. Custom and social pressure encouraged amicable settlement by arbitration. If the residents were quick to take offense and to insist on their rights as a matter of personal honor they were also accustomed to surrendering their conflicts to peaceful mediation. When disputes flared, business colleagues, friends, relatives, religious leaders, and respected men usually offered or were recruited to act as go-betweens and work out a reconciliation *(sulh)*. The mediators sought to reach a compromise in which no party lost face rather than to declare clear winners and losers.

Settling disputes through the services of informal arbiters was not only less confrontational but also less costly than appeal to the court. In court the winning party paid the fees. People expecting to win a suit faced the prospect of inflicting damage on themselves and reducing their net gain. Suing in court made sense for them only if no other acceptable recourse remained open. At the same time, the party expecting to lose could threaten to sue in court and by losing cause harm to his adversary. This improved his bargaining position and acted as still another inducement for the other party to settle through mediation. Nuisance suits designed to harass did come occasionally to court.[62] The judicial registers record claims, some of them probably groundless, that plaintiffs brought without any proof or possible expectation of judicial victory. The ashraf protested against this nefarious practice in 1770, demanding that those who bring vexatious suits be compelled to bear the court expenses themselves.[63]

Neither the private mediators nor the various restricted courts left a record of their modes of adjudication or their work load. Although none of them approached the shari'a court in importance, their very presence indicates something of the complex institutional setting within which law and justice functioned in Aleppo. A Muslim in a Muslim state submitting to the authority of a Jewish judge, a lay Ottoman governor adjudicating disputes belonging in the shari'a court, a private go-between negotiating a settlement without recourse to a formal court— these situations alone suggest the interplay of jurisdictions and the wide range of practices that existed within the community.

The legal institutions maintained a remarkable stability throughout the eighteenth century. Some laws did change during the period, but large segments of the legal corpus remained entirely unaltered. On a more basic level, there was no major shift in the sources from which society drew its laws, the processes by which it made and unmade rules, the notions of justice, and the approaches to law enforcement. Islam, so tightly woven into the whole complex of legal institutions, had clearly much to do with this stability. So also had the realities of power. The shariʿa was unchallenged in good measure because the state chose to throw its weight behind it and avoid tampering flagrantly with its rules. In the nineteenth century, when the state opted for reform even at the expense of the hallowed laws, the road was opened for the replacement of shariʿa laws with new codes, including many imported from Europe.

The state was also the key force behind the process of legislation. Its despotic ideology made no room for recognized public participation in the making of laws; those in positions of authority and influence enjoyed that prerogative. Even the customary laws were shaped by the more influential residents, and their range of choices was bound by government policies and preferences. In principle, all laws legislated by the state had to conform to the shariʿa, which represented a kind of constitutional yardstick for justice and morality in lawmaking. The religious standards did constrain the government, but not entirely. Official legislation occasionally exceeded their bounds, to the chagrin of the religious establishment. Expediency, the cultivation of political allies, and the overriding concern for maintaining order and control dictated their own priorities. Over the centuries the state's ideology and interests had come to have a profound impact on the legal institutions and on the relationship between power and individual rights.

JUDICIAL PRACTICE AND LAW ENFORCEMENT

THE SYSTEM OF law and justice as it actually functioned during the century is not fully explained by the formal rules and social ideals. It lent itself to a measure of manipulation; some residents paid bribes, fabricated evidence, and evaded justice. The police and criminal investigators labored with limited resources and solved only a portion of their cases. Considerations of personal gain affected the behavior of officials and were responsible for various abuses and irregularities in the execution of justice. In certain circumstances, especially in times of unrest, the authorities exercised their wide powers in the interest of order, often at the expense of the finer demands of the law. The official staff that made decisions changed constantly with the turn of administrations;

harsh and efficient individuals alternated with more lackadaisical types. With the periodic shifts in local circumstances the crime rate and the level of public orderliness rose and fell. Working in the midst of these different pulls and changes, the institutions showed their flaws as well as their inner strengths. The actual performance of the courts, the workings of the police and crime prevention, and the handling of suspects and criminals all reveal the realities of the law and law enforcement in the city.

In the shariʿa court, litigation followed an established set of procedures designed to give the parties their say and the judge all the necessary evidence on which to rule. The plaintiff began by making his claim. Unless the defendant confessed to the charge the plaintiff was asked to bring proof. He needed the testimony of at least two witnesses or relevant documentation to establish his claim; otherwise the judge dismissed the case for lack of sufficient proof. If the defendant made a counterclaim, he was called upon to prove it in like fashion. After both sides had rested their cases, the judge, without the aid of a jury, pronounced his verdict. It followed the burden of the evidence: unproved charges were dismissed while claims supported by adequate legal proof were accepted. Some cases were not so clear-cut: neither party could bring conclusive proof. In these instances the court encouraged a negotiated compromise. Mediators *(muslihun)*, whose identities were not spelled out in the protocols, worked out a settlement, and both sides announced their agreement to it with the judge's blessings.[64] The practice of mediation out of court thus came to the aid of conflict resolution in formal litigation as well.

This judicial process worked with remarkable speed. Many matters came before the judge on the day of the complaint or shortly after. The deliberations were usually concluded and the judge's sentence handed down in one or two sessions. The court scribe then wrote a concise summary of the proceedings in the register, and issued copies to interested parties. Judging from these summaries, residents who went to the shariʿa court could usually expect the trial to be fair as well as speedy. The rulings of several dozen judges in four courthouses over a quarter of a century are striking in their consistency; they followed legal principle rather than arbitrary choice. The shariʿa was too clear on most matters to leave much room for debate, while official orders and established customs received consistent judicial backing. The repeated testing of certain matters in litigation with uniform results created a good sense of what the court might do and so tended to reduce public uncertainty.

Although people were entitled to appeal the verdict of a deputy judge before the qadi few actually took that course, suggesting that they did not expect the outcome to change in their favor.

The pattern of verdicts rules out a decided court bias in favor of the strong and powerful. Government officials, members of distinguished families, ulama, and ashraf all lost cases to their social inferiors. Christians and Jews often prevailed over Muslims in litigation. In 1778 representatives of the Christians went to court to seek judicial protection against new dress restrictions that had been imposed on their communities by the interim governor despite an official edict from Istanbul confirming their existing dress code. Confronted by the qadi, the interim governor backed down. Mustafa Bey, the son of a pasha, sued a Christian for a debt and lost for lack of evidence; witnesses he brought proved false and were disqualified. Ibrahim Effendi ibn Ibshir Agha, in charge of the cheese tax farm in the city, was taken to court in 1757 by Jews who proved successfully that he was overtaxing them. Without official permission, the qadi reminded the revenue farmer, he could not alter the tax rates. A Muslim who made false claims against three Jews with the intent of harassing them suffered flogging by order of the judge.[65]

The opportunities for gross irregularities by the court were limited by various institutional controls built into the judicial process. Too many alert eyes and ears monitored court proceedings for unfair practices to pass unnoticed. Several notarial witnesses *(shuhud al-hal)* sat in on all deliberations for the express purpose of observing the procedures. When a court investigator went out to collect evidence from individuals or to examine a site in dispute, notarial witnesses accompanied him as observers. Deeds had to bear the names of these witnesses in order to be considered legal. The witnesses usually included one or two court officers, but the majority of them were Muslim men not in the court's employ: people with an interest in a case, neighbors and associates of the parties, and respectable residents who happened to be in court that day for other business. Their number stood commonly at six or seven, but in some cases as many as forty or fifty sat in court as observers.[66] Among them were porters and barbers as well as ulama and members of the elite. Without being expert in the fine points of law many of these witnesses could spot gross deviations from correct form.

The litigants themselves usually knew enough about their rights to defend themselves against open violation of the established judicial rules. Appearance in court in various capacities familiarized a good segment of the city's population with legal procedures. Many took care to prepare themselves in advance, even coming equipped with legal opinions (fatwas) from the jurisconsult which they presented to the judge in support of their case.[67]

Yet a certain measure of abuse did compromise the court's ideals of justice. One source of irregularity lay in the occasional admission of fabricated evidence. A certain proportion of litigants made inaccurate or contrived charges. Some admitted their dishonesty under questioning in court, or betrayed it by refusing to repeat their version under oath. But when backed by the doctored testimony of witnesses, such charges could give the necessary legal support to a case. According to the recorded summaries of the suits, the court checked on the credibility (ʿadala) of witnesses before allowing them to testify; a few were indeed disqualified for partiality or for accepting bribes.[68] Yet some litigants managed to hire witnesses to testify on their behalf and so to manipulate justice to their advantage.[69]

If money could buy witnesses it could also procure some behind-the-scenes cooperation from officers of the court, including the qadi. Residents managed through bribes to delay verdicts detrimental to them and to expedite cases when the decision favored them. These abuses testified to the venality within the court system. But they also proved that justice was still alive; the bribers worked to manipulate the timing of the verdicts because the contents could not be altered to their advantage.

Such bribery was one of several irregular ways in which qadis enriched themselves during their tenure in the city. Some actually took care to depart before the arrival of their successors in order to avoid demands for restitution of sums illegally obtained. Residents who suffered injustices succeeded occasionally in taking their case to the highest authorities and having the responsible qadi return part of his spoils. However, it often required making a trip to Istanbul and good connections there to mobilize such official intervention against a qadi.[70] When the qadi illegally seized a share of the estate of the wealthy merchant Bakri Chalabi Tabla Zadeh in 1773, the heirs took their case to the top officials in the capital. The qadi was ordered to return everything he had taken.[71] In practice, such recourse was not readily open to the mass of ordinary people, who lacked both the financial means and the political connections needed to pursue a grievance successfully.

Although venality and abuses tainted the image of the shariʿa court, its level of dishonesty was probably within the bounds of ordinary and acceptable judicial practice. In the milieu in which it was set the court

performed fairly well and served the cause of justice. Its protective
services were not lost on the thousands of people who over the years
recovered their rights with the judges' help. In the court, countless
women were able to obtain dowers and child support payments from
reluctant ex-husbands, creditors recovered overdue debts, and victims
of cheating and harm won compensation.

The shariʿa court appeared especially fair and just in comparison
with the judicial practices of the governors. The pashas left no records
of their sessions as administrative judges, but a stream of complaints to
the shariʿa court exposed something of their abusive practices. Some of
those found guilty and punished by administrative judges were subse-
quently able to prove in the shariʿa court that they had been condemned
and fined on the basis of false accusations. Some of them had also been
thrown in prison for a few months and even subjected to beatings.
Having failed to recover their financial loss from the departed governors,
their only recourse was to claim it from those who had falsely accused
them in the first place. They turned to the shariʿa court, where they
obtained this kind of compensation with the aid of witnesses and legal
opinions. Some of those sued in such trials actually admitted to having
made false accusations to the pasha.[72]

While the more upright governors refrained from accepting un-
founded complaints, many others took advantage of the opportunity to
pocket fines. The shariʿa court was left to rectify their abuses in imperfect fashion. The pashas were not made to account for their behavior or
to restore the fines they imposed unjustly. What judicial procedures
they employed in adjudicating disputes remain a mystery. Their arbitrariness, however, was such common knowledge in the city that making a complaint to the pasha figured among the familiar forms of threat
and blackmail. One man used this method to ward off a creditor for a
while; another tried it in order to force his former employer into rehiring
him. Three textile artisans who failed to get promoted to mastership
threatened to avenge themselves on their colleagues by making some
contrived complaint against them to the governor. Unwilling to take any
chances, their colleagues brought the three to the shariʿa court, where
they admitted their designs and pledged to pay back any damage they
might cause in the future by an unjust complaint.[73] Some who did not
get their way in the qadi's court vented their frustration through vexatious suits to the pasha. A man who claimed an entitlement to a stipend
from a family endowment and failed to prove his case in the shariʿa
court proceeded with his complaint to the governor, who found some
cause to fine the accused administrator of the endowment. The latter

then took the matter back to the qadi and recovered the fine from the author of the false complaint.[74]

For better or worse the governors affected the administration of justice in the city, and not only in their limited capacity as judges. As the officers in charge of security and order they touched the daily life of the community in other, more pervasive ways. A police machinery under their command kept an eye on the population and investigated offenses. It was hardly impressive in size. The governor's footguard (*tufenkjis*), who usually numbered some two or three hundred men, performed the routine tasks of urban police. Spread across a large metropolis this rudimentary force was naturally ill equipped to monitor closely the entire population. For these shortcomings in manpower the authorities compensated in two effective ways: they exercised a good dose of intimidation, and imposed various police responsibilities on the public.

Patrols of the pasha's footguard toured the streets and markets. They flogged wrongdoers on the spot or carried them off to jail to await sentencing and a monetary fine. Tips from informants put them on the track of unlawful activities. Many of those caught in their net paid dearly for their offenses. Hasan ibn Yusuf, caught in 1751 in the illicit company of a woman, was thrown in prison and then fined 1,150 piastres by the governor. This substantial sum, equivalent to the price of ten modest homes, he had to borrow from a wealthy merchant.[75]

For the governor and his subordinate officers hunting for offenders proved a profitable business. In a year's time they supplemented their personal income considerably from their share of the fines imposed on wrongdoers. Their zeal and the harsh penalties imposed bred wide-spread fear of the police—fear that was reinforced by their occasional arbitrariness and abusiveness. Especially under the more rapacious governors the police looked for excuses to punish people and impose collective fines, acting in essence as instruments of extortion. They subjected their victims to enough intimidation and abuse to render them eager to pay for their release. "Anyone who ended up in the governor's palace found himself in a hell," commented the chronicler al-Halabi on the harsh reign of 'Abdi Pasha in 1784, when multitudes were arrested. "He witnessed such frightful sights that he was only too willing to pay to free himself."[76] Some governors added to the intimidation by resorting to a few executions at the beginning of their term, or touring the city in disguise in order to surprise offenders. These practices sowed the desired amount of trepidation in the public.[77]

Policing by the authorities was only one element in a larger effort at law enforcement in which the population itself played a major role. The neighborhoods instituted standard security arrangements designed to control local movement and deter crime and immoral activities. Among them they erected barriers throughout the city that limited opportunities for mischief. At night gates closed off the quarters and even streets within them to unannounced visitors. Each neighborhood and market hired a watchman *(haris)* to monitor the movement of people into its precincts. The limited night life helped: people usually stayed home after dark, and those who ventured outdoors were required to carry lit lanterns or pay a fine if caught without one.

Occasionally undesirables did slip past the barriers and guards under cover of dark. In 1754 the residents of Altunbogha accused their neighbors in Oghlubey of keeping such lax control over the gate between the two quarters that thieves found their way in. They arranged for a night watchman hired by both districts to stand at the gate and inspect the traffic.[78] When in 1750 the owner of a workshop complex carved a door into a neighborhood street the local residents brought him to court for exposing them to an inflow of thieves who robbed their homes. The qadi ordered the property owner to seal the door.[79] Empty lots and ruined buildings in the neighborhoods, which tended to attract immoral activities, were also a cause of local displeasure. When charitable foundations leased out unused land to prospective builders neighbors welcomed the arrangement as a contribution to their security.[80]

The concern with local security grew out of occasional thefts from homes as well as the offensive presence of prostitution, drinking, and other forms of vice. Behind it, however, was also another driving force: fear of the authorities. Ill equipped to police the residents closely, the government resorted to a system of social control by which members of groups would police each other. It held each neighborhood and non-Muslim minority collectively responsible for the behavior of its members. Residents were expected to make local misdeeds known and find the offenders. The entire locality or group suffered a heavy fine for failure to report crimes and to uncover their perpetrators. When an angry mob killed the head of the millers' guild during the famine of 1735 an investigation failed to uncover the culprits, but that did not prevent the governor from imposing a large fine on the neighborhood that was the scene of the crime.[81]

Even illicit affairs and premarital pregnancies were among the matters for which an entire group was held accountable. The residents of Karlik, who in 1752 failed to inform the authorities about an affair between an unmarried local woman and her cousin, encountered the governor's wrath. Representatives of the neighborhood pledged before the authorities to report immediately any offenses of this sort in their locality.[82] Jewish maids who became pregnant out of wedlock were sent by their masters to deliver their babies in another town or were quickly married off locally, all to ward off a fine on the entire community.[83]

The principle of collective responsibility, which had its basis in the criminal codes, was a source of dread for the population. No one appreciated paying for the wrongdoing of others. The fear of official reprisals encouraged some covering up of misdeeds, but it also worked to a certain extent as an effective instrument of group control. People were prompted to spy on their neighbors in situations in which they would otherwise have been inclined to exercise civil inattention. They confronted neighbors who drank and sold wine, organized gambling activities, or ran brothels in their homes, warning them to mend their ways before they brought a financial penalty on the entire group. Sometimes they denounced them to the authorities and even had them expelled from the neighborhood. Many men and women whose behavior brought official wrath upon their quarter or threatened to involve it in trouble were taken by their neighbors to court to secure their removal from the locality; disgust with their conduct and fear of collective reprisals were both given as justification for such requests.[84] In one instance neighbors went so far as to enter a house in their quarter uninvited in order to catch the occupants in their suspected immoral activities. The scene before their eyes—several women sitting unveiled in male company—proved less compromising than they had apparently expected, but they proceeded to have the owners of the house expelled from the neighborhood.[85]

That collective responsibility encouraged policing within groups was evident also in the precautionary and preemptive measures that residents took against potential sources of trouble. One man and his wife pledged to their quarter to reform their immoral ways, not to allow two undesirable women to live with them, and to reimburse the locality for any fines they might bring upon it. Another resident was permitted to stay in his neighborhood only after other parties undertook to guarantee his behavior. In one quarter the residents secured from two sisters a promise to cover any future fines imposed on the locality because of their troublesome brother.[86]

Checking on the identity of those who moved into their quarter was another means by which residents exercised social control. Fatima bint

ʿAbdallah, expelled from her neighborhood for immoral behavior, moved
to another quarter, only to meet the scrutiny of her new neighbors. No
sooner did they discover her past record than she was ordered to leave.
In the quarter of al-Hajjaj five women who owned rental homes agreed
to lease their properties only to tenants approved by the headman and
residents, and to bear responsibility for all official fines their tenants
might bring on the neighborhood.[87]

In the limited privacy and intense social familiarity of the neighborhoods, where residents lived very much in the public eye, the weight of
opinion and group pressure could work effectively to deter crime and
vice. This, together with the security measures taken and official police
work, helps to account for the relatively low incidence of crime. The
entire setup reflected the manipulative powers of the authorities, which
skillfully compensated for their limited capacity to police the population
by relying on indirect means of enforcing law and order. The policing
exercised within groups and the cooperation of informants assisted their
work. So also did the practice of recruiting residents associated with
offenders to help the police. Relatives and landlords suffered fines if
they failed to produce wrongdoers sought by the authorities. In 1754
one Khalil ibn Bektash paid 25 piastres in fines after he could not locate
his tenant for the police.[88]

The fate of suspects and offenders who fell into the hands of the
authorities varied widely, although it usually promised to be unpleasant
to some degree. In the shariʿa court the judge usually punished minor
offenses with flogging, his sentence specifying the number of strokes to
be inflicted on the bare soles of the offender. Thieves were sometimes
punished by the amputation of a hand. The governor and the police
commonly imposed a fine as a penalty. Some residents experienced
arrest and incarceration, either for purposes of interrogation, or pending
a decision on their fate, or as part of their sentence. Their jail terms,
however, were usually limited to a few months at the most. Long-term
imprisonment was not among the penalties to which wrongdoers were
subjected, even in the case of severe crimes. Much of the city's prison
population was composed of debtors who were usually detained for two
or three months until they paid their debts or provided surety.[89] Although generally brief, the prison experience proved painful at least for
some: thrown into narrow cells shared by other inmates, they were
chained, beaten, and subjected to various forms of torture.[90] Their
experience may not have been that uncommon in a penal system that
accepted the selective use of torture in interrogation and punishment.[91]

For murderers, armed robbers, and other serious criminals death was considered a fit penalty. The pasha's subordinates conducted the investigations, turning the criminals over to the qadi for trial and the necessary sanction for execution. The hangings and beheadings, performed in public in front of crowds, were intended as demonstrations of justice and warnings to potential troublemakers; the corpses remained on display for several days to convey the message. The drama and public attention surrounding executions were particularly intense because such events tended to be infrequent.

Although the public favored strong measures against vicious criminals the authorities were required by law to ensure due process and to impose capital punishment only with the qadi's sanction. On the whole, however, the criminal codes allowed them wide discretion in disposing of individuals considered to be threats to public order. On the basis of collected testimony the court could establish that a person was a "troublemaker" and a "habitual criminal" *(sa°in bi °l-fasad, mustamirr al-darar li °l-°ibad)* and thereby make him a legal candidate for execution. Thrown into those conveniently broad categories were an armed robber, Khalil ibn Jabir, who repeatedly broke into homes and escaped with property, and a neighborhood headman, Krikor ibn Nerses, who instigated collective exactions. The qadi transferred these and other offenders to the pasha, who had them executed by administrative sanction *(siyasatan)* in accordance with the powers vested in him by the criminal codes of the state.[92]

How much attention the authorities paid to the legal niceties in cases involving human life depended very much on the scruples of the pasha and qadi as well as the political climate in the city. In times of unrest it was not uncommon for governors to resort to summary executions as a way of disposing of troublemakers and intimidating the public. When a mob attacked the qadi in 1765 the pasha ordered that two men caught as ringleaders be hung immediately. A swift public execution displayed the seriousness of official resolve to crack down on mischief, and usually had the desired pacifying effects.[93] Against gangs of armed bandits in the countryside the pashas sent their troops out with orders to kill and return with the decapitated heads of the criminals. While these passed as legal practices justified in the interest of keeping public order, there were official acts that flagrantly violated the accepted notions of justice. When he was transferred to another post in 1780 the oppressive °Abdi Pasha left in Aleppo illegally executed men as well as prisoners held in the citadel without legal convictions. From fear or complicity the qadi in office at the time had shut his eyes to the governor's abuses. The new qadi freed the prisoners and secured from the pasha's successor a pledge not to jail or execute anyone without legal cause in accordance with the shari'a.[94]

That the law enforcement system had its abusive sides is evident from the judicial irregularities, arbitrary arrests, extortionate fines, excessive torture, and illegal executions. The precise levels of this abuse over the century are impossible to measure. They clearly varied among administrations, and appear to have been generally higher in the less orderly climate of the latter part of the century. In any case, the abuse needs to be seen in the context of the contemporary norms of justice. Police intimidation, the penalization of a group for the wrongdoing of individuals, the use of force to extract confessions, and summary executions were among the more severe yet not illegal aspects of law enforcement at the time. The broad powers of the authorities increased the potential for abuse, especially since the institutional checks proved less than adequate. The qadis did not consistently exercise the counterweight necessary to constrain those pashas intent on getting their way at all costs. The central government, which pressed the pashas to enforce authority with a strong hand, tended to back their harsh actions and to accept after the fact certain violations of law committed in the name of order. Confronted with political upheaval and social unrest in many parts of the empire, it was inclined often to follow the logic of *raison d'état*, even if that compromised justice.

Yet the oppression experienced by the public should not be exaggerated. It bears remembering that the government's limited sphere of concerns kept it from penetrating too deeply into people's lives. The residents took for granted many of the official practices, both legal and irregular, developing a relatively high threshold of tolerance for government arbitrariness and harshness. Using the courts, patrons, bribery, bargaining, evasion, and other mechanisms of defense, they managed to obtain some protection and relief. The venality of officials was a weakness that they turned to some advantage: placed in the right hands in the proper amounts, money worked wonders in softening the harsher acts of government. The privileged and propertied groups were clearly more favorably placed to protect themselves against official abuses. Yet the readiness to resist and manipulate was evident at all levels, illustrating how much the passive "flocks" represented more an official ideal than a political reality.

CHAPTER 4

Economic Welfare: The External Sources of Wealth and Subsistence

LEPPO'S TOWNSPEOPLE LIVED in a world attentive to economic concerns, and to an extent driven by them. Their local leaders were a club of wealthy men. In their society, wealth opened the route to power, and power appealed as a sure avenue to personal enrichment. Material issues dominated their political life: taxes, food, extortion, markets, tax farms, and venal offices were the sources of factional fighting, popular protests, and endless competition. The records of the shari'a court, which preserve a rich slice of daily activities, display the prominence of economic matters; seldom is the word "piastres" absent from a summary of litigation or a notarial document.

Aleppo's economy clearly deserves attention in its own right. It was, by the regional standards of the day, a sophisticated system based on large-scale manufacturing and trade, and equipped with outlets for investment and profit making. Elaborate institutions regulated economic activities and ordered competition in the marketplace. Substantial transfers of wealth and services also took place outside the market, primarily within the family and by way of charity. Together with earned income they shaped the material conditions of the population and determined the distribution of wealth.

Yet the story of economic welfare in Aleppo must really begin with the description of a context extending well beyond the sphere of strictly local activities. The city was part of a larger economic system, and its fortunes depended very much on external events. During the eighteenth century four basic concerns linked it to the outside: food, rural resources, security, and trade. Its external ties stretched all the way to England and India, but a hinterland extending in a radius of some seventy miles from the city formed the truly vital sphere of urban interests. While the city drew great wealth from its external associations, it was also subject to constant shifts in the opportunities and benefits they offered. The availability of food, the degree of rural security, the level of revenues from the countryside, and the fortunes of trade fluctuated, even from one year to the next, setting in motion changes in the economic welfare of smaller or larger segments of the population.

In the eighteenth century the external conditions, in the hinterland as well as the regional and global scenes, posed problems for various urban interests. Aggressive tribal groups established a powerful presence in the countryside; peasants deserted their villages; the area of agricultural cultivation shrank; the supplies of food diminished; insecurity and extortion plagued the routes of trade and travel; and European commercial business shifted steadily to other centers. These developments, part of an interrelated set of events, had to do with movements of population in the area, realignments in the patterns of trade, and above all shifts in the balance of regional and global power. They created conditions over which people in Aleppo had limited or no control and which worked largely to their detriment. The urban population suffered their unfavorable consequences, in the form of famines, slumps, loss of business, and other troubles. At the time only the state commanded the ability to impose order, protect the peasants, subdue the tribes, secure trade routes, and respond to the enterprising commercial advancements by European powers, and it proved inadequate on all counts. As one actor on the larger political and economic scene, Aleppo was constrained by obvious limits on its power, limits which deserve some attention in light of the common image of regional domination associated with Middle Eastern cities.

A closer examination of Aleppo's external sources of wealth and subsistence—food, rural resources, security, and trade—helps to establish the city's role and limitations in its hinterland, the crucial linkages between its economic conditions and the larger political realities, and the level of integration of its economy into the regional and European economic systems. It throws light on some of the essential forces which shaped the material welfare of the townspeople, and on the types of benefits and dislocations experienced by different groups in the wake of developments originating on the regional and global scenes.

THE RURAL CONNECTION: FOOD

THE WINTER OF 1756 was ferociously cold in Aleppo, more so than anything people could remember. Thick snow descended on the city, and temperatures dropped well below the freezing point. Barely equipped to weather the discomforts of milder winters, many families suffered misery and loss of life. "It is so cold we cannot leave our homes," complained a local resident. "Every fruit-bearing tree in our city, especially the vine and olive, is dried up. May God deliver us from misfortune and misery."[1] Even the approach of the warm season did not brighten the public mood; the crop had failed that year, and fear of famine was acute.

In the course of 1757 basic foodstuffs, primarily bread, became steadily scarcer and dearer. Some grain was brought in intermittently, particularly from the private stores of the governor, who seized the opportunity to sell it to a desperate population at excessive prices. When winter arrived hunger and want were widespread in the city. The acute subsistence crisis triggered a slump in the local economy which only compounded the misery. Trade stagnated, the wheels of industry slowed, and thousands found themselves unemployed. Epidemic diseases began to rage among the weakened and malnourished residents, taking many lives. Impoverished and destitute people ended up in the streets; many of them died of starvation, cold, and disease.[2]

The conventional instruments of charity and poor relief were helpless in the face of this large-scale destitution. The French consul, depressed by what he saw, estimated in late May 1758 that more than 40,000 inhabitants had perished in the preceding six months.[3] A local priest assessed the victims of the famine at 87,000.[4] These improbable figures, along with the contemporary accounts of conditions, suggest how frightful the crisis appeared to those who experienced it. The prospects of outside relief seemed dim—large parts of Syria, Iraq, and Anatolia were suffering a similar fate. Stories reached the city of acts of cannibalism in Diyarbakr, and of people there as well as in Mosul and Urfa selling their children in order to survive another day.[5]

In the face of popular despair and unrest, the governor met in special session with the city's political leaders in April 1758, and arranged to import wheat from the area of Hama.[6] What supplies came in did little to relieve the misery. The price of bread and other basic necessities remained very high. Guards stood at the doors of bakeries to prevent

attacks by hungry mobs.[7] Bands of armed bedouin and disbanded soldiers *(kapısız)* roaming wantonly on the city's outskirts added to public
anxieties. Residents feared to venture outside the city. The alarm increased when gangs entered Aleppo and robbed passersby. In October
1759 the town gates were locked for fear of depredations.[8]

That winter a series of major earthquakes hit Syria. Aleppo's townspeople counted themselves fortunate for having escaped the devastation
visited upon Damascus, Sidon, Antioch, and numerous other settlements in the region. The succession of tremors kept the residents in
terror of an impending disaster until they subsided in the spring of
1760.[9] At that point their attention was already turned to the bubonic
plague which had made its appearance in the city. It raged there intermittently for two whole years, wreaking havoc on the helpless population, and killing many thousands.[10]

Survivors of the plague were left to recover amid persisting problems
of subsistence. Bread and other basic necessities remained exceptionally
expensive. In 1762 the qadi met with the heads of several guilds to fix
the prices of a host of food items.[11] Relief was short-lived. Despite a
good harvest bread became expensive again in the summer of 1764 after
wheat was transferred to relieve the severe shortage in Damascus. In the
succeeding months conditions worsened considerably. An exceptionally
dry winter followed by a heat wave destroyed the crops in the country.
There was little the townspeople could do except rest their hopes on the
communal prayers for rain. By spring the price of bread and other basic
foodstuffs shot up to new heights. The pasha sent out for wheat from
Urfa, but the quantities proved insufficient. Angry crowds rioted and
attacked bakeries. In July they mobbed the courthouse; troops went out
to disperse them, and had two men hung. The qadi himself was not
hurt; having sensed the vicious public mood he had already sought
refuge with the pasha. Dysentery and other diseases reached epidemic
proportions, aided by the acute shortage of water in the city. In despair,
some residents packed their belongings and migrated to other cities.

An air of gloom hung over the city when the new year entered.
Cannon blasts on the morning of January 30 announced the birth of a
daughter to the sultan. Usually a welcome pretext for public jollity, the
occasion stirred only a token celebration in the citadel. The abundant
harvest did not improve conditions. Bread remained scarce, and always
of an unappetizing quality. Tax farmers and officials resorted to the
common practice of withholding grain from the market in order to profit
from the artificial shortages. The governor himself prohibited the im-

portation of wheat from the countryside in the summer of 1766, until he had sold his own stocks, which he released for sale at a deliberately slow pace and at excessive prices.[12] Among the victims of his machinations were the city's millers, who under orders sold flour for his kitchen at a heavy loss. His year's tenure of office over, the pasha left the city without troubling to pay them.[13]

Hardships such as those experienced during these ten years were not the exclusive lot of one unfortunate generation; they recurred time and again throughout the century, as if part of the natural rhythm of life. At least twenty-five years, most of them in the second half of the century, are known to have been accompanied by major shortages of food.[14] The crises varied in duration and intensity: some subsided after a few months, while others lingered on for several seasons. In general, they tended to repeat the patterns visible in the scarcities of the 1750s and 1760s. They threw the community out of balance and set in motion an array of developments, revealing the vulnerability of the city to outside forces beyond its immediate control. Nowhere is this more evident than in the elemental dependence on food: the harvest was the heartbeat of the economy, the success of the annual crop determined the prosperity of business and the material welfare of the population. The effects of this dependence were complicated by the politics affecting the food supply, which reached especially intense levels in the second part of the century.

The food consumed in Aleppo was striking in its variety: in a good year the townspeople could find in their markets a wide assortment of breads, cereals, meats, legumes, vegetables, fruits, dairy products, nuts, pastries, and condiments. All of these had their place in the elaborate local cuisine, which delighted in the refinements of assorted dishes and rich mixtures of ingredients. Yet what any resident actually consumed from day to day depended in great measure on his financial means. Even in years of relative abundance he faced a hierarchy of food prices which set severe limits on his possible choices (see table 4.1). Some food items came in different grades and qualities which varied considerably in price. One could buy bread in the form of crispy doughnutlike cakes (ka‘k), or, for almost half the price, in the form of flat white flour loaves; for a third of the price of the cakes one could settle for bread deemed no longer fresh. The most desirable cuts of lamb cost three times more than inferior sheep's and goat's meat. Bread, grains, legumes (primarily lentils, chick peas, and beans), seasonal vegetables and fruits, milk, and yogurt fell within the lower price ranges; they composed the diet of large segments of the population. On the other hand meat, always at least three times more expensive than bread, grains, and legumes, appeared seldom on the tables of the lower-income groups.

Food prices fluctuated with the seasons and according to the success of the crop, but the price ratios between the different categories of foodstuffs tended to remain fairly stable, with bread maintaining its place as the staple food.[15] The agricultural land in the countryside was given mostly to wheat, supplemented by barley and legumes. In times of food shortage and famine an elemental preoccupation with bread dominated the public mind. "Since everything other than bread is expensive, the poor and the wage laborer can afford to eat only bread, and are delighted if it is available," observed Yusuf al-Halabi during the food scarcities of 1787.[16]

Subsistence crises created widespread misery and even starvation because they pushed even bread and other basic foods out of the reach

TABLE 4.1. Prices of Foodstuffs in Aleppo, January 1762
(prices in ʿuthmanis)

	Price per Ratl	*Price per Unit*
Bread, of different types and qualities	7–20	
Meat, of different types and qualities	18–54	
Chicken, of different sizes		24, 30, 36
Fish		20, 30
Rice	30	
Noodles	20	
Cracked wheat	15	
Mung beans	15	
Broad beans	10	
Chick peas	12	
Lentils	12	
Carrots	2	
Turnips	2, 3	
Yellow onions	4	
Green onions		0.1
Cauliflower		3.0
Pumpkin, large		10.0
Cabbage		2, 1.5

of the poor. Within a short span of time bread and other basic items could turn into virtual luxuries, especially when available only on the black market. In March 1787, at the height of the food shortage, bread and meat prices were three times what they had been six months earlier; other basic foods had also risen considerably in the interval (see table 4.2). The townspeople experienced equally dramatic increases in other difficult years. In 1729 the price of flour shot up from 12 to 60 piastres a *makkuk* (a unit of dry measure for grain). In June 1765 a *makkuk* of wheat stood at 30 piastres; a month later it was already 70, and by October it reached 100. The wheat supplies imported in 1771 to relieve the shortage brought down the price of wheat from 180 to 80 piastres a *makkuk*. In 1775 the prices of basic foods went up three times, and in 1783 the prices of fruits and vegetables rose to four or five times their normal levels.[17]

TABLE 4.1. Prices of Foodstuffs in Aleppo
(continued)

	Price per Ratl	Price per Unit
Celery root		0.2
Fruits, of various sorts	18–70	
Milk	14	
Yogurt, of different kinds and qualities	15–24	
Cheese	76	
Eggs		1.2, 1.5
Butter	150	
Olive oil	106	
Sesame oil	84	
Honey	81	
Pomegranate juice, of different qualities	63, 47	
Syrup of grape juice	38	
Sesame paste	50	
Vinegar	15	
Salt	4	
Nuts, of different varieties	57–180	
Pastries	46–96	

SOURCE: Aleppo court records.
NOTE: The Aleppo *ratl* was approximately 4.8 pounds; 120 ʿuthmanis (or akçes) were equivalent to one piastre.

Such sharp price increases strained the budgets of the poorer residents, who in the best of times struggled to keep themselves and their families adequately fed. They lacked the cushion of domestic food storages and substantial savings of the better-off families, who routinely stocked up on large amounts of grains, legumes, and other unperishable foods, both for convenience and as a defense against possible shortages. Their larger houses were equipped with storage rooms and underground cellars designed for this purpose. Such seasonal purchases in bulk called for outlays of money beyond the means of the poor, who were left at the mercy of the wild market and the profiteers.

Once even bread became scarce the lower classes suffered extreme hardship. Multitudes gathered daily at the gates of bakeries in the hope of obtaining a loaf or two. The bread sold in those periods of shortage was often a greyish, unappetizing product made of a mix of wheat, barley, rye, ground legumes and, the residents suspected, foreign material of all sorts. "The bread is so full of filth it is inedible," al-Halabi complained in disgust.[18] Yet the poor could not be too discriminating about their diet; in despair they ate anything that would keep them alive, including plant roots, cotton seeds, and apricot pits.[19] In the famine of 1787 hungry men and women roamed the streets, weak and wailing from hunger. Some were seen dropping dead in the marketplaces.[20] Further, widespread malnutrition bred dysentery and other ailments that carried away many of the weak; of the eight major attacks of plague in the eighteenth century five came during subsistence crises or right on their heels.

TABLE 4.2. Rise of Food Prices in Aleppo,
September 1786–March 1787
(prices in piastres)

	September 1786	*March 1787*
Wheat (1 *shunbul*)	8.00	14.00
Barley (1 *shunbul*)	5.00	10.00
Bread (1 *ratl*)	0.25	0.75
Meat (1 *ratl*)	0.75	2.25
Cooking oil (1 *ratl*)	2.00	3.00
Butter (1 *ratl*)	2.00	3.50
Rice (1 *ratl*)	0.75	1.00

SOURCE: Halabi, Murtad.

Economic troubles became particularly acute when food shortages persisted beyond a few months. The hardships that began with scarce bread deteriorated into a severe recession which affected all classes. Once want and destitution became widespread they cut into the purchasing power of the population, and slowed down the entire economy. Trade and artisanal production declined, and many found themselves out of employment at a time when a secure income was most needed. Even wealthy merchants went bankrupt as the city's fortunes suddenly turned.[21] Emigration increased considerably at such times. Rich families, who stood to lose from the dimmed economic prospects, were among those who left to seek their fortunes in other places.[22] The resident European merchants complained incessantly about the stagnation of business and financial losses occasioned by the recurrent subsistence crises. However, some trades, especially those fed by external demand, proved more resilient than others. In 1787 the silk industry continued to do brisk business despite the local hardships. "The artisans and those working in the silk craft are all employed," observed al-Halabi in his description of the generally depressing situation. "They are not overwhelmed by the high cost of living, being secure in their livelihood, which is just adequate to meet the cost of bread."[23]

The growth of food shortages into wider economic crises was especially hard on low-income groups who were not sufficiently secure financially to withstand the onslaught of protracted unemployment and high prices. Without adequate welfare institutions to back the sick, needy, and unemployed many soon fell into the ranks of the dependent. In mid-March 1787, at the height of one famine, al-Halabi observed that during one week "the number of the poor [*fuqara*'] multiplied beyond count in every community in Aleppo."[24] Multitudes of families were reduced to begging. Al-Halabi estimated that as many as three hundred people knocked on his door daily to plead for help. Many of the shopkeepers were so overwhelmed by the swarms of beggars who filled the marketplaces that they chose to keep their businesses closed. The better-off did respond generously, but as al-Halabi was quick to observe, this private charity could never quite meet the needs of the poor.[25]

In the absence of adequate income or outside support, many turned to theft as a means of survival. The rate of crime, usually low, climbed considerably in times of prolonged crisis. In 1787, for example, numerous bakeries and shops were robbed and many residents had bread loaves snatched from their hands in the streets. Theft reached such proportions that the authorities ceased searching for stolen goods and prosecuting thieves. To protect themselves, shopkeepers kept their merchandise at home or closed their businesses altogether. Families took their own precautions, bringing wheat to the millers in small amounts and baking their bread at home rather than having it done by the neighborhood bakeries.[26]

So much was disrupted in times of food shortage, yet the community was able to rebound fairly quickly. Once food became available again, prices returned to normal and life settled back into its usual routines. The subsistence crises did not leave behind them lasting structural changes in Aleppo's society. They were, after all, an old and familiar type of misfortune to which society had long adapted; they did not alter the system of belief, the demographic regime, the economic system, the role of the state in society, the institutions of welfare, or agricultural technology. But even if temporary the unsettling changes clearly took their toll on a more individual level; those who lived through the hardships gained a sense of the uncertainty and precariousness of existence. Many carried painful memories of privation, greed, and loss which colored their visions of life and human nature. The victims were left to rebuild their families and means of livelihood, while the profiteers found their pockets fuller and their social ambitions easier to attain.

Food supply problems plagued the city throughout the century, and if anything grew worse over time. Food prices crept up steadily, but in the late eighteenth and early nineteenth centuries they took dramatic leaps upward. The price of a *ratl* (approximately 4.8 pounds) of bread was set at around 10 'uthmanis in 1762, at 18 in 1773, and at 48 in 1787; in 1792, while grains were available, it stood at 60, or half a piastre.[27] In the span of thirty years the price that the townspeople paid for their staple food had thus multiplied six times. Such had never been the case in the first half of the century: both in the famine of 1697 and in the severe crisis sixty years later residents were overwhelmed when a *ratl* of bread shot up to one-third of a piastre. Yet in the famine of 1793 they had to cope with bread priced at a record one piastre, and in the next crisis just eleven years later paid as much as two piastres for a *ratl* of wheat.[28]

The price of wheat, which in great measure determined the cost of bread and many other foodstuffs, rose markedly, particularly during the late eighteenth and early nineteenth centuries. In 1729 a *makkuk* could be bought for 12 piastres; in bulk sales transacted from the late 1740s to the late 1760s prices ranged usually between 20 and 50 piastres in times when supplies were not acutely scarce; by 1811, 160 piastres was considered the normal price.[29] The peaks reached by wheat prices during periods of shortage mounted in like fashion: 60 piastres a *makkuk* in 1729; 160 piastres in 1758; 224 piastres in 1787; 480 piastres in 1811; and 576 piastres in 1820.[30]

A resident who kept record of the high food prices in the plague year of 1786 was prompted to comment later: "At the time, people considered these prices extremely high, but a few years after the plague they came to long for those prices."[31] And indeed, the cost of food soared, climbing wildly during the next severe crisis in 1792–1793, and reaching unprecedented heights in 1804, a year in which the city suffered what the experienced al-Halabi described as "a great famine the like of which has not occurred in this city."[32] Not only did prices reach new peaks during these years of famine; they failed to go down to their previous levels in subsequent years.

This economic deterioration had its roots in a complex of conditions that were readily apparent at the time. Al-Halabi could on occasion reiterate the traditional pious explanation of subsistence problems. "We accepted all this willingly because it is a strike by the Almighty," he wrote of the suffering of the 1787 famine. "We stand in submission to His sublime will. It is all part of what we justly deserve for our sins."[33] Fifteen years earlier he saw God's merciful intervention at play when unexpected supplies of grain flowed in to avert a famine.[34] Yet far from resting entirely on such interpretations, his commentaries on the crises he experienced betray the good grasp he and his contemporaries had of the mundane forces that rendered their community so vulnerable to the recurrent hardships.

The whims of climate were to blame for much of the trouble. Many of the subsistence crises originated in a failure of the crop due to inadequate rainfall or hard freezes. Aleppo drew its food from an agricultural zone sensitive to fluctuations of rainfall and temperature. For grains, legumes, and various other basic foods the city depended on the agricultural lands of northern Syria and southern Anatolia. The orchards and gardens on Aleppo's outskirts provided most of the seasonal fruits and vegetables consumed by the townspeople. The only important edibles imported from areas further afield were rice (from Egypt), coffee (from Arabia and the European colonies), sugar (from the European colonies), and some spices (from the Far East).[35]

In years of good rainfall and rural security the extensive agricultural hinterland produced a good supply of foods, and the residents could delight in abundance and low prices. Yet the climate rarely cooperated for long uninterrupted periods. Good parts of the hinterland, particularly the grain-producing steppe lands to the east and south of the city, received just enough rainfall annually (ten inches) to produce one crop. Here a small annual variation in rainfall made the difference between a successful harvest and a failed crop. Time and again during the eighteenth century inadequate rainfall destroyed enough of the crop to require the city to import grains from neighboring provinces and areas farther afield. Periodically, winter freezes and scorchingly hot springs and summers damaged the nearby gardens, making even basic fruits and vegetables scarce. Irregularities in the climate appear to have been especially problematic in the second part of the century. Whether they formed part of a larger climatic shift in the area toward drier, colder winters and hotter summers is not clear. Al-Halabi for one was sufficiently impressed with the spells of unusual weather to comment on them in his chronicle.[36]

Climatic accidents and other natural misfortunes such as attacks of locusts were only partly to blame for subsistence crises.[37] There were years of abundant harvest in which grain was nevertheless scarce and dear, due to artificial shortages created by hoarding and manipulation of the market.[38] The authorities assumed a certain responsibility for keeping the population supplied with affordable bread, partly by facilitating the transfer of grain surpluses from other areas, and partly by regulating the market to ensure stable prices and fair distribution. The actual benefits of official measures varied with the circumstances. Some crises lent themselves more readily than others to quick relief, and some administrations proved more effective than others in meeting the challenges.

The most effective answer to the problem of food shortages lay in the importation of grains. When the crop failure was limited to the Aleppo area, the city drew on the harvest of neighboring parts, such as Hama, Urfa, and al-Bira. In some years, however, drought affected large parts of the Middle East at once; poor harvests in the regions of Damascus and Aleppo, for instance, often coincided.[39] The city then depended on surpluses from farther afield. In 1787, when much of Syria, Iraq, and Anatolia experienced problems of subsistence, wheat reached Aleppo from the European provinces of the empire.[40] Competition with other stricken areas as well as problems of transportation complicated the task of relief in such circumstances. Overall, access to food surpluses within the empire helped, although the transfer of food among areas worked both ways. When neighboring provinces suffered shortages, they drew on the harvest of the Aleppo area, thus reducing the pool of food available to the city.

The prospects of prompt relief by way of importation depended on the cooperation of the authorities. Precisely because of the limited and unpredictable pool of wheat available annually for consumption the Ottoman government set restrictions on grain transfers among provinces. During the acute shortages of 1778 Aleppo had to petition Istanbul for permission to import wheat from neighboring al-Bira, where prices were far lower. Once the grain arrived in the city's markets, bread became far more affordable.[41] More serious obstacles arose in Aleppo itself, of course, on those occasions when governors and high officials prolonged the material hardships by prohibiting the importation of wheat until they had sold their private stocks at a high profit.[42]

Government officials and tax farmers came regularly into the possession of large amounts of grain as part of the dues and debts paid to them by villagers in the countryside; these were a precious commodity from which they could turn large profits by manipulating market conditions. In 1773, for instance, as food problems in Aleppo were mounting, Chalabi Effendi sent out orders to the hundred or so villages under his control as tax farms to withhold all shipments of grain, while he waited for prices in the city to rise. Such schemes were not always successful, however. In 1773, and again in 1792, grain imports from other provinces brought down prices, forcing the disappointed hoarders to release their stocks.[43]

The profiteering extended beyond hoarding into large-scale evasion of price controls. In times of scarcity, the authorities usually set a ceiling on the prices of bread and basic foodstuffs. Bakers and food merchants were required to abide by the official prices, or face prosecution; violations occurred, of course, their extent varying according to circumstances. In some crises the fixing of prices only drove food into the black market. The authorities, even when guided by the best intentions, lacked the necessary means to supervise the markets closely. Not all officials were as conscientious as the qadi who won popular praise for personally supervising the markets and punishing offenders during the crisis of 1778. The Janissaries and the governor's footguard assigned to supervise sales in the bakeries during the famine of 1787 set themselves up as middlemen, taking over the sale of bread and dough to the public at highly inflated prices.[44]

The effectiveness of traditional measures of price fixing and market supervision waned when Ottoman authority weakened and influence in the city passed to local factions. From the late 1780s profiteering and black market activity reached unprecedented levels as the Janissaries and ashraf seized virtual control of the food supplies and manipulated them recklessly. During the famine of 1787 they intercepted shipments destined for the city, bought them, and had them smuggled in to be sold on the black market at twice the set price. By the time the next famine came along in 1792–1793, their monopoly had tightened. They controlled all food imports and even the sale of bread at bakeries, little of which was to be found during daylight hours. Most of the sales took place at night, when the black market came to life. Residents purchased their bread on dark street corners from dealers who charged exorbitant prices for inferior loaves. Complaints to the governor led nowhere; even he submitted to the realities, buying wheat for his troops at black market prices. The absence of effective official control thwarted all prospects of relief. In April 1793, when a large caravan carrying a shipment of rice approached the city, a group of resourceful Janissaries rushed out to meet it, bought up its three hundred camel loads and smuggled them into the city, where they were sold at two piastres a *ratl*, double the set price.[45]

Such practices persisted for the next twenty years, until the government finally crushed the Janissaries and reasserted its authority. It was this wild profiteering, even more than the vagaries of nature, that produced the chronic food problems of the late eighteenth and early nineteenth centuries and determined the level of food prices. The popular protests against the behavior of the powerful, expressed in sporadic bread riots, attacks on qadis, and verbal abuse of governors and influential leaders, were minor eruptions of despair which left the root sources of the abuses untouched.

There were also real problems in the agricultural sector that worked to aggravate the food supply situation in the city. The peasantry in the north Syrian countryside labored under onerous conditions of indebtedness and insecurity which took their toll on the level of food production. At times entire villages abandoned their fields, and Aleppo felt the effects of the diminished crop. The food shortages in 1775 and again in 1783 were attributed in part to the oppression of the peasantry.[46] In 1811 wheat had to be imported from Urfa because, according to the French consul, the Aleppo agricultural region was no longer able to support its food needs.[47]

Whether the region had indeed ceased to be self-sufficient is not clear. However, the considerable extent of depopulation in the countryside was certainly particularly acute in the late eighteenth and early nineteenth centuries. The townspeople lacked the secure backing of a prosperous agriculture operating at full capacity and producing large surpluses of food. This condition grew out of developments in the countryside that affected not only the city's access to food but several others of its key interests as well.

THE RURAL CONNECTION: RESOURCES AND SECURITY

WHILE IT HAD little outward appearance of prosperity and luxury, Aleppo's countryside actually represented in its aggregate a vast source of wealth and economic opportunity. The expanses of cultivable land, the taxable produce, the countless peasants in need of loans, credit, and various goods—these were among the economic resources that tempted and enriched entrepreneurs. Aleppo, or rather certain groups in it, reached out and syphoned off a share of this rural wealth, by way of taxes, profits, rents, interest, and exactions of all sorts. Aleppo also had another concern with the countryside: the city's vital routes of communication with the outside world ran through it, and safety on the roads was essential to trade and travel. The fortunes of both urban interests depended on order and security in a rural world over which the city exercised only limited control. Both resources and roads were the focus of competition in which the city was one of several participants.

Land was the most obvious and abundant rural asset, but only a relatively small portion of the income and profit that urban people drew from the countryside came from it. The bulk of the agricultural land in Aleppo's countryside was state property *(miri)*, available for farming by peasants in return for taxes and dues. Some of it was *waqf* land, that is, property which had been endowed for the support of charitable causes or family interests, and was hence removed by law from commercial circulation. The small fraction of the agricultural lands open to private ownership *(mulk)* belonged to landlords in various localities in the province. Those in Aleppo used their properties as a source of rental income rather than as profit-making enterprises.[48] In relation to their other sources of income and wealth the rents were fairly modest in scale. Income from rural properties was a more important component of waqf revenues. The hundreds of charitable endowments and family trusts based in the city held between them a very considerable amount of real estate, including a good number of rural properties from which they drew rents and tithes. In the period between November 1751 and October 1753 the court audited the accounts of ninety-eight of the pious foundations dedicated to the support of mosques, public fountains, and colleges in the city. Rural properties produced as much as 22 percent of their combined annual income (2,746 out of a total of 12,426 piastres).[49]

When the Ottoman state finally opened up its lands to private ownership in the second part of the nineteenth century Aleppo's wealthy families rushed in, and within a few decades amassed vast amounts of land in the countryside. While barred from this avenue in the eighteenth century they were able to tap what was then by far the largest source of rural wealth—taxes. A small circle of well-to-do merchants, ulama, Janissary officers, high government officials, and great tax farmers (the aʿyan) controlled the collection of revenues from the villages in the province on behalf of the state. They invested in tax farms as a form of income-producing property. The annals of the court record transfers, partnerships, and subletting arrangements, some involving a share in a single village, others a dozen or more villages.[50] Many of the investors held the same villages for years. The steady conversion of one-year tax farms *(iltizams)* into lifetime grants *(malikânes)* during the eighteenth century opened the way for the emergence of a class of hereditary quasi-landlords.

The tax farmers drew their financial benefits only in part from what they skimmed off the vast pool of state revenues by way of legitimate remuneration for their services as well as by defrauding the administration and the peasants. They also profited handsomely from the stocks of grain in their possession, which were economic assets in their own right. Their tax collection tasks involved them, in addition, in a variety of lucrative financial dealings with peasants. They became moneylenders and patrons, routinely advancing taxes and dues on behalf of the villagers, covering the impositions frequently levied on them, selling them seed and fodder, and paying out their debts to urban creditors. The peasants turned to them most directly for the credit they so often needed to carry them over from one year to the next. Moneylending to villagers was an extensive business not limited to tax farmers alone; a number of other urban investors lent out large sums of money to peasants at high interest rates.

These involved economic dealings between urban figures and peasants are recorded in numerous notarial deeds drawn up by the parties.[51]

They give a sense of the scale of business and of the heavy dependence underlying the peasant's connection with urban patrons. In 1766, for instance, seven villages acknowledged a combined debt of 138,691 piastres to Chalabi Effendi. A large portion of it originated in loans that he had advanced to the peasants.[52] Over one hundred villages were under the control of this powerful tax farmer at that time.[53] The deeds, however, never recorded the interest charged and the profits accumulated by the tax farmers and businessmen, leaving the boundaries between exploitative dealings and transactions of regular exchange conveniently blurred. Only infrequently was the silence broken to reveal the actual realities behind the figures and dealings. In 1765 'Abd al-Wahhab Agha Shurayyif met with a group of peasants representing the village of Ram Hamdan, his tax farm for over twenty years. They owed him 37,111 piastres, which they arranged to repay in installments over a period of fourteen years. When their tax farmer died some two years later the peasants felt free to charge in court that the bulk of their debt was actually interest that had been disguised in the notarial deeds as legal credit. Their claim was apparently well founded; the court cut the debt to 'Abd al-Wahhab's heirs almost in half and spread out the repayment over a period of fifty years.[54]

The disguised transactions and undisclosed profits preclude any possibility of establishing the full extent of the rural wealth appropriated at any time during the century. The enormous scale of the investments, the competition for them, and the willingness of those involved to risk making deals in an uncertain environment all indicate that returns were high. Many members of the urban elite built their financial and political fortunes on rural resources. While not the sole source of their power, the rural wealth helped them reinforce their social position in the city, build up their clienteles, and increase their political influence.

The benefits of rural wealth went to a relative few. With the exception of the waqf revenues that supported communal institutions the bulk of the rural rents, taxes, interest, and exactions benefited mainly a small group of wealthy Aleppines and their clients. Little of this wealth returned to benefit the rural sector. Its recipients did not use the capital and land at their disposal to develop and finance agricultural projects or to improve the productivity of the agricultural sector. Their income constituted an outright redistribution of wealth from the country to the city. Only in the second part of the nineteenth century did wealthy Aleppines begin putting private capital into agriculture. Their investment was central to the intensification of production in the fertile lands north and west of the city, and to the resettlement of depopulated steppe lands to the south and east.[55] Private landownership, increased rural security, and the expanding opportunities for profit from agriculture, especially with the growing foreign demand for cash crops, introduced new incentives for urban investment in the countryside.

In the pattern of urban-rural relations that prevailed in the eighteenth century, groups in Aleppo relied on their economic and political leverage to exploit rural resources. The unequal premises of their ties with the countryside worked in their favor, but did not give them free rein to do as they pleased. In the countryside they faced a world with a will of its own, not a passive instrument in urban hands. While they exercised a considerable say in rural affairs, so also did government, the peasantry, and tribal groups. Conditions in the countryside showed clearly the extent to which forces outside the city shaped realities. The unhealthy state of agriculture and the widespread insecurity in parts of the countryside, conditions that seriously affected urban interests during the eighteenth century, were neither created by the city nor desired by it.

Much cultivable land around Aleppo lay deserted. Aleppo's governor was able to settle on vacant land in the province numerous peasants from Diyarbakr, Mosul, and Urfa who sought refuge from their famine-stricken areas in 1757.[56] In the middle decades of the century some fields and orchards belonging to pious foundations in the city appeared in annual financial audits as vacant properties yielding no income.[57] In the areas to the east and south of the city few villages remained inhabited. Even in the fertile lands to the north and west peasants abandoned their fields. By the early nineteenth century large tracts of formerly cultivated land lay fallow.[58] Contemporary observers spoke repeatedly about the great decline in the number of villages in Aleppo's countryside, and the numerous ruined and abandoned settlements that dotted the landscape.[59]

A combination of oppression, misgovernment, and insecurity accounted for this state of affairs. Some but by no means all of it originated in the city. Urban groups shared most directly in the financial exploitation that upset agricultural prosperity. The peasant in Aleppo's countryside labored under a crushing tax burden, especially during the costly Ottoman wars and the weakened state authority in the last decades of the century. He was subject to a host of impositions and levies; some were collected on a regular basis, and others were unanticipated exactions. In addition to dues levied on yields and property he paid his share of the large collective fines imposed for crimes committed in his village, covered the expenses of high officials and their retinues who happened to pass through his district, quartered troops on official mission at his own expense, helped to finance campaigns against tribes, paid protection money to bedouin Arabs, and succumbed to all sorts of extortion by officials and power figures. Borrowing at high interest from urban moneylenders only compounded his financial troubles. The overall burden proved too heavy for many peasants to carry. Some fled to escape their share of accumulated village debts; at times entire communities abandoned their homes and fields.[60] Tax farmers and moneylenders in the city took their losses or went out to negotiate compromises with the oppressed villagers. To avoid the likely prospect of mass flight from the land the authorities routinely granted insolvent villages a year's immunity from all legal claims by creditors.[61]

Insecurity also unsettled agricultural life to the point of pushing many peasants off the land. In addition to the normal dose of assaults, murders, robberies, and other violent crimes that accompanied village life peasants were exposed to the dread of organized attacks by armed bands.[62] Occasionally the peasants themselves turned to brigandage. In 1753 the peasants of Darat 'Izza, a village some twelve miles northwest of Aleppo, brought to court one of their members for participating in a series of gang assaults in which their crops were stolen and property set on fire.[63] Discharged soldiers posed a more serious threat to rural peace. Turning to banditry, they roamed the countryside, pillaging crops and terrorizing the peasants. In 1763 a group of them attacked the village of Safira, massacred its men, and raped many women before moving into neighboring settlements. An expeditionary force from Aleppo succeeded with difficulty in forcing their retreat, an accomplishment that earned the commanders official honors and occasioned victory celebrations. Three years earlier the pasha's troops had suffered defeat at the hands of these gangs, losing some one hundred soldiers.[64]

Government units occasionally threatened the peasants' security more than they assured it. Passing troops routinely quartered themselves in the villages en route to their destinations. The long succession of wars with Iran during the first part of the century subjected the peasants to constant visits of unruly armies who wreaked havoc on their lands. The provincial soldiers, occasionally dispatched for tours of duty in the countryside, also abused the hospitality of defenseless villagers to the point of causing them to flee. In 1780 the troops of the governor 'Abdi Pasha moved wantonly across the countryside, terrorizing and robbing the peasants. Many villages were deserted as their inhabitants fled for refuge in the hills. Seeking to repair the damage, the new governor called on the harassed villagers to return to their fields, giving them official assurances of safety.[65]

The tribal groups occupying Aleppo's countryside added considerably to the insecurity of the peasants as well as of travelers on the roads. They raided villages, laid peasants under tribute, robbed crops, pillaged travelers and merchant caravans, and collected tolls on roads under their control. The sedentary Kurdish tribesmen operated from their strongholds in the mountainous region extending between Alexandretta and ʿAyntab, in which they exercised virtually unchallenged control, especially in the second half of the century. They commanded the vital route from Aleppo to its port of Alexandretta and the coastal road into Anatolia. Their armed bands descended routinely upon peasants and caravans, and then retreated into the safety of the mountains. Still more formidable were the tribes of bedouin nomadic pastoralists who made the vast deserts and plateaus east and south of the city their domain. In the eighteenth century they claimed unchallenged mastery of the Syrian desert. A large-scale migration of Arab tribes into Aleppo's region reinforced their numbers and strength. At the turn of the eighteenth century tribes of the powerful ʿAnaza confederation from Arabia invaded the Syrian desert. They collided with the relatively peaceful Mawali bedouin, the long-time masters of the northern Syrian desert, cut them off from the Euphrates, and drove them westward into the areas of Aleppo and Hama. At the end of the century, in the wake of the Wahhabi movement in Arabia, a new wave of ʿAnaza tribesmen pushed northward. They pressed still more upon the Mawali and other tribes, pushing them to undesirable areas on the fringes of the desert.[66]

Years of warfare and the movements of displaced tribes caused widespread harm to settled life. Large tracts of cultivated land were overrun, and travel over vital roads was disrupted. Conditions did not settle when the eighteenth century drew to a close. Indeed, a particularly severe wave of tribal turbulence swept over the region in the first decades of the following century. Safety on the roads deteriorated, many villages were destroyed or laid under tribute, and residents were robbed on the very outskirts of and even within the city.[67] The cycle of defiance and insecurity was broken only in the 1850s, when the government launched a firm policy for the final pacification of the tribes. Along Aleppo's desert frontier the authorities erected a chain of fortifications which proved effective in containing bedouin assaults. Turkman tribes were settled in the plains of Antioch, while many bedouins took advantage of various government incentives and anchored themselves in tillable parts of the desert.[68] After years of defiance the Kurdish strongholds in the region of Alexandretta were finally subjugated in 1865.[69]

This kind of government vigor and assertiveness was absent in the eighteenth century. The government, the only regional force capable of providing order and security, proved an increasingly feeble and ineffective presence in the countryside, especially in the latter part of the century. It failed to protect the peasants from exploitation or to guarantee the security of roads and settlements. This weakness, together with the resurgence of the tribes, represented a real shift in the rural balance of power. The tribes emerged as formidable actors in the struggle over rural resources, skillfully using their mobility and martial talents to compete on their own terms over land, food, roads, and ultimately authority. Their challenge, which echoed a political struggle familiar to the region from ancient times, was part of a strategy of survival that worked to their advantage even if it appeared as sheer lawlessness to urbanites, peasants, and the government.

While the peasants in various parts of the countryside suffered the most from this political realignment, Aleppo also felt the effects. The desertion of land and the decline in agricultural production aggravated the city's food problems and curtailed urban opportunities for profit making in the rural sector. In addition, movement on the roads connecting the city with the wider region was complicated by the tribal presence. A certain paranoia and prejudice colored popular visions of the tribes and their menace to safe travel. "Four were born to do mischief: rats, locusts, bedouins, and Kurds," announced one local saying.[70] Stories of tribal pillage and robbery were common news items. The townspeople saw countless military expeditions leave the city to confront tribal defiance; on occasion they returned beaten or reduced in number. Baron de Tott, traveling in the area of Antioch on his way to board a boat in Alexandretta, found his heavy local escort "perpetually possessed with fears of the Turcomen, and anxious to avoid them"; the sight of a large tribal encampment visibly scared them. The heavily guarded party passed by the tribesmen, however, without suffering harm.[71] Many who took to the road experienced a similar blend of fear and relief on their journeys.

In the course of the century tribesmen did commit numerous attacks on travelers and merchants, who lost their belongings, their merchandise, and even their lives. But there was by no means permanent insecurity on all roads at all times; conditions varied considerably depending on the area and the time period. None of the major arteries connecting Aleppo with the wider region remained consistently impassable, and alternate routes were always available as a safe albeit inconvenient backup in times of danger. Roads given to tribal control were often cleared of danger for several months every year while the tribe was away on its seasonal migration. Some tribes, like the Mawali and Hadidi bedouin, were generally more peaceful and cooperative than others. Even the powerful and aggressive tribal groups did not invariably resort to plunder: both the Kurds and bedouin set up organized systems of tolls and tribute, which proved more advantageous to their long-term financial interests. Once the tribal system in the Syrian desert had stabilized in the second part of the century the bedouin chiefs tended to opt for an orderly system of taxing travelers and merchandise. The desert routes to Baghdad and Basra, important for Aleppo's trade with the east, enjoyed remarkable safety during that period, and were preferred even to the routes across the settled lands.[72]

The authorities as well as the travelers preferred a stable system of taxation by tribes to the permanent threat of robbery. The government itself used its leverage and patronage to strike deals with the tribes in the interest of ensuring rural security. In one of the most notable arrangements of the period, the authorities contracted with the Mawali to protect the settlements and roads between Aleppo and Damascus. In return for their services they honored the tribal chief with the official rank of bey and on occasion even pasha, and remunerated him annually with a large sum (known as the *ramiyya*) that was collected from villages as far south as Hims, as well as an allocation for personal expenses drawn from an urban tax farm.[73] The arrangement assured a measure of security in parts of the countryside during much of the eighteenth century. Periodically, however, order broke down, especially when governors were tempted to pocket the tribute and leave the Mawali to their own devices. In 1765 the Mawali seized 30,000 sheep and pillaged a caravan to protest the withholding of payments.[74] In the 1790s brigandage on the roads increased after the Mawali failed to receive the expected remuneration.[75] Judging from the frequency of recorded payments and transactions, however, the arrangement appears to have held fairly effectively through the period. The authorities ventured periodically into similar dealings with the Turkman tribesmen in the Antioch region, who agreed to protect the areas along their migration route in return for financial compensation.[76]

With a limited measure of success the government also bought assurances of security on the vital routes and mountain passes in the area of Alexandretta and Payas on the coast. In return for Ottoman recognition of their authority over their mountain strongholds the Kurdish chieftains agreed to spare travelers and caravans. Again, the arrangements broke down periodically, especially with the decline of state authority in the second part of the century. In 1764, following a series of attacks on caravans, Aleppo's governor traveled in person to the area of Payas. He gathered the local notables from the region and secured from them solemn pledges to maintain order. No sooner had he returned to Aleppo than the pillaging resumed; government troops battled the Kurds intermittently during the next year.[77] In 1772 Janissary troops on their way back to Aleppo from an imperial campaign were robbed of their possessions and animals in the same area. The Kurdish warlord then in control of the roads, Küçük Ali Oğlu, routinely collected transit fees from caravans and travelers, not sparing even qadis. Exasperated with his defiance, Istanbul ordered the pasha of Aleppo in 1786 to proceed to Payas with a large force and have the hardy chieftain executed. The campaign failed. When the leader died some time later the authorities honored his son with the rank of pasha in the hope of winning his cooperation, but with mixed success. He too taxed travelers, but without renouncing plunder when the prey was especially tempting. In 1791 he stopped the Aleppo Janissaries on their way to the city from the European front, and held seventeen of their leading officers hostage until a ransom of 37,000 piastres was delivered. A three-month siege of his stronghold that year failed to dislodge him. In 1798 he detained the Dutch consul to Aleppo for eight months, releasing him after extorting 25,000 piastres.[78] In the late eighteenth and early nineteenth centuries the coastal road was closed at times for months on end, and even the Mecca pilgrimage caravan had to negotiate its way through.

Negotiation and patronage worked to a certain extent in winning tribal cooperation, although the political relationships revolving around the tribal groups were too tense and the periodic arrangements with them too tenuous to form the basis of a stable and enduring order. Drought, feuding between tribes, shifts in tribal activities, changes in government policies, and mutual misunderstandings tended to unsettle conditions and restore insecurity to the roads. "Things are always the same in this regard," sighed the French consul upon one such breakdown of peace.[79] The government was clearly willing to use force to impose its will, but its strategy, relying on periodic expeditions rather than a permanent military presence in the rural trouble spots, proved of limited effectiveness. When successful, the campaigns won periods of peace, but they were not a substitute for constant surveillance. There was nothing to prevent the tribes from resuming their attacks and defiance once the soldiers were back in their barracks. The countless military confrontations during the period, many of which brought defeat to government troops, proved the uselessness of this method of handling the tribes.[80] Expeditions proved more successful against gangs of bandits and discharged soldiers, who lacked both the rural power base and the facility with desert warfare enjoyed by the tribal groups.[81]

Ensuring safe travel clearly lay beyond the abilities of the Ottoman government, let alone Aleppo. The townspeople had to adapt their behavior to realities that they could not alter. The practical wisdom accumulated over generations recommended several rules of thumb: travel in the safer company of a large caravan; plan the schedule around the migration pattern of the tribes; hire an armed escort; and take alternative routes, even if long and circuitous, to avoid trouble spots. With these precautions people navigated the hazards of travel, albeit without full assurance of safety. A transport business was available to travelers and merchants, equipped with the necessary services and skills; the caravan shaykhs in Aleppo even secured in advance guarantees of immunity from attack by the bedouin tribes. They engaged the services of *rafiqs*, representatives of the tribes who were on hand in the city to join caravans and act as human passports in return for gifts to their chiefs. So institutionalized were many of the arrangements that travelers often drew up written contracts with their caravan shaykh specifying services and costs.[82]

Trade and travel through the region went on, but at a certain inevitable cost. When pillage did occur, the property losses were often quite extensive, especially in the case of loaded commercial caravans.[83] Few recovered their stolen property. Obtaining the governor's willingness to send out his troops in search of bandits entailed payment without any assurance of return. After financing a useless search by the authorities for merchandise pillaged by Kurds in 1743 and 1744, the French traders in Aleppo chose the more secure course of buying protection directly from the Kurdish chieftains, thereby avoiding the expenses of fruitless expeditions which only excited the tribesmen's hostilities against them.[84] Loss of life was uncommon. Burckhardt, who spent many years on Middle Eastern roads, even complimented the honorable conduct of the bedouin: "They never maltreat the traveller who agrees to be robbed," he wrote cheerfully to his parents after being stripped of his possessions by a group of Arab tribesmen.[85]

Insecurity on the roads discouraged travel and imposed a surcharge on the price of many goods. On the whole, however, it had a relatively limited effect on the fortunes of the city's external trade. Competing commercial centers often shared a similar level of insecurity. And, as the correspondence of the resident French and English merchants shows, famines, plagues, economic crises, and wars in the region were usually far greater sources of worry and commercial disruption. These were unpredictable misfortunes which damaged the markets themselves, and over which the trader had virtually no control. As a major center of regional and international trade Aleppo routinely experienced ups and downs in commercial activity, its fortunes affected by developments in Europe, the Middle East, and Asian lands further to the east.

THE RHYTHMS OF REGIONAL AND INTERNATIONAL TRADE

AN ENORMOUS VOLUME of commodities arrived in Aleppo every year. Some of the goods originated in the surrounding countryside and other parts of the Middle East, others many miles away in western Europe and the areas around the Indian Ocean. They entered Aleppo laden on beasts of burden, in some cases part of caravans, like those from Baghdad, one or two thousand camels strong. To feed a city of Aleppo's size and to provide its thousands of craftsmen with raw materials naturally required considerable and regular supplies from outside. But only part of what arrived in the city or was produced there actually served local consumption. A good amount was reexported to other areas, with the city serving as a center of exchange and redistribution.

Aleppo's commerce with the outside consisted therefore of two rather distinct types of exchange. One involved the importation of goods for local use and the export of urban products. Literally vital to the city's survival, this activity was fairly regular and consistent. In terms of its geographical scope it was largely an intraregional trade, linking Aleppo in ties of exchange with other parts of the Middle East, and especially with the city's more immediate surroundings. The other part of the city's commercial relations with the outside consisted of its role as intermediary in a large but unstable transit trade of international scope. European goods arrived in varying quantities from London, Marseille,

Amsterdam, Livorno, and Venice via the Mediterranean ports of Alexandretta and Latakia. A host of goods originating in Iran, India, Iraq, Anatolia, and Arabia came in by caravan, through intermediary centers like Basra, Baghdad, Mosul, and Diyarbakr. Aleppo was the scene of busy bargaining and exchange that sent the European and Asian goods on to different parts of the Middle East, and the Middle Eastern and Asian goods on to Europe.

Aleppo's substantial business with Europe, which began as early as the fifteenth century, is by far the best known aspect of its commercial activities. The records kept by the Europeans—in the consular correspondence and the account books of trading houses—provide a mass of detail and figures unmatched by those for other components of the city's trade. This ought not to overshadow the fact that the intraregional trade remained throughout the eighteenth century the more important sphere of commercial exchange. The Middle East could still supply most of its internal needs by way of local production or exchange between different localities. Independently of the European business Aleppo participated as a prominent middleman in the regional exchange as well as in the substantial trade between Asia and the Middle East. The different types of commercial business varied in their patterns and their importance for Aleppo's welfare. All of them, however, tied the city to the dynamics— and uncertainties—of larger networks; the shifting rhythms of regional and international trends in the eighteenth century were felt in Aleppo, not always in pleasant ways.

Access to finished goods did not place Aleppo at the mercy of the outside as did its demand for food and raw materials. Its craftsmen, the biggest sector in the city's work force, labored in their small shops to manufacture a variety of textile, metal, leather, and wood products. These satisfied the daily needs of the urban population for anything from pots and shoes to fine jewelry and exquisite silk fabrics. As the largest manufacturing center in its region, the city was able to sell some of its products to the neighboring villages and towns, in addition to exporting its luxurious fabrics to the bigger cities, including Istanbul. Aleppo's textile workers thrived also on the large amounts of textiles brought to them from other localities for processing and dyeing. Even cities as large and distant as Konya, Urfa, and Mardin used Aleppo's artisanal facilities.[86] What finished goods the city imported for local consumption were relatively limited in quantity and specialized in nature: paper, clocks, watches, housewares, firearms, and chemical products from Europe; tobacco and carpets from Iran; and glassware and pottery from northern Syria. Of the imported finished goods only European cloth could potentially threaten the local industry. In fact, much of it was redistributed from Aleppo to other parts of the Middle East.

Foreign competition preoccupied most of the artisans far less than access to the raw materials they needed. Most of these—cotton, wool, hemp, hides, wood, coal, beeswax, sulfur, alkali, and other basic materials—were actually available in the more immediate areas of northern Syria and southeastern Anatolia. Silk, in great demand by the local silk workers, was brought in from Iran until the 1720s, when it was replaced by Syrian silk supplemented by occasional shipments from the Bursa area in western Anatolia. During the eighteenth century only a few crucial raw materials had to be imported from more distant areas: gallnuts (used in dyeing) from the Mosul and Diyarbakr areas; gums and drugs from Arabia; and metals and dyes from Europe. Despite their proximity, however, raw materials were not available to artisans in the desired quantities. The shortages appear to have had less to do with real scarcities than with the artificial quotas set by craft guilds in the interest of regulating production and prices. Many craftsmen resented the restricted and uneven distribution of raw materials. Those ready to take the risks of violating guild rules were able to acquire additional raw materials, and at better prices, by buying in other localities or on the black market.[87]

The bulk of the city's supply of food and raw materials came from the area stretching roughly from ʿAyntab in the north to Hama in the south, and from the Mediterranean in the west to the Euphrates in the east. Aleppo benefited from its location at the geographical center of this extensive hinterland; most of its daily needs were available within a radius of 65 to 80 miles. What this area could not supply the city acquired largely from other Ottoman lands, primarily in Anatolia and Iraq.

There was a limit to how much of its products or imports the city could hope to sell to the rural inhabitants, most of whom were peasants and nomads living at bare subsistence levels. Many of their basic necessities could be acquired from craftsmen in the villages or neighboring towns.[88] Aleppo was able to supply the more specialized goods that the better-off in the countryside could afford, such as jewelry, silver ornaments, and fine fabrics. It also offered clerical, educational, medical, and other services not available in the country. Among the regular patients of the city's surgeons were many villagers and residents of small towns in the hinterland.[89] The townspeople in turn went to the countryside for specialized rural services. Urban people who owned sheep and goats, for instance, entrusted their herding to nomads. Contracts occasionally allotted to the shepherds a share of wool or produce in lieu of wages.[90]

The trade with Europe actually intensified Aleppo's commercial links with its surrounding region and areas further afield, for which the city acted as an intermediary. In the eighteenth century virtually everything the city sold to European buyers, with the exception of some of its own fabrics, came from the outside: raw silk from northern Syria, Iran, and western Anatolia; wool and cotton largely from northern Syria; finished fabrics from northern Syria, southeastern Anatolia, and the Mosul area; camel hair from the Syrian desert and Iran; gallnuts from the areas of Mosul and Diyarbakr; pistachio nuts from northern Syria; and drugs and gums from Arabia and Basra. And most of the goods brought to Aleppo by the Europeans were actually reexported to other cities in Syria, Anatolia, Iraq, and Iran. These included cloth, primarily woolens; dyes, spices, sugar, and coffee from the colonies; raw metals; and small amounts of assorted goods such as firearms, clocks, paper, housewares, and chemical products. Along with the European goods Aleppo also forwarded to the interior some Iranian and Arabian goods, and large numbers of camels that came from the Arabian and Syrian deserts.

This pattern of exchange indicates two important aspects of Aleppo's commercial relations. First, long-distance trade oriented the city toward the lands to its north and east. Outside its own region Aleppo's important trade contacts extended to the centers of Iraq and southeastern Anatolia, and through them further east to Iran. The city's commercial ties with Mecca, Egypt, and even southern Syria were minor by comparison.[91] Second, Syrian and Middle Eastern goods in general dominated the trade with Europe. This was radically different from the original pattern of the transit trade during its heyday at the turn of the seventeenth century, when Venetian, English, and French merchants came to Aleppo to purchase not Levant products, but the Eastern commodities that were in great demand in Europe: Asian pepper and spices and Iranian silk. Well over half of what was bought of these goods for import to Europe went westward by caravan through Basra and Baghdad to the Mediterranean, from whence ships carried it to European ports. Aleppo, which commanded the shortest land route across the desert to Iraq, prospered as the most important center in the Levant for the westward distribution of these products, especially silk. But the tide turned after 1600, when ships of the newly established English and

Dutch East India companies began to transport Asian commodities by sea around the Cape of Good Hope, circumventing the Levant entirely. By 1630 pepper and spices ceased to arrive in Aleppo from the East; only Iranian raw silk continued to be shipped to the city. One century after its discovery the Cape route was finally employed successfully to alter the global patterns of trade.[92]

If Aleppo's commercial business with Europe continued to flourish in the aftermath of this rerouting of the pepper and spice trade it was because the Europeans had learned in the meantime of various Middle Eastern products saleable in their home countries, and proceeded to buy them in large quantities through the city. In the seventeenth century, Aleppo became the assembly point for Middle Eastern goods, primarily Iranian silk, rather than for Asian commodities. This transformation of its intermediary role was advanced one step further when it ceased to handle Iranian silk a century later. From 1722 internal disorder and several wars with the Ottomans and Russians plunged Iran into three decades of trouble. Silk-producing areas were ravaged, and the routes westward sealed by hostilities. The local weavers and the European buyers in Aleppo switched quickly to the use and purchase of Syrian silk from the producing areas around Antioch, the coastal plain, and Lebanon.[93] With the final disruption of the Iranian silk trade Aleppo's merchants lost access to a commodity that had blessed them with great profits for several centuries. And Aleppo's commercial horizons were narrowed still further in the process: the goods that it gathered for the Europeans were henceforth almost entirely of Ottoman origin.

In the course of a century or so Aleppo's original role in East-West trade had thus been radically altered. The city became a major market for the exchange of Ottoman and European goods, in which the Europeans maintained an interest until the last decade of the eighteenth century. France in fact increased its business in the city. Its purchases rose from an annual average of 736,00 livres in 1700 to 3,517,000 in 1789. French annual sales exceeded 2 million livres in the second half of the century. By 1780 France came to control well over half of the city's European trade, which exceeded 7 million livres; Livorno, Venice, and England controlled the rest.[94] But as France's share increased that of England declined. From the middle decades of the century England steadily lost interest in Aleppo, where it had been the dominant trading partner. The English were interested mainly in one commodity—silk. While the Iranian silks sold well in London, the less refined Syrian varieties that came to replace them proved less successful. They failed to compete with the superior Italian silk or the cheaper Indian and Chinese silks. The English reduced their purchases of Syrian silk, but did not replace them with other imports. When the Napoleonic Wars destroyed the thriving French trade in the Mediterranean, Aleppo's European trade declined dramatically, and did not revive until well into the nineteenth century.[95]

In the first decades of the eighteenth century, Aleppo's trade with Europe conformed to the "colonial" pattern of exchange commonly associated with Europe's commerce in the Middle East: it was largely an exchange of regional raw materials for European finished goods. The English bartered their cloth for raw silk. On the French side, only 10 percent of purchases in 1700 were finished goods (cloth); the remaining 90 percent were raw fibers, gallnuts, and drugs. In the course of the century, however, the pattern changed. By the late 1780s Aleppo was able to increase dramatically its sale of regional fabrics, which rose to constitute half of total French purchases. In the prospering trade with France Aleppo actually came to sell more finished goods than it imported.[96]

The trade with Europe was on the whole beneficial but not indispensable to the economies of Aleppo and the surrounding region. Only a relatively limited segment of the city's population was directly involved in this exchange. It included some textile workers, merchants, agents, and those providing various services. Government officials and tax farmers collected a percentage of the commercial profits. Outside the city, in towns from Hama to ʿAyntab and from Antioch to Mosul, spinners, weavers, dyers, and other craftsmen profited from the French demand for their fabrics.[97] The producers of silk, cotton, and gallnuts in the countryside also enjoyed several decades of European demand. Indeed, so intense was the pursuit of silk by the English that they were occasionally drawn into competition with the city's silk workers over access to it. When silk prices in London peaked the English merchants were willing to buy at prices that the local artisans could not match. But when their industry prospered the local craftsmen were able to bring their weight to bear on the market and overwhelm their competitors. In the 1740s, for instance, they readily purchased silk at prices that seemed utterly exorbitant to the English merchants.[98]

Imports from Europe do not appear to have seriously harmed local industries. English and French fabrics, the only goods capable of threatening local producers, did enjoy some popularity in the region. The French, especially attentive to tastes and needs, brought in a light and attractive woolen cloth which sold successfully for several decades. Aleppo reexported the bulk of European cloth throughout the Middle East, sending it as far as Iran.[99] It was dispersed too thinly to have a marked impact on any one locality, and for some sectors of the population it remained unaffordable or unappealing. Local industry continued to satisfy most of the population's demands. The days had not yet come when the British would dump massive amounts of their inexpensive cloth on the Middle East and dislocate the region's crafts. In the eighteenth century they sold only as much cloth as was necessary to finance their purchases of silk, which gradually declined. The Ottomans prohibited the transport of cash out of the empire, thus compelling the Europeans to take their profits home in the form of goods, or keep their sales down. When the English lost interest in Middle Eastern goods they decreased their cloth exports accordingly. The French, on the other hand, brought in large amounts of cash to finance their purchases. Merchants in Aleppo and other cities preferred the imported silver coins (mostly Spanish and Mexican) to their local currency and readily acquired them at exchange rates highly profitable to the French. What effect this had on the value of local money is not known. It certainly provided the French with advantageous terms and with profits that do not figure in the regular trade statistics.[100]

Although they came from lands more powerful and prosperous, and were protected by some extraterritorial rights granted in diplomatic treaties (known as the Capitulations) between their countries and the Ottoman government, the European merchants did not operate in Aleppo as exploiters of the native population. Indeed, they were not always successful in their business; some returned home penniless, their fortunes lost in failed ventures. Pitted against them were local traders skilled in the arts of negotiation and incomparably more familiar with regional realities. Furthermore, their European colleagues competed fiercely among themselves, each working for his own account or a particular trading house at home. They commonly undercut each other, despite periodic attempts to foster a unified bargaining front.[101] They also endured all the frustrations and uncertainties that accompanied long-distance trade in the region. It was not unusual for them to write home delighted letters about their prosperous transactions, only to pour out the most despondent complaints in the very next season. Along with their local counterparts they impatiently awaited caravans that never arrived, having been pillaged or delayed by hostilities on the eastern front. They missed good market opportunities because expected ships struck port too late or important letters were delayed a month or two. Subsistence crises and epidemics in Aleppo and other trade centers also periodically unsettled the routines of commercial life. "It hath put a stop to all business," complained an Englishman of the plague of 1761.[102] Twelve years later a severe plague in Iran and Iraq disrupted temporarily the shipment of goods to Aleppo from those parts.[103]

Aleppo's European commerce was clearly an unstable business. The types and amounts of goods exchanged fluctuated from year to year, their rhythms set by ever-changing conditions in various localities. These ups and downs, however, were not at the root of the periodic economic crises experienced by the townspeople in the course of the eighteenth century. Sophisticated as their city was, it remained vulnerable first and foremost to the vagaries of the regional food supply, not of the international trade cycle. Aleppo and the surrounding region were not deeply enough integrated into the European economic system to be seriously affected by its rhythms. In the eighteenth century two long-term developments actually helped to retard their involvement with European commercial activity: the Europeans showed growing interest in other parts of the Middle East, at the expense of Aleppo; and at the same time they shifted toward new global markets, at the expense of the Middle East as a whole.

In the eighteenth century the commercial center of Izmir in western Anatolia replaced Aleppo as the principal Middle Eastern trading station for both France and England. While Aleppo's share of the growing French purchases in the Middle East remained at a level of around 10 percent, Izmir was able to capture toward the end of the century as much as 38 percent.[104] Izmir's rise as Aleppo's commercial rival was connected with the problems that had begun to discourage the Europeans in Aleppo in the previous century: the periodic commercial disruptions caused by the Ottoman hostilities with Iran; unsafe routes; and heavy extortion. The caravans from Iran had more and more frequently been diverted to Izmir, which could be reached more safely and cheaply despite the distance.[105] In the eighteenth century Izmir established itself as the main Middle Eastern supplier of silk, cotton, wool, and camel hair to France. Aleppo continued to control the market for gallnuts and cloth. Izmir and Istanbul became the biggest buyers of French products in the region; it was these two cities, not Aleppo, that absorbed the bulk of French cloth.[106] The western Anatolian hinterland beyond Izmir was thus drawn into more vigorous trade with Europe than Aleppo's region.

On the whole, however, the Middle East was losing its commercial appeal to its traditional European partners. While both France and England were expanding their global trade at an unprecedented pace, and their demand for the sort of goods that the Middle East traditionally supplied, such as silk, cotton, and coffee, was actually growing, they were steadily turning elsewhere to get them. In the eighteenth century they discovered new markets with which the Middle East failed to compete, both in quality and price. The English turned to the West Indies instead of the Middle East for their cotton, and to Italy, China, and India for silk. The French also found alternative sources for silk and cotton; if they increased their purchases of cotton in Aleppo and else-where it was only because the West Indies could not satisfy the demands of their flourishing cotton industry. By the late eighteenth century the reorientation of European commercial activities away from the Middle East was far advanced. Only 5 percent of total French trade took place in the Middle East—a decline from 50 percent two centuries earlier; for the English it was a mere 1 percent, a decline from a high of 10 percent during some decades of the previous century.[107]

The Middle East had failed to capture a share of the growing Western demand for world goods. Its economic condition vis-à-vis the expanding power of Europe was so disadvantageous that its traditional export products were encountering foreign competition even at home. In the eighteenth century many people in Aleppo and the Middle East were drinking French colonial coffee instead of the Arabian coffee which had previously conquered the world. Regionally produced sugar, once a major export item, failed to compete with colonial sugar, which the French sold successfully even in Egypt.[108] These were some indications that the economic balance, like the political and military balance, had tipped in Europe's favor. Backed by the formidable advantages of its maritime discoveries and colonial possessions, Europe increasingly set the pace and direction of international trade.

Although aspects of the European ascendancy were visible in Aleppo and other parts of the Middle East before the industrial revolution it was really in the nineteenth century that the West reshaped the commercial fortunes of the Middle East and the region's place in the global economy. By the late nineteenth century about 90 percent of Middle Eastern trade was with Europe and the United States; the once-thriving Asian trade declined to insignificance. In this new setting non-Muslim merchants equipped with the necessary European contacts, languages and protections came to dominate the region's commerce while their Muslim colleagues lost their previous prominence. The exchange of

Middle Eastern raw materials for European finished goods became established as a clear pattern, the Middle East providing a ready outlet for
the flood of industrial goods from European factories. This new influx,
beginning in force around the 1830s, caused the first major dislocations
for Middle Eastern craftsmen, primarily in the textile business, who
could not compete effectively with some of the European products.
Many peasants became more dependent than ever on European demand
for their cash crops, and hence on the ups and downs of the larger
economic system into which they had been absorbed.[109]

As Aleppo's commercial relations with Europe indicate, these nineteenth-century realities ought not to be projected backward as if they
applied equally in the eighteenth century. Certainly in the case of
Aleppo the importance of the premodern European trade has been
exaggerated. The European merchants who settled there harbored rather
grand notions about the importance of their activities to the city's welfare. To their business, they believed, Aleppo owed its greatness and its
very subsistence.[110] This vision of the city and of the special European
role in it was repeated even by latter-day observers. Jean Sauvaget could
comfortably conclude his classic study of the city with the pronounce-
ment that Europe gave Aleppo "its only positive element of prosperity."[111] Seen against the overall economic base on which the welfare
of the population rested this view appears rather myopic. The city's
European trade was clearly only a small portion of its overall commercial
exchange, which in the eighteenth century was still predominantly
intra-Ottoman. And the commercial exchange was itself only one external source of wealth and subsistence in an economy that depended also
on various forms of nonmarket appropriation from the outside, and
whose prosperity was more sensitive to the success of the harvest than
to the trade cycle.

CHAPTER 5

Economic Welfare: The Market, Family, and Charity

T HE STORIES OF food, rural resources, and external trade only begin to explain the realities of economic life in eighteenth century Aleppo. Some of the main clues to the forces which shaped the material welfare of the residents must be sought in the complex world of institutions and activities which made up the local economy. The most visible part of the economic scene was the market, that sphere of exchange in which people used their muscles, skills, and capital to earn a living and make money. A multitude of commercial and artisanal businesses formed the mainstay of the city's economy, providing jobs and livelihood to the bulk of the population. Many men and women also drew income, in the form of profits, rents, and interest, from the investment of their savings in property and financial ventures.

For all its obvious importance, the market was by no means the only realm of economic behavior. Large-scale economic activities took place outside the market, and had a considerable bearing on the material fortunes of the residents. The family was the scene of vast transfers of wealth and services among members, through gifts, inheritance, stipends from trusts, marriage payments, divorce settlements, child support, and the provision of welfare payments and shelter to needy relatives, widows, orphans, and the elderly. The absence of a social security system and of hospitals, orphanages, and nursing homes established the family as the main agency of care and support. At the same time there were also considerable payments for poor relief outside the family, by private individuals and public institutions. A poor segment of the community depended on this charity for survival.

The market, family, and charity represented distinct spheres of economic activity, each with its particular institutions, mechanisms for allocating resources, distributive effects, and dynamics. When seen as related parts of a larger whole they bring out the full texture of the local economy and the array of forces which shaped the material welfare of the townspeople. The composite picture presents an elaborate economic system: a whole range of ideas, rules, practices, and interests, not all of them fully compatible with each other; dozens of occupations organized in separate trade guilds, each with its own binding regulations; different types of property and wealth; various outlets for investment and profit, each with its particular returns and risks; many participants in the making of economic decisions, ranging from government and trade guilds to communities and households; a variety of factor and product markets organized along different lines and responding to particular trends; an array of redistributive transfers flowing in different directions; a variety of formal and informal channels of charity; different household makeups and domestic arrangements; great contrasts in the economic opportunities and benefits of different groups and classes; and discrepancies between formal rules and actual behavior.

The norms and institutions governing economic behavior derived from different sources: the rules in the areas of the family, property, contracts, credit, and the waqf were based on Islamic law, while market regulation and fiscal arrangements were subject to rules legislated by the government and the trade guilds. Underlying the rules and the process of shaping them was a competition among several goals and norms current in the economic sphere: gain, efficiency, justice, freedom, and security. While all of them figured as valid principles in which rules could be grounded, the pursuit of one often had to be at the expense of another. The push and pull among these various goals surfaced in the daily struggles to mold economic arrangements and allocate rights, with disingenuous arguments often camouflaging selfish ends. Economic security tended to prevail often as an overriding concern, with free competition, equity, and efficiency being sacrificed in the process.

This complex economic scene, which remains a virtually unexplored aspect of the city's history, can clearly be understood best when seen against the larger ideological, social, political, and demographic forces that shaped the economic behavior and welfare of the townspeople. The market, family, and charity capture the essential elements of this scene.

The concern here is with their basic structures and daily workings, mostly during the period 1740–1770, rather than with long-term developments and trends. The uneven information available on these matters complicates the task of reconstruction. There are no works by contemporaries on the local economy, no surviving guild records or account books of shopkeepers and craftsmen, no records of family budgets, and no statistics on prices, incomes, rents, interest rates, trade, production, the work force, unemployment, savings, money supply, charitable contributions, marriages, divorces, births, deaths, or household sizes. Much needs to be pieced together from thousands of cases in the shari'a court records, which have preserved a vast body of raw details, including much quantitative information, on business, the family, and charity.

THE WORKING POPULATION

A FORMIDABLE NUMBER of Aleppo's residents made their living from work in the marketplace. Although no one at the time kept records on the size and breakdown of the working population, the main lines of its makeup are fairly clear.

Adult men formed the mainstay of the labor force, but among them also worked multitudes of children, women, and the elderly. Work usually began during childhood: young boys, some of them only six years of age, did odd jobs, ran errands, carried loads, helped craftsmen, and learned trades. Apprenticeship involved them in active work while they learned. Businesses in all sectors of the economy drew on the abundant pool of cheap child labor.[1] The law set no minimum age of employment; nor did it impose a mandatory age of retirement. In the absence of any system of social security or pensions people remained active as long as their health allowed, many of them working virtually until they died.

Economic necessity forced many women to work in the marketplace. Female labor was limited exclusively to the lower-income groups, which often had to forego the luxury of keeping their women, and the status of their families, uncompromised by employment. Some women worked in the textile industry, usually doing the spinning and preparation of thread in their homes for craftsmen. Others engaged in trade, selling wool thread, bread, wine, wheat, and other commodities, or roaming the city as peddlers of trinkets and various articles for women. The majority, however, worked in various service occupations as dancers,

singers, professional mourners, wet nurses, midwives, bath house attendants, prostitutes, tutors, fortune-tellers, bonesetters, marriage brokers,
cleaners, and, above all, as domestic servants. Young girls nine and ten
years of age were sent by their parents to be maids in other households
in return for their keep.[2]

Perhaps half of Aleppo's labor force, if not more, worked in manufacturing, with fewer making their living from trade and still fewer by
providing services. A limited number of residents also engaged in agricultural work in the orchards, vineyards, vegetable gardens, and tobacco
fields on the city's outskirts. As a sophisticated metropolis with many
families of means, Aleppo naturally demanded all kinds of goods and
services and supported a vast array of trades and professions. Its craftsmen processed foods and manufactured a countless variety of products
from leather, cloth, wood, metal, and stone. The retail shops carried
merchandise of all sorts, both locally produced and imported. Services
ranging from floor washing to surgery were readily available.

This formidable and diverse labor force operated in a world of small
and highly specialized enterprises. The marketplace had no factories,
business corporations, department stores, or supermarkets. Production
and trade were organized in small stores and artisanal workshops in
which the merchant or craftsman usually worked on his own, or with
help which seldom exceeded two or three employees, and possibly a
business partner. These small enterprises were as a rule highly specialized: there were merchants who sold only saffron, others who dealt
exclusively in lemons, and still others who handled eggs; some dyers
specialized in a single color. Each type of footwear, whether slippers,
shoes, or wooden clogs, was the work of particular craftsmen. The
brokers and auctioneers who handled commercial transactions in the
markets usually specialized in one particular commodity.

The narrow professional specialization, so characteristic of all branches
of the economy, was not a mere product of choice. A comprehensive
system of monopolies parceled out business in the marketplace to different trades, giving each of them exclusive rights in certain areas while
prohibiting their encroachment on the spheres reserved for others. The
defense of narrow professional territory and interests was formally institutionalized by the organization of the various trades into guilds (sing.
ta'ifa), each equipped with its headman and collectively binding rules.
Some of the guilds incorporated an entire professional group; others
were organized more narrowly around a segment of a trade. Thus the
porters in different caravanserais formed separate guilds, each with its

own shaykh. The silk spinners who worked in one large workshop made up one guild, while their colleagues scattered in shops throughout the city formed another. There were several guilds of dyers, organized according to the colors or types of cloth in which they specialized.[3] The fragmentation was a perfectly logical aspect of a setup designed to guard and regulate the professional interests of people who shared specific realms of activity. The porters in the caravanserai for wheat (Khan al-Hunta) or the dyers specializing only in imported cloth had certain concerns which were distinct from those of their colleagues, and hence best handled by a separate organization.

There are 157 professional guild organizations known to have existed in the middle decades of the century. The list, compiled from references in the court documents, leaves some professions unaccounted for. No mention of guilds appears for singers, dancers, wet nurses, midwives, domestic servants, and prostitutes. In fact women, who dominated these professions, do not figure at all among the listed members of guilds, with the exception of one Karima bint Nasr Allah who belonged to the guild of starch manufacturers in 1762.[4] Christians and Jews, on the other hand, did belong to the guilds of their particular trades. The Jewish butchers, who handled specially slaughtered meat, formed the only guild organized along religious lines.

Despite the contemporary emphasis on professional specialization, the majority of trades and guilds actually fell into one of three areas of production and trade: food, textiles, and construction. These branches of the economy involved the basic necessities of life as well as luxury goods, and accounted for the bulk of demand and expenditure. The poor used up most of their income just on feeding themselves, while the better-off spent larger amounts on food, even if smaller shares of their income. Shops for the preparation and sale of food abounded in all parts of the city. The thousands of houses, commercial structures, and public buildings needed for shelter supported a large construction industry, which included many specialized craftsmen as well as dealers in various building materials. Repairs alone accounted for enormous expenditures every year, as structures tended to deteriorate at a fairly rapid rate.[5]

By far the largest number of craftsmen were employed in the textile industry, which surpassed all other branches of manufacturing both in the size of its labor force and the value of its output. Domestic consumption and foreign demand for its fine products combined to make Aleppo the principal center of cloth production in Syria and possibly in the entire Arab world with the exception of Cairo. The city manufactured large quantities of silk, cotton, and woolen fabrics. Cloth from other towns, especially in Anatolia, arrived to be finished by local artisans. Thousands of men, women, and children working in hundreds of specialized workshops participated in the processes of spinning, weaving, smoothing, dyeing, printing, embroidering, and tailoring. Cloth dominated the business of the export-import traders, while numerous shopkeepers catered to the constant demand for clothing, both new and used.

Only a relatively small body of people made their living by providing business services to the thousands of artisanal and commercial enterprises that formed the mainstay of the economy. There were auctioneers, weighers, brokers, moneychangers, porters, and caravaneers who handled much of the daily business of exchange, and accountants who kept the books for the larger traders, but no banks, accounting firms, investment consultants, advertising agencies, or insurance companies. The small scale of most enterprises and their limited needs restricted the call for specialized business services. Personal services employed many more people, who benefited from the demand for spiritual guidance, entertainment, education, medical care, and domestic help. The ulama, a relatively small group, doubled as clergymen, teachers, clerks, legal experts, copyists, and scholars, and often held multiple positions in these different capacities.

By far the largest service occupation was composed of the servants and domestics, who found ready employment in the better-off households. Even the moderately comfortable families permitted themselves the luxury of a maidservant, while the affluent often kept in their employ a host of cooks, attendants, pages, and servants, some of them slaves, who catered to their whims and displayed their status.[6] More than any other aspect of the work force, this abundance of servants highlighted the immense economic inequalities in Aleppo's society.

Most of the working people in the city were employed in the private sector. All of the manufacturing and commercial businesses were privately owned. The government did not invest in housing projects, in transportation enterprises, in health, education, and welfare facilities, in urban services, or in public works. The bulk of its expenditures went to administration and defense. The body of government employees, which included administrators, soldiers, and clerks, was therefore quite limited, with a good portion of it composed of nonnatives. The presence of the provincial authorities in the city, however, did contribute to the demand for various goods and services in the marketplace, and was hence of some importance to the urban economy.

Some residents worked for public institutions, usually on a part-time basis. The hundreds of mosques, religious colleges, Sufi lodges, and public water fountains maintained staffs of teachers, leaders of prayer, preachers, janitors, clerks, and administrators, paying them small wages drawn from their particular endowments. In 1751–1753, for instance, a sample of 98 public institutions employed a total of 398 people in addition to the administrators, and had total annual expenditures of 14,762 piastres on wages, repairs, equipment, rents, and so on. Like government, the public foundations added to the level of demand in the marketplace.[7]

The public employees of the period were not exclusively part of the public sector; many of them worked in the private sector as well. Members of the ulama commonly moved in both spheres at once; they tutored, copied manuscripts, and even operated shops in the market while holding posts in government and public institutions. The Janissaries and the tax farmers also functioned in both sectors of the economy.

A high proportion of the men and women who earned income in the marketplace was self-employed. The small scale of individual businesses and the limited size of the public sector worked to restrict the proportion of wage employees, but without reducing it to a negligible presence. The working children and the vast army of servants and domestics alone made up a formidable body of employees. Master craftsmen relied often on hired help in their shops. The more prosperous merchants hired salesmen to assist in their stores and warehouses, and to travel on business. Bath houses maintained staffs of attendants, guards, and men responsible for the furnaces and water supply. Many men provided seasonal labor for the agricultural enterprises on the outskirts of town. Even porters hired children to help when their strength began to wane.[8]

Employees were a common feature of the marketplace. Indeed, most of the economically active residents, including the self-employed, worked at some stage in their lives in the employ of others, whether as apprentices, wage employees, or journeymen. In order to limit competition, most professions restricted the number of independent enterprises that could be operated in their line of trade. In the crafts, only the masters could open their own businesses. Ceilings on promotion to the rank of master compelled the others to earn their living as employees. Some spent years working for others while awaiting their turn for a business license; others lacked the capital or will necessary to set themselves up in a business of their own.

Self-employment brought with it the advantages of higher status and freedom from the dictates of superiors. It also meant a better income than that of the employees in the same trade. The earnings of employees were highly uneven, but generally low. What chance references to wages appear in the court records are too fragmentary to allow any comprehensive profile of incomes in the marketplace. However, they do indicate the orders of magnitude and the considerable variations between the different areas of employment during the 1750s and 1760s. Servants, at the bottom of the pay scale, earned their keep only, or 1–2 piastres a month (which may have included room and board); watchmen, 2–3 piastres; a laborer in an orchard, 3.75 piastres; employees in various industries, 4–6 piastres; an assistant to a shopkeeper, 8 piastres; administrative and personal assistants, 6–12.5 piastres; and salesmen for import-export merchants, 17–20 piastres.[9] How much more was earned by the employers of these people, or for that matter by any self-employed person, is unknown. That a surgeon collected between 3 and 12 piastres for a single operation for removing bladder stones points to an earning power many times that of the wage employees.[10] The recorded commercial dealings of the great merchants, which involved tens of thousands of piastres, are more impressive still.

The small sample of known wages cannot illustrate the income differences between members of one profession and another, or between colleagues in the same trade, or between employees and the self-employed. However, the wide range of incomes found within just the layer of employees indicates the great variations in opportunities and fortunes in the marketplace. These variations corresponded to areas of employment, with earnings rising as one moved up successively in a hierarchy composed of less-skilled manual labor, manufacturing, retail trade, skilled professions, and long-distance trade. Artisans in general enjoyed lower incomes than retail merchants, while both categories lagged well behind the export-import traders.

INDUSTRY, TRADE, AND MARKET REGULATION

THE GREAT DIFFERENCES in income, like the highly diverse makeup of the labor force, were symptoms of the city's complex market economy. A practical spirit comfortable with the pursuit of profit and advantage ran through business activity. But alongside this economic orientation existed a tendency to regard the market as a socially subversive and unjust force in need of taming by external controls. It found live expression in a mass of rules which regulated in detail various aspects of economic activity and set limits on free competition. This regulation originated not in centralized planning from above, but in a diffuse mechanism of policymaking which gave the guilds a considerable say. Behind the rules were certain ideological notions about economic behavior as well as the push and pull of competing interests—those of producers, traders, consumers, professions, tax farmers and, not least, government. The rules were not fixed and rigid; they were modified in response to conflicts between different interests and changes in market conditions. The institutional arrangements and economic realities of the period shaped the scale and organization of industry and trade, the prospects for economic growth, and the matrix of opportunities and constraints within which the working people operated.

The manufacturing sector on which a major portion of the population depended for a living displays perhaps most vividly the underlying limits and strengths of the economy. Local industry was made up of a multitude of small artisanal enterprises, labor intensive in their organization and low in their level of productivity. Yet the model of the small workshop operated by a craftsman who owned his tools, bought raw materials, worked on them by himself or with the help of a few employees, and then sold his products on the market did not entirely dominate industrial production. In the textile industry especially other patterns thrived, encouraged by the larger market, the more intimate involvement with merchants, and the peculiarities of cloth manufacturing. These conditions actually favored capitalistic modes of production, but such did not emerge in any developed form.

The state of technology had much to do with the generally low level of productivity in industry. The craftsman labored with hand tools and rudimentary equipment operated manually. With the exception of grinding stones and presses driven by animals, and water mills along the river, mechanical energy remained alien to the work place. Textile artisans used manually operated looms *(nawls)* and wheeled implements *(dulabs,* and *chalkhs* or *charkhs)* for spinning thread and finishing cloth, but also resorted to more rudimentary techniques such as beating newly woven fabrics with wooden hammers, a professional specialty of the *daqqaq.*[11] Europeans found the technical standards of the craftsmen low, but not necessarily the quality of their workmanship. "Their tools are coarsely made; but natural ingenuity often supplies the want of such, as might easily be procured from Europe," commented the resident English physician Alexander Russell, adding that the artisans "greatly admire the finished hardware, and cabinet work, brought from England."[12] On the other hand, the local silk and cotton stuffs, often embroidered with silver and gold thread, were renowned throughout the region for their exquisite quality, and won the admiration of Western visitors.[13]

Like other parts of the Middle East, including great manufacturing centers such as Cairo, Aleppo witnessed no significant technical progress during the century.[14] Tools and routines of work passed from one generation to the next with little variation, the apprentice imitating his elders and in turn transmitting his acquired skills to new trainees. What improvements originated in the creativity of the artisan or the adoption of new techniques diffused by the migration of craftsmen from other parts of the region were too minor to revolutionize production in any trade. Local artisans continued to produce their goods slowly, submitting to a schedule that appeared unchangeable.

Much of what the craftsmen manufactured went to satisfy a local market which was limited and often uncertain. The purchasing power of large segments of the population was restricted at the best of times. During the unpredictable slumps and subsistence crises that hit the economy periodically the mass of poor had little to spare beyond what they spent on bread and basic necessities. This set additional constraints on the productivity of industry. For a shoemaker to produce one hundred pairs of slippers for stock without any prior guarantee of purchase was highly risky, even if he could manage such an investment of capital. Craftsmen followed the safer and more affordable course of producing their goods in small amounts at a time. Working on order, a practice common in all areas of manufacturing, helped them to overcome the twin problems of risk and burdensome investment. They tailored clothes, crafted jewelry, unholstered divans, and performed a host of other jobs in response to orders placed by customers, and often with materials supplied by the customers.

In the textile industry most of the artisans worked on demand. The process of cloth production, which involved a series of successive operations divided among many specialized crafts, favored this mode of work despite the larger market. The poor women who labored in their homes to prepare the raw silk and cotton for spinning, the spinners who prepared the thread, the weavers who produced the raw cloth on looms in their homes or workshops, and the host of other craftsmen who took part in finishing the fabric—all these usually worked with material that others gave to them along with instructions regarding the desired quality, dimensions, color, or style of the finished product. Merchants rather than the artisans themselves commonly owned the material and marketed the cloth. The craftsman's business was therefore determined to a great extent by the business of the merchant who gave the work order, provided the materials, undertook the distribution of the cloth, developed the markets, determined the type of product, and exercised quality control over the activities of the artisan. The craftsmen did work with their own tools and equipment, but not in all cases. Some of the more elaborate equipment, such as the *dulabs* used for smoothing cloth (*saql al-aqmisha*) or for embroidering it with gold and silver thread, were too expensive for most craftsmen to purchase, their prices ranging from 125 to 500 piastres. The artisans rented them from the owners, who included well-to-do merchants, ulama, and women, as well as the heirs of better-off craftsmen who occasionally chose to hold on to the more costly equipment they inherited.[15]

Some of the more enterprising craftsmen in the textile industry did venture into the market. Among the spinners who worked in the large establishment known as al-Dulab al-Kabir were some who, in addition to taking orders, also bought silk, made the thread, and sold it. The practice caused some friction in the guild; in 1756 the members agreed that no spinner would engage in both modes of business simultaneously.[16] In many of the crafts artisans were not entirely free to take advantage of the market and expand their business at will. The guild organizations of which they were part often imposed limits on how much they could produce. In the interest of guaranteeing a livelihood to all members, even if unequally, the guilds sought to control competition, most directly by regulating the access of members to raw materials and work orders.

In many crafts the artisans usually bought the raw materials needed for their work. Their business relied at the outset on the ready availability of supplies adequate to meet their work potential. The rope makers, for instance, depended on hemp, the oil pressers on sesame seeds, and the carpenters on wood, materials that were imported into the city in amounts that tended to fluctuate with the availability of supplies and their distribution in the regional markets. By the regulations of their guilds, these artisans as well as members of other crafts were required to purchase their raw materials through their headmen, each receiving a certain allotted quota at a fixed price. Rules prohibited them from buying their materials independently without reporting their purchases and, sometimes, sharing them with their colleagues. In some guilds the members received equal shares of the available supplies, but more commonly the senior members enjoyed the right to larger portions.

The more successful artisans found these arrangements barriers to the expansion of their businesses; therefore they occasionally evaded the rules. Some of them managed somehow to acquire excessive shares of the imports; others ventured abroad and returned with their own stocks. When violations were discovered, the guild leaders and members usually proceeded to the shariᶜa court to reaffirm the rules and to condemn their manipulation, which unfairly allowed some to corner the market, push up prices, and deprive the poorer members of their livelihood.[17]

The craftsmen who worked on order submitted to similar restrictions. The arrangements in their guilds often provided for all the job orders to go through the headman, who had them distributed among the members according to an established quota system. The artisans were prohibited from taking work independently, or were required to report extra earnings, which counted against their quota, and even to share them with their colleagues.[18] These practices, commonplace in the textile industry, substituted for the allocation of jobs by market competition. Each artisan had his guaranteed share (*qism*) in the overall output of his craft, with the security as well as limitations that the arrangements implied for his business. In some of the crafts, such as the spinning of thread and the beating and smoothing of cloth, the artisan's share was tantamount to private property that the owner could sell or pass on to his heirs. These assets commanded high prices. A smoother of cloth with an entitlement to approximately 9 percent of his craft's business was able in 1769 to sell half of his share to a colleague for almost 400 piastres.[19]

These collective controls were not adopted uniformly by all the guilds, nor were they necessarily a permanent feature of those that did opt for them. The same guild might alternate periodically between the collective distribution of work and free competition. Different practices could prevail within the same profession and across professions: three guilds of dyers followed the principle of free competition while a fourth regulated access to jobs.[20]

The internal politics in the guilds, not only market conditions, affected the choice of arrangements governing the allocation of business. The printers of kerchiefs grew tired of arguing over the distribution of work among them and decided in 1747 to return to their previous "custom" of letting the members fend for themselves. The cloth printers, on the other hand, moved in the reverse direction in 1764. Here too the pressures for change came from within. Some of the craftsmen could not hold their own in a situation of free market competition. Their resentment at their loss of livelihood burst out in conflicts with their more successful colleagues, who finally agreed to have the business parceled out to all members through the agency of the shaykh. Similarly, the manufacturers of starch reached an agreement in 1767 to have all their shops produce equal amounts of starch every day and sell their output at a set price, "in order to equalize the rich and poor members of the trade." The poorer artisans, they explained, were unable to compete with their better-off colleagues under free market conditions, and their business suffered.[21]

Collective controls over output were clearly not shaped solely by the economic benefits presented by a cartel organization. Behind them, on occasion, lay social considerations, not purely material ones. The inequalities within the guilds excited tensions that could translate into corrective action by the group. The weaker artisans who lacked the entrepreneurial spirit, professional reputation, and privileges of their more successful colleagues looked for support in collective measures of protection. They invoked ideas of fairness and group solidarity to argue for economic security, even if not equality, for all. By redistributing the business in the trade, collective protections had a certain leveling effect. They also reduced social tensions, although in some cases they became the source of bickering. In a milieu in which restrictive practices enjoyed acceptance, guilds that chose to operate on the principle of free competition experienced nagging demands from the weaker members for protection. Some artisans went so far as to take their more successful colleagues to court for refusing to share with them the business they were attracting. They received no help from the judges, who viewed the rules adopted by the guilds as the guiding norms.[22]

Whether they obtained their business by competition or a quota system, and whether they prospered or not, artisanal enterprises operated with low concentrations of capital and wage labor. There did exist manufacturing establishments that asembled in one place several dozen artisans and much equipment, but these were rare and, more important, organized along lines bearing no real resemblance to the modern industrial factory. They consisted actually of many artisanal enterprises operating almost independently of each other in one place. Such, for example, was the tannery (*al-dabbagha*) on the open grounds near the river. The tanners, who numbered at least fifty-seven men in 1754, all worked there, but as many independent enterprises rather than one centrally directed operation.[23] Their common establishment provided access to free water and space, and removed an offensive industry from the main residential areas. Several similar setups existed in the textile industry, most notably al-Dulab al-Kabir, where sixty-five silk spinners and their employees worked in 1756; Qaysariyyat Ismaʿil Pasha, which assembled thirty-three beaters of cloth and their employees in 1767; and Qaʿat al-ʿUjaymi, with its numerous looms and *dulabs* for smoothing cloth. In all of these establishments the artisans worked on their own, usually under collective guild arrangements which allocated to them fixed shares in the overall output. In Qaʿat al-ʿUjaymi, which housed the largest concentration of textile equipment, the looms and machines belonged to numerous craftsmen and investors rather than to any single proprietor.[24]

It is these large workshops that Dr. Russell saw, and to which he referred as "large factories, where a great many looms are kept under the same roof."[25] These unusual concentrations of many artisanal enterprises in one place had to do with practical considerations: merchants were able to place their large orders in one location rather than split their material between numerous scattered shops; craftsmen had easy access to a pool of expensive equipment that they needed to rent; and tax farmers could monitor output and collect their dues more easily. The large textile establishments rationalized production, but only to a certain extent. They did not go so far as to bring together several stages of cloth manufacturing. The guild system, premised as it was on narrow professional monopolies, set up institutional barriers to enterprises combining several distinct crafts.

The intimate involvement of merchants with textile production had a marked effect on the organization and fortunes of the industry, but did not lead it into developed capitalistic patterns. The merchants gave the artisans the working capital, marketed the products, and perhaps coordinated between the different enterprises handling their materials and cloth. But there is no evidence that they organized production themselves, or invested substantial capital in the existing artisanal enterprises.

The manufacturing sector as a whole benefited from little outside investment. The well-to-do directed large sums into trade, real estate, moneylending, and tax farms, but not into industry, which promised them less lucrative returns. The *mudaraba* partnership, equivalent to the European commenda, provided a commonly used arrangement by which investors put capital into business enterprises as silent partners. Judging from the recorded settlements of terminated partnerships, only a small number of craftsmen attracted such investments. One ʿAʾisha bint Rajab, a widow, put some capital into her brother-in-law's soap manufacturing business in return for two-thirds of the profits. In 1746, ʿAbd al-Rahman ibn Muhammad had some money invested with an Armenian craftsman who produced printed kerchiefs; he took five-sixths of the profits from the venture, which lasted four months. Two years earlier, the merchant ʿAbdallah Chalabi Haykal Zadeh entered into a silent partnership with his son and a Christian; he put up the capital while they worked to produce cloth and sell it. The partnership lasted four years. Another invested 300 piastres in a pickle making business.[26]

The limited infusion of outside capital reflected industry's weaknesses, and in some respects compounded them. With the various economic and institutional barriers that constrained its overall development, manufacturing could hardly become a field of fortune building like trade, or more precisely long-distance trade. The commercial enterprises of the *tujjar* were of a different order. The large investments, the extensive traveling, the transportation of merchandise across seas and deserts, the speculation in commodities and credit, the far-flung networks of agents and business contacts, and the complex transfers of money and bills of exchange all testified to a sphere of business broad in its horizons and prospects.

Unlike industry, long-distance trade rested on developed capitalistic practices. Merchants worked with large concentrations of capital in the form of stocks, credit, and cash. Their access to capital and the scale of their business benefited from the convenient credit practices and the networks of trust current in the business world, from partnerships with other merchants, and from the cash often placed with them by savers who wished to partake in the profits of commercial ventures. They managed their elaborate dealings with a relatively rudimentary organization. Even the most prosperous of them worked from modest offices in caravanserais, where they also rented storage space for their merchandise, and employed a small number of accountants, salesmen, and trusted agents to handle their financial and commercial affairs. The company as a corporate entity existing independently of the merchant was not known.

The *tujjar* formed only a segment of the commercial sector, and were hardly representative of it. Most merchants were retailers who spent their days selling goods in shops in the neighborhood markets and larger bazaars, or peddling their wares in the streets. They as well as the barbers, porters, brokers, and others who sold their services in the market differed from the *tujjar* in several key respects: the scale of their business was markedly smaller; they specialized in particular lines of goods or services, whereas the *tujjar* diversified their trade according to opportunities; and they did business in a setting more restrictive than that of the *tujjar*, who were not subject to guild controls. Their economic and institutional milieu resembled in many ways that of the craftsmen, although here too there was a diversity of practices and experiences that defies generalization.

The world of retail trade was dominated by small merchants who worked on their own or with the help of a partner or assistant, and kept small stocks in shops which could not accommodate much merchandise anyway. As among the craftsmen, some were more successful and established than others, even within the same trade; they seized the better locations and occasionally expanded beyond a single store. Available information on the butchers, whose shops were surveyed and listed by the court in 1762, illustrates well the inner variations. Most of the 146 Muslim butcher shops, but by no means all, were owned each by a single butcher. As many as twelve butchers ran 2 shops each, three butchers ran 3 shops each, one butcher ran 4 shops, and one ran 5 shops. At the same time, 5 shops were each operated by two partners, and 1 by three partners.[27]

Conditions made it possible for merchants to expand their business, but not to spread it into spheres reserved for others. As in industry, the guilds jealously protected their monopolies. In 1755, when some dealers in shoe leather ventured into the sale of shoes, they were taken to court by the shoe merchants for encroaching on their exclusive area of trade. The shoe dealers presented an old order from Istanbul confirming their monopoly, and won the qadi's support.[28] The principle that all business is divided according to established monopolies set basic limits on competition in the marketplace. To these were added other constraints, exercised by way of price controls and the collective allocation of business. Such measures, however, were not adopted in all trades at all times. By agreement or evasion, competition remained a living force in many areas of market exchange.

The organized allocation of work practiced by some guilds at times followed territorial lines. Each coffeehouse had an assigned area to which it could send out its coffee vendors. The water carriers and the sellers of licorice drinks allotted to each member an exclusive district in which to practice his trade. The bakeries each distributed bread exclusively to shops in assigned locations. Despite occasional violations these rules ordered competition by securing for each member of a trade a share of the market.[29]

Arrangements to the same effect were adopted by some other guilds:

the slaughterers in the city's slaughterhouse worked by a quota system; the porters in some caravanserais agreed, following disputes, to divide work and wages equally; the felt merchants divided equally among them the orders placed by the European merchants and the commander of the pilgrimage, and prohibited any independent sales to these buyers; and, likewise, the dealers in used shoes arranged in 1770 that their sales to merchants from outside would be divided equally among them, with their shaykh coordinating the transactions.[30] The shearers of animals decided in 1764 to abandon free competition because some members failed to hold their own; they agreed to have their shaykh assign all jobs by turn.[31] As in the crafts, measures to limit competition often grew out of frictions among members of a profession working in the same place or experiencing highly uneven success in the marketplace.

The parceling out of rights and monpolies in the market appeared perhaps in its most elaborate forms among the brokers *(dallals)* and weighers *(qabbans* and *kayyals)*. The members of these guilds enjoyed exclusive jurisdictions in particular markets, caravanserais, or districts of the city. Many of them held their monopolies by way of lifetime tax farms purchased from the state. In return for an advance sum and annual payments to the treasury they obtained the exclusive right to collect certain fees for weighing wholesale goods or brokering their sale. The government occasionally extended such monopolies to new markets as a way of increasing its revenues. In 1755, for instance, it sold the monopoly for the brokerage of copper to one Ibrahim ibn Jamil and his son, entitling them to a commission of 1 percent on all cash sales and .75 percent on credit sales. The thirteen Jewish brokers who had been handling the sales of copper lost their jobs.[32] Such monopolies were treated as valuable forms of property which the owners sold on the market or passed on to their children; quite a few of them remained within the same family for decades. In 1755, two brothers and a son of each held the brokerage of potash, which had previously been in the hands of their father, and of his father before him. They possessed a deed dating back to 1709 confirming their family's long control of the monopoly.[33]

The allocation of rights in the market, whether by the guilds or the government, was a practice actually restricted to some trades during certain periods. Most of the shopkeepers were perfectly free to sell their goods or services to whomever they wished. What could set some limits on their freedoms was the regulation of prices, but even this practice was highly selective, touching some areas of business during particular periods. There was no across-the-board regulation of the prices of all goods and services by any government agency or public body. The authorities did resort to fixing prices, but their controls applied almost exclusively to food, and usually only during periods of scarcity. Of the hundred or so items whose prices were fixed by government order in 1762, firewood, cotton, and horseshoes formed the only nonfood articles.[34] Only some guilds chose to impose uniform prices on their members, often in response to inner frictions. In 1768 the porters in a caravanserai agreed on a uniform charge per load when their competition became too fierce. The producers of starch set a fixed price for their products when they decided in 1768 to reduce inequalities.[35]

Conditions in the market set limits on the actual resort to direct price controls. Most of the handmade goods were too unstandardized to be uniformly priced. Even where uniform prices could be fixed their enforcement posed problems. Neither the government nor the guilds were equipped to monitor the markets closely to prevent cheating and black market activity. The leading butchers were able to run a racket (known as the *duman*) which manipulated meat prices for some fifteen years until a crackdown by the authorities in the 1760s.[36]

Most important was the fact that the forces of the market were deemed too powerful to be tamed by price controls. Prices fluctuated constantly in accordance with supply and demand, and even the court expected merchants to adjust what they charged to the fluid market conditions. On several occasions, craftsmen complained in court against merchants who had raised the price of certain raw materials. After establishing that the market price had indeed gone up and that the craftsmen had been charged a fair price, the judges upheld the right of the merchants to sell without taking a loss.[37] Traders were expected to sell at "a fair price" *(thaman al-mithl)*, which was understood as the going rate in the market rather than some arbitrarily decreed price. Bargaining, an established market ritual, served to refine the price levels of many goods. Under these circumstances, a customer who purchased something voluntarily had no claim against the seller regarding the price, unless he could prove that the latter had deceived him intentionally. The few customers who did complain that they had been overcharged all left the court empty-handed.[38]

To pronounce competition as nonexistent would therefore misrepresent the reality of Aleppo's economy and, more specifically, the impact of the guilds on it. Suppressing competition entirely was neither the aim of all guilds nor the outcome of their actions. Generalizations about the extreme restrictiveness of the Ottoman guild system with regard to competition can do injustice to the complexity of this organizational scheme as it actually functioned in Aleppo.[39] The basic premise of the system—that professional groups have a recognized claim on a parcel of the marketplace and the right to regulate their access to it—was indeed restrictive. Yet this monopolistic principle, which guided economic policy in the city from at least the sixteenth century, did not predetermine how much control the different trades actually imposed in their particular spheres of the market.[40] In practice there was a patchwork of economic practices and arrangements, some restrictive and others not. What is called the "guild system" represented not a monolith, but dozens of individual organizations governed by different and often diametrically opposed market rules which changed over time and were, in addition, given to a measure of evasion.

In making rules for their particular trades the guild organizations enjoyed a limited, but not negligible, autonomy. They devised their codes of entry and promotion, their modes of allocating raw materials and work, and their pricing policies. With this decision-making authority in their command they effectively substituted for direct government regulation. The official inspection of the markets and regulation of their standards, a traditional institution that had accompanied society for centuries, was no longer a living practice. The venerable office of the *muhtasib*, or market inspector, lapsed in Aleppo sometime before the eighteenth century, most likely because its functions had passed entirely to the guilds.[41]

The guild system operated outside government, but not independently of it. The latitude of the guilds was restricted by the interests of other groups, by the existing laws, and by the economic policies and interests of the state. Although not entirely instruments of government, they did submit to various forms of official oversight which affirmed the limits of their independent authority. The guild members made their choice for the position of shaykh, but their nomination had to be confirmed by the qadi. The central government issued official appointment letters to the headmen, and held them responsible for order within their organizations. Disciplinary action against members also rested with the authorities. Members of a trade occasionally took troublesome colleagues to the judge, who imposed a punishment or fine. No member could be expelled from his guild without the court's approval. Such extreme measures against colleagues did occur, but quite infrequently. For the period 1746–1770, the judicial records show only forty-eight cases of expulsion, for reasons ranging from violation of guild rules and abuse of public trust to professional incompetence and cursing of the shaykh.[42]

Evasion clearly set certain limits on the effectiveness of restrictive market regulations adopted by guilds. Some enterprising merchants and craftsmen were tempted to encroach on the spheres of others, to cheat on set prices, and to exceed their quotas of raw materials and business. The hundreds of recorded violations may represent a small sample in comparison with the number of undetected evasions. Behind the failure of guilds to ensure full compliance lay in part their lack of a policing apparatus. On a more basic level, the evasion testified to the instincts of enterprise and profit making that thrived unsuppressed under the lid of restrictions.

The conflicts that erupted among and within trades over violations gave expression to the rougher sides of market life. When argued out in court they also brought into the open the kinds of economic and social principles by which guilds justified their rules and restrictions. Violations were condemned for an array of possible evil effects: pushing prices up, harming the poorer members of the trade, encroaching on the spheres of other professions, cornering the market, harming customers or the urban poor, reducing tax revenues, causing scarcities of raw materials, contributing to the unemployment of colleagues, provoking punitive action by the authorities, compromising the quality of products, and, most commonly, violating guild rules and customs.[43] The rules, argued their defenders in effect, served good purposes, protecting the larger interests of producers, merchants, customers, government, and society as a whole. From the condemnations of deviations can be deduced principles that, even if evoked at times to camouflage selfish ends, represented the desired guidelines of economic policy and guild regulation.

What impact the guilds exercised on the opportunities and welfare of their members depended in great measure on the particular arrangements they adopted. Some trades followed policies of protecting their weaker members from going under, or of sharing opportunities and even incomes on an equal basis. Others left their members to fend for themselves under conditions of free competition, or distributed benefits according to openly inegalitarian standards. The mix of practices mirrored the different and often incompatible tendencies that coexisted in the economic culture. The pursuit of personal gain had its venerable place alongside a social ethic favoring restraint, and a stress on hierarchy and privilege. Guilds devised different types of balance among these values, modifying their rules when one tendency or another gained favor among the influential members.

Making and modifying guild arrangements were political processes. Decision making rested with a small, privileged group at the top, and tended naturally to reflect its interests. The shaykh exercised a major say in shaping policy and overseeing its execution. He distributed raw materials and work, approved promotions, fixed prices, and allocated taxes. A number of senior members, known as the *ikhtiyariyya*, or elders, acted as an informal executive committee of sorts which supervised the shaykh and participated in policymaking.[44]

The shaykhs depended on the good will and backing of their influential colleagues. With the exception of a few cases in which shaykhs enjoyed hereditary control of the position by way of a government grant, their tenure of office was hardly permanent.[45] Some held their position for several years, but in many cases the turnover was relatively rapid, following short terms of service lasting several months or a couple of years. Death removed a few shaykhs from office; more commonly, however, they resigned. At least a few of them left under the pressure of internal opposition, having lost the trust of their colleagues. Competition for the office and its benefits by influential members occasioned some intrigues and politicking which found their way into the court chambers.[46]

As inherently hierarchical bodies, the guilds often promoted economic inequalities, or at least institutionalized them. Beyond this impact on the distribution of opportunities and incomes the guilds had a considerable effect on economic productivity. The various barriers set up by the monopolies were economically inefficient. They narrowed the horizons of possibility and stifled the potential for productive ventures which threatened to violate the sacrosanct lines between professional domains. The government enforced these practices as essential elements of its economic policy.

Yet for all their importance the guilds shaped the fortunes of the working population only to a point. People did not function in the marketplace as members of guilds to the exclusion of all else. They had to deal with the limits set by the rudimentary technology, the small markets, and the shortage of capital, all of which the guilds may have perpetuated but did not create. They also faced economic crises, shortages of raw materials, changes in external demand, and other economic developments that originated outside the city and were beyond the control of the guilds or anyone else. The government presented still another formidable reality that shaped their opportunities and material welfare. Although largely withdrawn from long-term planning and extensive direct regulation of industry and trade, the government did take an active interest in the general condition of the economy. It had a vital stake in preserving a climate of social peace, and also in drawing to itself some of the wealth in the market by way of taxes. Through regular taxing and exploitative appropriation the government exercised a marked effect on the welfare of individuals and the climate in the marketplace.

The artisans and merchants were charged regular taxes assessed on their business activities according to set rates and criteria. Overcharging on these dues was uncommon; guild members often came to an agreement with their tax farmer on the terms of payment, and sued him when he tried to exceed the rates set in the imperial tax registers.[47] In addition, they paid to the governors the *ordu bazaar* and *mashyakha* taxes, which were imposed as lump sums on the guilds. Collective fines *(gharamat ʿurfiyya)* and sums exacted by officials and power figures in the city added substantially to the burden of the regular taxes.[48]

The authorities appropriated still more from the trades by less direct methods. The governor's household and staff routinely paid below-market prices for the food and other necessities they purchased from local businessmen. The millers, for instance, took a loss of 1,900 piastres from the sale of wheat to the pasha's kitchen in 1767. The guilds so exploited absorbed the losses by distributing the burden among members. They followed the same course when governors forced their stocks of wheat and sheep on them for above-market prices. These forced sales *(tarh)*, which primarily affected the butchers and millers, involved substantial losses. In 1752, the butchers were forced to buy from ʿAbd al-Rahman Pasha 2,123 heads of sheep for 8,885 piastres; they recovered only 3,430 piastres from selling them.[49]

The official tax figures, based as they are on the regular impositions alone, conceal the full extent of appropriation. The overall burden weighed heavily on many of the artisans and merchants. Some guilds sank into indebtedness, and resorted to borrowing money in order to finance their taxes and their losses from dealings with the authorities.[50] Inner conflicts flared up within guilds over the distribution of the load among the members. Janissaries, ashraf, ulama, and others with tax exemptions escaped various collective impositions, shifting their shares onto their unprivileged colleagues. Some guilds, however, adopted egalitarian principles of distribution, sometimes under orders from the court when it heeded the desperate pleas of the disadvantaged members.[51]

FIGURE 5.1. *A residential street in Aleppo.*
Photographer: Ihsan Sheet

FIGURE 5.2. *A portrait of the leading Ottoman officials in the city. Seated from left to right are the qadi, the commander of the Janissary corps, and the governor, attended by a servant.*

From A. Russell, *The Natural History of Aleppo.* London, 1794.

FIGURE 5.3. *A page from a shariʿa court register, showing three entries, each followed by the names of notarial witnesses.*

FIGURE 5.4. *Several courtyard houses seen from above, illustrating the physical proximity of neighbors.*

From Jean Sauvaget, *Alep*. Paris: Librairie Orientaliste Paul Geuthner, 1941. By kind permission of the publisher.

FIGURE 5.5. *A musical band in performance.*
From A. Russell, *The Natural History of Aleppo*. London, 1794.

FIGURE 5.6. *The annual balance sheet of a mosque's charitable foundation, listing its revenues and expenditures (from the Aleppo court records).*

The unequal distribution of taxes contributed to differences not only in incomes but in business opportunities as well. Those released from various impositions found themselves better equipped to invest and to compete. In the silk industry, for instance, the Christian artisans lost their traditional predominance when many Janissaries and ashraf entered the crafts and turned their tax exemptions to economic advantage.[52] The heavy tax burden took its toll on the productive capacity of the economy. In periods of acute fiscal exploitation business stagnated, shops closed, and merchants fled to other towns.[53]

INVESTMENT AND PROPERTY

WHETHER INDUSTRY AND trade languished or prospered certainly mattered to a population so heavily dependent on them for its livelihood. The thousands of commercial and industrial enterprises created the jobs, distributed the goods, manufactured the products, and generated much of the wealth in the community. Investment in these enterprises absorbed large amounts of capital, although for various institutional and economic reasons it was not open to everyone.

There were three other important areas of investment besides trade and manufacturing from which some residents drew income: tax farming, moneylending, and real estate. They provided the main outlets for savings in a society that viewed putting money to work as sensible. Large amounts of local wealth found their way into these three spheres, and produced considerable profits. Tax farms, which often involved large-scale investments in state finances, were lucrative but accessible to a very select group. The money and real estate markets, on the other hand, attracted a larger crowd that included small savers as well as wealthy investors. They enjoyed profits from rents and interest payments.

The four major spheres of investment formed fairly discrete categories of economic activity, each with its particular institutional arrangements, risks, benefits, market trends, and participants. They were by no means mutually exclusive: the wealthy, who had not only more money to invest but also a wider range of lucrative options than the small savers, often spread their investments over all areas. As essential components of the market they help to broaden the view of the urban economy and its structure. In the absence of any global figures on investments and profits it is impossible to assess with any precision the relative economic weight of the four spheres or the shifts in their importance over time. However, the economic and institutional conditions that shaped the opportunities for investment in each area can be reconstructed from the numerous bits of information scattered in the judicial records.

Economic conditions and institutional arrangements made it possible for many of the townspeople to set up their own commercial and artisanal businesses, to finance the necessary capital investment, to hire help, and to cope with the financial costs of keeping their enterprises going. But they also set limits on entry into the world of independent business and on the potential for expansion. The markets for business permits, shops, tools, labor, business credit, and investment capital, all essential to the economic prospects of work and enterprise, display the current advantages and barriers.

For a resident to start a business of his own required a permit. Known as a *gedik*, the license usually conveyed the right to practice the trade in a particular shop or establishment. It also conveyed the right to use the tools and equipment in the place, known often as *taqwima*. When the owner of a coffeehouse transferred his business license (which his guild identified variously as *gedik* or *taqwima*), he actually sold with it the stools, coffeepots, cups, and other equipment with which he had worked. The guild of bath house owners kept a detailed written inventory of the equipment *(taqwima)* in each of the establishments, specifying the number of towels, clogs, mirrors, mules, and other items they contained; the business license for a particular bath house included the equipment in it. In trades that parceled out guaranteed shares in the business, the *gedik* of a member included his right to his particular quota. When a beater of cloth sold his *gedik*, he transferred a specific entitlement rather than a mere license to operate a business in the craft.[54]

The permits and the material advantages attached to them were neither easily accessible nor inexpensive. The guilds restricted the number of licenses they issued. In the crafts, which allowed only the masters to work on their own, the skilled employees had to wait their turn patiently for promotion and the privilege of opening their own shops. Three journeymen in the guild of cloth beaters must have expressed fairly common frustrations when they complained to the qadi in 1767 that they were prevented from becoming self-employed despite their proficiency in the craft. The shaykh and masters who opposed their promotion defended their position on the basis of the rules of the trade, which they spelled out in the courtroom: the guild has only thirty-three slots for masters; when a vacancy opens the master's son enjoys the first priority; if there is no son, a journeyman can advance, but only on the condition that he is professionally competent, of honest character, and acceptable to the masters. With the law on their side the masters were able to fend off the disgruntled journeymen.[55]

Not much is known about the practices of promotion in the various crafts, the periods spent waiting for work licenses, and the flexibility of the number of permits issued. The ceilings put on promotion clearly stood as a barrier to the advancement of skilled journeymen, holding them in a position of prolonged subordination. Even when vacancies opened up relatives often enjoyed an advantage over outsiders. *Gediks* were private property which the owners sold, passed on to their heirs, and even used as collateral to guarantee loans they took. Some families held on to them for long periods, thus closing off the opportunities of other candidates. One textile craftsman sold his *gedik* to his son. Three men who inherited their father's *gedik* divided it equally among them after resolving to pursue the craft. The son of another craftsman transferred the *gedik* he inherited to three of his nephews. Yet heredity was by no means absolute; in many cases families sold the *gediks* they inherited to unrelated individuals.[56]

How much artisans and businessmen had to pay for their work licenses varied widely according to the line of business, the location, and the equipment and privileges attached to the permit. A seller of grains acquired a *gedik* in a store for 40 piastres while a baker paid 600 piastres for the right to practice his trade in a bakery. *Gediks* with a guaranteed share in a guild's business commanded relatively high prices, ranging usually from 100 to 400 piastres. The larger commercial enterprises also involved considerable capital outlays on the permit and equipment: 150 to 530 piastres for coffeehouses, 280 to 520 piastres for bath houses, and 150 to 600 piastres for bakeries. These establishments were often run by two partners, who between them could finance the investment. The fact that fractions of *gediks* commonly appeared for sale on the market gave artisans and traders affordable access to business enterprises.[57]

The relatively low cost of most tools and equipment also helped people set themselves up in business with minimal investment. Few had to invest even 100 piastres to equip their stores and workshops. The small merchants in the markets needed little more than some shelves and containers, and occasionally weighing scales. The tools and equipment were generally simple and inexpensive to produce, a fact reflected in the prices of those found in different shops: a barber's, 22.5 piastres; a cloth beater's, 30 piastres; a dyer's, 45 piastres; a jeweler's, 60 piastres; a coffee grinder's, 65 piastres; an oil dealer's, 80 piastres. Looms, on which so many depended for their livelihood, cost relatively little: four looms together with a shop sold for 62 piastres, while a room equipped with six looms in a workshop complex sold for 180 piastres. Spinning wheels cost between 40 and 100 piastres. Those highly expensive textile manufacturing machines not affordable to the small artisans were available for rent for a piastre or two a week split among several craftsmen.[58]

The investment in equipment, like that in *gediks*, was a recoverable expense rather than a loss. In the absence of technical innovations, tools and implements did not depreciate in value due to obsolescence. Nor did they deteriorate rapidly or require major outlays for maintenance. Artisans often acquired used tools and eventually passed them on to their sons, sparing them the need to invest in equipping themselves. One notable exception was the multitude of animals used for transportation and moving machines. They had a limited life span and required constant expenditures on food and shelter. Porters, millers, pressers, and others invested in them, paying usually 13 to 20 piastres for an ass and 50 to 70 piastres for a mule.[59]

Most business enterprises required a place of work in the marketplace. The city made available thousands of commercial buildings scattered in numerous locations and fit for various uses. For the majority of trades the cost of a place was generally low. The standard practice was to rent. Much of the commercial real estate in the city was privately owned by hundreds of investors; some of them actually used their properties for their own business, while many others, including women, held them as sources of rental income. The hundreds of charitable foundations and family trusts held the remainder of the commercial properties as endowments which they rented out on the market. Their combined assets were considerable: a sample of ninety-eight foundations audited by the court in 1751–1753 controlled a total of 448 commercial buildings, including bath houses, workshop complexes, and caravanserais as well as small shops. The endowed real estate, which could not legally be bought or sold, was by definition available only for rent.

The real estate market in which businessmen acquired their shops worked by free competition. Neither prices nor rents were subject to regulation. The prices of commercial buildings on the market tended to place their ownership beyond the means of the smaller artisans and merchants. This certainly applied to the larger establishments, whose

prices in piastres, as recorded in hundreds of sales deeds from the 1750s
and 1760s, ran quite high: mills, 270–600; presses, 600–700; a bakery,
770; coffeehouses, 1,000–1,800; workshop complexes *(qaysariyyas)*, 550–
2,800; and bath houses, 1,800–8,200.[60] A standard shop cost usually
between 50 and 200 piastres, although some ran as high as 400 piastres.
The particular market conditions, the specific circumstances surrounding the transactions, and the physical condition of the shops all affected
the price, but the location had an important bearing as well. Shops in
the main bazaar and other important markets were generally more
expensive than those in the less central locations. The particular use of
a shop, which was usually fixed on a long-term basis, also affected the
price. The play of these various factors resulted in a wide range of prices
for shops in the same market and for shops designated for the same
trade in different locations. Thus, in the 1750s barber shops sold for
prices ranging from 90 to 330 piastres, dyeing shops for 100 to 675
piastres, and shops for the sale of coal for 32 to 90 piastres.[61]

The better-off businessmen often bought their places of work, which
gave them the benefit of security of location as well as a good credit
rating in the market. Some of the weavers and textile craftsmen, who
did not require large shops in prime locations for their work, purchased
small rooms *(odas)*, available for 20 to 40 piastres, in the workshop
complexes scattered around the city.[62] However, most artisans and men
of business in the marketplace were tenants for whom rents mattered
more than prices. Although lease agreements were not notarized in the
court as were sales deeds, the annual balance sheets of the charitable
foundations have preserved a vast sample of data on rents. In the 1750s
the rents on a standard shop stood at a low level of between 5 and 15
piastres a year. Only the tenants of the larger establishments paid
considerably more: 50–100 piastres for mills; 45–100 for bakeries; 30–
350 for workshop complexes; 100–450 for bath houses; and as much as
850 piastres for caravanserais. Tenancy thus allowed the owners of
business enterprises to benefit from the use of their premises without
spending annually more than 8 to 14 percent of the cost of the property,
and without the added expenses on taxes and repairs that came with
ownership.

Conditions in the labor market were also beneficial in many respects
to industrial and commercial enterprises. The craftsmen and merchants
could draw at little cost on an abundant pool of child labor to help with
menial tasks, errands, and other time-consuming chores. Parents were
only too eager to find employers who would take in their sons and train

them. In the crafts, the masters benefited from the presence of skilled artisans compelled by the ceilings on promotion to seek employment under others. Without the guild restrictions many of these captive artisans would have been the competitors rather than employees of the masters. In addition, employers were not subject to burdensome restrictions on the terms under which they could hire and fire employees. The authorities imposed no minimum wage, nor did the guilds set a fixed pay scale binding on all employers in their respective trades. Employers bore no responsibility for providing retirement, medical, and other types of benefits to their employees. They negotiated the wages and terms of employment with their employees, and enjoyed the freedom to lay them off at will. The records of the shari'a court contain no suits by employees over unfair wages and no complaints or collective arrangements by guilds regarding wages and employment. On several rare occasions employees sued in the hope of being rehired or assigned more lucrative work. The court invariably sided with the employers, upholding their right to hire and assign work as they pleased.[63]

If the markets for labor and fixed capital favored business investment, setting up an enterprise and running it successfully remained nonetheless costly affairs. In relation to the means and ambitions of businessmen, capital was scarce; its pursuit occupied businessmen at all levels, from the small struggling shopkeeper to the wealthy export-import trader. Conditions in the market made it possible for them to work with some capital in addition to their own. They acquired it by resorting to business credit, loans, and partnerships, all of which were common practices in the marketplace of the day.

Much daily business ran on credit. Craftsmen and merchants routinely deferred payment for the raw materials and merchandise they purchased, repaying their debts from the proceeds of their sales. In this way they were able to extend themselves beyond the limits of their available cash, in effect financing their business activities with borrowed capital. Among merchants, the charge on deferred payments ranged usually between 10 and 12 percent a year. Almost every page of the judicial records bears testimony to the widespread resort to credit. Businessmen came routinely to the court to draw up contracts, to register revised schedules of repayment, and to sue uncooperative debtors. When they died, their estates often included business debts owed both by them and to them.

The pursuit of capital was a major cause of the abundance of partnerships. Both merchants and craftsmen often established joint enterprises with partners who promised to bring cash, professional skills, customers, or connections into the business. Such an addition to a venture strengthened the ability to compete while helping at the same time to spread the risks. Partnerships were most common in lines of trade that required heavy capital investment or that benefited from a relatively good demand. Expensive establishments such as bakeries, mills, coffeehouses, and bath houses were usually run by two partners. In industry, partnerships were by far most prevalent among textile artisans, whose volume of work was often high enough to make a partnership with two or three colleagues a profitable proposition. But it was above all merchants, especially in the export-import trade, who worked with partners as a matter of course.

The partnerships of the period were by and large limited in their scope: they involved usually only two partners, and rarely more than four; they were set up for specific ventures; and they tended to last for relatively short periods. The most common type of commercial partnership, indeed, was the *shirkat ʿinan*, which created limited mutual liabilities suitable for specific short-term ventures.[64] The recorded amounts of capital brought in by partners ranged from ten piastres to thousands of piastres. Merchants and craftsmen occasionally set up partnerships with kin, usually brothers. But this was hardly the dominant pattern. Indeed, many of them involved joint ventures between Muslims and Christians, and between Muslims and Jews.[65] Differences of religious affiliation did not stand in the way of trusting relations and common enterprises between businessmen. In fact, they may have been an asset, since each partner could provide connections and clienteles from a group not fully accessible to the other.[66]

Judging from the vast number of recorded loans, borrowing money was also a common practice, although what amounts of borrowed funds went to finance investment rather than consumption cannot be determined. Merchants and craftsmen seeking loans depended on private sources; government provided no credit to help finance business investment. The family offered one important source of funds. Many men borrowed money from relatives, particularly from their wives. Even well-to-do businessmen used cash borrowed from family members. The merchant Musa Agha al-Amiri, among the wealthiest men in the city, borrowed 6,700 piastres from one of his wives. Family funds may very well have helped to finance many artisanal and commercial enterprises.[67]

Borrowing money on the market was possible as well, although the terms could often be demanding. The shortage of cash, and various risks associated with lending, worked to push up the cost of money. How much businessmen borrowed, and how this outside capital and its costs affected their enterprises, is unclear. More readily visible are the workings of the money market itself and the opportunities it offered for investment.

The demand for credit, whether for consumption or investment purposes, drew small savers as well as wealthy investors into the business of lending money at interest. The absence of banks and elaborate credit organizations left the ground open for savers to profit from the demand for loans. The professional moneychangers *(sarrafs)*, the great majority of whom were Jews, did act as bankers, taking deposits, making transfers, and lending money. Some savers put their money with them at interest. However, the moneychangers supplied only a portion of the credit in the market; many of the borrowers obtained their cash from nonprofessional lenders. The business of the moneychangers revolved more often around the world of high finance and commerce than of petty borrowers. It was through them that the local and European merchants made and received payments; even the governor's office and the sharicta court each employed its Jewish banker. When the moneychangers fled from the city in 1775 for fear of extortion by the rapacious cAli Pasha, merchants were unable to transfer funds from their accounts, and commercial activity slowed down.[68]

Economic practice in the city and the wider region accepted as perfectly fair that a lender should draw some compensation from making the use of his money available to others. Even Muslim legal opinion, for centuries uneasy about the usurious aspects of moneylending, had come to legitimize the taking of interest within certain bounds. The sharicta court regarded interest of around 10 percent as legal profit *(murabaha sharciyya)*, and rates well in excess as prohibited usury *(riba)*. The guardians charged with managing the inherited funds of minor children and retarded relatives reported to the court on their returns from lending their money on the market. So also did the charitable foundations endowed with cash, whose involvement with interest loans had sparked a legal controversy among Ottoman jurists two centuries earlier. The amounts they reported were usually around 10 to 12 percent, but in some cases stood as high as 18 percent.[69] In 1762, the indebted butchers' guild borrowed from an official 6,810 piastres for six months at an interest of 500 piastres. This financial return on the loan, amounting to an annual interest rate of 14.7 percent, was reckoned as "legal profit."[70] Interest rates ranging between 10 and 20 percent were accepted as legitimate at different times in other parts of the empire.[71]

The current legal norms applied a flexible standard which released lenders and borrowers from the fear of official censure as well as from pangs of conscience as long as they stayed within bounds. Those bounds were conveniently defined by trends in the credit market rather than by some arbitrary and fixed rate. The interest accepted in legal practice as legitimate corresponded to the standard rates current in low-risk loans between trusting parties, which stood usually at around 10 to 12 percent.[72]

In practice, much higher rates also prevailed in the market. In the recorded loan contracts lenders and borrowers left out mention of interest, but subsequent disputes between them occasionally brought into the open usurious practices. One woman charged 24 piastres a year on a loan of 122 piastres (20 percent interest), collecting 144 piastres over a period of six years. A baker who lent a colleague 80 piastres charged him 36 piastres a year (45 percent interest). A borrower who took a loan of 400 piastres was charged 80 piastres in each of the first three years (33 percent annual interest), 70 piastres in each of the following two years (29 percent interest), and 40 piastres in each of two subsequent years (16.7 percent interest). Another borrower paid 30.75 piastres in ten months on a loan of 16.5 piastres (224 percent annual interest), while still another paid in one year 45 piastres on a loan of 15 piastres (300 percent interest). These dealings came into the open when the debtors decided to denounce their demanding lenders, all of them Muslims, who were ordered by the court to return everything they had collected.[73]

While legal rates of interest obtained in some types of transactions they clearly did not determine the level of gain of all lenders. Lenders and borrowers agreed on all sorts of rates, depending on the familiarity between them, the terms of the loan, the perception of risk, and the current cost of money. For all intents and purposes the credit market operated freely without effective regulation. There was no way for the authorities to monitor transactions or discover the illegal aspects of any loan unless the debtor chose the highly unusual course of betraying them. Borrowers were willing to pay high rates for money, attracting men and women equipped with savings to benefit from the opportunities for easy profits. The English merchants in the city found even 10 to 12 percent to be very attractive lending rates, and engaged extensively in lending out their surplus money to local merchants and officials. In their home country and in western Europe in general interest rates stood at 2 to 5 percent, having declined steadily from a level of 9 to 12 percent in the sixteenth century as the supply of capital improved.[74] Dr. Alexander Russell, the resident physician to the English merchant community, was able to leave Aleppo in the early 1750s with 60,000 piastres worth of goods that he had accumulated, as he noted in a statement, "by the practice of my profession, and by the interest of money."[75]

Investment in moneylending promised relatively high returns, but it was also risky business. Lenders encountered occasional delays and at times lost their funds due to default by borrowers. Even loans to prominent businessmen and high officials were not entirely safe. "I can not name 50 persons in the place of such who at times do borrow mony [sic] that are fit to be trusted with at interest and the best of them only pay when it suits them," wrote an English merchant, with some exaggeration, about the frustrations of moneylending.[76] The lenders dealing with small borrowers from low-income groups took especially high risks, and charged accordingly. They often had to revise the payment schedules, and when they lost patience, took the borrowers to court and had them jailed. This act of last resort also failed often to produce the money. Many of the imprisoned debtors were certified by witnesses to be insolvent, and found difficulties in producing a trustworthy guarantor to back them. They languished in prison for extended periods even for small sums: three months for a 20-piastre debt; sixty days for 10 piastres; thirty days for 6 piastres; four months for 3 piastres.[77]

Careful lenders intent on seeing their money again took precautionary steps to protect themselves against the risk of default. They often insisted that the borrower produce a guarantor *(kafil)* who would pledge in writing to repay the debt in case the borrower failed to meet the terms. When problems did arise the guarantors were actually taken to court and ordered to repay the debt themselves. In 1751, for example, one ʿUmar ibn ʿAbdallah paid a 784-piastre loan that he had guaranteed; a few months later, Nasli bint ʿAbdallah paid 300 piastres on behalf of her nephew, who had recruited her as guarantor for his debts.[78]

Lenders also sought to secure their loans by taking collateral, usually the borrower's most valuable possession: his home. They took the property as security *(rahn)*, which by law gave them the right to possession, and then formally permitted the borrower to continue using it.[79] With such collateral the lender acquired some leverage over the debtor, although not the remedy of automatic foreclosure. To obtain this added advantage some lenders took property as security with the formal provision that it become theirs if the loan was not repaid by a specified deadline. In many cases they actually secured an advance transfer to them in writing of full ownership of the property, with an oral understanding that they would return the title when the debt was repaid.

With the title to a house or other property formally in his hands, the lender had a firmer hold on the debtor. In case of a legal dispute the debtor faced the burden of proving, against the written documents, that the sale was actually a conditional one *(bayʿ bi ʾl-wafaʾ)*. Even when he managed to produce witnesses who backed his claim he still faced the hard choice between repaying the loan immediately and losing his pledged property. Such conflicts, which erupted time and again, forced some hard-pressed debtors to give up their homes.[80]

Moneylending was accompanied by elaborate dealings and occasional frictions. The transactions themselves present a highly diverse picture: borrowers both urban and rural, rich and poor, Muslim and non-Muslim, male and female; sums ranging from one piastre to tens of thousands; lending periods of two months and of ten years; loans secured and unsecured; and rates of interest spanning a remarkable range. The amounts that inventors directed to moneylending varied with their available savings and their particular preferences. ʿAbd al-Wahhab Chalabi al-Tibi, a mentally disturbed man of means, had some 30,000 piastres loaned out by his guardian to various individuals in 1767.[81] The wealthy often had large sums tied up in loans. To them turned large borrowers like villages, guilds, and religious communities, which often needed huge sums on short notice to finance collective fines and taxes.

How much income was produced every year in the form of interest must remain unknown, although it was certainly of more than negligible economic importance. The beneficiaries, more readily visible, represented a wide-ranging group: wealthy merchants and tax farmers, for whom large-scale credit dealings were a common part of daily business; charitable foundations, which drew income from lending out relatively minor sums; and many smaller and larger investors, both Muslim and non-Muslim, who sought a profitable outlet for their savings.

Women, who were largely absent from direct involvement in commercial and artisanal enterprises, figured prominently among the suppliers of credit. They made deals with borrowers outside the family circle, secured their loans, drew up contracts, and sued in court to protect their rights. Women from wealthy families possessed considerable savings to invest. Fatima bint Niʿma, married into the prominent Jabiri family, lent 1,000 piastres to one man, taking as security his house and the equipment in his mill. Amina bint ʿAbd al-Qadir made a loan of 1,050 piastres secured with a home and some jewelry as collateral. Saliha bint ʿAli Chalabi al-ʿUjaymi was able to spare as much as 6,400 piastres on a secured loan.[82] Some women also participated in large-scale moneylending to villagers in the countryside. In 1753, Fatima bint ʿAli Agha and her brother Muhammad Agha collected debts of 14,303 piastres from one village and 8,630 piastres from another.[83]

Alongside the wealthy women were also smaller female investors who lent out lesser sums.[84] Some Christian women even put money with European merchants in return for interest. When the French trading house of Beraud Frères collapsed in the early 1740s, several Christian widows lost their savings. Under pressure from them the French consulate agreed to reimburse the lost sums to avoid the unwelcome prospect of legal suits and government intervention.[85]

Like men, women put their money to work in the ways open to them. Men accepted them as guarantors for loans and sought them out for their own funds. In moneylending women found one accessible avenue for investment and a good source of income. Their activated savings, in the form of credit, thus circulated in various sectors of the economy.

Besides moneylending, and often in competition with it, thrived another major source of investment income: real estate. It promised lower margins of financial profit, but the compensating advantages of greater security and attractive social rewards. Immense wealth drawn from all classes of the population found its way into real property. The patterns of this ownership and investment can be reconstructed from the court archives, which preserved a record of property sales and related transactions unmatched in its comprehensiveness by that for any other major market of the period.

During the 1750s, a thousand or more residential properties changed hands annually. They made up about 80 percent of the total body of transactions in the real estate market; the remaining 20 percent were split more or less evenly between commercial and agricultural properties. The residents enjoyed open access to ownership. The law recognized the right of all free individuals, regardless of age, sex, religious affiliation, class, or origin, to acquire and own real property; even the European merchants in the city owned houses and other real estate. The legal rules also placed no barriers on accumulating property or deriving income from it. A highly developed body of shariʿa laws anchored in a respect for private property defined the different bundles of property rights and the modes of acquiring, using, and transferring them. Effectively enforced by the court, these rules provided the institutional framework that ordered the economic activities surrounding real estate. Neither Islamic law nor the authorities imposed price controls in this market. Sellers usually put their properties with real estate brokers, who advertised them in public places and took bids. The shari'a court itself regarded the best offers obtained by such open advertising as indicators of a property's "fair price" *(thaman al-mithl).*[86]

Only a portion of the mass of real estate owned by the townspeople was rental property. The income-producing assets included most of the commercial buildings, virtually all of the orchards and other agricultural properties on the city's outskirts, and a small proportion of the dwellings. Most of the houses were actually inhabited by their owners. As a rule, the townspeople were not tenants; even the poor families usually owned their houses. Homeownership was widely distributed in the population rather than being concentrated in the hands of a small group of landlords. This reality shaped not only the opportunities for investment in property but also, in a more basic way, the makeup of personal fortunes. Underlying it were social attitudes and economic conditions which made the ownership of one's home a cherished and affordable goal.

The townspeople grew up in a culture that placed a high value on homeownership. They saw in a privately owned home several compelling advantages over tenancy: it was a safe form of equity; it improved one's credit standing; it secured freedom from dependence on landlords, from rental payments, and from the prospects of eviction; and it conveyed a measure of social prestige. The prices of dwellings placed homeownership within the reach of most people. The city offered a wide selection of houses in a remarkably broad range of prices, among them numerous modest homes suited to the financial means of the poorer residents. There were magnificent mansions which sold for as much as 11,500 piastres, and mean dwellings which cost as little as 8 piastres. The majority of houses fell into the lower price ranges. In the 1750s, 30 percent of the dwellings sold annually went for less than 100 piastres, and about 60 percent of them cost less than 200 piastres (see table 5.1).

The standard dwelling of the lower classes—a small courtyard house of one to three rooms, a kitchen, and perhaps a cellar—usually cost 50 to 150 piastres. The poor who could not afford an entire house of their own settled for part of one. Rather than rent a place they bought a room or two in a courtyard house (which in the more comfortable segments of society accommodated a single household), along with rights to the yard and the draw well, usually for 5 to 30 piastres.[87] Although not ideal, such forms of private housing widened the access of residents to homeownership. Even the bedouin who took up residence in apartment complexes *(qaysariyyas)* organized around shared courtyards usually bought rather than rented their inexpensive dwelling units.[88]

Many residents owned shares of houses, acquired by purchase or inheritance. Multiple ownership was common, among family members as well as among unrelated people. Every co-owner was free to sell his interest, or part of it. The properties sold on the market therefore included numerous shares in dwellings, expressed in numbers or fractions of *qirats*, of which twenty-four constituted a whole. Shares as small as one *qirat* and even less changed hands in real estate transactions. This fragmentation not only spread homeownership very widely throughout the population, but also allowed the townspeople to acquire affordable shares in homes and gradually expand their holdings.[89] Helpful too were credit arrangements reached between buyers and sellers. Although the institution of the mortgage was unknown, buyers of homes were able sometimes to put down only part of the cost and spread their payments over a period of some months and even years.[90]

For most residents the private home represented the single most valuable personal possession. The full value of the 1,284 residential properties sold between June 1750 and May 1751 amounted to 361,317 piastres. This small fraction of the total value of Aleppo's houses indicates the immense wealth sunk into residential property, most of which

TABLE 5.1. Prices of Houses Traded in Aleppo in Three Selected Years, 1750–1759

Price (in piastres)	*1750–1751*		*1755–1756*		*1758–1759*	
	Number of houses	Percent of total	Number of houses	Percent of total	Number of houses	Percent of total
1–100	409	31.9	305	31.1	378	36.3
101–200	337	26.2	232	23.6	262	25.1
201–400	298	23.2	232	23.6	215	20.6
401–600	122	9.5	117	11.9	89	8.6
601–800	41	3.2	34	3.5	26	2.5
801–1,000	20	1.6	11	1.1	25	2.4
1,001–	57	4.4	51	5.2	47	4.5
Total	1,284	100.0	982	100.0	1,042	100.0

SOURCE: Aleppo court records.

served for personal use rather than as a source of rental income. Both rich and poor, Muslim and non-Muslim, men and women shared this mass of property. In monetary terms, the wealthier segment which owned the more expensive homes naturally controlled a disproportionately high share of the assets. Women owned less than men, but figured nonetheless quite prominently among the homeowners. They constituted 40 percent of the buyers and sellers involved in the 1,284 sales of houses registered for 1750–1751; at least one woman appeared in 67 percent of these transactions.[91]

The desire for homeownership and the widespread access to it severely restricted the market for rental housing. The several hundred rental homes made available on the market by the charitable foundations and some individual investors met the limited demand of local residents as well as merchants, officials, and others who came to the city for temporary stays. Investment in real estate for income was directed more commonly to commercial and agricultural properties, for which there was a thriving rental market. A relatively small group owned the rental properties and enjoyed their financial and other benefits. The rental market excluded the mass of poor individuals who struggled to acquire even their own homes. It also excluded the non-Muslims who, with the exception of a few odd consular interpreters, did not invest in rental properties. Of the 796 individuals who bought or sold agricultural and commercial properties in 1750–1751 only 22 were Christians and Jews. In the sphere of real property, the non-Muslims put money almost exclusively into homeownership; indeed, the Christians boasted some of the most handsome and expensive houses in the city.[92]

Investment in income properties attracted some small investors who bought a shop or two, or held onto property they happened to inherit. But it attracted most notably the city's wealthy, who sank large sums into real estate of all kinds. Some of them were big landlords with title to dozens of commercial, industrial, and agricultural properties, as well as to some houses. Ahmad Effendi al-Kawakibi, the prominent alim and one-time head of the ashraf, owned considerable portions of his neighborhood of al-Jallum al-Sughra, in addition to properties in other parts of the city and in the countryside.[93] Mustafa Effendi al-Jabiri and his brother Yusuf Effendi, prominent ulama from a distinguished family, bought numerous properties in the poor neighborhoods outside the western city walls, and engaged in large-scale building and renovation in the area.[94] The merchant Musa Agha al-Amiri purchased dozens of properties, most of which he eventually dedicated for the support of the

mosque he founded.[95] Several other wealthy men invested in real property on a similarly large scale. None, however, matched Chalabi Effendi, who was by far the largest landlord in the city, and the owner of
many agricultural properties as well. His numerous dealings fill many
pages of the court records.[96]

Wealthy men invested large sums in real estate, sometimes spending
several thousand piastres in a single transaction. They owned the most
expensive commercial buildings, such as the baths and *qaysariyyas*, and
put some of their capital into construction and renovation. Their large
inventories of property eventually passed to their wives and children,
who sold off their shares or kept them as investments. Through inheritance, women acquired valuable real estate from which they drew income. But many of them actually purchased rental property, from kin
as well as unrelated sellers. In 1750–1751, for instance, women made
up one-third of the buyers of commercial property and one-seventh of
the buyers of agricultural property. And, as the deeds indicate, many of
the commercial and agricultural properties sold by women had originally come into their possession by way of purchase.[97] The better-off
women often held shares in expensive bath houses and orchards, in
addition to a smaller or larger collection of shops and dwellings.[98] Those
of lesser means invested in a shop or house, and even rented out rooms
in their own homes to lodgers.[99]

The rent from leasing a room amounted to as little as 4 piastres a
year; a bath house, in comparison, could yield several hundred piastres.
The financial benefits varied widely with the sum invested and the
productivity of the property. The annual returns in rents that investors
could expect from a property ranged between 8 and 14 percent of the
capital invested. Expenses on taxes and maintenance, however, reduced
the benefits considerably. A house valued at 100 piastres yielded 9
piastres a year in gross rent (9 percent). Another house purchased for
530 piastres produced 45 piastres in rent (8.5 percent), but 11.25 piastres
paid in taxes on it reduced the annual returns to 6.4 percent. An orchard
bought for 700 piastres was rented out for 100 piastres a year (14.3
percent); maintenance expenses of 20 piastres reduced the returns to
11.3 percent. Another orchard acquired for 300 piastres was rented out
for 35 piastres a year (11.6 percent); the tenant undertook to cover all of
the expenses. A deteriorated bath house which a charitable foundation
sold with official permission brought 600 piastres; under waqf management it had yielded 54 piastres a year in net income (9 percent). Another
deteriorated bath house valued at 1,100 piastres yielded 150 piastres

(13.6 percent).[100] Property taxes reduced the income from rent by anywhere from 2 to 38 percent.[101] This outlay, along with inescapable expenditures on repairs, lowered the net returns from real estate to a general range of 6 to 11 percent.

The attraction of real property clearly lay not entirely in its financial returns, which were modest. The security of an assured income from a durable asset immune to serious mischief appealed to many investors. So also did the social prestige conferred by tangible and public symbols of wealth. Speculative calculations of capital gains from future resale may have also weighed with some investors. For the smaller savers, including widows and orphans without the benefit of income from employment, real estate provided primarily the benefit of regular cash payments which helped to improve their material welfare. For the great landlords, who enjoyed the bulk of property income, real estate was more often an outlet for wealth acquired by other avenues than it was a source of wealth. They built their fortunes from commercial ventures, moneylending, and tax farms, all of which absorbed large portions of their capital. State finances afforded them a lucrative sphere of investment, one accessible only to a privileged few.

A small group composed exclusively of Muslim men controlled the urban and rural tax farms available to investors. To acquire even a modest farm required contacts, luck, and a considerable amount of cash. Many of the tax farms were held as lifetime grants *(malikânes)* which the owners could sell at will or pass on to their heirs; they often remained for decades in the same family. Their prices varied widely, but in general called for a substantial investment. A share of one-eighth in an urban farm was transferred in 1756 for 6,000 piastres.[102] Investors often owned only portions of tax farms, sharing the income from the revenues with their partners.

The level of profit from tax farms cannot be estimated. It was clearly very high in the case of the rural farms, which required immense investments but also opened up great opportunities for profit from the exploitation of the peasantry, large-scale moneylending, and the manipulation of the food supply. The great fortunes and social prominence of the aʿyan reflected the rewards of these ventures. Urban tax farms offered more limited opportunities for financial gain, and attracted men of lesser status and means. But whether it enriched or provided a comfortable income, tax farming was more a redistributive type of activity than a genuinely productive one for the urban economy. It attracted considerable local capital and produced large profits, but did not develop into a necessary gateway to fortune-building. Musa Agha al-Amiri, for instance, accumulated his immense wealth largely from trade, without venturing into tax farming. Commercial enterprises, real estate, and credit operations absorbed his capital.

Despite variations in individual preferences and opportunities the directions of investment show a distinct pattern: trade, real estate, and finance (in the form of credit and tax farms) attracted the bulk of invested fortunes, while industry and agriculture were generally unappealing as outlets for capital. In the areas of finance and long-distance trade, investment took developed capitalistic forms. A substantial portion of society's total wealth, however, found its way into the noncapitalist avenue of real property. For social as well as economic reasons, real estate exercised an extraordinary appeal which established it as a major form of property.

The meaning of what figured as property in Aleppo needs to be approached in terms more inclusive than simply physical things of value like coins, real estate, and personal possessions. Tax farms, monopolies, *gediks*, and membership in guilds were valuable assets which also formed the objects of property. The bundle of rights associated with each of them had become broad enough over time to recognize even hereditary privileges and the power of transfer. An intricate web of relations surrounded these forms of property, which were often held in joint ownership.

As the pursuit of property and investment indicates, many residents were able to accumulate savings and ready to put them to work. It is less clear, however, to what extent the potential savings in the community were actually mobilized or channelled to productive uses. If the financial institutions and credit facilities of the period, which included no developed banks, proved inadequate to tap some savings, or if the available investment opportunities appeared unattractive or risky to certain savers, then a portion of the savings would have remained idle. Gold and silver, regarded as assets of lasting value, exercised a fascinating appeal which encouraged some hoarding, in the common forms of jewelry and precious coins. This hoarded wealth remained out of circulation, and did not stimulate exchange and economic growth. It may be that capital was scarce in part because it was underdeveloped, that what was missing was not so much surplus money above consumption needs as the incentives, investment opportunities, and financial facilities needed to mobilize it to the fullest extent. The pressure to spend on consumption, felt particularly strongly among those with the largest amounts of savings, also worked to limit capital formation.

THE FAMILY AND MATERIAL WELFARE

M ANY ECONOMIC ADVANTAGES came to people in Aleppo by way of their families. Tax farms, rights to entry and promotion in guilds, shares in a craft's business, and tax exemptions often passed by heredity, while relatives participated in the supply of credit and business partners. The family had a bearing on economic welfare in a still larger sense. Within it took place nonmarket transfers of wealth, benefits, and services on an enormous scale. The meaning of these economic activities can be understood best against the particular structure of local families and the dynamics which shaped them. While the evidence in this area is singularly inadequate, and untested assumptions abound, the material in the court records helps to unveil the complexity of the family structure and to reconstruct its main outlines.

The residents experienced family life primarily as members of specific households. They spoke often of *ʿaʾila* or *ʿiyal* in referring to the domestic group which shared a common residence, mutual responsibilities, and a presiding head, usually but not invariably a male. It was this unit which embodied family authority, obligations, and intimate ties in their most intense forms, and which consequently shaped the welfare of the townspeople most directly. Yet the larger circle of kin extending beyond the immediate household was also a meaningful part of one's family life. A sense of common descent and family pride, stronger in some individuals than in others, linked residents to the members of their larger family group, with whom they were often also closely associated as playmates, friends, business partners and even spouses. The ties with kin outside the household were not entirely voluntary. Needy individuals could claim support from relatives according to a hierarchy of obligations established by Islamic law. Many people in Aleppo made welfare payments to economically dependent relatives and even sheltered them in their homes.

The boundaries between the household and the larger circle of kin were somewhat fluid, although real enough to be recognized by law and social practice. In 1755, when one Muhammad ibn ʿUmar was found murdered, his father's suspicions fell on a fellow resident who disappeared from the city. Frustrated in his efforts to bring the suspect to justice he took his father to court in the hope of compelling him to produce his son. The suspect's father was not forthcoming. "My missing son Ahmad does not reside in my household [*ʿiyal*], but lives separately from me in a different neighborhood," he excused himself. "I don't know his whereabouts—he is a mature adult who goes where he pleases without notifying me." The judge agreed with him that he was under no obligation to make his son available. In 1768 the official representative of the Jacobite Christians received an order from Istanbul banishing him and his family to Alexandretta. His married daughter appealed to the court for an exemption from the order on the grounds that it did not apply to her. "I am not part of his household [*ʿaʾila*], but belong to the household of another man, my husband Jirjis," she explained. The qadi accepted her reasoning and allowed her to stay behind.[103] On the basis of affiliation with a separate household a married woman could thus escape a banishment order imposed on her father's family, and a father could absolve himself of responsibility for his son's criminal conduct.

During the eighteenth century the structure of local households was shaped most profoundly by several conditions current in the city: almost universal marriage; early age at first marriage; frequent break-up of families due to divorce or the premature death of spouses; common remarriage; high fertility; and high mortality, of children and adults alike. Behind these realities were certain ideals, norms, and customs, as well as the dictates of the demographic regime. Economic factors also had a marked bearing on the household structure, the level of wealth of residents determining their options and their access to various ideals.

Aleppo's households were organized predominantly around a core of parents and their offspring. The vast majority of men and women in the city married, sometimes more than once. They grew up in a culture which directed them into marriage as a natural course. Religious norms, which promoted marriage as a holy duty incumbent on every healthy individual while forbidding sexual relations outside married life, reinforced the strong pressures from the family and the larger community. Ulama, priests, and rabbis all took wives. Celibacy enjoyed no popular appeal; even among the Christians only a few odd men and women chose to withdraw into monastic life. The ideal was to marry, and to marry young. Even minors, defined legally as children who had not reached puberty, were wed or engaged; the law imposed no minimum age of marriage. Girls usually became wives between the ages of fourteen and seventeen, while men, especially in the lower classes, appear to have entered wedlock at an older age in order to prepare themselves for the financial burdens of married life.[104]

The practice of universal and early marriage restricted the number of single-person households. So also did the fact that single adults, whether unmarried, widowed, or divorced, tended to reside with relatives, especially in the case of females. It was usually men lacking close family, particularly transients and immigrants, who took up lodgings on their own, usually in apartment complexes or rented rooms. The majority of residents, however, lived at most times with others, in households which were either nuclear units organized around one married couple, or extended ones composed of parents, their unmarried children, and their married sons with their wives and offspring. Each of these two basic types of household was subject to a range of variations. While it is impossible to arrive at a precise profile of the domestic organization in a period lacking household censuses, the many bits and pieces of information scattered in the judicial records reveal the general outlines of household structure and the processes which shaped it.

One observation emerges at the outset: the extended household, often assumed to be the standard form of domestic organization in past Middle Eastern communities, was not universal or even predominant in the city. Although a desirable mode of family living, its actual prevalence was severely limited by three sets of factors: insufficient economic means; the natural workings of the family cycle; and demographic circumstances and familial crises. The majority of residents may have actually spent most of their lives in households with only one married couple rather than in extended units.

A family's level of wealth had much to do with its ability to create and sustain an extended household. The tendency of newly married couples to reside with the parents, usually of the groom, was common in all classes. It grew partly out of the practical necessity of helping out young couples in need of initial support. But it also reflected a form of domestic living cherished for social reasons. The extended group of parents and children who remained united in a single residential unit demonstrated a laudable familial closeness and cohesion. The arrangement also reflected honorably on the family head, who commanded the authority and material comfort necessary to hold the family together. The well-to-do were best equipped to realize these familial ideals; unlike the poorer segments of the population, they could provide private rooms to accommodate additional married couples comfortably. The truly elaborate extended groups, with several sons and their families living under the parents' roof on a sustained basis, thus appeared most commonly among the better-off. In the lower classes, newly married couples could not count on a prolonged stay with parents; circumstances launched them more rapidly than their wealthy counterparts into separate nuclear households of their own.

Even if all couples were able to afford and maintain extended households, only a portion of the domestic units, including those of the wealthy, could possibly be extended at any one time. Extended households broke up into nuclear units in the normal course of things, most commonly when the senior generation died or when the family grew too large to be accommodated in a single dwelling. Such fission fragmented even the great extended households of the elite. When the father died, the mother often continued to hold the family together even though ownership of the house and estate was now fragmented among the heirs; some residences were known, like Dar al-Sitt Karima (House of Lady Karima), by the name of such matrons.[105] With the death of both parents, however, the extended household ceased to exist, and the married brothers usually moved out to set up separate nuclear households.[106] The newly formed nuclear households could evolve in turn into larger extended units, which eventually would undergo fission themselves.

The transition from one household type to another as a normal feature of the family cycle meant that only some households could be extended at any one time. Demographic accidents and familial crises reduced the number still further: some parents had no surviving sons to extend their households, and many children lacked the option of such an arrangement, having lost their father, and even both parents, by the time they entered marriage. In the conditions of high mortality current at the time, numerous married men and women died young, while their own parents were still alive and their children still minors.[107] Such circumstances usually aborted the possibility of an extended household. The surviving parent often remarried and started a new family. Because of the laws of custody or the preferences of the parents, the orphaned children usually ended up in the households of their grandparents, aunts, uncles, brothers or other kin, and were unlikely to join their father's new family when they themselves married.[108] Divorce, another common occurrence, had many of the same disruptive consequences. It broke up households altogether, dispersing the parents and even the children in different households. The chances of the married children joining their parents in an extended unit were again rendered remote.

The contingencies of family life, along with the domestic cycle and the level of wealth, thus worked to promote nuclear households in some families and extended units in others. They also tended to complicate the scene further by introducing variety into the makeup of households of both types. The nuclear households ought not to be thought of stereotypically as neat units composed of two parents and their children. Nor were the extended groups made up necessarily or exclusively of two parents, their unmarried children, and the families of the married sons. The labels "nuclear" and "extended" capture basic principles underlying domestic organization, not the precise contents and size of the households themselves. Missing members as well as the addition of various kin and unrelated individuals modified the composition of households, creating all sorts of incomplete or augmented units.

Many households were headed by single parents; death, and to a lesser extent divorce, removed one of the spouses from the home. Some included divorced or widowed sisters and daughters of the household head, who usually returned to their families of birth when they were relatively young. The multitudes of children from broken homes augmented local households still further. Some of them lived with a remarried parent, adding stepchildren to the household. Others were put with kin; many households included siblings, nephews, nieces, grandchildren, and cousins of their heads. This population of children often floated between households according to the currents of family events. The experience of Fatima bint Khalil, a twelve year old girl who lost her father in 1758, was not uncommon. For a year she lived with her mother, who then remarried and passed the girl to the custody of her maternal grandmother. Hardly a year was over when Fatima was moved again. Her paternal grandfather sued her custodian for child neglect and convinced the court that the girl ought to be brought into his household (*'iyal*).[109]

Households with only one parent, or with stepchildren, or with an orphaned nephew, or with a divorced sister were not actively pursued ideal types of domestic organization. They represented adaptations to contingencies and pressures within the larger family circle. The divorce, premature death, and remarriage of parents not only resulted often in the breakup of the affected households, but also dispersed their members among existing households, changing their composition and size as well.

Among the better-off, households were enlarged by voluntary additions reflecting luxurious living. Many middle-class families kept live-in maids, attendants, wet nurses, and other domestic help, while the very wealthy often accommodated slaves and concubines in their households. Polygamy was also found more commonly in the better-off families. Although Muslims were permitted to have up to four wives, polygamy was restricted in actual practice to a small minority of households, at least in part because of economic constraints. To pay the additional dower of a second wife, provide her with a room of her own, and support her daily needs was not within the means of many men. Most of them were certainly unable to make the domestic investments of Muhammad al-Rifaʿi, who set up each of his three wives in a separate house. His son Muhammad, a distinguished religious scholar (d. 1847), followed the same arrangement with his two wives: he shuttled between their separate houses, seeing them on alternate days.[110] The uncommon mention of polygamous marriages in the court records indicates something of the low incidence of the institution. The practice was forbidden entirely to Christians and rare among Jews, who were permitted another wife only when the first one proved barren or produced no son.[111]

In light of the great variations in circumstances the size of the city's households ranged between striking extremes. At one end were single-person households, present in limited numbers. At the other end, in small proportions too, were domestic groups that numbered several dozen members. The household of the merchant Musa Agha al-Amiri, for instance, included forty concubines as well as a host of slaves and attendants. Four wives and thirteen children survived him when he died in 1763.[112] Most households were clearly of a more modest order. The estimated average size of the city's households, which numbered roughly 15,000 in the middle decades of the century, was seven members.[113]

The relatively large average size is explained in part by the features of many local households noted above: the occasional accommodation of married children and their offspring; the absorption of relatives; the tendency of single adults to reside with family; and the inclusion of domestics and other nonkin. Above all, however, it was the relatively large number of children that inflated the size of households. The judicial records contain numerous listings of the children who survived a deceased parent. A sample of three hundred families shows a number of children ranging from 1 to 13 at the time of the parent's death. The average stood at 4.8 children per family (see table 5.2). More than half of the families had 4 or 5 children; only a fifth had 3 or less. The figures undercount the number of children actually born to the deceased parents, who had lost some along the way. Among the children listed were some from a previous marriage of the parent.

This high fertility reflected in part the advantages attached to children. Parents valued children, especially boys, as sources of pride and delight, as the carriers of the family line, and as insurance in their old age. The prospect of motherhood appealed to women, whose leverage and status in the family improved considerably once they bore children and assumed the responsibilities of raising them. The high rates of infant and child mortality encouraged parents to produce a surplus of children to compensate for anticipated deaths.

Some of the children, however, were unplanned. Parents did display a desire to limit births, often for economic reasons, but lacked guaranteed means of realizing it. Women consulted doctors and tried out various medicines reputed to act as contraceptives; some nursed their children until they were three or four years old in the hope of preventing conception. These attempts often proved disappointing. Only a few were willing to take the risks of an abortion: the operation, performed by midwives, was too hazardous to the mother's life to become common practice. A less drastic course, such as taking drugs considered to have abortifacient effects, usually proved ineffective. Popular beliefs that abortion and drugs produced sterility tended to reduce their appeal.[114] What birth control was practiced by couples, together with lactation, divorce, the premature death of spouses, malnutrition, and poor health, did set some limits on fertility, but without freeing families from the

TABLE 5.2. Number of Children Surviving a Deceased Parent in 300 Aleppo Families, 1746–1771

Number of Families	Number of Children
7	1
16	2
37	3
80	4
84	5
34	6
22	7
9	8
3	9
3	10
2	11
0	12
3	13
Total children	1,448
Children per family	4.8

SOURCE: Aleppo court records.

threat of excess children. The economic burden weighed so heavily on some poor parents that they put one or more of their children with other unrelated families willing to raise them at their own expense until they reached puberty.[115]

When seen against these realities of fertility, and the demographic and economic conditions in general, the household structure in Aleppo becomes more comprehensible. The differences in size and composition can be explained more readily in terms of variables such as level of wealth, stage in the family cycle, demographic accidents, and other contingencies than as reflections of distinct family types grounded in separate ideals. In the sphere of domestic life all social groups appear to have shared the same core of ideals and norms. Even the various religious groups differed little in the essential characteristics of their domestic organization and values. Due to religious prohibitions non-Muslim households contained no concubines and, with rare exceptions among Jews, were not polygamous. But otherwise the variations in customs and beliefs were not marked enough to foster distinctly Muslim, Christian, or Jewish types of household. A domestic organization such as the extended household was not something prescribed by Islam; it was found among local Muslims and non-Muslims alike, and also in the Christian lands along the northern Mediterranean.

Because of the many variations it is impossible to speak of a single family cycle that captures the sequence of experiences of all people in Aleppo from birth to death; alongside the households which followed undisturbed the socially desired course were others whose development was halted or redirected. Whatever their precise patterns, the various stages and events of family life involved transfers of wealth and services of considerable economic importance. The larger circle of kin, not only the household, took part in these activities. The extended *household* may not have been a reality for most people at most times, but the extended *family*, in the sense of the larger network of relatives, certainly was, even if its members did not live under the same roof. The institutional framework within which the economic transfers took place is fairly clear: Islamic law, extremely detailed in its regulation of family matters, defined the rights and obligations in the areas of marriage, child care, divorce, inheritance, and support of needy kin. It is the actual behavior and conditions which need to be reconstructed.

The story must begin with the central institution in which family life was anchored: marriage. The value that people in Aleppo attached to marriage was perhaps most evident in their wedding celebrations. "There is no other occasion on which the people of the East display so festive a spirit, and such prodigal expense, as on the marriage of their children, especially of the eldest son," observed the resident English physician Russell, clearly impressed with weddings he attended in the city. "In regard to the middling people of every denomination, it is certain that the expense lavished on their marriage feasts, is extravagant, beyond all proportion to their condition. The female apparels and jewels are likewise sumptuous, much above the fortunes of the persons who wear them."[116]

The wedding put a joyous seal on a match arranged by the families of the bride and groom, often after considerable inquiries and negotiations. Once agreement was reached the families drew up a written contract which stipulated the terms, and especially the size of the *mahr*, or dower, to be paid by the groom to the bride. This marriage payment, required by Islamic law, ranged in the middle decades of the eighteenth century from one piastre to one thousand piastres or more. By local custom, the groom paid half the dower in advance while holding the rest as a debt to be paid to his wife when he divorced her or died. In the better-off families, the bride's father supplemented the dower with an additional customary gift to the girl. The total amount received from the father and groom was used to purchase the clothing, jewelry, bedding, and other articles which formed the bride's trousseau (*jihaz*).[117]

These payments and material preparations loomed large in prenuptial arrangements, for symbolic as well as economic reasons. How much was settled on the bride affected her economic security during marriage and the standard of living she will expect to lead. It also measured the value placed on the girl and the status of the families involved. The parties as well as the larger public judged the social importance of the match partly by material standards. Three days before the wedding the bride's trousseau was sent to the groom's house, ostentatiously displayed for public viewing. Its size, and the lavishness of the wedding, were status symbols which became the focus of much social competition. The better-off families in particular felt pressured to bargain for high dowers for their daughters, to lavish sizable settlements on them as a way of attracting bids from men of good status, and to spend heavily on the festivities.

The social competition inflated the costs of marriage and placed heavy financial burdens on men looking for brides. Many men were unable to come up immediately with the sums needed to seal an acceptable match; they made down payments on their dowers, and then proceeded, sometimes over a period of several years, to make payments to their fiancees, in addition to periodic gifts intended to demonstrate their good intentions. Some engagements fell through due to delays in completing payments or to other causes of friction.[118] The inflation of marriage costs and the obstacles placed in the way of the poorer families prompted the leaders of the Christian communities to issue periodic regulations setting ceilings on marriage payments and prohibiting various costly festivities as well as ostentatious displays of clothes and jewelry. The Jewish community exempted its unmarried men from communal taxes as a way of allowing them to save for marriage. This measure, tantamount to a subsidy of marriage expenses, proved counterproductive in the early nineteenth century, when Jewish bachelors were found to delay marriage in order to avoid sharing in the heavy tax burden. The communal leaders also prohibited a customary festive visit of the groom's family to the bride's house, partly because it occasioned large expenses which the poor could not afford.[119]

The transfers of wealth accompanying marriage went from men to women, who upon marriage acquired some property and valuables recognized as their own. The matrimonial regime, which was premised on a separation of funds of husband and wife rather than on community property, protected their rights to everything they brought into the marriage or accumulated by way of inheritance, gifts, investment or employment in the course of their married life; their husbands had no claim to the ownership or management of these assets. The conjugal regime also released wives from any obligation to share in the household expenses. The husband was required by Islamic law to provide his wife with lodging, food and clothes, and to maintain his children. Women left without support for themselves and their children during an absence of the husband were entitled by the court to be reimbursed by him for their daily expenditures according to a specified daily rate; that rate could include the expenses of domestic service if the wife was accustomed to such a luxury.[120] This setup allowed married women to save and accumulate private assets which could serve as economic insurance in times of need. Keenly conscious of the precariousness of marriage, they guarded what they owned, even taking care to have written documents drawn up when they lent money to their husbands.

While favorable to women and protective of their material welfare in many respects, the economic arrangements of marriage also had their negative side, evident when the marriage broke up. Upon divorce, a wife was entitled only to the deferred half of her dower and to support for the first three months following the breakup (a period intended to establish whether she was pregnant). She had a right to whatever she owned, but not to alimony payments or to a share of her husband's wealth, however substantial. The three-month support amounted in the 1750s and 1760s to a minor sum ranging between 2 and 7 piastres.[121] The deferred dower was often a pittance too. Of 384 divorce settlements recorded in the court in the twelve-month period between June 1750 and May 1751, 50 percent involved dowers of 10 piastres or less; 80 percent of the women were entitled to 30 piastres or less (see table 5.3). As many as 248 of the divorcees actually forfeited their dowers and temporary support as part of the settlement.

Divorce exposed some of the underlying weaknesses in the position of women. Not only did they obtain little monetary compensation when their marriages broke up; their power of maneuver in marital relations was markedly inferior to that of their husbands. The man could repudiate his wife without her consent or any legal proceedings, while she lacked a corresponding power to initiate divorce. If the wife pressed her husband for a divorce and made his life unpleasant he could still use his veto power to wrest material concessions from her as a price for his

TABLE 5.3. Size of Dowers Owed to Women Divorced in Aleppo,
1750–1751

Amount of Dower (in piastres)	Number of Women	Percent of Women
1–10	199	51.8
11–20	68	17.7
21–30	44	11.5
31–40	19	5.0
41–50	22	5.7
51–60	2	0.5
61–70	2	0.5
71–80	2	0.5
81–90	1	0.3
91–100	8	2.1
101–	2	0.5
no data	15	3.9
Total	384	100.0

SOURCE: Aleppo court records.

agreement to end the marriage. Indeed, in most of the recorded settlements the couples resorted to the type of divorce known as *khulᶜ*, in which the husband released his wife in return for a monetary consideration by her. Wives usually sacrificed their deferred dowers and three months of support. Some even made cash payments to their husbands and absolved them of the obligation to provide child support.[122] By using their property as leverage many women were thus able to buy their way out of unwanted marriages despite their legal disabilities. They also made sure that their husbands fulfilled their obligations under the settlement reached. When ex-husbands proved recalcitrant or short of cash, their former wives sued them in court, or allowed them to pay in installments, or took their share in the dwelling in lieu of their debt.[123]

The financial obligations may have deterred some husbands from divorcing their wives, especially when the owed dowers were substantial. Social pressure also worked to reduce the frequency of divorce; when marital quarrels broke out relatives often intervened to restore domestic peace and keep the couple together.[124] Divorce remained nonetheless a fairly common occurrence. If the recorded settlements represent the full number, some 300 to 400 divorces took place annually during the 1750s. They involved mostly Muslim families, Christians and Jews appearing in disproportionately small numbers.[125]

Each case of divorce created dislocations which touched the couple, the children, and often the larger family. But still more disruptive in its effects was another frequent occurrence: the premature death of a spouse. When the wife and mother died, the family was left without its main source of domestic care; with the death of the husband and father, the family lost its chief breadwinner. The precise effects on the survivors depended on the economic circumstances of the family and its stage in the domestic cycle. Their material welfare, however, was bound to be affected to a larger or smaller degree. Premature death led frequently to the breakup of households and to the remarriage of many of the widowed. It also created frequent problems of child care and financial support which fell on the shoulders of various relatives. Similar repercussions were common in the case of divorces. Death, however, also set in motion the process of inheritance, which altered the distribution of property within the family and the economic means of the heirs far more drastically than the financial transfers upon divorce.

For women the economic consequences of a broken marriage were usually more immediate and acute than for men since they lost their source of daily support. Those among them who lacked personal funds to provide for themselves turned to their fathers and male relatives, who bore the legal responsibility to care for them. The safety net of the larger family proved important in these times of crises. However, the kin of poor women were usually too poor themselves to provide financial support on a permanent basis, and remarriage therefore emerged as the most indicated solution. And indeed, many widows and divorcees took this course. The court records abound in references to remarriages, by men as well as women. While the proportion of people who remarried, their ages, and their motivations are unknown, several features appear more clearly: men remarried more frequently than women; having children from a previous marriage was not an obstacle to remarriage; and remarried women were still young enough to bear more children.[126]

Remarriage was more readily accessible, and perhaps also more desirable, to men.[127] Unlike women, they could marry over a wide age range. The more established and economically secure among them were actually considered attractive prospects for young girls even when the age difference was substantial. Older women had a smaller range of choices available, and those of them past child-bearing age lost much of their appeal as marriage partners. The burden of raising young children from a broken marriage was a powerful inducement for fathers to remarry, but less so to mothers. Indeed, mothers had some reason to avoid remarriage: they often lost custody of their children by remarrying, unless the new husband happened to be one of a small category of kin defined by Islamic law. When women remarried it may have been often from economic necessity. For materially secure widows, remaining single actually provided a level of independence and freedom unachieved at any other stage of their lives. They no longer faced the encumbrance of pregnancies and could make decisions without the control of a husband.

Remarriage, accepted as normal and practical in Aleppo's culture, helped countless men and women to restore their material security and rebuild their domestic lives. Many residents married twice and even more times, although none probably broke the record of Mustafa al-Khujaki, a Sufi shaykh who had gone through twenty-two marriages by the time he died in 1740.[128] With remarriages often came new children, who added another layer of complexity to the network of family ties. Stepparents, stepchildren, half-brothers, and half-sisters thus became a normal part of one's circle of relatives.

Behind the fresh start of a remarriage there remained the legacies of

previous marriages in the form of children. The multitudes of orphans
and victims of broken marriages saw their domestic milieu and personal
dreams altered by the crises and rearrangements in their family life.
Some continued to live with a parent; many others grew up in the
homes of relatives, who made the daily decisions affecting their welfare.
Legal battles over their custody shifted them occasionally from one
household to another. The issue of their financial support *(nafaqa)* posed
problems as well. Those orphans who had some inherited property were
maintained from their assets, which were managed by a guardian of the
property *(wasi)*, usually the surviving parent, an uncle, a sibling or a
grandparent.[129] When orphans had no funds of their own and no father
to assume the responsibility for support, the obligation passed to the
larger family. Uncles, grandfathers, adult brothers, and other relatives
were called upon to provide child support payments, which usually
ranged between one and two piastres a month. Some found the financial
demands unmanageable; when taken to court by the orphans' mother,
they proved that they were too poor, passing the burden on to the next
blood relative in line.[130]

The care of orphans illustrates well the workings of the extended
family as an agency of welfare and support. Those who brought up the
children, managed their property and paid for their needs included not
only parents but other kin as well. The sacrifices made by relatives
originated in a strong sense of family cohesion as well as in social
pressures. But they rested also on legal obligations. The shari'a placed
the responsibilities for supporting the weak and needy on their kin, and
the court enforced the financial obligations. The support provided by
relatives extended beyond orphans to other categories of dependent
persons, including divorcees, widows, the mentally incompetent, and
needy parents. The court imposed on people welfare payments for the
support of their mothers, and also of their fathers when they could no
longer earn a living.[131]

This flow of material benefits within the family, in the form of cash
payments, shelter, nursing, and other services provided to relatives,
amounted to a substantial redistribution whose magnitude in monetary
terms defies calculation. Of no lesser economic importance were the
intrafamilial transfers of wealth by way of inheritance. Many widows
and orphans were able to support themselves from what they inherited,
without depending on charity. But beyond providing a source of income
and material security for the vulnerable members of families deprived of
their breadwinner, inheritance affected the distribution of wealth in
society as a whole.

A complicated set of rules based on Islamic law defined who had rights to the possessions of the dead.[132] Two characteristics of the system determined most directly its economic consequences: it tended to split estates among a relatively large number of male and female heirs who might include, depending on circumstances, spouses, parents, children, siblings, and more distant relatives; and it allocated the shares unequally, most notably by giving to males usually twice as much as the corresponding females. Spouses, for example, inherited only a portion of each other's property: the wife received an eighth of her husband's estate if he had descendants and a quarter if he had none; the husband was entitled to twice these shares, but to no more. Children always inherited, but their precise shares depended on their number and the presence of other legal heirs. Actual cases recorded in the judicial documents illustrate the large and varied pool of heirs who received shares in the estates of relatives: the wife and ten children of the deceased; the husband, five children, and father of the deceased; the wife, daughter, mother, and five siblings; the wife and four nephews of the deceased; the three wives and five children; the sister, uncle, and aunt; the sister and three sons of a cousin; the wife, two sisters, and seven cousins of the deceased; the wife, daughter, maternal grandmother, and two sisters of the deceased; the wife, two sons from her, and two daughters from a concubine of the deceased.[133]

The property of deceased residents thus ended up often in the hands of several relatives, who each received only a small share. Some of the property of married people left the immediate conjugal family, with portions going to parents, siblings, and other relatives. Because the circle of legal heirs was wide and mortality high people often inherited several times in the course of their lives. In some cases their share amounted to a mere five piastres, while in others they benefited from considerable wealth which improved their economic lot. The distribution of inherited property favored males, but without giving them a monopoly over this source of wealth; women shared the benefits of inheritance, which helped them to increase their personal assets, to invest, and to exercise leverage within their families. Although less advantaged than the males, they were clearly not subjected to any systematic denial of their rights as heirs.

The partible system of inheritance had its egalitarian aspects, but it also militated against the transmission of large fortunes from one generation to the next, hence retarding the accumulation of capital. The great wealth of 'Abd al-Wahhab Agha Shurayyif was split among his wife and thirteen children, seven of whom originated in a previous marriage.

Musa Agha al-Amiri had his fortune fragmented among four wives, seven sons, and six daughters.[134] Although considerable, the amount inherited by each of the heirs was only a fraction of the patrimony. Even in the case of formidable estates the heirs tended to take their individual shares rather than maintain the property intact under long-term collective control.

The Islamic law of inheritance, which applied also to the Christians and possibly the Jews, gave individuals only limited discretion as to how their estate would be distributed.[135] They could will no more than a third of their property, and any bequest to one of the legal heirs required the consent of the others to be valid. Some did draw up wills, although no record exists of their precise terms. Making gifts to children and other relatives offered another strategy for circumventing the rigid rules of inheritance. In addition to the transfers of property registered openly as acts of donation *(hiba)*, some of the sales of real estate by parents to children were possibly veiled gifts. When in 1757 Shukr Allah Shidyaq divided among his wife and six children the large house he had owned for forty years, his seven sales transactions with his kin may have disguised premortem gifts made by an old man.[136]

Whether before or after death, wealth usually passed hands in the family by way of a direct transfer of ownership over assets. Some residents, however, chose a more elaborate mode of distributing their property: they endowed their real estate holdings and designated relatives of their choice as lifetime beneficiaries of the rental income, with the distribution of the stipends becoming operative upon the death of the donors. Some allocated income to relatives from endowments made partly or chiefly for the benefit of a public cause such as a mosque or water fountain; others dedicated their endowments exclusively to their relatives, setting up in effect a family trust *(waqf dhurri)*.

The family trust, which rested on the same institutional arrangements as the charitable endowment, was actually an uncommon way of transmitting wealth. Only 97 such trusts were established in the period 1746–1771, 38 of them by women. Several drawbacks rendered this course unattractive despite the advantage of discretion in distributing one's wealth: the capital of endowed property could not be realized; the property tended to deteriorate from wear or neglect, reducing the overall income; and the number of beneficiaries had a way of multiplying in successive generations to the point of reducing the individual stipends to negligible sums.

In most of the family trusts it was the children of the donor and their descendants who enjoyed the income, in some cases concurrently with other relatives; other categories of relatives, especially those outside the immediate conjugal unit, followed far behind (see table 5.4). The donors usually included both their male and female descendants among the beneficiaries. However, only in a minority of cases did they provide for equal distribution; more commonly they allocated to the girls half the income of the boys.[137] Wives, the second largest category of beneficiaries after the children, were often allocated a fixed allowance or the right to reside for life in an endowed house, but on condition that they remained unmarried.[138]

Some of the family trusts survived for decades, their financial benefits passing to new generations which often did not know the donor. Several hundred men and women in Aleppo drew annual income from this source, although in uneven amounts. The balance sheets of trusts audited by the court in the 1750s record individual stipends ranging from 5 to 240 piastres. The variations had to do with the marked differences in the overall wealth of the foundations and the manner of its distribution. The assets available to the trusts ranged between 1 and 44 properties, their total income between 13.5 and 663.5 piastres, and the number of their beneficiaries between 2 and 20.[139] In each trust one of the beneficiaries served as administrator and handled the management of the properties and funds. The holders of this office, who usually collected an additional allowance, often included women.[140] Quarrels over the post of administrator, over alleged mismanagement, and over the

TABLE 5.4. The Beneficiaries of 97 Family Trusts Founded in Aleppo, 1746–1771

	First	*Alternate*
Children and descendants	74	4
Wives	15	2
Husband	5	0
Grandchildren and descendants	3	1
Siblings and descendants	6	7
Siblings' children and descendants	7	10
Parents	1	1
More distant relatives	3	8
Freed slaves and descendants	5	7

SOURCE: Aleppo court records.

distribution of stipends brought the beneficiaries of trusts to the court on occasion. Unlike inheritance, the family foundations kept alive long-term associations among those kin entitled to shares in the endowed property.

The transfers of wealth, care, and support within the family no doubt shaped personal relationships and were shaped by them; the affective aspects of family life are too obscure to determine in what ways. It is impossible to say how much companionship and intimacy developed between spouses, what the sexual habits were like, whether children were spoiled or treated harshly, how authority was exercised within domestic units, and to what extent the patterns varied among groups. Affective ties in the local family may very well have been less intense than those in its modern counterpart, even though it fulfilled broader functions. People in Aleppo lived often in large, fluid, and impermanent households, spread their family ties into the larger kin group, and entered marriage without the opportunity to establish romantic bonds with their spouses. Love and intimacy may have not figured in their conception of the family and its functions as much as practical considerations of survival, mutual care, and social advantage.

POVERTY AND CHARITY

THE SUPPORTS AND benefits provided by the family in Aleppo acted as an essential safety net, but without safeguarding all residents from want. There were some who knocked on doors and stretched their arms out for a coin or piece of bread, and others who died from hunger and malnutrition in times of famine. These people lacked the backing of family, or rather, of family equipped with the means to support them. They turned to the community for help.

The funds that went toward poor relief in Aleppo were limited, and could provide only for the immediate needs of the most destitute. No single welfare agency managed the distribution of this aid. The resources, which came almost entirely from private rather than government funds, were disbursed by countless almsgivers and by dozens of separate foundations organized within neighborhoods, trade guilds, and religious communities. This complex setup rested on voluntary charity, not mandatory redistribution; only the non-Muslim minorities resorted to communal taxation to finance poor relief.

The purposes, beneficiaries, mechanisms, and effects of poor relief in

Aleppo are best understood against the general milieu in which the system functioned. Several conditions determined its particular shape: the considerable extent of material deprivation; the current notions of poverty, charity, and social justice; the lack of government responsibility for the needy; the limited public resources available through voluntary contributions; and the solidarity of smaller groups. These features persisted throughout the century, and along with them the traditional patterns of poor relief.

Poverty, in the general sense of material want as judged by the current standards of the community, was not in itself a burning public issue. That multitudes of people lacked the means to afford adequate nutrition, housing, clothing, and other basic comforts was taken as a natural condition. The reigning ideology did not see it as the objective or duty of society to wipe out this structural poverty. Neither the Ottoman government nor the local leaders professed a sense of obligation to ensure a decent standard of living for the poor, and no pressure from below worked to push them toward greater responsibility. The lower classes demanded that the government redress specific material grievances, mostly in the areas of food and taxes, not that it strive toward socioeconomic equality and undertake a major redistribution of wealth in favor of the poorer segments of society.

Some sense of social responsibility, however, was shown toward those among the poor who could not support themselves and faced real danger or even death if left without assistance. This category of poor, whose numbers cannot be estimated with any precision, fluctuated in size according to the economic fortunes in the city. Its members included widows, orphans, the elderly, the sick, the blind, the crippled, the mentally retarded, and others without the capacity to provide for themselves. These dependent individuals, whom the community identified most immediately as the *fuqara'* (poor), were considered deserving of help by others when their families could not support them. It was to them that poor relief was directed, with the minimal intent of saving them from acute hardships.

The needy expected and received little help from government by way of poor relief. Of the immense patronage bestowed by the state only some crumbs reached them. For instance, over the years a few qadis who served in the city allocated small allowances from the court revenues for the support of needy individuals. The court registers for the entire third quarter of the century record only twelve such acts of generosity, each on the order of about two piastres a month. The beneficiaries included a retiring court clerk, a woman who undertook to raise a foundling, and poor individuals, some of them described as pious.[141]

Such welfare payments, born of individual whim rather than official obligation, did not amount to much. The real help to the poor came from the generosity and spirit of mutual aid within the urban community itself. The better-off donated to various public causes; their contributions were evident in the hundreds of mosques, churches, colleges, water fountains, and other public services that dotted the urban landscape, all of them founded and maintained by private philanthropy rather than the government treasury. This tradition of generosity, of which help to the poor formed an important element, was not totally unselfish. All religious communities harped endlessly on the duty and virtue of charity and sacrifice for the larger good, placing heavy moral pressure on the rich to give of their substance to the less fortunate. Donors were rewarded with public respect and good reputation; the practice of charity also promised to win them divine favor and improve their lot in the hereafter, thus serving as "a peculiar species of fire insurance."[142] Within the religious meaning attached to it, the issue of poor relief involved not only the material condition of the needy in this world but also the spiritual fate of the rest of society, especially the rich, in the next.

Most charity took the form of casual almsgiving and customary liberalities rather than payments through poor relief institutions. Poor men and women habitually knocked on private doors or approached people in the streets and markets. For many residents, putting a coin or piece of bread in their hands was an almost unthinking reflex. The begging poor relied on this as well as the special acts of charity expected by custom at certain times. On Fridays, when the Muslims celebrated the weekly communal worship, beggars lined the main streets to benefit from the generosity of the crowds headed for the mosques. On these days and on other religious occasions the well-to-do distributed food and money to the poor who gathered outside their homes. Marriage celebrations and death rituals were also accompanied by customary acts of charity to the poor.[143]

Begging was accepted as a legitimate means of survival for the poor. In times of famine and economic hardship many impoverished people were reduced to stretching out their hands. The community made no attempt to keep them off the streets; it had no houses of correction to lock up beggars or put them to work. Indeed, there was a guild of professional beggars *(shahhatin)* headed by a shaykh officially appointed in the shariᶜa court. Its members, who claimed to lead pious lives, roamed the city and countryside begging for alms. A professional code regulated their public conduct. In 1759, the headman of the guild complained in court against a group of beggars who annoyed the public with improper demands, and proceeded to appoint a supervisor to watch their behavior.[144]

While much of the almsgiving was random, some of the poor enjoyed the patronage of particular individuals, who undertook to support them with regular charitable allowances *(sadaqa)*. Such payments often extended over long periods, establishing a dependence which the beneficiaries proved reluctant to sever, some even taking their benefactors to court. In 1755 a number of Jews sued several of their wealthy coreligionists who had been subsidizing their poll tax payments for refusing to continue this voluntary arrangement. Two years later, one Ishaq ibn Yaᶜqub went so far as to sue three men who had supported his late father with an allowance of half a piastre a week because they would not extend the same generosity to him. A Christian who was receiving from a coreligionist 15 piastres as charity every two or three months was unhappy when his conversion to Islam brought an end to the payments.[145]

Almsgiving, in its casual and arranged forms, made up the core of poor relief in Aleppo. The many small payments and generosities accounted for much of the help available to the needy. They were supplemented by aid distributed through specialized institutions. The Muslims had almshouses attached to some of the mosques for the reception of pious men, as well as poor funds organized on a neighborhood basis. Both sources of aid were financed from endowments made by generous residents. The almshouses depended for their support on rental income from real estate donated by the founders or subsequent benefactors of mosques for the specific purpose of distributing food to the needy. The assets of the neighborhood charities consisted most commonly of endowed cash, supplemented on occasion by some real property. The administrators of these foundations lent out the cash, usually at an interest rate of about 10 percent, and used the proceeds as well as any income from rents to subsidize the share of the poorer residents in the collective neighborhood taxes and expenses.

How much aid the poor could expect from these local charitable foundations varied from neighborhood to neighborhood, but on the whole was quite limited. The foundations in the better-off quarters benefited from larger and more frequent donations than did the poorer districts. In the 1750s, the prestigious neighborhood of Suwayqat Hatim boasted the best-endowed foundation, with an annual income approaching 200 piastres. Its assets included over 900 piastres in cash as well as a bakery and two shops. In contrast, the low-income quarter of al-Hajjaj had a mere 15 piastres in annual income available for its poor residents. Operational costs, which included unpaid loans and expenditures on the repair of buildings, ate into the net income of the foundations. The waqf of Suwayqat Hatim, for instance, had to spend 1,217 piastres on the renovation of its properties in 1767.[146]

In the course of time residents added money and property to their neighborhood charities, but their voluntary donations, on which the foundations depended entirely, were too small and limited to raise this institutionalized poor relief above its rudimentary level. The endowment of property or money for aid to the poor was rather uncommon. Of the hundreds of charitable endowments made during the eighteenth century only a handful went to the poor.[147] The donors preferred to support houses of worship, public water fountains, schools, and other causes, often designating poor relief as a second or third choice; the poor were to benefit only after the mosque or other preferred cause had ceased to exist.[148]

The non-Muslims, especially the Jews, went a certain way to overcome the limits of voluntary charity. Like their Muslim neighbors, they gave alms and endowed property to support the poor, but at the same time also used communal authority to raise funds for collective ends, including poor relief. The four Christian communities each maintained a waqf endowed with real estate whose rental income went to cover the poll tax payments of the poorer members. In the middle decades of the century these foundations raised between them some 800 to 850 piastres a year, a sum that could subsidize the share of as many as 300 lower-income taxpayers.[149] When collective fines and impositions fell on the Christians, the wealthy families customarily shouldered the burden of their poorer neighbors. The communities also used for poor relief a portion of what they raised from dues as well as customary contributions made by members on the occasion of religious holidays, masses, weddings, and funerals. Some of the needy members received welfare allowances or leased endowed houses for little or no rent.[150]

The idea of a collectively organized system of poor relief drawing its resources from taxes rather than voluntary contributions alone took its most elaborate forms in the small Jewish community. The Jews maintained special funds that helped poor families with their burial expenses and with maintenance when breadwinning members fell sick. The money came from taxes collected regularly by the community, supplemented by donations. The power to tax gave the community not only considerable funds but also the ability to handle emergencies. During the plague of 1787, when some five hundred members perished, the community spent over a thousand piastres on poor relief, and in the midst of the crisis imposed an emergency tax to replenish the funds. The communal tax system assessed the share of each member according to his means, thus placing the main burden on the better-off.[51] Among the charitable activities organized on a collective level was the payment of subsidies to support the purchase of meat by poor families.[52]

Poor relief employing nonvoluntary means of redistribution appears as a feature specific to the non-Muslims, particularly the Jews. It was not found in the larger Muslim population, nor in the other important corporate units of society—the neighborhoods and guilds. Indeed, few guilds had even waqfs for the support of poor members. The hundreds of records and transactions involving charitable foundations make mention of only two waqfs established within trade guilds, both of minor size. One consisted of fifty-five copper plates which were rented out, the other of a sum that over a period of nine years yielded 290 piastres in interest.[53]

The different approach to poor relief among the Jews and Christians had its basis not only in their long tradition of tight communal organization but also in their sense of insecurity as minority groups. Experience taught them that conversion to Islam, the greatest threat to their collective self-preservation, was most likely to tempt the destitute, who in desperation might seek an escape from the financial burdens of dhimmi status. Under the circumstances it was hardly accidental that the socially weak groups, not the dominant community, invested most heavily in organized poor relief. They possessed the interest, the political will, and the social institutions needed to extend the boundaries of charity beyond the voluntary arrangements of the Muslim milieu.

These differences between groups add yet another layer to the evident complexity of Aleppo's system of poor relief. Within the same urban population coexisted various modalities of aid to the needy: private and public, casual and formal, voluntary and compulsory, direct and indirect. The aid itself took a range of forms, including money, food, and subsidies for housing, taxes, and meat. Seen against this elaborate system the actual amounts of aid appear rather unimpressive.

Sums on the order of a few piastres could not pull the recipients out of poverty, nor exercise in their aggregate any dramatic impact on the overall distribution of wealth. Yet their importance for the material welfare of poor individuals should not be underestimated. For those in dire straits even a piastre or two could provide a margin of security and make the difference between surviving and going under.

Within the context of its minimal ends, the local system of aid to the poor helped to keep a layer of the materially deprived afloat and to safeguard social peace. It was ill equipped, however, to handle the large-scale want created periodically by subsistence crises and economic slumps, which unsettled the normal balance between affluent and needy. The increases in charity could hardly meet the enormous problems of survival. People actually starved or took to stealing, which illustrates the ultimate limits of voluntary assistance. In times of crisis poor relief failed to meet even its already minimal aims of caring for the immediate needs of the most destitute.

The limited scale of poor relief reflected not so much the lack of resources in the community as the absence of the necessary commitment, both ideological and political, to a larger conception of social welfare. Beliefs in fairness and social responsibility toward the weak were clearly part of the cultural baggage of society; they found expression in various controls and sacrifices evident in market behavior, family relations, and charitable acts. Their objectives, however, were limited to modest amelioration left largely to families, communities, and guilds to achieve. While some redistribution in favor of needy members did take place within these units, only government was in a position to transfer wealth between income groups on a large scale. Such a course of action was precluded by the conservatism and narrow social concerns of the state. The propertied and influential segments of the community, who were allied with government, had both a vested interest in the existing order and the political means to perpetuate it. They showed generosity to their dependents and subordinates, but not because they recognized the structure of privilege which benefited them as manifestly unjust. Their conception of social justice took the current privileges and inequalities as natural aspects of their world.

CHAPTER 6

*The Mind: Religion, Learning,
and Popular Culture*

ONEY, POWER, AMBITION, exploitation, conflict—these surface again and again in the story of Aleppo's society. They
were indeed essential qualities of the place and time; but this
was also a community that paid much heed to spiritual matters and
religious expression, directed energies to learning and scholarship, and
made room for entertainment and worldly pleasures. These concerns
expose another face of the society, and lead into the inner core of the
culture in which local minds were shaped.

The Middle Eastern culture of which Aleppo was part formed a
composite of several elements, two of which—Islam and higher learning
—have drawn almost exclusive scholarly attention, and have hence
come to appear as the totality of the cultural scene, or at least that part
of it worthy of study. The label "Islamic," which is often applied to this
premodern culture, suggests explicitly that it had its basis in the faith
and doctrines of Islam. And indeed, religion along with high learning,
which was itself dominated by religious subjects, occupied a revered
place in Aleppo's culture. But for all their importance they did not
entirely mold the local mind. The townspeople lived in a community
rich with skills, knowledge, customs, tastes, beliefs, pleasures, and
aspirations that evolved outside the shadow of religion and were not
shaped by books. Neither highly educated nor even fluently literate,
most Aleppines were largely untouched by the erudition of written
texts. Alongside the literate tradition of the few thrived a vibrant oral
tradition that dominated the popular culture. Religion penetrated into

this milieu, but without wrapping everything in its spiritual cloak. Popular beliefs, secular scholarship, and worldly pleasures appeared alongside religion, and occasionally in a state of tension with it. Although no one stood up to challenge religion, the mainstream of society chose not to let it get too much in the way of fun and diversion. The culture had its built-in pull between incompatible desires, its daily maneuverings for a balance between the self and the community and between the spiritual and the worldly.

In this eclectic milieu the oral, the illiterate, the popular, and the nonreligious occupied an important place, and ought not to be dismissed or belittled in favor of the written, the literate, the high, and the religious. The various elements actually fed on each other, and tend to illuminate the culture best when seen as parts of a whole rather than as self-contained spheres. Education, for instance, cannot be understood just in terms of formal learning when much of what people knew and believed came neither from books nor from classroom instruction. Nor can the richness and diversity of the cultural scene be fully appreciated without attention to the important place of superstition, magic, food, dress, music, pastimes, and popular wisdom.

Variations in the cultural makeup of different groups added to this complexity. The townspeople were not formed of a uniform mental mold: some were naturally more literate, educated, well-traveled, pious, superstitious, or inclined to pleasurable pursuits than others. Customs, styles, and tastes varied somewhat with class, sex, and religion. Yet the common collective heritage and experience of the townspeople far outweighed these differences; a concord on essentials united all groups. The culture did show creativity and certain changes, but its basic features maintained a remarkable stability over the century. Penetrating more deeply into the spheres of religion, learning, and popular culture opens up several essential aspects of Aleppo's world: its categories of belief, knowledge, and cultural expression; the processes by which they were acquired and transmitted; the subcultural variations among groups and classes; the elements of innovation and creativity; and the underlying causes of the cultural stability.

RELIGION AND BELIEF

IN HIS ADOLESCENT years ʿAbdallah Qaraʾli was gripped by a profound desire to pursue the monastic life. His family was wealthy, respected, and well established in business, but pursuits of a different sort absorbed his young mind. He dreamed of a serene and pious existence in some remote monastery on Mount Lebanon, where he would follow the discipline of high devotion. His father, who sent him to European missionaries in the city for a rigorous Christian education, balked at this ascetic bent. "He feared that I would become ignorant of the affairs of the world," reminisced ʿAbdallah in his memoirs. He finally prevailed on his father to let him seek his own ways. In 1694, in his early twenties, he left Aleppo for Lebanon, where in the course of some years he set up a new and vigorous monastic order.[1]

Three years after ʿAbdallah's departure, a Melkite priest in the city lashed out at the sinful ways of his congregation. The members, he complained in his angry exposé, were guilty of numerous forbidden practices: they drank ʿaraq (an alcoholic spirit), took opium, smoked, played musical instruments, shaved their beards, put their trust in superstitious talismans, and exorcised evil spirits. His moral assault did not reduce the community to shame; if anything, it made the priest the butt of popular ridicule for his excesses. "It is hereby forbidden [*haram*] to eat the three daily meals, to drink water when thirsty, to rest and sleep, to go to bed without slippers, and to respond when asked a question," wrote a member of the congregation in sarcastic parody of his clergyman's exaggerated demands.[2]

The practical voice of Qaraʾli's father and the anticlerical retort of the Melkite wit echoed a general disposition to set limits on spiritual demands, to make room for needs other than the religious. A popular saying gave support to this same attitude: "Excess is obnoxious—even in religious worship."[3] Aleppines absorbed a strong dose of spirituality and a concern for the afterlife—but they were also very much preoccupied with this world. While some among them pursued a life of piety and insisted on the virtues of restraint, sobriety, and denunciation of pleasure, many others were inclined to good humor and a sense of fun and gaiety. Alongside the stern demands of orthodoxy thrived an easygoing mentality comfortable with superstitious practices and the pursuit of pleasure in measured, well-tempered ways.

In a society aspiring to a moral life guided by high religious precepts such inner tensions were normal; they ran through all the religious communities. Behind them was not an irreconcilable conflict between a religious orientation to life and a competing secular outlook. The debates revolved around the intensity of observance, not over the right to unbelief. No local or regional movement during the period challenged the core of religious beliefs or the central place of religion in society. The townspeople inherited a world in which religion was woven into laws, institutions, and daily practices. Their empire proclaimed itself an Islamic state committed to the cause of religion and the faithful. A religious code of laws governed behavior in many spheres of life. Clergymen officiated at weddings, funerals, and circumcisions, providing proper spiritual blessing for these important rites of passage. In the courts it was again men of religion who adjudicated disputes and handled notarial business. The religious establishment enjoyed official honors and public respect. Society looked up to its members as models of righteous conduct, and turned to them habitually for advice and support when faced with personal problems. Participation in prayer and ritual was taken for granted; over two hundred and fifty mosques scattered throughout the city opened their doors to worshippers.

In affirmation of the importance of religion, schools for young children were geared almost entirely toward religious instruction. In fact, no strictly secular institutions of learning functioned in the city. Muslim families sent their boys to the elementary Koranic schools (*maktabs*) to acquire a foundation in the faith. Sitting on the floor with other children, they recited the Koran, committing verse after verse to memory. Neither literacy nor a broad education nor even an understanding of the Koran's text were the desired ends of this instruction. What rudiments of reading, writing, and arithmetic were acquired in the process remained ancillary to the religious indoctrination. The maktab was seen primarily as the social instrument for breaking in a child, for teaching him the necessary virtues of godliness, discipline, and subordination that ought to guide him throughout adult life. The pupil completed his course of learning when he had memorized the Holy Book, and a merry public celebration announced his graduation to friends and neighbors. Christian and Jewish boys attended corresponding parochial schools which also focused on the rudiments of faith.

A few years of this elementary instruction formed the only formal schooling of most children. In the larger scheme of things this education was supplementary to the real training for life—acquiring practical skills and a profession. Most occupations required no literacy or higher learning, and life was too short and material burdens too heavy for most people to make the pursuit of studies beyond the elementary level an affordable luxury. The demands of survival and financial security thrust most children into the workplace early in life; what proportion of the local boys attended the religious instruction, how regularly, for what length of time, and with what result is unknown. The religious thrust of their training, however, mirrored the cultural priorities of the community: if effort, time, and money were to be expended on shaping the minds of children in a formal school setting they ought to go toward religious instruction before anything else.

That Aleppo's culture accorded a central place to religion was readily demonstrated in local education, law, official ideology, and social institutions. The individuals living in this society experienced religion as a feature built into their corporate and institutional structures. They also experienced it as something meaningful at the personal level. Religion came with a rich body of traditions and writings, elaborate rituals of worship and celebration, and a set of beliefs in God and the divine scheme for mankind. These elements shaped the mental and emotional makeup of individuals, colored their outlook and interpretation of events, and affected their social identity and behavior. In practice, there was no single type of religious experience that was characteristic of all: individuals varied in their knowledge of faith, the intensity of their religious observance, and the depth of their beliefs.

Only the professional men of religion and a small lay group boasted a solid familiarity with religious texts and traditions, having gone through varying stages of higher education. Some of them devoted their careers to studying, teaching and writing on religious subjects. Below this educated elite were some who in the course of their adult lives absorbed portions of religious lore, by reading books or attending study circles and lectures in a mosque, church, or synagogue. Many others, however, could claim little more than a bare familiarity with the rudiments of their faith. They lacked the necessary time, literacy, or inclination to participate in educational activities; questions of theology and scriptural interpretation were remote concerns.

For the majority, the religious experience tended to be expressed in acts of worship more than in intellectual reflection. They observed prayers, fasts, and other rituals as part of their normal routines. When the call to prayer echoed from the minarets during the day many Muslim shopkeepers and artisans performed their religious devotions in their place of work, and then casually resumed their mundane labors. Observance was deemed an unquestioned requirement binding on all; social pressure helped to enforce it. Such was the expectation of conformity that Jews who failed to attend the synagogue on the sabbath were assumed to be sick, and expected their friends to check on them soon after the morning service.[4] Religious holidays and celebrations, plentiful in all communities, were occasions that the townspeople actually relished. They afforded breaks from the routine and opportunities for jollification and socializing. People closed shop, dressed in their finest clothes, and paid visits to friends and relatives. A host of customary religious events, manufactured over the centuries to commemorate and show faith, provided them with welcome pretexts for outdoor picnics and group pilgrimages. The festive air was always at its height during the feasts surrounding Ramadan, with their happy celebrations, lively street fairs, and generally relaxed pace of living.

Even in this generally observant society people varied in their level of religious devotion. Some erred on the side of laxity, and suffered the reprimands of the court and their religious leaders. Others went to the other extreme, observing their religious worship in the strictest manner. Differences were evident even among the ulama. Some of them insisted on a life to extreme modesty and devotion; they ate little, spent their days in study and prayer, and denied themselves frivolities and comforts.[5] In the larger society, the more pious often supplemented the standard prayers, fasts, and rituals with additional devotional exercises, usually in the circles of religious fraternities. Many Muslims, but by no means all, met regularly in Sufi lodges to pray, study, and lose themselves in spiritual trances. A revered shaykh initiated them into the order and its mystic secrets, and guided them through the tortuous path toward unity with God. The ulama took active part in these mystical devotions, and even headed the lodges, many of which were branches of regional orders like the Naqshbandiyya, Sa'diyya, Rifa'iyya, and Qadiriyya.[6] Even these pious settings were not immune to immorality. Ibrahim ibn 'Umar, administrator of a Sufi lodge, turned the *dhikr* devotional rites into homosexual orgies. He also acted as pimp for his wife and other women. Outraged residents had him expelled from his neighborhood in 1768.[7]

Similar variations in the levels of observance were also evident among Christians. Laxity penetrated even their religious fraternities, which by their nature attracted men with a stronger religious bent. The group of Armenian celibates who founded a religious brotherhood in 1752 pledged to follow a strict social code consistent with pious living. The members were prohibited from sitting in coffeehouses, going out to the gardens on the outskirts, smoking or playing in the street, keeping disreputable company, or staying overnight in other homes without permission from the head of the brotherhood. Over the years many of the devoted young men who joined the fraternity broke these rules to pursue pleasurable activities current among their peers. The journal kept by the brotherhood recorded their sins and the disciplinary punishments administered to them. In a session held in 1772 the guide admonished some of the brothers for taking snuff and falling asleep during a sermon.[8]

All faiths considered certain elements of observance essential and mandatory, yet conservative and liberal viewpoints coexisted on these matters, offering people a certain leeway in the expression of their spiritual devotions. But unbelief, the conscious rejection of religion as a belief system, was not a recognized possibility, a legitimate cultural alternative. There may have been some skeptics and unbelievers who dared not say what they really thought, but judging from the overwhelming weight of religious expression, belief was meaningful for most individuals, even if in varying degrees. Those who studied religion, read works about it at their leisure, attended lectures, joined the devotions of brotherhoods, and led a life of observed piety clearly took religion seriously. It occupied their attention and time, touched their outlook and emotions, and affected their behavior.

Even for those who practiced their faith in moderation and engaged in little serious reflection the religious experience amounted to more than going through the motions of external ritual. The central premise of religious faith—that a divine authority existed beyond the self, with unmatched power to affect the personal fortunes and afterlives of all individuals—was part of the cultural baggage of this society, not as a philosophical abstraction but as a living belief residing in the minds of people and shaping their outlook and behavior. The residents were ready to detect the hand of God in everyday events. They interpreted plagues, earthquakes, and other disasters as acts of providence. Their religious leaders linked such adversities to the moral defects of the public; misfortune, they insisted, was the logical consequence of sin. The world was a moral order reflecting God's purposes, and was physically sensitive to the conduct of human beings. In times of difficulty people acted on these religious beliefs, turning to prayer, supplication, and fasting as routine ways for obtaining divine mercy.

The belief in divine providence helped to clarify the riddles of existence and indicate the path to ultimate salvation. But it was not quite sufficient in itself to explain or provide a defense against the hazards of a world that appeared uncertain and capricious. It formed only one layer of belief in a culture that harbored a rich arsenal of popular notions about the supernatural: people also believed in the work of fate, evil spirits, spells, and omens. They seriously feared that others driven by envy or malice would seek to harm them, and that even their evil wishes and intents could manufacture misfortunes. The power of these beliefs was evident in the host of magical means commonly used to ward off evil and predict the future. They carried horoscopic almanacs indicating fortunate and unfortunate days of the year, according to which they planned their daily activities. Talismans and amulets commonly served as shields against the evil eye; they accompanied their owners at all times. On the windows and doors of homes hung charms against mosquitoes and other pests. Sorcerers, geomancers, astrologers, and casters of spells practiced their trades throughout the city, providing their expert services to troubled customers.[9] One Rahma bint Yasin, who in 1757 fell out with her husband, turned to a practitioner of geomancy (*ʿilm al-ramal*) for help. He promised to use his spiritual powers to make her husband more affectionate toward her. Disappointed in his efforts, she finally sued in court, and recovered the substantial payments she had made to him.[10]

For favorable intervention on their behalf people also commonly turned to the dead. Dozens of tombs within the city and in the cemeteries on the outskirts were deemed holy sites, the abode of saints who enjoyed divine grace and could intercede on behalf of the living. People worshiped and pleaded for favors at those graves, some of which drew large annual pilgrimages of devotees. All sorts of legends and powers were associated with these saints. The residents of the quarter of al-Dudu, for instance, believed that an ailing pack animal would be cured if walked seven times around the local tomb of one al-Tirmidhi.[11]

These beliefs and practices formed part of popular religion. They were not culturally marginal or confined to the lower classes; well established, they thrived alongside orthodox religion. Indeed, the distinction between orthodox and popular religion was far from clear-cut in the public mind. Amulets cast their protective spell with the aid of religious verses, while the tombs of ulama, some of them within mosques, were the common sites of popular pleading. Some men of religion practiced divination; the alim ʿAbd al-Latif al-Rammal, for instance, supported himself by working as a geomancer.[12] Over the centuries Islam was stretched to accommodate and tolerate a variety of popular practices; the interpenetration blurred the boundaries between the two components of religion, which fed on each other.

The importance accorded to popular religion did tend to increase as one moved down the social scale, and from the urban to the rural population. It appears also to have been more prevalent among women than men. The popular practices were generally viewed as a field of female creativity and expertise, and the corpus of superstitions was even referred to in jest as "the women's book" *(daftar al-niswan)*. One saying paid humorous tribute to the magnitude of female superstitious lore: "The women's book was loaded on a camel, but it was not able to carry the burden."[13] The prominence of women in popular religion coincided with their subordinate role in orthodox religion, suggesting a basic difference in the cultural expectations of males and females. Women were expected to be God-fearing and moral, but were not sent to religious schools or assigned an active role in communal prayers and worship. Muslim women did not even attend the mosques. With their religious education and active participation in ritual restricted, women perhaps turned more readily to popular religion as a channel for spiritual expression.

POPULAR CULTURE

WITHIN SHORT WALKING distance of any neighborhood mosque stood a coffeehouse. In atmosphere and cultural pursuits the two places of assembly seemed worlds apart. Men chatting, playing backgammon, sipping hot coffee, and smoking water pipes filled the coffeehouses until the late hours of the night. A band of musicians entertained the crowd with popular songs and airs. At certain hours a storyteller occupied the stage, captivating the audience with adventurous tales; at others, a satirical puppet show excited laughter from the viewers. This worldly milieu of the coffeehouse, occupied by the very same people who filled the mosques at prayer time, presents one aspect of a popular culture with its particular pastimes, entertainments, indulgences, and mental escapes; its forms of cultural and artistic expression; and its lore of songs, plays, stories, jokes, and proverbial wisdom. These were variously refined and crude, light and serious, upper class and lower class, masculine and feminine. On the whole they had little to do with religion; indeed, moralists took a dim view of some of them. Nor did their absorption depend on literacy and high learning; the mass of the uneducated acquired and shared them without recourse to the written word. This largely oral culture was governed by a strong continuity over the period, but it also made room for creativity and responsiveness to changing conditions in society.

A rich fabric of cultural preoccupation and expression was woven around that most elemental of human needs: food. Food's availability and cost were matters of chronic apprehension; they were ever-present in routine conversation and affected the general mood. On another level, food figured in this culture as a pleasure, even an art, and was rich in symbolic meaning. One resident gave expression to these sentiments in a long poem praising the local cuisine and its delicious creations. Themes associated with food ran through the popular lore, expressing appreciation of good eating as well as a keen consciousness of the symbolic and vital aspects of food.[14] Eating was most immediately associated with home and family. The community had no restaurant culture; going out to eat was an unfamiliar practice. Food was also the cornerstone of hospitality and celebration, and guests were served food and refreshments as a matter of course. Lavish displays of food reflected the festive spirit in weddings and other parties; charity also commonly took the form of donations of food to the poor.

The local cuisine boasted a great variety of dishes and a rich blend of ingredients, and often involved elaborate preparation. The residents knew and used many kinds of meats, fruits, vegetables, legumes, grains, dairy products, spices, nuts, sauces, condiments, pastries, and drinks. Ninety-eight food items appeared on a list of controlled prices drawn up by the court during the famine of 1762.[15] The physician to the English merchant community, impressed with the culinary variety, compiled a list of 141 local dishes.[16] Many of them required experience and hours of work to prepare, especially since virtually everything had to be cooked from scratch. The art of cooking was a field of female expertise, with skills passed on from one generation of housewives to the next by oral transmission rather than written recipes and cookbooks. With some variations due largely to dietary laws, the same cuisine was shared by members of all religious communities. The tables of the poor reflected but faintly the elaborate setups characteristic of the comfortable homes, but the differences displayed variations in financial means more than in taste. In its general features the cuisine remained stable throughout the century. New dishes and drinks may have joined the corpus of favorite foods, but they did not signal any major shift in taste or in the place of food in the culture.

Clothing was another major preoccupation: a rich variety of fabrics, colors, headgear, jewelry, and cosmetics adorned local bodies. Fond of the bright and gaudy, the townspeople crowding the public places made a gay and colorful spectacle.[17] Because of its reflection on status and rank dress was the object of an almost obsessive attention. The style and color of the turban alone indicated anything from occupation and lineage to religion and tribal affiliation. Fine silks, furs, and jewels bespoke a high social position. Their cost placed them beyond the means of the poor, who had to make do with cheaper linens, costume jewelry, and even secondhand clothing bought in the market. A special pleasure was associated with one's appearance in new clothes. In the Muslim feasts surrounding Ramadan and on other special occasions there was customarily indulgence in new clothes, which were displayed to the congratulations and compliments of others. Items of clothing and pieces of fabric were common types of gifts exchanged even among the wealthy.

That clothing mattered was particularly evident in female circles. Women paid keen attention to dress, showed off their clothes, and even borrowed jewelry and dresses from friends to wear on special occasions. In order to display their wardrobes women came to wedding parties equipped with several changes of clothes.[18] Moralists complained about these feminine frivolities and excesses; the Christian clergy issued periodic regulations requiring greater modesty of dress and forbidding the borrowing of clothing or the wearing of perfume in public.[19] These sumptuary rules failed to suppress the pleasures associated with dress or the popular attention to the currents of fashion. Although the basic mode of dress remained unchanged until the spread of European clothing in the nineteenth century, colors, fabrics, and particular items did go in and out of fashion periodically. Both the upper and lower classes responded to the shifting trends, which often originated in Istanbul, Iran, and other parts of the region. Furs had a special appeal among men in the eighteenth century; some contemporaries saw in this and other bows to the dictates of fashion a sign of moral degeneracy.[20]

Some echoes of moral disapproval or official restriction accompanied many of the popular pleasures and pastimes of the day. They ran against the mainstream of a culture that accepted fun and diversion as legitimate activities with a recognized place alongside work and responsibility. A variety of pastimes and entertainments provided healthy antidotes to a life heavy with routine and mental pressures. The amusements of the period were largely of a sedentary sort: playing indoor games, socializing over a cup of coffee or a festive meal, and enjoying performances by professional artists. Sports and physical activity held no special attraction, and Aleppo was a city without public playgrounds, sports clubs, or athletic teams and competition. The popular entertainments also revolved heavily around company rather than solitary amusement and stimulation. There was not much that most people could do on their own to occupy their leisure hours in a stimulating way. Very few played musical instruments, and the habit of private reading was confined to a small segment of the population; there were, in any case, no newspapers, magazines, or books of general interest. In this largely oral culture, in which communication depended heavily on face-to-face contact, people felt the need to come together more often. Friendly company promised not only a welcome diversion but also an indispensable source of information. By talking to others one was sure to pick up some piece of news or gossip that could satisfy idle curiosity or prove useful. The sociability that characterized popular pastimes and entertainments was visible in indoor gatherings as well as in the routine assemblies of company in the orchards, bath houses, and coffeehouses.

Visiting with relatives and friends figured among the most common ways of passing time. People often invited guests to their homes, and spent hours chatting with them while eating, smoking, and drinking coffee. Chess, backgammon, and other popular games helped to occupy the time.[21] Some amused themselves with arithmetic riddles, of which a few examples appear in the handbook of a local resident.[22] Often people stayed with their friends overnight or even for several days. It was particularly common to send children for overnight visits at the homes of relatives or friends. Moralists disapproved of these forms of socializing for fear that they might result in illicit contacts between the sexes.[23]

On the occasion of weddings, circumcisions, and other happy celebrations social gatherings assumed a different order. Families threw big parties, opening their homes to multitudes of guests whom they treated to abundant food and entertainment. Musicians played popular songs, professional dancers performed their sensuous dances, and clowns amused the audience with their mimics and occasionally obscene humor. The women celebrated in separate quarters of the house, entertained by females. Their revelry tended to be noisier than the men's.[24] Nuptial festivities usually lasted several nights. Customs anchored in age-old traditions regulated these events; they changed little over the decades. Different classes acted out the customs in their own style. To the higher ranks, proud of their refined ways, the celebration of both familial and religious occasions by the masses appeared noisy and crude.[25]

The privately owned gardens and orchards on the outskirts of town were popular places to which people retreated to socialize and spend time in agreeable sloth. Muslims and non-Muslims celebrated various customary feasts there, turning each occasion into a lively picnic. In return for a fee the owners of the orchards allowed the visitors to spend the day in the cool shade of the trees. The better-off rented them for parties, often bringing musicians, dancers, and clowns for entertainment. Women were especially fond of these social outings, which gave them an opportunity for outdoor relaxation and freedom. Moral opinion, however, was reluctant to grant them unrestricted license. In the middle decades of the century excursions to the outskirts by women were prohibited by the authorities except on Mondays and Thursdays, and in times of unrest were prohibited altogether, to the great displeasure of the confined women.[26]

The public bath houses also doubled as places of amusement and socializing, again especially for women, and a rich lore of popular sayings and stories centered on this social institution.[27] During Ramadan, when people customarily went out at night to celebrate the holiday, the baths as well as the coffeehouses were kept open until the early hours of the morning to provide places of entertainment. Parties of women and children brought food and entertainers along with them to the baths, and spent the day socializing in the relaxed atmosphere, their excited voices reaching the streets. On happy domestic occasions the better-off families rented the bath houses for private parties for female relatives and friends. Wary of the excesses of such revelry, the Christian clergy issued periodic regulations prohibiting women from feasting in the baths.[28] The local historian al-Ghazzi, always attentive to the moral image of his city, counted the habit of spending too many idle hours in the baths among the deplorable traits of its inhabitants—especially the women, who went in at noon and did not emerge before sunset.[29]

The sociability that ran through the popular culture appeared perhaps at its best in the coffeehouses (*qahwas*), which served as the main gathering places for men. These brightly painted establishments, which ranged in size from modest rooms to handsome halls with water fountains spouting at their center, were found in every neighborhood. People could be seen in them at all hours of the day. After dark, when all businesses closed and streets emptied, the coffeehouses held out as the only spots of organized night life. Their clientele, drawn largely from the lower classes, flocked to them for companionship, relaxation, refreshment, and live entertainment.[30]

The free and relaxed atmosphere of the coffeehouses at this time betrayed little of the controversy that had accompanied their rise to popularity in the sixteenth century. Moralists had then condemned the spread of coffee drinking, and even more the emergence of the coffeehouse, an institution that they associated variously with impiety, lewdness, and indolence.[31] As late as the 1630s Sultan Murad launched an empirewide crusade against the coffeehouses in an effort to eradicate the habits of coffee drinking and smoking. The banned establishments remained closed for some years, until the furor gradually settled;[32] the battle against a popular institution which had taken deep root throughout the region had clearly been lost. In the eighteenth century the coffeehouses operated freely, with only periodic restrictions when behavior in them exceeded the bounds of legality. In 1764, for instance, the governor commanded that the coffeehouses be closed after sundown because of problems with wine drinking and prostitution. The order, apparently ineffective, was reissued three years later by another governor.[33] However, almost nothing was done to curtail the routine amusements and diversions associated with the coffeehouse—socializing, coffee drinking, smoking, music, the performance of plays, and story telling—despite the persisting misgivings of some about their morality and decency. The cultural importance of the coffeehouse rested on its unmatched status as the main public forum for these various activities, all of which figured also in other contexts and formed essential parts of contemporary culture.

No social occasion passed without the ritual coffee drinking and tobacco smoking, which were usually enjoyed simultaneously. Both coffee and tobacco were offered to any guest as a matter of routine hospitality, and were consumed upon waking up in the morning, after meals, during breaks in the day, in the course of social visits and business negotiations, while relaxing in the coffeehouse, and upon retiring at night. Both habits, acquired already in the early teens, were almost universal, shared by young and old, men and women, rich and poor. Those pious people who condemned them as vices failed to lessen their great popularity with the mainstream of society. No refreshment competed with coffee even in the summer months, when the townspeople continued to drink several cups of it a day, always hot and unsweetened. Vendors employed by the coffeehouses toured the streets and markets, selling the beverage to shopkeepers, artisans, and the general customer. Smoking filled many hours of the day with a stimulating diversion. To increase their pleasure, people experimented with various mixtures of tobaccos and types of pipes. In the middle decades of the century the better-off acquired a fancy for the fine Iranian water pipe (*kalyan*), which was more attractive, convenient, and expensive than the local variety (the *nargileh*). The taking of snuff also gained considerable popularity in the second part of the century.[34]

Smoking did not stop at innocuous amusement and diversion: by mixing drugs such as hashish with their tobacco, smokers took a recognized route to mental escape. While alcoholic drinks and opium were also known to be effective, their actual use remained relatively restricted and almost entirely hidden, due largely to powerful Muslim prohibitions and to limited availability.[35] Smoking tobacco mixed with intoxicating drugs, on the other hand, was widespread and open. People indulged in this pleasure in the coffeehouses, in their shops, and in other public places. Muslim religious opinion, which condemned the practice, aroused only sporadic and piecemeal official intervention against it. In 1762, for instance, an unidentified "group of Muslims" appealed to the qadi to outlaw the sale and public smoking of tobacco mixed with drugs because of its harmful moral and physical effects. The consumer of this tobacco, who smoked it with a water pipe in his shop or in a coffeehouse, lost his mental faculties and became so intoxicated that "he dropped unconscious and was only waked up and restored to health by pouring water on his head." The practice led to neglect of prayer and religious observance, and exposed passersby to offensive smoke. The concerned citizens came equipped with a legal opinion from the mufti supporting the prohibition of the sale and public smoking of the harmful tobacco. The qadi accommodated them by outlawing the smoking in public, but did not go so far as to prohibit the sale of the tobacco. At least for a period some effort was made to enforce the new restriction. Three months after the original proclamation the qadi punished several men caught smoking the intoxicating tobacco in public. On this occasion he also prohibited the coffeehouses from serving it to their customers.[36]

The coffeehouse helped to satisfy the desire for socializing, relaxation, and escape. In its capacity as a music club and theater it also provided performances that engaged the hearts and minds of the public. Of the various modes of artistic expression music aroused perhaps the deepest passions. Although conservative religious opinion frowned upon it as a profane pleasure, music delighted people of all classes. It highlighted every festivity and soothed the emotions. It drew people to the coffeehouses, where the finest bands played during many hours of the day. The wealthy kept personal performers, who played in their homes and lulled them to sleep with soft music.[37]

The local musical tradition, which enjoyed renown throughout the Middle East for its richness and erudition, included a vast repertoire of folk, popular, and art music geared to various tastes and occasions.[38] There were romantic, mournful, and jovial songs, and alongside them also a high classical tradition, based on lengthy modal improvisation, which expressed more controlled and reflective moods. The varied tones of stringed instruments, flutes, and percussion, played solo or in small ensembles, interpreted musical pieces and accompanied singing. The entire art, with its repertoire and technical skills, was passed on by oral transmission rather than formal study. The classical treatises analyzing musical theory were not accompanied by works on practice or, in the absence of a notation system, by written collections of the repertoire. In the culture of the period training in musical performance did not figure among the ingredients of good education. The professional performers came from the lower ranks of the community, although some men of standing and Sufi shaykhs did compose and play instruments for personal enjoyment and spiritual inspiration.[39]

Many new songs and musical pieces appeared on the local scene during the century, some imported from the wider region, others the creations of locals. As none of them was recorded on paper, it is impossible to determine to what extent they expressed new styles, reflected new sensibilities, or voiced popular responses to particular social and political developments. In any case, they remained untouched by Western influences; few residents ever had the opportunity to hear European music. The local musical tradition was shared by all groups; what particularisms rural migrants, women, the upper class, or the various religious communities brought to their music were outweighed by the common musical culture that united them. The better-off entertained their parties with the same popular bands that catered to the masses. Non-Muslims figured prominently among contemporary performers, appearing often in mixed ensembles. Even the liturgical melodies of all three communities rested on the same system of Arab modes or *maqams*, which also guided secular composition.[40] When Mahmud al-Rifaʿi (d. 1760) chanted the Muslim public call to prayer in his melodious voice, non-Muslims were among the enchanted listeners who crowded the nearby streets to hear him.[41]

Professional storytellers, who appeared regularly in the coffeehouses, took listeners into imaginary worlds of heroes and adventurers. They related their tales with drama and expression, often breaking off at a moment of great suspense in order to force the captive crowd to the coffeehouse the following day for the next installment. Like the readers of the Koran, the storytellers imparted elements of the literary culture to a largely illiterate audience. They drew their material from the repertoire of the *Arabian Nights* and medieval epics, on which they improvised creatively to produce interesting variations.[42]

A different tone was heard in the shadow plays (*khayal al-zill* or *karagoz*), which were performed to the delight of viewers in coffeehouses and at private parties. Light, bitingly satirical, and frequently obscene, they provided humorous commentary on the present rather than escapes into an imaginary past. One skilled puppeteer operated the figures on the stage, giving each its distinct voice and mannerisms. The stories centered around the character of Karagoz, an ordinary man whose mischief and experiences were rooted in the realities of the day. This crude form of theatrical art, which was popular throughout the Middle East and survived in Aleppo until the coming of the cinema in the 1930s, lent itself to a variety of cultural expressions. Some of the plays presented innocent, silly sketches, but they were also often character-ized by sexually explicit language and obscenities, except when the audience in a private party included women. Other sketches centered their plots around current events of general interest, with government corruption and scandalous behavior among the mighty coming under satirical attack. When the Janissaries returned in disgrace from the Russian campaign of 1768, Karagoz ridiculed their performance to great public applause. Such criticism had some effect on public opinion, and some even appealed to the authorities to prohibit the performers from introducing their characters on the stage.[43] The viewers took pleasure in watching their superiors humiliated on the stage, as they took pleasure also in the loose language, despite the objections of moralists.[44]

That moral opinion found fault with the plays and with so much else that gave pleasure and engaged the mind—elaborate dress, overnight visits, coffee drinking and coffeehouses, smoking, music, and outings by women—is not nearly as striking as the unrelenting vigor of the popular pursuits. In a world so suffused with religion they thrived as a largely autonomous segment of the local culture, and held out against the pressures of religion to gain ground at their expense. This popular culture was clearly not a marginal area of nonconformity nor a strictly lower-class region. It represented a set of attitudes, values, tastes, cus-toms, and practices shared, and considered legitimate, by the broad spectrum of groups and classes that made up the community.

Differences of class, religion, and sex made for some variations in the way in which different groups participated in this culture, but did not alter the fact of their participation in it. The upper-class families in-dulged in fine cuisine, attention to dress, various entertainments and other worldly pursuits, even if with a style and emphasis of their own. While their men did not visit the coffeehouses, they enjoyed at home the performances of musicians, clowns, storytellers, and dancers, who were often maintained as part of their households.[45] Like the rest of the community, they too were entertained by professional performers who came invariably from the poorer classes, enjoyed low occupational status, and performed much the same artistic material regardless of their audience. Women took part in the popular culture not less than men. The segregation of the sexes, the restrictions placed on women, and the general differences in social roles fostered some variations in the cultural milieus of men and women, but not two different cultural worlds. The three religious communities also displayed some distinctions of custom and taste, but again within a common cultural setting.

The popular pursuits of Aleppines reveal an appreciation of the comic, the satirical, the sensual, the adventurous, the romantic, the rhythmic, the intoxicating, and the aesthetic. The performers and artists, themselves, are an unknown lot; nor was written record kept of the contents of their songs, plays, jokes, stories, and musical pieces, so that the precise ideas and feelings, the changes of taste and fashion, and the creative spirit that infused the popular culture are inaccessible. Only one component of the popular lore—proverbial wisdom—was committed to paper. Encapsulated in thousands of sayings, maxims, proverbs, aphorisms, and stories, it gave practical advice on everything from dealing with one's mother-in-law to the dangers of laziness. People heard and repeated this lore at appropriate moments as part of routine speech. With the aid of memorable rhymes in the local colloquial, it explained, warned, moralized, and condemned. Some of the imagery was colorful and unabashed: "You can't fry eggs just by farting"; "Shit on us, neighbors, we're going to the bath house tomorrow anyway"; "If you don't shit on someone who pisses on you he will claim that you have no bottom."[46]

A strong strain of social realism ran through popular wisdom: life is neither easy nor fair; humans are by nature self-seeking; the poor and weak have the worst of it; and quick wit and shrewdness are necessary to protect one's interests. Along with some stress on faith and trust in God the advice included a heavy emphasis on self-help: be on guard to prevent being exploited, cheated, and robbed; and be ready to respond and defend yourself when threatened.[47] The world as it is, not as it ought to be, inspired this lore; like religious beliefs and norms, it formed part of the contemporary manual for living. Both cultural categories resided in the mind, probably without clear-cut distinction. In the personal handbook of one local resident over six hundred sayings, including many crude ones, appear comfortably sandwiched between pious poems composed in the high literary Arabic style.[48]

The messages and symbols of popular culture, like those of religion, required neither literacy nor higher learning, but were passed on from generation to generation by oral means, and reached all levels of society. In the extent and manner of their diffusion they differed from high learning, which throughout the period was confined to a narrow, literate segment of the population.

LITERACY AND HIGHER LEARNING

ALEPPINES INHERITED A massive body of writing from their intellectual predecessors. texts on religion, medicine, philosophy, language, history, geography, and a host of other fields. But this legacy was felt in only a limited and uneven way by most Aleppines, as only a narrow segment of the population commanded the skills of literacy and had access to or interest in an education broader than the elementary religious instruction, and fewer still participated in the act of serious writing.

The relatively small minority of the literate varied widely in their linguistic skills. A few boasted a true mastery of literary skills, which in some instances extended to a knowledge of Turkish and Persian as well as Arabic. At a level below them were the scribes, clerks, accountants, and others whose professions called for solid linguistic proficiency. Many others in various walks of life possessed elementary skills in reading, writing, and calculating, used mostly as working tools in daily activities. A majority of the men and almost the entire population of women remained outside the ranks of the functionally literate; others read and wrote for them. This condition of restricted literacy remained a consistent feature of the community throughout the century. Elementary education was not reformed to lay heavier stress on literacy, nor did new conditions emerge that rendered literacy indispensable or even more attractive to the larger public.

In practice, only a portion of the literate became members of a book-reading public. Books did not penetrate deeply into people's lives, and only in part because of restricted literacy. Both their availability and contents severely limited their cultural impact. Copied and illustrated by hand, the books were expensive and scarce. Only the better-off families and those with a long tradition of learning owned sizable collections, some of them containing several thousand volumes, acquired by purchase or by copying of extant manuscripts. They jealously guarded their treasured texts, and often refused to lend them out. In the middle years of the century some people of means driven by a desire to build private libraries were able to outbid scholars and to inflate the price of manuscripts offered for sale in public auctions.[49] The only institutions that resembled public libraries were the book collections, usually the gifts of generous donors, of colleges, mosques, and churches. The largest of these libraries, in the Ahmadiyya College founded in 1752, held only some three thousand volumes, donated from the personal collection of its founder, Ahmad Effendi Taha Zadeh. Readers could consult these texts only on the premises during four days of the week; yet despite this and similar restrictions imposed by other institutions, many books were stolen and lost over the years.[50]

The kind of information available in contemporary books was not, in any case, of particularly wide appeal. Most of the works were of a specialized nature and directed at narrow readerships. Texts on Koranic commentary, jurisprudence, theology, philosophy, religious traditions, grammar, medicine, musical theory, biographies, poetry, or history could have had no mass audience even if literacy had been more widespread. Fiction, light literature, and reference works designed to entertain and inform the wider public were virtually nonexistent. And the language itself barred easy access to the available books: the literary Arabic was too removed from the spoken dialect to be readily understood by readers without considerable linguistic training.

Literacy and the habit of private reading would probably have been more attractive if there had been interesting written material, including newspapers and magazines, readily available at an affordable price. In this respect the official refusal to permit printing did much to abort both the spread of literacy and the development of the written culture. A religious ban on printing in Arabic by Muslims, enforced by the Ottoman authorities, was in effect in the region throughout most of the century. In 1706 several Christians set up in Aleppo the first Arabic press in the Middle East. It published a few texts of a strictly religious nature before closing down. The experiment was continued by Christian clergymen in Lebanon, on the same limited and parochial scale.[51]

The absence of printing not only kept books costly and scarce but also helped preserve traditional monopolies on knowledge and authorship and limited the dissemination of both information and works of imagination. Authors continued to write specialized works for small audiences and to depend for their livelihood on patrons rather than on a large reading public. The masses for their part continued to see written literature as having little direct relevance to their lives. Within their largely oral culture they were able to obtain most knowledge, skills, and news without much recourse to the written word. Oral transmission, not books and classrooms, shaped their stock of knowledge, or what amounted, in a real sense, to their education. They learned from parents, peers, elders, religious leaders, and masters. From them they absorbed what they knew about artisanal skills, business practices, cooking, child rearing, money, home cures, weather, and a multitude of other matters. They listened, watched, imitated, and occasionally improvised. Even the literate worked within this oral culture rather than in some autonomous milieu of their own organized mainly around written communication.

Yet despite the restricted literacy the larger public was not entirely isolated from the written word. Writing was essential in some respects to the workings of the social order. Orthodox religion rested on the written word. Texts, not human memory, were the recognized authorities on religious laws and traditions. The ulama saw themselves as the carriers and transmitters of texts rather than as human substitutes for them. The faithful, including the mass of illiterates, shared in the reverence for the written scriptures and holy books as the ultimate anchors of the divine message. Government administration also relied heavily on writing for its record keeping and correspondence; like the religious establishment the state nourished the demand for men with literary skills. The use of written documents was widespread in the public at large. Marriage contracts, title deeds to homes and property, leases, letters of appointment to public positions, partnership agreements, credit notes, divorce settlements, letters of tax exemption, and records of court verdicts were normal personal papers in the possession of people in all classes. The illiterate as well as the literate took care to keep written and signed records in matters involving important rights and obligations.

Such daily contact with the written word did not extend into widespread public exposure to the higher learning embodied in the texts. Some bits and pieces of the written literature did filter down orally to the illiterate, by way of lectures, public readings, and story telling. But high learning remained the preserve of a few: from the larger public, heavily illiterate, the circle narrowed to the limited pool of the literate, which in turn narrowed to the small nucleus of the learned. This educated element was a mixed group composed of lay people as well as professional men of religion. Its members displayed varying levels of learning and intellectual ability, but tended to share a common core of knowledge and a similar world view. Although some ventured into strictly secular fields of learning, the nonreligious subjects were on the whole in a rather neglected state. Few men in the city could speak with much certainty about physics, chemistry, or mathematics; even history, geography, and philosophy received rather superficial attention. The contemporary curriculum of higher education provided a limited diet tailored mostly to the training and tastes of ulama. Arabic and various fields of Islamic studies, which boasted a formidable classical literature, were its main ingredients. In keeping with the cultural priorities of the community higher education was geared primarily to training professional men of religion who would lead the prayers, preach in the mosques, run the shariʿa courts, instruct the younger generation, and do scholarly work on Islam. This general orientation, and the processes by which learning was acquired and transmitted, defined the meaning of education in Aleppo and shaped the thought of the local intelligentsia.

The process of higher education followed an inherited pattern which underwent no major modification during the century. Students worked in classes offered in the colleges (*madrasas*) or by way of individual tutorials with scholars; those serious about their education traveled to study with experts in other centers of learning, notably Cairo, Istanbul, Damascus, and Mecca. Some thirty-one colleges existed in the city in the middle years of the century. The impressive number says little about the actual vigor of local education. Most of the schools were modest establishments with a staff of one or two teachers and a handful of students; from lack of funds or proper direction some were forced to close their doors or to operate mostly as places of worship rather than learning. Their annual financial accounts as audited by the court reveal their limited budgets and educational services.[52] A few schools equipped with better financing and reputations were able to attract good teachers and to provide scholarships as well as boarding to students. Two new colleges of an impressive order—the ʿUthmaniyya and Ahmadiyya—joined the ranks of local schools in the eighteenth century. Their emergence was not necessarily a reflection of a growing demand for higher education. These as well as other schools were founded by private philanthropists often driven by interests not necessarily pedagogic, such as perpetuating the donor's name, winning social standing and divine grace, and providing sources of income for their descendants.

One's teachers mattered much more at the time than the institution in which one studied. The age had its known experts in different fields, many of whom taught on a private basis; winning access to their circles was the ambition of aspiring students. Contemporary biographers, always attentive to the training of learned men, sketched the academic credentials of their subjects by listing the teachers with whom they worked. How a man fit into the chain of transmission was thought to affect the quality of his education, and certainly shaped his public reputation. A traditional learning strategy guided the acquisition of knowledge: under the guidance of teachers students worked their way through each classical text with the purpose of understanding and absorbing its knowledge. Criticizing or questioning the work lay outside the scope of proper learning. Even at this level students and teachers resorted frequently to memorization as a learning tool; some scholars impressed their fellow men by reciting whole texts from memory. Once a student demonstrated his comprehension of a text his teacher conferred on him a certificate *(ijaza)* attesting to his mastery and entitling him to transmit the work to others. A certificate from a distinguished scholar covering a host of works was a source of pride for its owner and was useful as letter of recommendation.

Hundreds went through this educational process in the course of the century, the majority of them men who ended up in the religious establishment in various capacities. Many of them obtained an adequate foundation of knowledge and then proceeded to careers as mosque functionaries or court clerks. A lesser number who were endowed with an intellectual bent devoted their lives to study, teaching, and writing. The biographies of the most distinguished ulama reveal a common core of learning which underwent no change in the course of the period. All studied the Koran, Koranic commentary *(tafsir)*, Islamic traditions *(hadith)*, jurisprudence *(fiqh)*, and literary Arabic. Mastery of these fields, each with its subcategories and array of classical texts, required many years of work. To this standard curriculum some students added more specialized areas of religious study such as Sufi mystical thought *(tasawwuf)*, the techniques of dividing estates among heirs *('ilm al-farā'id)*, and the techniques of determining the precise hours at which prayer should take place *('ilm al-miqat)*.[53]

A certain unknown number of lay people also acquired a measure of higher education, but did not constitute an educated class clearly distinct from the ulama in learning and modes of thought. The two elements overlapped in academic background, scholarly interests, and social connections. The physicians, astrologers, scribes, poets, and various lay men of good breeding who boasted an education were tutored mostly by ulama, and in accordance with the reigning conceptions of good education received substantial training in religious subjects. ʿAbdallah Agha Ibn Miru (d. 1770), a member of a merchant family who distinguished himself by writing a local chronicle, studied Islamic law and tradition as part of his education. The physician Mustafa ibn Mansur, who learned the medical profession from his father, also studied with ulama, and in the course of his career gave lessons to ulama in the arithmetic techniques of calculating prayer times. ʿAbdallah al-Yusufi, an accomplished poet, studied with his father and went through a solid course of study in religious and linguistic fields with distinguished ulama. He worked as a seller of coffee beans in the market, but for a period was called to substitute as a preacher in a mosque. At the same time, men within the religious establishment engaged in nonreligious pursuits. ʿAbd al-Rahman Effendi ibn Muhammad Effendi, who served as a preacher, leader of prayer, and muezzin, also treated patients in a local hospital. Ahmad al-Khallasi was both a religious preacher and a medical doctor.[54] Personal interest led a few ulama to the study of nonreligious fields such as astronomy, geometry, chemistry, genealogy, and history.[55] But there was no lay academic community of specialists in these or other secular fields who saw themselves as distinct in methodology and orientation from religious scholars. In the absence of a strictly secular curriculum and academic specialization a gap did not emerge between scientific and religious learning.

The learned circle of the day was almost entirely a men's club. Women attended neither the colleges nor even the Koranic schools. Feminine occupations did not demand literacy or higher learning. Maryam bint Muhammad al-ʿAqqad (d. ca. 1805) was the only woman of the century to have occasioned a biographical notice for her learning: working with her father and local ulama, she acquired a knowledge in Islamic studies that impressed her contemporaries.[56] Some women of good breeding, who were usually given a basic education through hired tutors, may have ventured into further reading and study; their environment, however, was hardly supportive of women's education.

The educated took pride in learning, relished popular respect for their knowledge, collected books, read, and occasionally tried their hand at writing, some of them with accomplishment. Poetry and books circulated among them, and groups assembled to discuss and study. The community of learning brought even Muslims and Christians into the same circles. The educated kept notebooks (*majmuʿa*, pl. *majamiʿ*) in which they assembled a miscellany of papers and writings: poems, quotations, sayings, historical notes, genealogies, biographies, and educational certificates.[57] The children raised in this more learned milieu acquired from early age a comfortable attitude toward books and reading. The wealthy gave social recognition to scholarship by supporting scholars with allowances and providing them with homes and even wives.

Yet Aleppo's educated men were not part of an intellectual world drawn to new frontiers and experiences. Education dipped them in a stable pool of knowledge undisturbed by great waves of exploration, discovery, or doubt. It instilled in them a reverential sense of an established order within which they must take their place and whose values they must preserve. Their approach to learning took past attitudes as the starting point of correct reasoning: heeding the sure voices of the past and emulating them were the paths to wisdom. They did not claim greater wisdom than earlier generations nor did they place a premium on innovation. In the course of the century they and their counterparts in the larger region produced a large body of writings; it attested to creativity, but little innovation. Their real cultural accomplishment lay more in keeping alive the inherited learning than in contributing something new to it. Religion, the Arabic language, and poetry dominated their literary output while other fields, notably the natural and social sciences, received at best marginal attention. The areas on which they chose to reflect and write, their level of creativity, and the relation of their writings to the existing learning are revealing not only about the consciousness of the educated class, but also, in a broader way, about the priorities and self-imposed limits of Aleppo's cultural world.

The numerous writings on Islam—the area of leading scholarly interest—did not redefine the role of religion or set new directions for its development. They added more drops to the laden bucket of traditional works. Now into its second millennium, Islam was settled into an intellectually conservative attitude, its path already charted and its traditions codified. Some religious scholars produced their commentaries on the classical commentaries, published their legal opinions, and wrote essays on spiritual and moral questions. Whether combs manufactured from tortoise shells were permissible was a theme pursued in a piece composed by ʿAbd al-Jawwad al-Kayyali (d. 1778). Very few ventured into the heavier fields of theology and philosophy.

Religious subjects dominated Christian and Jewish writings as well. Catholic priests trained in Western languages began to translate European scriptural commentaries and other religious works into Arabic. The bitter schisms in the wake of conversion to Catholicism nourished,

in addition, a new output of polemical literature which had no counterpart in the other faiths.[58] Jewish writings also remained bound by
traditional religious concerns. In the Jewish community collections of
legal opinions (responsa) and scriptural commentaries written by local
rabbis formed the exclusive published output during the period. Some
of these works were issued in print by Hebrew presses in Livorno and
Istanbul.[59]

After religion it was language and literary expression that attracted
writers. The period had its linguistic experts who mastered Arabic
syntax, grammar, and rhetoric; most of them were ulama. Their attention to language preserved the traditional art of flowery and formal
expression which was the hallmark of conspicuous erudition. Poetry,
governed by an obsessive attention to rhyme and meter, offered the best
medium for personal expression and the display of linguistic abilities.
The hundreds of poems composed and circulated by local men covered
many themes: praise of learning and piety, congratulations to friends
and officials, and description of earthquakes and political events. Some
poems gave expression to the personal emotions of writers disturbed by
impoverishment, misfortune, or grief over the premature death of their
children; against the cruelties of life they advised refuge in God. Several
Christians joined the circle of accomplished Muslim poets, indulging in
an art whose mastery had previously eluded Christian writers.[60]

Poetry was virtually the only literary medium that expressed personal
sensibilities and agonies. Works of introspection and individuality such
as autobiographies, diaries, and memoirs were otherwise strikingly rare.
The attenuated individualism in contemporary culture may have stifled
such excessive attentions to the self. Educated men felt particularly
disposed to suppress individual whims and to display conformity to
communal models. They saw themselves as links in a long chain of
learning, and took pleasure in modeling themselves after virtuous figures. The individual was worthy of glorification when he displayed
society's ideal qualities, not just by virtue of being himself. Following
an old literary tradition, contemporaries wrote and collected biographical notices *(tarajim)*, but with an eye not so much to the individuality of
the subjects as to the virtue they represented. Ulama were characteristi-
cally the largest single group about whom biographical notices were
written. The accounts of them as well as of virtuous lay figures stressed
their piety, learning, and communal devotion, holding them up as
examples for others to follow.

The moralistic orientation of the biographies placed them in part within the sphere of the religious literature. Because their subjects made distinguished contributions to the community and shaped events, the contemporary culture conceived of the biographies also as part of another field: history *(ta'rikh)*. Immersed in old texts and past traditions, the educated absorbed a certain regard for the collective memory of the past and its preservation. Yet their respect for the venerable discipline of history was not matched by prolific writing. A few of them left behind chronicles that recorded local events as they observed them, but no known text devoted to reconstructing aspects of past history. Their urge to keep a record of events, in the form of occasional notes jotted down in personal handbooks or as regularly maintained journals, was channeled primarily into what they considered the real stuff of history: the dramas of power and politics. They tended to cast their gaze at the lower levels of society only in periods of popular revolt, famine, plague, or other major crises.

The interplay of different subjects of concern in local historical writing appears in vivid ways in the chronicle of Yusuf al-Halabi (d. 1806), who kept a detailed record of local happenings during the eventful years of 1771–1805. The author began his narrative with straight political history, jotting in the margins occasional observations about irregular weather, or about births, marriages, and deaths in families he knew. With the approach of the famine and plague of 1786–1787 he became increasingly preoccupied with these unsettling developments, gradually filling the margins all around the political narrative with information on food prices and the progress of the pestilence. And then, as if submitting to the dictate of those events that seemed to matter most, he shifted the account of the famine and plague into the main text, delving in detail into the turmoil and popular misery he witnessed. For a short spell political history gave way to social history.[61]

While history attracted some reflection, the physical and natural sciences were almost completely neglected. There were no scientists who carried out serious theoretical or empirical research in physics, chemistry, biology, or botany. The community remained bound by a limited understanding of nature and the environment. Faith in progress, in the human potential to control nature and bring about an improvement in conditions, was not part of its cultural environment. Only medicine occasioned some written studies. Several local doctors composed works on medical subjects, including the treatment of eye diseases, the benefits of certain fruits, the responsibility of the physician to his patient, and various ailments and bodily conditions. If the empirical knowledge acquired by contemporaries contributed to the ancient and medieval learning that still guided medicine, it certainly failed to deliver society from its many health problems. Ibrahim al-Hakim, a prominent local doctor, was prompted to complain in a poem about the helpless and thankless nature of his profession.[62]

This was not an age of scientific breakthroughs, technological innovations, new visions, or major shifts in the world of thought and belief. Traditional interests and approaches maintained their hold over high learning. This stability was reinforced by the city's contacts with the outside, which are essential in general for understanding the dynamics of the culture and aspects of the local mindset.

MENTAL HORIZONS
AND OUTSIDE INFLUENCES

THE MENTAL HORIZONS of many in Aleppo were limited not only by the lack of literacy and formal education but also by restricted contact and familiarity with the outside. That the city was cosmopolitan by contemporary standards, that economic interests and administrative tasks linked it to the outside, that it meshed with the population of its region and shared the common traits of Middle Eastern culture, that its fortunes were shaped so profoundly by external developments—none of these say much about the place of the wider world in the minds of Aleppo's residents. Most of them actually saw little of the world and were poorly informed about external affairs. They tended to be provincial in outlook, their minds shaped most heavily by local experiences. Wider horizons were more common among those who had professional and economic interests abroad, traveled extensively, corresponded, read, and studied. Only some relatively small groups drawn largely from the upper ranges of the community developed that level of contact with the outside.

Men involved in the business of long-distance trade were accustomed to thinking in broad geographical terms. Information on markets, roads, currencies, political conditions, taxes, tastes, and competitors in distant areas was crucial to their success. An extensive correspondence with agents and partners helped them plan their enterprises. Through contacts abroad the local silk merchants were able to learn fairly soon about the rise of silk prices in London, then more than two months of travel away; the English traders in the city were often frustrated in their hopes of quietly turning to advantage such favorable economic trends in their home country.[63] The familiarity of the local merchants with the outside world came above all from first-hand observation. The Frenchman Volney was impressed to find that even the wealthiest merchants in Syria spent a good part of their lives on the road. "Traveling is their education, their science," he exclaimed.[64] The commercial ventures that made Musa Agha al-Amiri and his cousin ʿAbd al-Qadir fabulously rich took them on travels all the way to India. Qasim al-Khani spent ten years on the move between Iraq, Mecca, and Istanbul before he grew restless and traded his business for a life of religious study.[65]

Something of the merchant's worldly exposure and network of affiliations was shared by some of the more prominent ulama, whose professional lives dictated a nomadic schedule and extensive external contacts. Almost all of them spent part of their careers abroad. Their student days initiated them into a routine of travel. They moved about the region to sit at the feet of learned teachers, men who were dispersed in many localities and often on the move themselves. Mecca and Istanbul, Cairo and Damascus were among the common stations in the peripatetic system of higher education in which they were trained. After the completion of their studies they continued to venture abroad in order to lecture, to attend master classes, to confer with colleagues, to acquire books, to seek employment, and to cultivate patrons. Their friendships and professional ties brought them together with colleagues. On his visit to Aleppo in 1791 the distinguished Damascene scholar Muhammad Khalil al-Muradi befriended many of the local ulama, and spent many days of study and conversation with them.[66] Mustafa al-Jabiri and his son ʿAbdallah, members of an Aleppine family known for its learning, had stayed in his home when they visited Damascus in 1770 and again ten years later.[67] The ulama also maintained a correspondence with colleagues elsewhere, exchanging letters and poetry as well as scholarly material. The death of respected figures occasioned poems of eulogy from students and colleagues throughout the region.[68]

Most of Aleppo's townspeople were not, like the merchants and ulama, thrust into the world beyond the metropolis. Their training, work opportunities, and professional lives confined their daily pursuits to the city. Less educated and less widely connected, they lived in a much more closed world. Only a relative few had traveled extensively. Most people ventured on trips abroad only infrequently, and seldom beyond the confines of the Middle East. The religious pilgrimage to Mecca and Medina was apt to rank as the most extensive and memorable journey of one's lifetime. In a metropolis where almost every desirable good, service, and vocational training was right at hand the need to travel was limited. More important, traveling was not deemed a pleasurable and entertaining pastime. Too many difficulties, perils, and expenses quelled the urge to make long excursions out of town.

A trip even within the region qualified as an adventure of sorts; it was a slow, strenuous, costly, and occasionally dangerous affair. Travelers had to manage without wheeled vehicles, spending hours on the back of a horse, mule, or camel. There were no paved roads but rather tracks that had been trodden into hard paths by countless generations of beasts of burden. The neglected condition of the roads became fully evident in the rainy season, when many parts became virtually impassable.[69] Brigands and hostile tribesmen rendered some routes unsafe, forcing travelers to resort to circuitous paths or risk being stripped bare. And the distances seemed immense. Unless he was equipped with a fast horse—a luxury reserved for official couriers and the more wealthy— the traveler could not normally expect to cover more than twenty to thirty miles a day. Even a visit to Damascus was a major enterprise, requiring about seven days on the road, and two or three extra days for rest. Travelers who returned safely from a long journey deserved the congratulations and parties that customarily awaited them at home.

Without the benefit of frequent firsthand observation most Aleppines acquired their familiarity with the outside indirectly, primarily by way of oral communication. Neither the elementary schools nor the religious colleges did much to acquaint students with the affairs of the world. Written media played no important part in diffusing news and information to the public, and illiteracy set limits on the practice of regular correspondence with acquaintances outside. Information filtered into the city with the constant traffic of visitors: villagers and nomads came to trade and settle official business, bringing with them news from the countryside, while merchants from cities in Iraq, Anatolia, and Syria were common visitors. The city's location at the intersection of important routes drew to it also numerous transit passengers who stopped temporarily to rest and make preparations for the continuation of their journeys. Among them were government officials, couriers, merchants, troops, European travelers, and Muslim pilgrims headed for Mecca.[70]

The modes of communication as well as travel conditions in the region did not undergo any major changes in the eighteenth century. Exposure to the outside and familiarity with it remained limited; even among the best traveled and educated these seldom extended far beyond the Middle East. Europe was distant and almost entirely unknown at first hand even in this major center of East-West trade. Only a few odd men—Christian and Jewish merchants who visited some European cities on business and Catholic clergymen who studied in Rome—had had some glimpse of the Western world. And only a handful of non-Muslims mastered any European languages to read writings from the West. But without visiting Europe or acquiring its ideas and ways the local Christians who converted to Catholicism or came under European consular protection developed a new consciousness of the West. Their contacts with the few European missionaries and merchants in their midst stretched their horizons to a world beyond the Ottoman Empire, a world now brought closer by new affinities and hopes. But even they acquired little more than a superficial familiarity with Western society and culture.

With their external contacts confined by and large to the Middle East, the townspeople were exposed mainly to the trends and influences of a region with a stable culture similar to their own. Those residents who traveled in the region, heard news of its affairs, studied with ulama elsewhere, read books by contemporaries, and conversed with fellow Middle Easterners were not apt to absorb ideas and impressions that challenged their basic outlook on things. The wider cultural milieu of which their city was part acted as a cushion that actually reinforced the basic premises of their culture. Developments and innovations did occur in the region, but they were limited to certain aspects of the culture and touched some groups more than others. New Middle Eastern fashions and tastes found at least some segments of Aleppo's population receptive. The upper-class families were attentive to trends among their peers in other great cities, primarily in the imperial capital. They indulged in the affectations of a life-style of ever-changing dictates, and as models of good taste they inspired imitation by groups lower down on the social scale. In a more general way, some of the clothes, food, songs, music, plays, stories, games, and pastimes that captivated the townspeople at the time were probably imported in the course of contacts with other localities in the region.

The Middle Eastern imports did not alter the essential aspects of local culture. Their limited and selective influence is well illustrated by the city's architecture, which absorbed some innovations without altering its basic forms. Mosques, colleges, and other structures of monumental nature adopted the Ottoman minaret and some decorative styles current in Istanbul. These were integrated into the local traditions of architecture, which continued to predominate. Out of more than a hundred surviving Ottoman monuments only four were built in the Ottoman imperial style, the last of them in the eighteenth century ('Uthmaniyya College). In domestic architecture the basic form and conception of the traditional courtyard house withstood change. Only the great residences of the rich adopted an ornate stone decoration which originated in Istanbul and bore touches of European influence.[71] Overall, architectural innovations inspired by external trends affected in limited ways the homes of the upper classes, who could afford them and to whom they appealed, and a handful of public monuments sponsored by them more than they did the bulk of routine construction, which continued to follow traditional local practices.

The cushion of a culturally stable region accounts in part for the continuity in the basic features of Aleppo's culture. In the eighteenth century no major shifts occurred in the place accorded to Islam in society, nor were there great changes in the popular way of life, the distribution of literacy and education, the makeup and concerns of the intelligentsia, the structure of knowledge, or the outlook on essentials. This stability appears more striking when set against the new trends that began to alter aspects of the culture in Aleppo and the Middle East in the following century. Western dress, food, music, and theater took root. Appreciation of literacy and broader education increased; printed books, European writings, literary societies, newspapers, and periodicals appeared on the scene. More people ventured abroad to study and observe. A small lay intelligentsia espousing secular views began to make its voice heard in public circles.

These were sharp breaks with the traditional culture, not organic outgrowths of it. They reflected the overwhelming new impact of European culture, which played no significant role in the eighteenth century, when there was yet no unfavorable comparison of the culture with the European, no articulated doubt or discontent with local ways. Internally, a change in the policies and social functions of the state helped to set the new trends in motion. The state opened new secular schools, permitted Arabic printing, sponsored the translation of Western works, introduced official newspapers, sent students to Europe, curtailed the influence of the religious establishment, and in general gave legitimacy to a new interest in European ways and values. In the eighteenth century the government threw its considerable weight on the side of continuity.

The success in maintaining a stable cultural milieu meaningful to all groups was linked inextricably to the realities of power, and not only at the level of state policy. It clearly took active social investment, not mere inertia, to keep the essentials in place. People in Aleppo were socialized early to obey authority, conform to the community's expectations, respect religion and tradition, and suppress various individualistic whims. The community watched them continually and exercised effective social control. Many of their norms and institutions were presented as divinely ordained and hence immune to human challenge. Their moral leaders and learned men advocated conformity with the cultural ideals rather than changing them. The absence of printing imposed by the powerful helped to perpetuate the mass illiteracy and in general avoided the breakdown of the traditional constraints on the expression and diffusion of knowledge. Under these combined pressures and circumstances the townspeople were apt to remain secure in their values. During the century they aspired to attain the best that the society made possible, not to escape or reject it.

Within this stable cultural milieu people thought, wrote, experimented and improvised, responding to social whims and the press of events. Serious scholars worked to add something, however small, to their fields of interest and expertise. Performers faced audiences eager for variety and the thrill of some novelty. New products appeared in the bazaars and attracted buyers. Because so much was unrecorded, especially in the sphere of popular culture, we are apt to underestimate the extent of contemporary innovation and creativity. Stable though it was in many respects the "traditional" culture was clearly not frozen in its tracks.

CHAPTER 7

The Body: Health, Disease, and Death

"**D**EATH IS CLOSER than the veil is to the eye."[1] This ominous local saying spoke with the authority of experience. A good portion of the city's population died prematurely—in infancy, childhood, and early adulthood. Various illnesses and epidemics, among them the violent bubonic plague, carried off the majority of the victims, though the townspeople turned to a whole array of measures to help them prevent and treat diseases and to cope with death. "Everything is fixable—except death," sighed another popular saying, voicing a cliché that must have carried particular meaning in a world helpless in the face of high mortality.[2]

This unyielding condition of high mortality ranks among the essential realities of Aleppo's society in the eighteenth century. Its presence and dynamics left distinct marks on the material welfare, social relations, emotional texture, and general outlook of the population. In the absence of figures it is impossible to put the meaning of this condition in precise quantitative terms. What the average life expectancy of the townspeople was, to what extent the death rates of different social groups varied, how the rates of mortality and morbidity fluctuated during the century, how the patterns of mortality affected fertility and migration, how much disease and death cost the economy—these questions cannot be answered. The available evidence is largely qualitative, but concrete and telling nonetheless. The story of the family illustrates well the unsettling effects and material dislocations of high mortality.

Problems in the areas of hygiene, nutrition, public health, and medical care help to explain the vulnerable state of the body in Aleppo. Yet in a more basic way the key appears to lie in the state of the mind: the townspeople lacked the scientific and medical knowledge necessary to repulse the fatal attacks of diseases and epidemics. Poverty certainly played an important role in subjecting the bodies of many to weakening conditions, but a purely economic explanation would miss the cultural roots of a vulnerability which plagued the rich as well as the poor. The community saw no major improvement or breakthroughs in this area during the entire century. It did not generate from within, or import from outside, new weapons of defense which could improve bodily health and prolong life. Scientific inquiry in the city and the wider region languished, and government, the institution best equipped to initiate and direct public action, did little to promote improvements in medicine, public health or scientific knowledge.

Yet the inadequate understanding of the body and the forces of nature was not an indication of a simple setup. Health, disease, and death were the focus of a rich body of ideas and practices, and occasioned large investments of energy and money. Public institutions of health and sanitation accompanied private attention to physical well-being. People resorted both to scientific medicine and popular healers, pharmaceutical drugs and magical cures. Elaborate customs of burial, mourning, and commemoration surrounded death, and various beliefs thrived about the meaning of one's departure from the world of the living. Religion shaped many of the current attitudes and practices, but many others drew on nonreligious sources, and even offended pious opinion. The thinking and behavior in matters of health and death varied somewhat among groups: there were some noticeable differences between Muslims and non-Muslims, men and women, rich and poor. A probe into the roots and effects of the high mortality, the state of health, and the responses to death thus leads beyond strictly material issues into important aspects of the culture and inner workings of Aleppo's society.

DISEASE, PLAGUE, AND HIGH MORTALITY

SHA῾BAN IBN YA῾QUB was married for a few years when his wife died prematurely, leaving him with three children. He remarried and in the course of time added seven more children to his progeny. Two of them had not reached puberty when he passed away. Soon after his death one of his young boys died, followed by an older son who left behind a wife and six children, two of them still of minor age. Ahmad ibn Aslan saw his wife die, and then in succession his three sons. One of his nine orphaned grandchildren passed away some time after her father's death. As'ad ibn Ibshir died when five of his nine children were still of minor age. In the next five years two of them perished as well. Yaman bint Rajab lived to see her husband die, and following him all her three children.[3]

These fragments of family history, replicated in page after page of the city's court records, capture the reality of high mortality and early death in Aleppo's society. Death was not associated only with the old, but took a heavy toll on all age groups, including children and young adults. It struck with little heed to the principle of seniority; children often lost a parent whose own mother or father was still alive.[4] That "death does not discriminate," as a local saying observed, must have appeared especially true in this capricious milieu.[5]

This high mortality accompanied the residents throughout the century as a built-in, permanent feature of life. It shot up periodically to catastrophic levels, carrying off a sizable portion of the population in a short time. The average life expectancy of the residents in the best of times could not have exceeded forty years, a limit barely reached even in those cities of contemporary Europe with the lowest mortality rates. Some Aleppines did live to old age: the biographies of distinguished ulama of the eighteenth century, for instance, indicate that of thirty-nine whose ages at death are known with precision, fifteen died in their late fifties and in their sixties, ten in their seventies, eleven in their eighties, two at the age of ninety, and one at the age of one hundred and five.[6] Yet these men were hardly representative of the larger community. As prominent figures whose accomplishments took a lifetime to achieve, they tend to display longevity almost by definition; many promising men never made it simply because death cut their careers short. Comfortable circumstances—better than average working conditions, housing, nutrition, and hygiene—also helped these men navigate the hazards of life more successfully and enjoy longer life-spans than the less fortunate. No group, however, including the most privileged, succeeded in sheltering itself from the ravages of high mortality. Even the renowned local physician Ibrahim al-Hakim (d. ca. 1785) watched all of his four sons die in their youth from diseases that he could not treat.[7]

Diseases and epidemics more than anything else accounted for the high mortality and early death of so many. The toll from accidents, violence, and natural disasters was relatively small in comparison. From year to year a number of individuals drowned in domestic wells or in the river, fell off roofs and out of windows, were fatally hit by horses or donkeys, died as a result of work accidents, were suffocated by charcoal fumes, and fell victim to assaults and murders.[8] Some lost their lives in the periodic political violence of the period, or in executions for offenses. Major fires and floods were rare, and seldom caused loss of life.[9] Earthquakes shook the city on several occasions during the century, but only one, in 1723, is reported to have caused deaths.[10] A truly devastating earthquake was to hit Aleppo in 1822, leaving in its wake large-scale damage and casualties estimated in the thousands.[11] Suicides, too, appear to have been quite rare. Of the dozens of court investigations into suspicious deaths only one case, involving a prisoner found strangled in his cell in 1755, was established to have been suicide.[12] If others also took their own lives, but had the socially reprehensible fact of suicide concealed or undiscovered, they could not have been many.

All of these paled in comparison with the effect of disease on a population ill equipped to understand, prevent, or resist its fatal effects. A host of sicknesses afflicted the population almost chronically. Various ill-defined fevers appeared seasonally with almost unfailing regularity. Their victims ran high temperatures, and suffered variously from headaches, painful joints, coughing, diarrhea, vomiting, temporary deafness, and general weakness. Some of these fevers proved fatal, and because they often assumed epidemic proportions deaths were many, especially among children. Dysentery was common, working particular havoc in years of famine. There were epidemics every few years of smallpox, measles, scarlet fever, and whooping cough. Those fortunate enough to survive them were often left disfigured or burdened with persisting complications. Large numbers also suffered from chronic disorders and illnesses: birth defects; eye diseases and infections that impaired vision; toothaches and loss of teeth; deformities due to poorly treated fractures and dislocations; loss of limbs from neglected wounds and gangrene; kidney and bladder stones; ringworm, rashes, and other skin diseases; intestinal worms; epilepsy; venereal diseases; and mental disorders. Almost every resident carried on his face or body permanent scars from the "Aleppo boil," the result of a commonplace infection transmitted by the bites of sand flies.[13]

Childbirth also accounted for a constant loss of life. Much could go wrong during pregnancy and delivery that contemporary obstetrics could not resolve. Mothers and babies often died in the course of childbirth or from complications during its aftermath. The risks to mother and child proved especially high because women married early and often gave birth in adolescence, when their bodies were ill equipped to handle the physical strain. In the middle years of the century the physician to the English merchant community, Dr. Russell, observed a particularly high infant mortality among the local Jews, who also tended to marry at even a younger age than their Muslim and Christian neighbors.[14] The link between early marriage and high mortality also appeared evident to the local scholar al-Ghazzi from the conditions he observed in the early twentieth century. He condemned the practice of early marriage for causing unnecessary deaths as well as the physical frailty of mothers and babies. He too found the Jews to be the most common practitioners of premature marriage and childbearing.[15]

To the constant ravages of various sicknesses the bubonic plague *(taʿun)* added deadly strikes which pushed the already high mortality rate to catastrophic levels. A pestilence of unmatched destructiveness, it left more of a mark on the period than any other disease. No epidemic disease was more dreaded by the townspeople, and even in years of respite its appalling features lived on; those who survived its visitations carried with them memories of indescribable misery and desolation. Endemic in areas on the fringes of the Middle East, the disease sprang to life periodically in localized outbreaks and regional epidemics after the Black Death in the mid-fourteenth century. In the course of the eighteenth century the city suffered eight epidemics extending over fifteen years (in 1706–1707, 1718–1719, 1729, 1733, 1742–1744, 1760–1762, 1786–1787, and 1793).[16] This cycle did not end when the century drew to a close: four epidemics hit the population in close succession during the first three decades of the nineteenth century (in 1802, 1807, 1814–1815, and 1827).[17]

Plague epidemics appeared in the city on the average once every ten years during the eighteenth century. In comparison with the four plague epidemics in the sixteenth century and the five in the seventeenth, there was a considerable increase in their frequency, a trend characteristic of the Middle East in general.[18] Yet even in the eighteenth century some generations suffered more frequent visitations than others. Those who lived in the first forty-five years of the century experienced five epidemics. In the following forty-five years the number of eruptions dropped down to two. Then the frequency of attacks picked up dramatically; in the forty-year span between 1787 and 1827 five epidemics struck the population. The frequency of plague outbreaks appears to have passed through three phases, shifting roughly from a ten-year cycle to a twenty-year cycle and then to an eight-year cycle.

The frequency of plague epidemics mattered; each could mean several thousand fatalities and massive suffering. Contemporaries found some outbreaks to be milder or more virulent than others, but were generally always impressed with their toll on life. They issued staggering casualty estimates: 120,000 (in 1719 and 1761), 40,000 to 50,000 (in 1733), and 34,200 (in 1787).[19] After the plague of 1787 residents speculated that 100,000 or more Muslims had died.[20] A Carmelite missionary noted in his order's journal that as many as 162,500 people perished in 1719—an observation that duly prompted him to marvel at the inexplicable sight of busy crowds in the streets.[21]

These impressive contemporary figures seem a better measure of subjective horror than of actual mortality. The few counts of burials available from the period point to more modest levels of mortality in the general range of 13 to 20 percent. During the plague years of 1761 and 1762, Dr. Patrick Russell counted 7,767 and 11,883 burials respectively, based on reports provided by observers stationed in the cemeteries. Driven by a scientific curiosity about a disease that puzzled the entire medical community, the English physician treated the sick and assembled a massive body of empirical data which won him recognition as a leading authority on the plague.[22] His figures, by his own admission not entirely accurate, suggest a level of mortality in the range of 15 to 20 percent for the years 1761–1762. A local resident who kept a daily record of burials in 1743 arrived at 18,170 deaths, pointing to a similar level of mortality.[23]

More accurate figures available for the non-Muslim communities confirm those numbers: In the course of the plague of 1787 Yusuf al-Halabi kept a daily count of the Christian burials, obtained from the gravediggers and the administrator of the cemetery. From May to August, when the epidemic raged most violently, the number of dead was 2,475, a figure that al-Halabi raised to 3,000 to make up for unrecorded burials.[24] This number represented some 13 to 15 percent of the Christian population, which at the time took more precautions against contagion than the Muslims. A count of plague victims that the Jewish community conducted among its members in the same year for the purpose of organizing a relief fund confirms this general level of mortality: the number of dead came to approximately 500 people, which represented about 15 percent of the community.[25]

Aleppo was spared the far higher rates of mortality associated with the pneumonic plague, a vicious variety of the disease that did not appear in the city during the eighteenth century; this, however, gave little comfort to the townspeople, who saw heavenly wrath unleashed upon them even with the milder scourge. Scores of funeral processions thronged the streets, and the cries of mourners tore the peace of night. Old and young lay prostrate with chills, fever, vomiting, inflamed swellings, delirium, and the sense of impending death. In many families the contagion attacked several members, carrying off some while sparing others. No one knew of a sure treatment for the disease or could venture a satisfactory medical explanation for the recovery of some of the sick. Physicians could only attempt to treat the symptoms, following a set of traditional medical practices which promised no cure and occasionally hastened the patients' demise. Many doctors chose to admit their helplessness and avoided tending the ill altogether in the hope of saving themselves.[26]

Even in such an atmosphere of uncertainty and fear the community conducted itself in a remarkably controlled fashion. Personal grief did burst out uninhibitedly; in 1762 the qadi felt compelled to forbid women from shrieking in funeral processions in order to protect the peace of the sick.[27] But on the collective level the plague epidemics produced no breakdown of civil order, no political instability, no social tensions, no crisis of faith. No one was to blame for the misfortune; no one stood to benefit from it; all seemed equally liable to be affected. The plague excited the same basic fears and hopes in people from all walks of life; yet attitudes and responses to the disease did vary considerably among groups—differences that grew more pronounced during the eighteenth century as new notions took root and altered established patterns.

In the aftermath of the Black Death Muslim scholars arrived at a set of notions about the plague that came to dominate public discourse on the subject. The disease, they asserted, was a blessing and martyrdom; it was inflicted by God, not spread by contagion; the Muslim faithful should not flee for protection.[28] If their views were guided in any way by a practical wish to prevent an economic and psychological breakdown they produced the desired effect. There was no panic or mass flight from the city. The markets remained open and most people went about their business normally. As in other contemporary Middle Eastern communities, in Aleppo also many Muslims behaved with a calm disregard for the dangers of contagion, paying visits to the sick and mixing promiscuously with others without due precautions. There were, however, Muslim families, particularly the wealthier ones, who took the hazards of contagion quite seriously. They confined themselves to their homes or moved out of town temporarily, making sure to manufacture some legitimate pretext. This tendency of a segment of the Muslim population toward precaution and self-help was part of a larger shift in conduct that occurred mainly among local non-Muslims.

The Christians and Jews had occasion to observe at first hand the highly successful example of protective behavior taken by the resident Europeans, with whom they became intimately associated as employees, clients, business partners, and coreligionists. The Europeans routinely and strictly quarantined themselves in their compounds during times of plague, and had an excellent record of survival which inspired imitation. The practice of confinement grew increasingly common among Christians, who were in any case not bound by the Muslim ideological approaches to the plague. In 1787 al-Halabi went into domestic isolation along with many of his coreligionists. Emerging after ninety-one days of hiding he found that only four of those who had taken similar precautions had not survived. He lived to experience the succeeding pestilence in 1793, when many Christians again confined themselves to their homes "as was customary."[29] In the plague of 1807 some Muslims as well as the Christians went into hiding.

In addition to isolation, other precautions of a less extreme form also took root among non-Muslims: they refrained from visiting sick relatives and friends, avoided attendance at funerals, and even removed themselves from their homes when family members fell ill.[30] In the interest of protecting the public health one of the Christian communities went so far as to deny its clergy who died in the plague of 1787 the customary privilege of burial in the church. An ugly confrontation erupted when the family of one of the deceased priests took offense at this uncharitable measure and, with the help of the authorities, had the body buried in the church.[31] If this practice of exclusion from church burials contributed to public health in times of plague it was not quite as important as the long-standing local custom of burying the dead promptly, usually within a day or so.

With the increase in precautions taken by the public against the plague an important change of attitude and behavior was beginning to emerge, one not confined to Aleppo alone.[32] It was limited, however, primarily to the well-to-do and the non-Muslims, confinement being an avenue more readily accessible to that small economically secure segment of the population who could afford the luxury of two or three months of voluntary unemployment. The authorities, furthermore, provided no guidance or encouragement to any organized effort to promote physical protection against the epidemics. They imposed no quarantines, nor did they favor confinement. Indeed, during the plague of 1807 the governor actually ordered all of those in hiding to return to work. After some negotiation the Christians obtained permission to remain in confinement in return for a large collective payment.[33]

Only the European merchant communities took organized measures to control contact with merchandise and people from infected areas; they withheld transactions and shipments until their physicians had issued clean bills of health. Their cumbersome precautions occasioned a certain loss of income for themselves as well as for their local business associates, who tried time and again to conceal worrisome information about the epidemics in the interest of restoring normal commercial activities.[34] The Europeans sought to encourage official measures of quarantine, but without success. In 1786, when the plague raged in large parts of the region, they requested the qadi and the interim governor to forbid entry into the city to a caravan arrived from an infected area. An order to this effect was issued, but in the absence of any real enforcement many of the travelers ignored it.[35]

The leadership's concern with the plague tended to surface most commonly in the traditional stress on spiritual reform: only belief and righteous conduct, they contended, would assuage God's wrath and bring relief from the scourge. During the plague of 1762 the qadi issued an order enjoining all Muslims to be religiously observant and threatening the negligent with immediate punishment. He also decreed that before making their public call to prayer the muezzins chant nine times a particular Koranic verse believed to have special power in combating the plague.[36]

Those who broke away from the traditional approaches and adopted an attitude of active self-help were able to survive the deadly epidemics with greater success. The plague did penetrate the homes of upper-class families, but on the whole caused relatively little damage in their ranks.[37] The Christians also must have died in smaller proportions than their Muslim neighbors.[38] Such comparisons pale, however, beside the overwhelming fact that many thousands of residents lost their lives to this one disease in the course of the century, and that even without the violence of the plague, other diseases took a consistent and heavy toll on the population. The underlying causes of this vulnerability lay in the state of health and medicine.

HEALTH CONDITIONS AND MEDICAL CARE

ALEPPINES SUFFERED FROM many bodily malfunctions, but not completely for lack of attention to their physical well-being. They held
a rich store of notions about the virtues of cleanliness, the nutritional
value or harm of various foods, the general threats to public health, the
efficacy of drugs and treatments, and the causes of different ailments.
When indisposed they took medications and consulted physicians. That
the pursuit of good health was so often frustrated had to do in part with
the inability of many to afford reasonable standards of nutrition, hygiene, housing, and medical care. In a more basic sense many health
problems stemmed from a generally inadequate scientific and medical
knowledge; even the physicians were at a loss to explain or cure a
multitude of common ailments. During the eighteenth century there
were no dramatic advances in medical science or in basic conceptions
about health, and widespread vulnerability to disease and early death
remained standard.

At the level of personal health care, deficiencies in nutrition and
hygiene were most directly responsible for the vulnerability to various
diseases and disorders. In combination the main components of the local
diet—grains, legumes, vegetables, and dairy products, with the addition of meat, fruits, and nuts among the better-off—were an essentially
nutritious diet. Many in the lower-income groups, however, could not
always afford adequate amounts of food nor the elements of a balanced
diet. All too often food shortages and high prices reduced them to a
dependence on bread—if they could get their hands on it at all. At least
during these numerous subsistence crises malnutrition was widespread.
Various diseases became common, and with the weakening of their
bodies many died. In the absence of refrigeration the risks of consuming
spoiled food were also relatively high, despite the resort to various
means of preservation and storage.

The state of personal hygiene was equally mixed. The public bath
houses, in which people routinely did their washing, always teemed
with customers. Ranking among the great ancient institutions of Middle
Eastern society, they testified to the culture's deeply ingrained appreciation of personal cleanliness. In the bath houses one could get a good
scrub and massage, have body hair removed, and enjoy a relaxing break
from the daily routine. Yet many apparently visited the bath only once
a week or fortnight, a lapse that rendered them vulnerable to various

skin disorders, which were especially widespread among children.[39] The sanitary arrangements in the bath houses also left something to be desired. That people rinsed their bodies off in a pond of standing water shared by others rather than in a shower of fresh water may have actually helped to spread diseases. At home conditions were not entirely safe either. Many houses were infested with mice, rats, scorpions, fleas, and other pests. The domestic toilets proved offensive, especially in the hot summers.[40] In the lower classes families lived in overcrowded conditions which may have posed threats to health as well as privacy.

At the level of public health, the threats were generally limited, but nonetheless serious. One major health hazard grew out of the compact physical environment. Population densities, especially in the poorer districts, were high, giving aid to the spread of epidemics. On the other hand, the environment was free of serious problems of industrial pollution. The few activities that produced noxious smells and wastes, such as the lime works, tannery, and slaughterhouse, were placed in outlying areas removed from the main concentrations of population. In the absence of heavy machinery, electric power, and dangerous chemicals people faced limited threats to their health and life in the workplace. Far more important than occupational accidents were the daily working conditions associated with different professions. Those in the lower classes who did exhausting manual labor, spent many hours in the hot sun, and took few vacations subjected their bodies to a level of wear that weakened their resistance to diseases. Their life expectancy was probably lower than that of residents employed in more comfortable circumstances.

An efficient system of sanitation helped considerably to reduce the threats to public health. "In Aleppo, we find a cleanliness unknown to the other cities of Turkey, even to the capital itself," observed Baron de Tott in his stop there during his official tour of the region in the late eighteenth century. Other visitors shared this impression.[41] The rubbish in the houses and streets was picked up by garbage collectors *(zabbalin)*, most of them employed by the public bath houses. So intense was the demand for this cheap fuel that each bath house was assigned exclusive rights to the waste of one particular district of town. Bath house operators were tempted on occasion to encroach upon the territories of colleagues or to bribe the garbagemen hired by other bath houses into selling them what rubbish they collected. The local potters also tried to buy illegally some of the rubbish intended for the baths; when caught on one occasion they had to pledge in court to burn only wood in their ovens. The competition ran particularly high over dung, which the bath houses actually purchased from the stables and mills.[42]

The zealous collection of refuse and its disposal by burning were a blessing for public health in the city. So too was the limited market production of processed food. People bought most of their food in the form of raw ingredients which they cooked at home. On occasion, individual producers of foods cheated by reducing certain expensive ingredients or substituting others for them, but without necessarily posing any health threat to consumers in the process. Such adulteration was admitted in 1770 by several makers of sweet juices, who cut the seasonings and sugar, and mixed flour in their drinks. The violation of guild standards and consumer trust, not public health, were at issue in the court hearing on their case.[43] The adulteration of food assumed hazardous proportions most commonly in the case of bread sold in times of scarcity, when bakers tended to substitute various unhealthy ingredients for the precious flour and to subject consumers to illnesses. In 1787 three people died and several fell sick after eating adulterated bread bought in a neighborhood bakery. Following public complaints the authorities arrested the baker for interrogation.[44]

Of all items of consumption water posed the greatest potential threat to public health. Open aqueducts carried drinking water into the city from the river and from springs several miles north of the city. An underground system of canals and pipes distributed it to fountains, public institutions, and some homes in different parts of town. The system was cleared annually of silt and dirt, but nothing was done to purify or disinfect the supply. That the quality of water could affect the health of its consumers was known, if only in a crude way. Around 1740 the governor ordered that the Helena Springs be disconnected from the public system after "top doctors and experts on the quality of water" determined that its water was the cause of diseases and fevers.[45] Within the city unhealthy practices contributed to the contamination of the water. To increase the water pressure the technicians who oversaw the public system pushed horse dung into the pipes, until the bath houses complained about the offensive effects on their premises.[46] In the early twentieth century the technicians had not considerably improved their methods, having adopted the use of rags collected from refuse heaps to regulate the pressure. "No custom equals this one in its ugliness and harm to health," complained a contemporary historian.[47] Acute shortages of water also afflicted the city periodically, leaving the poorer townspeople without sufficient water for their most basic needs. In such times diseases spread rapidly and took a toll on the unhappy population.[48]

The concern with the quality of water, the regular collection of refuse, the zoning of offensive industries, and the complaints about unhealthy bread all reflected a local conception of health which extended to the collective level. The community recognized certain activities to be in the interest of public health and others to be harmful to it. People were required to refrain from activities that threatened the health of others, and were entitled to protection against such threats. In practice, though, the extent of regulation of public health was quite restricted. The limited or nonexistent hazards in some areas, and the unperceived problems in others, set limits on collective measures of control. Aleppo had no agency or officials dedicated to matters of public health. The government made no investment in public medical care, nor did it undertake routine supervision of health conditions in the city. Its intervention in issues of health, always minimal, usually came in response to public complaints.

Such complaints were actually rare in comparison with the grievances aired in court from time to time about defective products, offensive noises, and threats to security and privacy. When residents did raise the issue of health it was often in order to reinforce concerns of a different sort. A group of local bakers, for instance, used the argument of public health protection in 1768 to help defend a strictly economic interest of their own. Troubled by the commercial success of several colleagues who produced a new variety of bread, they obtained a court order banning the innovation. They argued that it violated local custom by introducing a product outside the four types of bread traditionally baked in the city, and that its production adversely affected their business. Eating this new bread, they added, was harmful because it was sold not fully baked.[49] Objections to the smoking of tobacco mixed with drugs used considerations of public health to buttress primarily moral concerns.

In many other instances the issue of public health was striking mainly in its absence or irrelevance. The authorities prohibited the consumption of wine by Muslims because it was forbidden by religious law, not for health reasons. They issued periodic orders designed to enforce the Muslim standards of modesty in the public bath houses; health standards in these establishments enjoyed no corresponding attention. In 1770 the guild of pastry makers prohibited its members from employing Christians and Jews because non-Muslims could not be expected to uphold the required standards of purity in the guild's products. At issue was the observance not of health standards as such but of Muslim religious norms of purity *(tahara*, as opposed to *najasa*, or impurity).[50]

Moral health clearly prompted regulation far more than physical health, perhaps because, while the paths to moral perfection were charted and well established, improved physical well-being seemed a more elusive goal. The scientific understanding of the townspeople offered no proven means of deliverance from the high incidence of disease and early death. They turned to the medical experts for help, but without a firm trust in their powers or an expectation of medical progress. Local medicine stood helpless in the face of the most common ailments. The physicians in the city were still applying medieval Arab knowledge, which itself was anchored in ancient Greek medicine. Theirs was a limited understanding of the human body and the nature of disease. Barred by religious prohibitions from performing autopsies, they lacked a firsthand familiarity with the internal organs and the finer aspects of human anatomy. The rich array of medicaments at their disposal, composed of careful mixtures of herbs and powders, included many items of dubious efficacy.

Unable to treat or even diagnose many diseases, the physicians sought to relieve rather than cure. Even then they took care not to administer any drastic measures for fear of taking a risk with the patient's life. If the patient expired while under their care they could face the unpleasant prospect of a charge of malpractice. Such concerns were most acute among the surgeons, who cut into bodies without the benefit of anesthetics, antibiotics, or any guarantee of the patient's survival. Before undertaking a hazardous operation, such as the removal of bladder stones, they routinely secured from their patients an agreement in writing to waive the right to sue for malpractice.[51]

Medical care was organized around private practice rather than public institutions. A host of self-employed doctors and surgeons, many of them Christians and Jews, treated the local sick. They paid house calls and received patients in their clinics. Even in the case of serious diseases the sick stayed home for treatment and care. Institutional medical care was almost nonexistent; there were only two public hospitals—the Maristan Nur al-Din, founded in the twelfth century, and the Maristan Argun, established two centuries later. Supported by funds from charitable endowments and equipped with no more than sixty small rooms altogether, they divided their limited resources between treatment of the Muslim poor and confinement of the insane.[52] Unlike the physically sick, who were kept at home in the care of relatives, the mentally ill who were deemed too dangerous to the general public were taken into confinement and even put in chains. The two hospitals housed the Muslim insane; the churches provided similar institutional refuge for mentally unstable Christians. One Christian committed his mentally disturbed wife to the church, "according to the accepted custom," when her conduct rendered her a public hazard in need of isolation from society.[53]

Institutional care was clearly intended for the marginal—notably individuals mentally or economically deprived—rather than the mainstream of society. It attracted correspondingly marginal public support. Private philanthropists, who financed the construction and maintenance of many mosques, water fountains, schools, and other public institutions, allocated little to the expansion of hospital care during the century. No new hospitals were built, and none of the hundreds of recorded charitable endowments of the period donated property for the support of the existing ones. Most of the townspeople were left to pay for medical treatment and drugs from their own pockets, without the benefit of government support, public subsidies, or health insurance. Only the small, tight-knit Jewish community maintained a special sick fund, drawn from a tax on its members, which subsidized the health expenses of the poor.[54] For those at the lower end of the income scale, medical costs could be a considerable financial burden, especially when surgery was involved. In the 1750s and 1760s an operation to remove a stone from a child's bladder or urinary tract cost usually from five to ten piastres, a sum equivalent to a month or two of a laborer's income.[55] The costs of even routine medical care could run high in the large families of the day. The very poor lacked the benefits, however limited, of regular medical attention, which could only increase their already high health risks.

Only part of what Aleppines spent on physical care and therapy went to the physicians and surgeons. They also employed barbers, bonesetters, midwives, faith healers, and other practitioners of popular medicine, who provided a host of therapeutic services. The medical experts enjoyed higher professional prestige, but not a monopoly over the art of healing. Unlike their competitors, they had to be officially certified in order to practice. While this formality testified to a perceived boundary between the learned medical profession and those on the fringes, the actual distinction was not very sharp. The two groups shared much in terms of knowledge and methods, and fed on each other. Doctors applied many remedies based on popular traditions and superstitions which were passed off as authoritative modes of therapy. They acquired their skills by apprenticeship rather than formal schooling; some lacked a good basis in medical texts or obtained their license without benefit of the required qualifying examination.[56] At the same time barbers handled bloodletting, scarification, and other practices recommended by learned medicine, and midwives boasted an unmatched empirical expertise in obstetrics, all without formal medical training.

People often resorted to the popular healers because the physicians were not manifestly so superior. Indeed, in some areas their treatment did more harm than good, and their medications proved useless or worse. Faith healing and magical cures thrived because people could not put their full trust in medicine. They sought to safeguard themselves against diseases and to obtain relief from their afflictions through a variety of avenues that went beyond the strictly medical. During three days every April crowds flocked to the gardens on the outskirts of town in the belief that this would guarantee a year free of headaches. Some women of the lower classes made it a point to wash in the fountain of ʿAli Bey at dawn during three Saturdays in July as a safeguard against disease for the rest of the year.[57] To prevent illnesses or seek cures men and women in all classes commonly put their trust in amulets, pleaded with saints, and consulted fortune-tellers and astrologers. Believing in the power of invisible spirits over the body, sick people often turned to exorcism and faith healing. In addition to employing doctors, the Jews called in rabbis to pray at the bedside of the sick in order to help combat the work of evil spirits, and even hired Muslim holy men to apply their powers of divine intercession and exorcism.[58]

If these popular practices failed to cure troublesome diseases, resort to them was not an entirely irrational course inasmuch as it could at least infuse some psychological security into minds tormented by worry and uncertainty. The struggle to stay alive and well certainly drove the residents to explore all possible resources: medical, pseudomedical, magical, religious, and psychological. These they did not see as mutually exclusive or contradictory. In their understanding of health and disease, spiritual forces, both good and evil, were part of the overall scheme, a notion that was echoed in their attitudes toward the mentally ill, whose abnormalities they attributed most immediately to the invasion of the body by invisible spirits. The raving madman carried within him an evil spirit, an ill omen, which rendered him almost subhuman and made it necessary to remove him from public sight. On the other hand, the innocuous imbecile who muttered religious verses encountered no such fearfulness. Seen as divinely inspired by the presence of a good spirit, he symbolized a mysterious blessing from which others could possibly benefit.[59] But whether the object of veneration, fear, or ridicule, the bizarre behavior of the mentally unstable indicated the work of spiritual forces on the body. Manipulating these outside forces, with the help of experts in matters spiritual, was hence as essential a part of health care as medical attention to the physique.

The mysterious interplay of the physical and the spiritual helped the townspeople to make some sense of conditions that science and medicine failed to explain. Sound and dubious notions about health coexisted in their minds, indeed even in the minds of the most learned men. The distinguished scholar al-Muradi could solemnly advise conscientious Muslim jurisconsults to avoid sour apples, vinegar, and broad beans because they produced dullness of mind. Reading tombstone inscriptions, he also warned, led to forgetfulness.[60] At the same time smoking tobacco was considered of therapeutic value for certain eye diseases. It was prescribed for Hasan al-Tabbakh when his eyesight began to fail— bitter medicine for a pious man who had campaigned most of his life against the vice.[61]

Major changes in health care began to occur in the nineteenth century, when the importation of European ideas and practices steadily eroded traditional local medicine. Government entered the field of public health with new regulations regarding sanitation and quarantines; the first modern hospitals were built; and the first local physicians trained in modern European medicine began to practice in the city. Improvement did not show immediately. The plague continued to attack with even greater frequency, and was joined in the 1830s by cholera, a new scourge that carried away thousands of people in the course of many subsequent epidemics.[62] And old ways persisted alongside the new: in the early twentieth century practitioners of traditional medicine were still treating the sick.[63]

LIVING WITH DEATH

UNTIL THE RAVAGES of disease were checked the level of mortality in Aleppo remained high. A familiar reality to which the community had long adapted, its continued presence in the eighteenth century did not in itself produce any important changes in the city's political system, economic organization, family patterns, system of welfare, demographic regime, or world of thought and belief. But while it left the basic structures of society unaltered the high mortality was nonetheless the source of major personal dislocations. These were most readily visible in the countless orphans and widowed people who faced problems of shelter, upbringing, and financial support. Their material and social needs activated a system of welfare and protection based largely on the larger family. Relatives sacrificed money, effort, space, and privacy in order to fulfill their responsibilities toward needy kin.

The attempts to deal with the survivors and their welfare problems formed one level of response to death. There was yet another set of responses, focused on the dead themselves—their bodies, their memory, and the meaning of their departure. Commonplace as death was, people did not react to it casually. Outbursts of grief were common, the women especially giving uninhibited expression to their feelings. The larger community was drawn into the family's crisis, giving death a more public character. Elaborate customs of burial, mourning, and commemoration came into play, with the investment in honoring the dead varying with social class. Despite some differences of custom, all religious groups in Aleppo shared the same basic approach to death and the dead. Religion profoundly shaped their mortuary rituals and their interpretation of death, but practices and attitudes inconsistent with orthodox opinion also thrived. Death brought out some revealing sides of the mind and the world of the living.

People usually died at home with relatives around them. In their last hours a clergyman often sat at their bedside, praying for their souls and comforting the distraught family. Once the person expired the women of the household broke into distinctively loud, high-pitched cries which echoed throughout the neighborhood and announced the tragedy to the public. Within a day or so the family completed a whole set of rituals for the removal of the corpse. After the body was washed, wrapped in shrouds, and prepared for burial it was carried in a public procession to the appropriate house of worship for a religious service, and from there to a cemetery, where it was buried after prayers led by a clergyman— the elaborateness of the burial ceremonies and tombs, and the location of the place of burial, varying with the wealth and social standing of the deceased. Much open emotion and grief surrounded the funerals as they passed through the city streets. The women cried and gesticulated in agony, with professional female mourners *(na'ihat)* hired by the family leading the sorrowful scene. Among the Jews, who prohibited women from accompanying the corpse to its burial place, funerals tended to be much quieter, prompting a local saying to liken a solemn and hasty affair to a Jewish funeral.[64]

The burial marked the first act in a process of mourning and commemoration that could last for many months and even years. Family members resorted to several common practices and rituals designed to honor the dead person, keep his memory alive, and help themselves deal with the loss. Widows and close female relatives changed to plain black clothes; the men usually made little or no alteration in their dress. It was considered proper for the bereaved to avoid parties and festive occasions for a time; the Jews also stayed away from work during the first week of mourning. Friends and neighbors came to pay their condolences, some bringing meals to feed the bereaved family or helping in other ways. On set days after the burial the family held customary memorial services for the deceased—the Muslims on the third, seventh, and fortieth days and on the anniversary; the Christians on the third, ninth, and fortieth days as well as after six months and a year; and the Jews on the first, seventh, and thirtieth days and on the anniversary. On these occasions the relatives and friends attended special religious services for the dead person in a house of worship, and visited the grave. The family also held open house, hosting visitors and distributing food and money to the poor, who came by to avail themselves of this customary charity.

The wish to pay homage and commemorate found expression also in the universal practice of identifying the grave with a personal tombstone. The more modest stones carried the name of the deceased, the date of death, and a verse or two from the scriptures. The elaborate epitaphs that graced the tombs of the wealthy and distinguished included words of tribute as well as specially composed eulogies.[65] Much of the initial grief of the bereaved focused on the grave. The women especially paid frequent, sometimes even daily, visits to the tombs of recently departed relatives, where they chanted laments and addressed the dead with words of love and sorrow. Although the pain gradually subsided and normalcy resumed its course, religious customs worked to keep the memory of the dead and concern for their souls alive. In all communities certain religious holidays involved customary visits to the graves of relatives, and prayers for the souls of dead kin were woven into the liturgy.

Clearly, death was not treated as taboo. Nothing displayed this more vividly than the uninhibited outbursts of grief that accompanied burial and mourning. It was the bereaved women who brought their emotions and anguish out into the open, in sharp contrast to the reserve and control displayed by the men. The women were altogether much more prominent in the performance of the death rituals. They did most of the visiting of the graves, handled the preparation and distribution of food, and submitted to greater alterations of their dress and routines than the men. That men were conditioned by upbringing to control their emotions and that the traditional division of labor between the sexes placed many of the obligations associated with mourning in the women's sphere may not explain fully why the women participated so much more than the men in the performance of the death rituals. Women may very well have been more deeply affected, both emotionally and socially, by the loss of close kin. A woman's identity and her social position were defined largely in terms of her kin, primarily the men. She also developed closer ties to her children and other kin than her husband. Because these relationships were so central to them, women were more threatened by the death of parents, siblings, husbands, and children. The visits to the grave, the anguished talks to the departed, and the general process of mourning and commemoration may have helped them maintain for a time something of the old ties with those who had given their lives definition and meaning.

Two modes of outward response to death thus coexisted in the culture: one of resigned self-control, more commonly associated with men; the other of uninhibited expression, associated with women. A state of some tension prevailed between the two types of response. While in a sense the women did the mourning for the larger family and performed a cathartic function on its behalf by letting out the emotions of grief, opinions in male and religious circles considered their conduct excessive, irreligious, and manipulative, and hence deserving of some social control. The English resident physician Russell, who as an outsider found the women's outbursts of grief exaggerated and often feigned, noted that local men in general "strongly express their disapprobation of these wild demonstrations of sorrow, regarding them, in some degree, as impious."[66]

Muslim religious opinion advocated more solemn and controlled forms of mourning, and generally condemned the popular superstitions and unsanctioned practices that had taken root in mortuary rituals.[67] Christian religious circles harbored similar disapproval of women's behavior in times of mourning. Moral regulations issued by the Maronite archbishop in 1807 prohibited women from attending funerals, issuing their customary cries of grief outdoors, and visiting the cemeteries "with the pretext of mourning."[68] That many women saw the visits to the grave-yards as welcome opportunities to go outdoors and share mundane talk as well as their grief with other women aroused the monitoring instincts of male domination against them even in this sphere. In the middle decades of the century, the authorities restricted the excursions of women to the graveyards, as also to the picnic sites in the orchards, to Mondays and Thursdays only.[69]

Death was a public event; the open advertisement of the tragedy, the condolence visits of friends and neighbors, the distribution of food to the poor, the help of friends—all these involved the larger community in the misfortune of the family, and gave the bereaved some needed external support. By their acts of charity to the poor—a feature charac-teristic also of happy domestic occasions—the mourners on their part affirmed their links with the community and commitment to its values. This public character given to death was quite in keeping with the general disposition in the culture to externalize important family events and rites of passage. The rituals and festivities of marriage, for instance, were celebrated in an equally public manner, with processions and open displays of the bride's trousseau in the streets.

Yet as public performances the death rituals were also subject to social evaluation. The family was expected to fulfill various obligations and to demonstrate proper honoring of the deceased. The better-off felt particular pressure to perform the rites in an elaborate way in order to uphold the family's reputation. Considerable costs were involved, and some families, of course, could do much more than others. There were expenses for shrouds, washing and preparing the corpse for burial, a casket (used by the Christians), the digging of the grave, the tombstone, the services of the clergy and professional mourners, and the food distributed and the meals served. The poor, for whom even the elemen-tary burial expenses were substantial, dispensed with the luxuries of charity, mourners, and elaborate graves. The wife and two sons of one ʿAbd al-Rahman ibn Mustafa spent 45 piastres just for preparing his body for burial in 1752. This sum came from the man's modest estate of 436 piastres.[70] The Jews subsidized the burial expenses of the poor members from a community chest which, like the sick fund, drew its money from a communal tax. During the plague of 1787 the leaders ordered the collection of an emergency tax to help meet the heavy demands on the fund by the scores of bereaved families.[71]

The graves themselves displayed perhaps most vividly the effects of social differences. Like the dwellings of the living so also the resting places of the dead varied in richness and prestige of location. The mass of people of little wealth or distinction were laid to rest amid the ocean of tombs in the vast burial grounds on the outskirts of the city, sometimes in a location quite a walking distance from it. Theirs were modest graves topped with nothing more than relatively plain tombstones. They told something about the humble status of their occupants, just as the mausoleums, the tombs covered with pillared domes, the finely carved marble monuments, and the lengthy epitaphs testified to a more privileged class of dead. The more wealthy and distinguished also boasted burial locations carrying special honor and prestige, notably in private or family cemeteries, within the grounds of religious institutions in the city, next to close kin, and in proximity to the tombs of revered holy men. Some made their choices and burial arrangements during their lifetimes, even endowing property for a special cemetery or tomb to be maintained by hired groundkeepers; others benefited from arrangements made by their ancestors or from honors conferred by tradition.

The merchant and philanthropist Hasan Chalabi al-Hamawi arranged to be buried in a special tomb in his own neighborhood of al-Bayyada, near the mosque and water fountain that he renovated in the second half of the century.[72] When he founded the grand Ahmadiyya College in 1754, Ahmad Effendi Taha Zadeh provided for a family graveyard to be kept next door to it. He, his father, his wife, and his son Muhammad Effendi were all buried there. His brother ʿUmar Effendi founded a mosque with a family graveyard in which he and several family members were buried over the years. The wealthy Muhibb family maintained a private cemetery on the northern outskirts of town. Mustafa al-Hafsarjawi, an alim who enjoyed their patronage, was honored at his death with a resting place there. The Kawakibis had their family burial grounds within the mosque of their ancestor Abu Yahya; members of the family have been laid to rest there until recent times.[73]

Special honor was attached to burial within the walls of religious institutions. There were few mosques, colleges, and Sufi lodges in the city without one or several tombs in which a privileged few were buried, including not only the founders and their descendants, but also some of their more distinguished scholars, teachers, preachers, guides, and other staff members.[74] To be buried next to close kin was also deemed important: in the public cemeteries many of the wealthy and ulama were laid to rest next to their fathers, grandfathers, siblings, and other relatives, in a conscious display of familial solidarity.[75] Honorable too was burial

near the tombs of renowned holy men, to which people of piety and
wealth were attracted. In the course of time cemeteries such as Maqbarat
al-Salihin on the southern outskirts of town ended up with a heavy
concentration of distinguished men and gained a special prestige in the
eyes of the living.[76] The tombs of saints, which were scattered within
the city and on its outskirts, were the objects of worship and the
destination of pilgrimages by many residents who saw them as sources
of divine grace. A local religious scholar, Shaykh Abu 'l-Wafa' al-Rifa'i
(1765–1847), went to the trouble of surveying the numerous holy tombs
and paying homage to them in a long poetic composition.[77]

The attention to the body and its physical resting place, varying
according to the means and pretensions of the deceased and his family,
was accompanied by the less tangible concern for the soul. Spiritual
notions about the meaning of mortality strongly colored the approach to
death and the dead. Religion, so much a part of the mortuary rituals
and customs, mustered the full weight of its eschatological vision to
make sense of the ultimate horror of human existence. The clergyman
who chanted prayers at a deathbed or by an open grave or in a memorial
service uttered words and concepts familiar to the listeners: the immor-
tal soul, eternal life, paradise, heaven, God's mercy. Death was not the
absolute end of life, but a transition by God's will to another world in
which the soul lived on. It brought blessings for those who earned
divine grace. In daily speech the common word for the deceased was *al-
marhum*, literally, "he who had been granted God's mercy." People said
"he passed away into God's mercy" (*intaqala ila rahmat Allah*, and in the
colloquial, *irtaham*) to mean "he died."

By denying the finality of death and integrating it into a sacred order
that transcended everyday experience, Islam and the other faiths equipped
their adherents with a framework which in effect legitimized death and
helped to mitigate its terror. They encouraged the acceptance of death
and resignation to it. The men of religion who officiated in the rituals
introduced a strong touch of solemnity and calmness which may have
had a comforting effect on the bereaved. Men and women of all classes
believed in the afterlife, and showed active concern for the fate of their
souls and those of relatives. Yahya Chalabi ibn 'Umar Chalabi endowed
four shops in 1770 for the purpose of hiring four men to read daily
portions of the Koran for his soul as well as the souls of his deceased
relatives. Others also sacrificed some of their private property for this
sole end of buying protection in the afterlife for themselves and others.[78]
Many Muslim men and women who made endowments for the support

of public institutions or their families included allocations of money for such Koran readings for their souls and those of dead relatives.[79] The soul lived on after bodily death, and could benefit from the prayer and good deeds of the living.

People found the religious vision of death a psychological support when faced with the pain of grief, and their faith in science and medicine was too weak to pose a formidable challenge to this spiritual interpretation. The fact of precarious existence they accepted as an inescapable feature of their world. Their belief that human action could not essentially break the cycle of suffering and death directed their cultural energies more intensely toward making sense of the realities. Religion helped to fortify their defenses, but even it could not adequately explain what often seemed so arbitrary and unfair.

For all its promised blessings death remained in the public mind a misfortune and curse. No mass glorification of death or pursuit of martyrdom swept the community in the eighteenth century. "Better a thousand nights of misery than one under the tombstone," declared a local saying in a clear affirmation of the will to live.[80] When death struck, people sought to rationalize it, usually as a relief from suffering. Among the wise quotes in one resident's personal handbook was one reflecting on the possible virtues of death: "This death which man so abhors and hates may at times be beneficial. It gives peace to the elderly man burdened with years and to the young boy suffering from disease. . . ."[81] "For someone afflicted with a prolonged illness the grave is a refuge," stated a saying in the same vein.[82] Death, according to another line of rationalization, could be seen as conferring honor on the deceased because the angel of death chose only the best, leaving the worst behind.[83]

Aleppines, in their responses to death, drew on both sacred and earthly elements without making any clear-cut differentiation between them; nor did they isolate death and the dead from the world of the living. The common sight of family members dying at home, of funerals passing in the streets, and of publicly expressed grief exposed the townspeople from an early age to the raw side of death. Graves, too, were a natural part of their landscape, and because of the lack of urban parks, recreation grounds, and open spaces, the cemeteries on the outskirts of town offered welcome places of retreat and play. No walls or fences hid them from view or barred entry into their grounds. People ventured into them to take evening strolls and to play outdoor games among the endless tombs. In 1749 one Jabbur ibn Barakat lost an eye in a cemetery while slinging stones at a target with his friend.[84] Even on special religious holidays for commemorating the dead Christians flocked to the graveyards equipped with food and musical instruments, turning the occasions into lively communal picnics.[85] The sense of respect for the dead was not accompanied by inhibiting taboos or by an attitude of joyless solemnity: in the cemeteries the living and the dead coexisted in casual harmony.

CHAPTER 8

The Urban Experience: Space, Services, and Public Spirit

I
F ALEPPO'S RESIDENTS failed to make their environment health-
ier, they did manage fairly successfully to make it functional and
pleasant. Their urban landscape, considered of impressive proportions by contemporary standards, was attractively built, endowed with
a network of public services and communal institutions, and laid out
with an eye to various needs, including convenience, security, privacy,
and protection from the elements. Considerable efforts and sums were
invested in managing this urban complex, regulating the use of its public
and private space, administering its collective services, and carrying out
construction and repair work.

The city's layout and architectural forms, which conformed to patterns typical of Arab cities in the region as a whole, are fairly well
known; large parts of the premodern city, including homes, markets,
public buildings and streets, still stand today amidst the vast new
metropolis which has come to envelope them in the twentieth century.
The premodern physical arrangements tell much about the urban vision
and collective preferences of the community, but they are not sufficient
in themselves to capture the dynamics and actual experiences of eighteenth-century urban life. They leave unexplained how these arrangements were shaped, how they in turn shaped the behavior and spatial
perceptions of people, how the daily tasks of municipal administration
were handled, and what the politics and economics of urban activities
were like. Nor do they reveal the inconveniences, nuisances, violations
of rights, conflicts, and water shortages which formed part of the urban

scene, or the financial problems of public services and the uneven distribution of their benefits among classes and parts of the city.

A closer look at the realities of development, services, and the use of space helps to move beyond a view of the city as a mere artifact and see some of the underlying processes which shaped it and the urban experiences of the townspeople. There were collective ideals and priorities that guided choices, and rules that regulated activities so as to avoid harm to the public or the rights of individuals. As in other areas, Islam shaped some of the norms and institutions, but not every aspect of the urban scene. Essential physical features of Aleppo and other cities often labeled Islamic—the courtyard house, the seemingly chaotic street pattern, the compact construction of buildings nestled back-to-back—actually dated back to the ancient pre-Islamic cities in the region. Adaptations to the climate, level of technology, and practical needs lay behind many arrangements. The city was run without a municipality, without central planning, and without more than minimal government involvement in managing urban affairs and financing services. Hundreds of charitable foundations (waqfs) formed by philanthropists supported services and communal institutions, displaying one of many aspects of the public spirit and activism essential to understanding the workings of the city. Involved in the activities and decisions which shaped the landscape and the quality of life were property owners, investors, builders, creditors, taxpayers, neighborhoods, guilds, philanthropists, charitable foundations, concerned citizens, and government officials. The economic aspects of the daily processes—the availability of resources, the financial health of the foundations, the distribution of services, the limits set by poverty, the levels of public and private investment in construction —also had an important bearing on the state of urban affairs. Important too was the large size of the city, which affected the tasks of administration and financing as well as the distribution of land uses and the public's familiarity with the city.

In the eighteenth century the dynamics of urban life perpetuated the existing arrangements rather than altered them. There was no marked change in the appearance and layout of the city or the modes of managing its affairs, and the built-up area saw no major expansion. Yet even in this context of a stable urban vision and landscape the information available on the city's daily workings is highly uneven. No official or public body produced maps, cadastral surveys, systematic data on construction and services, or reports on urban issues. The residents themselves left little more than sporadic comments on their urban experiences, while much of the politics surrounding urban issues was played out in informal settings that escaped written records. Many matters, however, passed through the shari^ca court, which acted in some respects as a municipal office. The judicial records contain a vast body of raw information, including the financial accounts of public institutions, which have not been examined yet. What can be pieced together from this detail sheds light on the urban experience in Aleppo, and in a more general way, on essential aspects of the city's economy, politics, and culture.

USES AND PERCEPTIONS OF SPACE

O PEN COUNTRY SURROUNDED Aleppo—orchards, cultivated fields and, most of all, vast burial grounds stretching as far as the eye could see. The hilly terrain, a pleasant mix of browns and greens, rolled gently into the distance. Along the western edges of the city the Quwayq River made its way southward in a verdant valley. A sleepy stream through much of the year, its waters could swell unpredictably in the wet season to flood the land and neighborhoods around it.

Only a portion of Aleppo was divided from the countryside by the city wall. Heavy ramparts enclosed only the oldest section of the town, an almost square area in whose approximate center rose the ancient citadel (see figure 8.1). Extensive districts stretched beyond these walls to the north and east; to the south and west isolated neighborhoods were scattered amid the open country. The old walls, reminders of a time when Aleppo was of more modest size, had lost much of their defensive value by Ottoman days. Without the benefit of government attention sections of them were crumbling, but the nine gates carved in them still served as important passageways. Guards locked them every night, and in times of political unrest the inner city often sealed itself off from the outside. No new walls were built to enclose the other parts of the city. The homes of residents living on the very periphery bordered right on cemeteries, gardens, and open country.[1] Yet the line of blank exteriors of the buildings on the outer edges did form a solid wall of sorts. Some two dozen roads cut through it at different points, with secure gates *(bawwabas)* at their extremities. During the popular revolt in 1819 it took Khurshid Pasha and his troops over three months to break their way into the city through these gateways, after which, in control once again, he vengefully ordered that they be demolished.[2]

1	al-Abraj (L5)	49	al-Masabin (E6)
2	al-A'jam (J9)	50	al-Mashariqa (A6)
3	al-Akrad (H3)	51	al-Mawardi (J3)
4	Akyol (K2)	52	Maydanjik (M11)
5	al-Almaji (J2)	53	Muhammad Bey (al-Takashira) (M10)
6	Altunbogha (K8)	54	al-Mushatiyya (N4)
7	'Antar (L3)	55	Mustadam Bey
8	al-'Aqaba (E6)		(al-Mustadamiyya) (K6)
9	al-'Aynayn (C5)	56	al-Nuhiyya (K2)
10	Bahsita (al-Yahud) (E4)	57	Oghlubey (al-Bab al-Ahmar) (K7)
11	al-Ballat al-Fawqani	58	Qadi 'Asker (N5)
	(Akrad al-Ballat) (N7)	59	Qal'at Halab (Citadel) (J7)
12	al-Ballat al-Tahtani	60	Qal'at al-Sharif (F10)
	(al-Qattana) (N8)	61	al-Qasila (K10)
13	al-Bandara (G5)	62	al-Qawanisa (B5)
14	al-Basatina (H2)	63	al-Safsafa (L9)
15	al-Bayyada (K6)	64	Sahat Biza (G9)
16	Chukurjuk (M5)	65	Sajlikhan al-Fawqani
17	Chukur Qastal (al-'Aryan) (K4)		(Harun Dada) (N5)
18	al-Dabbagha al-'Atiqa (F5)	66	Sajlikhan al-Tahtani
19	Dakhil Bab al-Maqam (H11)		(Aghajik) (N6)
20	Dakhil Bab al-Nasr (G5)	67	al-Sakhkhana (L11)
21	Dakhil Bab al-Nayrab (J10)	68	Saliba al-Judayda (F3)
22	Dakhil Bab Qinnasrin (E9)	69	Shahin Bey (J5)
23	al-Dallalin (N3)	70	Shakir Agha (Shukr Agha) (N5)
24	al-Dudu (M7)	71	al-Shamisatiyya
25	al-Farafira (H5)		(Qastal al-'Aqrab) (M3)
26	al-Farra'in (N4)	72	al-Shamma'in (C5)
27	al-Hajjaj (Jubb Qaraman,	73	al-Shari'atli (Qastal al-Harami) (J1)
	al-Bakraji) (M6)	74	al-Shaykh 'Arabi (M3)
28	Hamza Bey (M4)	75	al-Shaykh Yabraq (L2)
29	al-Hawarina (K11)	76	Suwayqat 'Ali (G6)
30	al-Hazzaza (F1)	77	Suwayqat Hatim (F6)
31	Ibn Nusayr (L6)	78	Tall 'Aran (Sahat Hamad) (M9)
32	Ibn Ya'qub (al-Sighar) (M4)	79	Tatarlar (O4)
33	al-Jallum al-Kubra (E8)	80	Turab al-Ghuraba' (H3)
34	al-Jallum al-Sughra (E9)	81	al-Warraqa (Jisr al-Salahif) (C6)
35	Jami' 'Ubays (al-Maghazila) (G10)	82	Kharij Bab al-Nasr
36	al-Jubayla (K5)		sub-districts (G1, G2, G3)
37	Jubb Asad Allah (E6)		'Abd al-Hayy, 'Abd al-Rahim,
38	al-Kallasa (C10)		al-Arba'in
39	Karlik (O3)		al-'Atawi al-Kabir, al-'Atawi
40	al-Kattan (N11)		al-Saghir, Bali,
41	Khan al-Sabil (L5)		Banqus (Bani Muhibb), al-Ghattas,
42	Kharabkhan (K3)		Jisr al-Ka'ka
43	Kuchuk Kallasa (K3)		al-Muballat, al-Mugharbiliyya,
44	al-Ma'adi (H11)		al-Qawwas
45	al-Magha'ir (D13)		al-Qir, al-Shimali,
46	al-Malindi (M3)		al-Tabla
47	al-Maqamat (G12)		Tuma 'Abd al-'Aziz, Tuma Bishara,
48	al-Mar'ashi (J4)		Tuma Hidaya

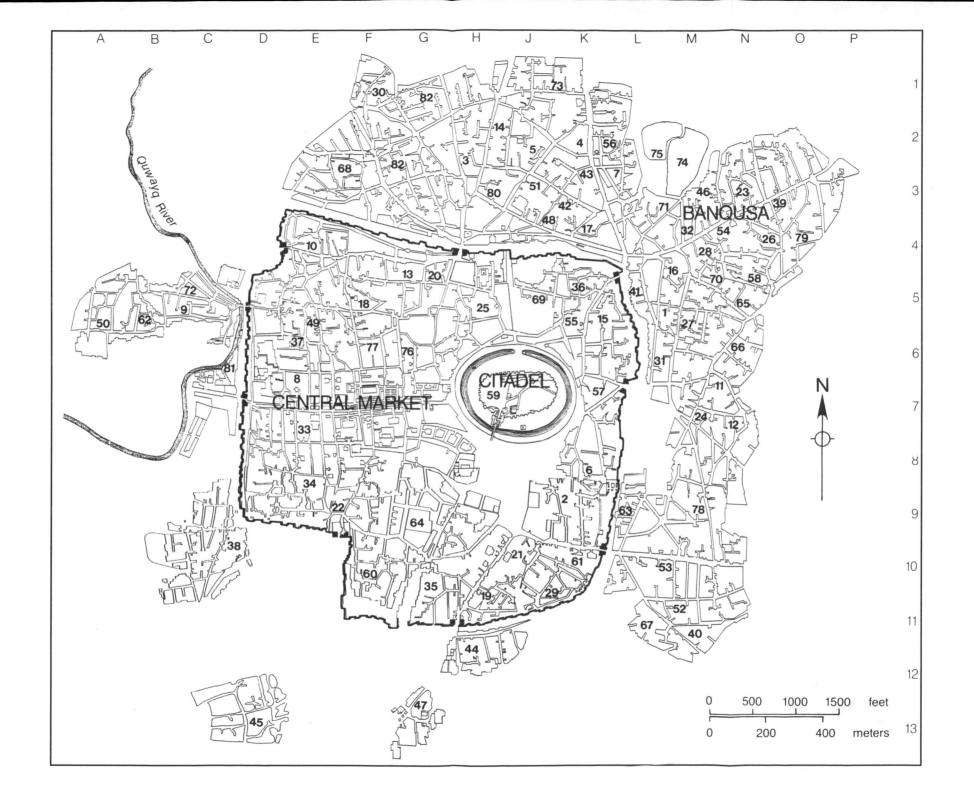

The distance from one end of Aleppo to the other, in any direction, was a mile and a half or two miles at most. The built-up area of the city covered only some 365 hectares (about one and a half square miles).[3] Much, however, was packed into this space, and for the residents, who measured distance on a pedestrian scale, it appeared of vast dimensions. For most people, transportation meant walking: wheeled vehicles were not in use in the city, and animals eased the travel of only a minority of residents, their prices and upkeep placing them beyond the means of the poorer classes. In any case, movement from one part of the city to another was slow, and all residents sought the convenience of a short walking distance. In fact, large numbers did enjoy the advantages of close proximity to shopping and places of employment. Compact construction, which economized on space, and the diffusion of most daily needs throughout the residential neighborhoods were the two most distinct adaptations of the urban layout to this collective need.

From a distance and from within Aleppo appeared a densely built place. Its houses did not exceed one floor above ground level, and only an occasional minaret or domed structure broke the uniformly low line of flat rooftops. But no space separated the buildings: each stood attached to the neighboring ones, together forming solid blocks of dwellings in a tight mosaiclike pattern. One could cross large parts of town by moving on top of the adjacent roofs. Relatively few open spaces outside of the streets offered relief from this compactness; the city provided no public parks or recreation fields. By far the largest unbuilt areas were two open grounds, one at the entrance to the citadel, the other east of it, outside the wall. The latter area, right next to the slaughterhouse, served as the main animal market. Here and there at the junction of two or three main streets one also encountered an open space that qualified as a public square (*saha*) and usually served as the location of neighborhood stores and markets. Only ten such squares boasted a presence worthy of a distinct name.[4] A few small cemeteries, mostly in the intramural city, withstood the pressures of urban development. Some private gardens and orchards also interrupted the built-up area; most of them were located just outside the walls, on what had once been the moat (*khandaq*).[5]

In addition to leaving few urban spaces unbuilt, the community economized on space and collective resources by adapting existing institutions for a multiplicity of uses. Coffeehouses doubled as music clubs and theaters. The baths were places of amusement and relaxation; families even rented them for private parties to celebrate happy domestic occasions. People used the mosques as social centers as well as places of prayer and meditation; they frequented them to chat, to seal business deals, and to relax. The orchards and cemeteries on the town's outskirts substituted as picnic areas, parks, and playgrounds. Young and old ventured to them for a change of scenery and an escape from the congestion and bustle of the city. Such multiple use of space allowed the community to satisfy a variety of personal and social needs without recourse to specialized institutions requiring additional space.

The street system also contributed considerably to the economy of urban space and helped reduce walking distances. Streets occupied only about 10 percent of the urban area.[6] Although highly irregular their pattern had its inner logic. Several major roads crossed the city; they served as the main arteries of traffic, connecting different parts and leading from the intramural center through the gates into the outskirts. Secondary roads branched out from them to tie adjacent districts together. Markets, workshops, and public facilities lined these important routes. But the majority of streets, especially in the residential areas, were narrow winding alleyways, some of them not more than four feet wide. Viewed as no more than functional accessways, they were kept to the minimal width required to allow pedestrian and animal traffic. Shade as well as economy of space were among the benefits of these narrow alleys. Tall blank walls interrupted by shut doors flanked the resident's path as he walked along their cobbled floors; here and there vaults covered the streets, giving them the aspect of subterranean passageways.

This street system did more than any other physical feature to shape the ways in which the townspeople related to their built environment. Much of the daily traffic in the city was channeled by design into the major streets, and away from the many small neighborhood alleyways. Indeed, close to half of the city's total street length was made up of culs-de-sac useless for anything but limited local traffic.[7] The less busy and frequented parts of the city assumed a more private character which the residents actively promoted, and with legal support. Islamic law recognized the dead-end street as a private way belonging jointly to the abutters, who could by common consent even close it off to outsiders. This type of street differed in status from the throughway, which the law defined as a public road immune to any obstruction. Sales deeds always noted whether a property opened onto a blind alleyway (*zuqaq ghayr nafidh*) or a throughway (*zuqaq salik*). In 1750 a group of residents sued the owner of a workshop complex (*qaysariyya*) for opening a back door from his property into their street in addition to its original gate-way into a different road. Criminals, they complained, used this new access to do mischief in their area. They demanded that the door be sealed off on the grounds that it had been cut into a blind alleyway without the permission of its "owners." The judge accepted their claim that the street was "a private way for the exclusive use of the residents," and ordered the owner to seal the disputed doorway.[8] In various parts of town the residents of culs-de-sac installed gates designed to control access into their immediate living areas. These barriers, like the gates at the entrance points to the neighborhoods, were intended to keep out criminals and other undesirables.

The street system and the density of the environment clearly did more than economize on space and reduce the walking distance of the residents. The use of party walls helped to lower the costs of construc-tion and housing. Narrow streets gave protection from the heat and sun. The physical barriers to movement, the lack of open spaces, and the watchful eyes of residents worked to discourage mischief and increase security. Along with these benefits, however, the residents had to accept certain costs. The intense physical proximity played havoc with human life during epidemics. It also exposed the homes to a good level of neighborhood noise—from activities and conversations in neighboring courtyards, from children playing in the streets, from neighbors chat-ting across their rooftops or calling out for their children, from peddlers announcing their wares, and from the din of business in nearby work-shops and markets. Above all, it set severe limits on personal privacy. People lived very much in the public eye. Face-to-face encounters with neighbors were frequent and unavoidable, a close familiarity that had its pleasant aspects but tended to create an overbearing atmosphere of gossip, prying, and social control.

The practical approach that shaped the basic form of the landscape also guided the distribution of land use within it. A functional logic governed the location of houses, shops, markets, mosques, baths, schools, and other activities. It rested on two major lines of differentiation: one between the large nonresidential city center in the heart of the intra-mural section and the predominantly residential areas divided into neighborhoods around it; the other between activities diffused through-out the city and activities concentrated in particular locations, most notably in the city center.

The central district, located along a belt stretching between the citadel and the western wall, was in many respects the functional heart

of the city. Into its dense nonresidential area were crammed the establishments of commercial exchange and religious learning, of state power
and legal justice, as well as hundreds of shops and many caravanserais,
mosques, religious colleges, and public baths. Here were the prestigious
Great Mosque with its vast courtyard; the citadel, which represented
imperial power; the governor's palace below it; and the qadi's Great
Courthouse and two other branches of the court. Noise and busy traffic
filled the area during the day; with the approach of night a heavy silence
descended over it as shoppers, businessmen, and officials returned to
their homes.

Although thousands of residents converged daily on the central business district, the area did not monopolize the supply of all daily needs
and services. Rather, it performed the more specialized functions. Economically, the center dominated the wholesale business and the retail in
specialized goods. Much of the wholesale trade took place in caravanserais *(khans)*, large structures built around open courtyards and equipped
with rooms for the storage of merchandise as well as offices and lodging
for merchants. Most *khans* specialized in particular commodities and
monopolized their sale in the city. Such centralization allowed the tax
farmers to monitor the transactions in particular commodities, and helped
the guilds to control the distribution of goods among their members
according to their assigned quotas. Of the city's sixty-one caravanserais,
twenty were concentrated in the central bazaar, and twenty-seven others in close proximity to it. These handled a wide range of commodities,
from cloth and soap to eggs and cheese. Six other wholesale establishments specializing in various food items (including molasses, onions,
flour, and raisins) were located in the Banqusa market to the northeast;
the remaining eight caravanserais (among them Dar al-Ghanam, which
handled sheep) were scattered in the other districts.[9]

The central business district also dominated the retail in specialized
goods. Within its confines were thirty-seven covered markets *(suqs)*
stocked with goods both imported and of local manufacture. Residents
came here to buy clothes, shoes, jewelry, spices, copper utensils, per-
fumes, drugs, pins, nails, muskets, Chinese porcelain, and European
watches. Not far from the central bazaar, in the area of al-Qasila southeast of the citadel, five other markets offered specialized goods, mostly
saddles, shoes, and other leather goods. The only other commercial
center with specialized markets was in Banqusa, where six *suqs* supplied
thread, poultry, flour, and wood and iron products, and generally pro-
visioned the caravans which departed from Aleppo.[10]

For their routine needs the townspeople did not have to venture to the Banqusa market or the central bazaar. Most basic goods and services were available to them close to home, usually within their own neighborhoods. In this and other respects the neighborhood unit *(mahalla)* formed a central feature of their physical landscape and social life. In the middle years of the century Aleppo had eighty-two distinct quarters, each made up of several adjoining streets and their buildings, and identified by its own name. These small cells, which varied in size and social composition, usually accommodated one hundred to two hundred households. No walls marked the boundaries of a neighborhood to differentiate it physically from its surroundings; the backs of the buildings on its periphery were actually attached to those in neighboring quarters.[11] That, however, did little to dilute the distinct identity of quarters. Heavy gates, shut every night and guarded by watchmen, controlled entry into each of them. Each had its own appointed headman, and acted as a collectivity responsible before the authorities for collecting taxes, maintaining security, and looking after public facilities within its precincts. And each had its own mosque, food stores, and other services. There was no neighborhood without at least some single shops selling bread, fruit, vegetables, spices, butter, tobacco, coffee, coal, firewood, and the versatile services of a barber. Many of these shops stood next door to houses, or were carved into the outer walls of dwellings. In at least forty-four different locations in neighborhoods throughout the city such shops were concentrated in organized markets, thirteen of which were located conveniently at the city gates.[12]

The retail business of the neighborhood shops and markets, clearly geared to the daily needs of the residents, differed markedly from that of the central bazaar. Yet the distinction was not absolute. The central bazaar area and the other specialized markets included many grocery and barber shops. These catered conveniently to the thousands who worked and shopped daily in these busy centers, and to the neighboring quarters as well. As many as 23 of the city's 146 Muslim butcher shops were located in the central bazaar in 1762. The rest were scattered throughout the city, with two particular areas of concentration (14 in the Banqusa market and 18 in the Judayda market).[13]

Just as the central market was not entirely specialized in its wares, the neighborhood was not entirely residential. The mixture of land uses in the quarters was yet another feature of an urban layout geared to a localized life of limited mobility. Residents were clearly not averse to the presence of shops near their homes. They had to go out almost daily to buy fresh, perishable food items or to have their bread baked, and assembling a basket of basic foodstuffs required making the rounds of several specialized shops. Easy access lightened the burden of these chores. Because proximity to place of employment was also a desirable convenience the residents accepted the presence of manufacturing establishments in their residential areas. One Ahmad ibn Muhammad, who operated two textile workshops which he had built outside his home, did arouse his neighbors' wrath, and in 1755 was ordered by the court to leave the quarter. Not the workshops themselves but the insolence of their occupants to women who passed by provoked the local opposition and the ensuing legal suit.[14] Many of Aleppo's artisans labored in workshops dispersed among houses; many others, especially in the textile industry, worked at home.[15] The production of cloth, for example, was distributed in all parts of the city: within the walls and in the northern district craftsmen concentrated on silk stuffs, finer fabrics, and dyeing; the eastern district abounded with weavers and spinners specializing in the processing of wool and cotton. Textile workshop complexes (*qaysariyyas*) operated in all districts, most abundantly in the area north of the city walls.[16] Carpenters, blacksmiths, and members of some of the smaller crafts tended to be more localized; their members worked in particular markets where they also sold their products.

Most local crafts did not produce the offensive smells, noise, or pollution that would warrant their segregation in a separate industrial zone. Only a few industries were removed to the outskirts or away from the main centers of population. All slaughtering was done in one large establishment (*al-maslakh al-sultani*) conveniently situated near the open grounds of the animal market in the southeast. For reasons connected with the monitoring of meat production for purposes of taxation the authorities prohibited the slaughtering of animals anywhere else.[17] The city's tanners worked their skins and hides in a large complex near the river outside the western wall—a location that had the advantage of abundant water and space in addition to distance from the residential areas. Until the late sixteenth century the tannery had been within the city walls, in the quarter known after its transfer as the Old Tannery (al-Dabbagha al-ʿAtiqa).[18] Just south of the tannery, in the neighborhood of al-Kallasa, craftsmen processed in kilns lime excavated in the vicinity. Still further from the centers of population were the manufacturers of rope and catgut concentrated in al-Maghaʾir, an area which produced "a most offensive stench" during certain months of the year.[19]

With places of employment so widely distributed in the city, proximity to work was made accessible to many. Like the localization of shopping, this too reduced the spatial mobility of the population. Nor did the residents need to walk far to pray, study, bathe, and amuse themselves. Of all public facilities none were more abundant than places of worship. Over 250 mosques were scattered in all parts of the city; some neighborhoods, especially in the intramural city, boasted several. Muslim religious fraternities assembled for their devotions and studies in some thirty-four Sufi lodges dispersed in all districts.[20] The non-Muslims, limited to one institution per community, did not enjoy nearly the same easy access to their places of worship. The Jews were able to live in proximity to their synagogue in Bahsita, but at the cost of extraordinary residential crowding in its vicinity. The Christians, however, were far too numerous to be able to attain residential proximity to the seat of their four churches in al-Saliba. Scattered throughout the northern part of the city, some resided more than a kilometer from their church. Although an inconvenience by contemporary standards, it was probably not quite as severe as portrayed by the Maronite archbishop, who complained in a report that some of his flock took as much as forty-five minutes to get to the community's only house of worship.[21]

The bath houses, not quite as abundant as the mosques, were accessible throughout the city, but were definitely concentrated in the more central locations. Of forty-nine identified bath houses thirty-two were located in the intramural city, largely in the area around the central bazaar. Of the baths outside the walls, seven were in the area of Banqusa, seven in various parts of the northern district, and the remaining three in the western neighborhoods. Many, especially those in the extramural districts, had to go some distance to get to a bath house. The Christians in the north, for instance, routinely used the baths in the walled city; in 1752 several of them were reserved for the exclusive use of Christian women, along with baths in the Christian areas of residence in the north.[22]

The children who attended Koranic schools did not go far from their homes. Their classes usually met in mosques or in school buildings *(maktabs)* in their own neighborhoods. The institutions of higher education, on the other hand, were much more centralized. Of thirty-one colleges offering classes in the mid-eighteenth century all but four were situated in the intramural city. The old part of town remained the center of higher learning and the seat of government. The governor and the qadi, the high officials and the imperial garrison, the tax offices and the prisons were all located within the walls, along with the residences of the urban elite associated with the state. Only one branch of the shariᶜa court operated outside the walls, in the busy center of Banqusa.

By the eighteenth century at least half of the city's population had made its home in the districts outside the walls. Removed as these residents were from close proximity to the old city center they remained in many ways linked to it by daily or periodic needs which no other section of the city could satisfy. Employment, shopping, bathing, college classes, litigation, and politics continued to draw them into the urban center. A main road leading to the nearest city gate and from there to the bazaar area was within easy access to them no matter where they lived. With urban expansion, however, came also a good measure of decentralization. The extensive districts to the north and east of the intramural city were self-sufficient in many respects, especially in daily necessities and routine services. For their residents, and for the townspeople in general, the more immediate locality tended to dominate the pattern of movement and activity.

One consequence of such a localized life was a partial familiarity with the place. "Everyone in Aleppo knows that half of those living in one part of the city are almost totally ignorant of the monuments and old sites in the other part," sighed a native scholar in 1940, frustrated in his search for Muslim landmarks in the old city. "Many of the inhabitants of Bab al-Nayrab do not know where the quarter of al-Saliba is located, and likewise, many of al-Saliba's residents are ignorant of the location of the neighborhood of Bab al-Nayrab."[23] The whereabouts of districts just a mile or so away from their homes no doubt were unknown to many residents in the eighteenth century as well. Not unlike urbanites in other regions and periods, their perceptions of the environment were to a large degree partial and rudimentary. The objective city as such did not exist in their minds; they knew or remembered what was physically distinctive and what was generally useful in their everyday patterns of spatial behavior, and their cognitive maps of the city mirrored the spatial patterns of regular activity. There were of course those whose work or curiosity took them into many areas of town and who knew the city much better than others, but most people never saw some parts of the city, which thus also remained perceptually invisible. A middle-class Christian businessman from al-Saliba and a poor Muslim laborer from the area of the Nayrab Gate would have had little cause to ever visit each other's districts of residence.[24]

The townspeople moved in their city's labyrinthine maze without the benefit of any street or guide signs, building numbers, or maps. They

oriented themselves in terms of a well-known and commonly understood system of coordinates. Walls, gates, districts, streets, and landmarks helped them to locate places and to direct their way to them.
Most of these physical and spatial elements had names that gave them
recognizable identities and proved particularly useful as a set of collective guiding symbols because of their remarkable stability—some of
them dated back to the early medieval period—and because they often
contained useful locational clues.[25]

To identify the location of a house, for instance, one provided an
address whose level of detail could vary. Real estate deeds of sale, in
which precise definition mattered, routinely used more descriptive addresses, such as "in the quarter of al-Malindi outside the Banqusa Gate
outside Aleppo."[26] The elements used in this type of common address
expose the local perceptions of space: the city's walls and gates, for
instance, served as basic geographical markers. The distinction made
between the walled city, which was often referred to as Aleppo proper
(Madinat Halab), and the sizable urban areas outside it had no legal or
administrative basis, but it proved useful for narrowing down the location of places. The dyers' guild even adopted this dividing line as the
basis for distributing work among its members: half the cloth went to
the craftsmen working within the walls, the other half to their colleagues
outside them.[27] The nine gates, each known by name, provided useful
reference to more specific parts of town; these were employed as a
system of coordinates. Markets located at the gates were conveniently
named after them: there was the Market Inside the Nasr Gate and the
Market Outside the Nasr Gate. Several neighborhoods were also named
after the gates near which they were situated.

Many streets had no commonly known names. Even sales deeds only
infrequently included a street name in the address of a property. The
quarter, although a less specific spatial unit, was most commonly used
by residents to identify location. It was deemed a sufficient address:
once in the neighborhood people were assured of easily finding their
way to a precise destination simply by asking around. The quarter
names, all of them old and familiar, originated from a variety of sources:
craft specialties (furriers, soap works, couriers, caravan guides, candle-
makers); personal names (Hamza Bey, Ibn Ya'qub, al-Mar'ashi); local
landmarks (caves, tombs, mosques, gates, fountains, markets); and social
groups (Persians, Jews, Kurds, Hawranis). By the eighteenth century
many of the names had lost their original relevance. They remained in
use, but alongside them proliferated additional labels for the same dis-

tricts. Almost all of these were practical names identical to the names of local institutions and landmarks. People often referred to their quarter by the name of its main mosque (al-Bakraji for al-Hajjaj, Harun Dada for Sajlikhan al-Fawqani, Aghajik for Sajlikhan al-Tahtani), or of the principal fountain in the locality (Qastal al-ʿAqrab for al-Shamisatiyya, Qastal al-Zaytun for ʿAntar, Qastal al-Hajjarin for al-Masabin). Local markets, squares, gates, and religious institutions substituted in similar fashion for quarter names.[28]

By association residents extended the name of a local landmark to their general district of residence; it identified the locality more concretely than a traditional name of inexplicable origin. This flexible and somewhat loose practice manufactured a pool of practical labels which found their way even into formal documents. Street names, coined by local usage, were likewise anchored in concrete aspects of the landscape rather than in abstractions, and served the same practical end of guiding spatial orientation. Almost all of the streets were named after a distinguished individual or family associated with the place (for example, the Street of the Amir family); after a prominent local landmark (for example, the Coffeehouse Street); or after a physical feature of the street (for example, the Long Street). Some landmarks were so widely known that they were sufficient to identify the location of a nearby place without the aid of a quarter or street name. A list of the city's Muslim butcher shops drawn up by the court in 1762 included these laconic addresses: "Bahramiyya" (a mosque), "near ʿUthmaniyya" (a college), "Coppersmiths" (a market), "Khan Abrak" (a caravanserai), "near the *qaysariyya* of al-ʿUjaymi," "near al-Qawwas Bath House," "Halawiyya" (a college), "the Fountain of al-Chawish," and "near the house of Ibn Hatab."[29]

CONSTRUCTION AND DEVELOPMENT

IN 1911 A cadastral surveying team dispatched from Istanbul labored in Aleppo to assign names to the city's streets and numbers to its buildings.[30] Its efforts at ordering the landscape only confirmed to residents that a new wind was blowing over the urban scene. After a lull of almost two centuries their town was expanding outward again. The new residential districts, which began to spring up on the outskirts in the second half of the nineteenth century, bore little resemblance to the older sections. Wide streets laid out in a grid pattern and lined with multistory apartment buildings replaced the traditional courtyard houses and the narrow, winding alleys. Their inhabitants were native families, many of them non-Muslim, for whom this new milieu represented the modern world, which they were eager to join.

And, indeed, the changes on the urban scene signaled a sharp break with the past, the adoption of imported European models rather than a logical outgrowth of the traditional vision. As in most other areas of local life, this Westernization was new. Urban development in Aleppo in the course of the eighteenth century consisted of renovation and new construction carried out within the traditional set of choices in an unexpanding city. In the process the environment was modified in a multitude of small ways, but without altering its overall layout, appearance, and size—reproducing rather than reshaping the existing scheme of things. While this urban development lacked the novelty of the subsequent period it was quite important both economically and in terms of the processes that shaped it.

The bulk of construction involved the repair and renovation of existing buildings. Not only were many of the city's buildings old, but they also tended to deteriorate at a relatively fast rate, largely because the construction materials other than the stone used for exteriors held imperfectly against the elements. Strewn about the city were ruined structures *(kharabas* or *khirbas)* that had fallen victim to neglect and the forces of nature.[31] Walls cracked and indoor paint peeled off. Water and drainage pipes, made of clay, leaked and threatened the foundations. The lime coating on the roofs decomposed with the winter frost, causing damage; the flat roofs caved in under the weight of snow accumulations; violent hail storms shattered glass windows. Heavy rains flooded the houses in low-lying areas and weakened their supports. When the Quwayq overflowed its rushing waters devastated entire neighborhoods in its vicinity.[32] In January 1776 al-Halabi witnessed the effects of unusually heavy rains. "The old houses collapsed," he commented in his chronicle. "The central bazaar was closed down because of water leaks in the shops, the mud in the markets, and the collapse of buildings right and left."[33] The greatest threat to buildings clearly came from winter weather, which residents blamed, even in court documents, for the deterioration of real estate.[34]

The endless cycle of repair acted as the metabolic process by which the city renewed itself. Other types of construction, described in numerous court documents, accompanied it. From year to year some houses were turned into shops, and some commercial buildings were modified to accommodate new lines of business. Some homes acquired additions as their owners expanded into adjacent dwellings or built a room or two above ground level; others were partitioned into two separate residences. Here and there old dwellings were knocked down and replaced by fresh residences. The period produced some very handsome houses striking in their size, breadth of conception, and decorative features.[35] However, additions to the impressive inventory of mosques, colleges, and other public institutions were few. The ʿUthmaniyya College (1730), the Ahmadiyya College (1754) and the Hajj Musa mosque (1763) ranked as the most notable of them. Their construction, the work of philanthropists, stimulated little additional urban development because existing real estate donated by the founders formed their main source of income.[36] The case was different in the sixteenth century, when the founders of several major institutions had the supporting real estate newly built as well. Four governors founded mosques, and in the process also added as endowments hundreds of new shops and other commercial facilities which together almost doubled the surface area of the central market.[37] No eighteenth-century philanthropist replicated this level of new construction.

Even in a century of halted urban expansion vast sums were spent on construction, to replace buildings and, more commonly, to repair and renovate them. In the absence of any comprehensive figures the financial records of the charitable foundations provide a sense of the magnitude of investment in the maintenance of public buildings and rental real estate. Deterioration and decay haunted the administrators without respite. On the average, one-quarter to one-third of the annual rental income they collected was eaten up by outlays on renovation and repairs, and even that level of expenditure often proved inadequate. Many of the foundations found themselves in deficit, reduced to borrowing hundreds of piastres from private individuals to finance urgent construction work.

The overall level of demand from the public and private sectors supported a construction industry of considerable economic importance. It provided livelihood to a large body of people engaged in several specialized crafts and trades. The sites of major construction teemed with stonecutters, masons, plasterers, painters, carpenters, blacksmiths, sawyers, stone carriers, and water carriers. A large number of wage laborers (*faʿala*, Turk. *ırgat*) swelled the ranks of the industry. Many producers and suppliers provided the building materials. Stone, the chief building material, which came from quarries conveniently located on the outskirts of town, was available in several varieties, each handled by specialized dealers. There were also suppliers of lime, marble, timber, baked bricks, gypsum, nails, hemp, copper, glass, and a variety of other materials. The versatile guild of druggists supplied the paint.[38]

The process of urban development was fed by the multitude of private property owners and the charitable foundations, which between them controlled virtually all of the land and buildings in the city. The state was an insignificant proprietor, and invested little in construction and renovation. Neither did it finance housing or commercial projects, or contribute to the construction and maintenance of most public services and facilities. Mosques, schools, hospitals, water fountains, and an array of other communal services depended for their foundation and upkeep on endowments by private philanthropists. Neighborhoods maintained the streets and gates within their precincts from funds collected locally. The government concentrated its outlays on the repair of its own facilities and fortifications, such as the citadel and the governor's palace.[39] This narrow scope of government investment in construction was quite in keeping with traditional Ottoman practice. Even in the heyday of imperial power the state treasury allocated relatively minute sums to construction and repair: the state budget for 1527–1528 provided only some 3 million akçes out of 403 million for construction throughout the empire.[40] Urban areas usually gained only a minor share of that investment, which tended to focus mostly on trade and pilgrimage routes, bridges, ports, and dockyards.[41] In the eighteenth century Aleppo showed signs of official inattention even to state installations. Visitors were quick to note the neglected state of the citadel and of what official documents pretentiously called the "imperial walls" *(al-sur al-sultani).*[42]

It was therefore not government but numerous individuals and charitable foundations who made the daily decisions affecting urban development. Their interests determined the level of investment in the urban environment and the uses to which land and buildings were put, as well as their physical appearance. On the face of it, their activities appear to have been subject to little systematic regulation: the city lacked a public agency for urban planning, an official master plan, elaborate zoning ordinances, or anything more than rudimentary government supervision. Yet those who modified buildings or changed land uses were hardly free to do as they pleased. They were bound by a set of laws that defined the rights of other individuals and of the larger public. If their activities caused harm to others, they could be taken to court and ordered to rectify the damage. Some official oversight, exercised primarily through the court and the builders, also worked to ensure conformity to the desired standards.

The community accepted several fundamental norms for the use or modification of space: it must not encroach on the property of others or threaten domestic privacy, the morals, health, and security of the public, the safety of neighboring buildings, and the freedom of movement in public ways. Shari'a law as well as local custom backed these norms. Violations, judging from the complaints that came before the court, tended to be limited in number, representing a normal level of friction rather than a breakdown of order. Litigation tested and reaffirmed the norms and public commitment to them. When Ahmad ibn Husayn turned his stable into a grinding mill in 1768, his neighbor complained that its vibrations threatened his house; in court Ahmad agreed to close down the mill and give the property to some inoffensive use.[43] Bakers who lined a main street with bread stalls provoked repeated complaints by residents inconvenienced by the obstruction of a public way (*tariq al-'amma*).[44] A large group of residents succeeded in having a new bakery in their neighborhood closed down after a court investigation established that the place harbored criminals and men who harassed female passersby.[45] When vacant properties and empty lots attracted prostitutes and criminals the court responded to demands by offended neighbors that the owners rectify the situation. One Husayn ibn Abu Bakr even obtained permission to fence at his own expense a ruined mosque across from his house in order to keep away the idle troublemakers who assembled there.[46]

Domestic privacy was a matter of particular sensitivity. The community regarded the indoor activities of the household as private and the home as a protected sanctuary free from unwelcome observation. The design of dwellings reflected this concern: regardless of size, they were laid out around a central courtyard, with all rooms and ground-level windows opening inward; tall blank exterior walls barred all observation from the outside. Islamic law recognized unlicensed observation as offensive behavior. Builders as a matter of course watched for the effects of any change they made on the privacy of neighbors. The possible compromise of the females of the household made violation of domestic privacy a particularly offensive act. One group of residents sued a man for dumping dirt against the exterior walls of their homes, on the grounds that their courtyards and women were thereby exposed to the view of outsiders who climbed on the mounds.[47] The segregation of the sexes was expected to apply even in public places. In 1754 the qadi ordered that a shop for weighing wool be closed after the competitors complained that the owners allowed their male and female customers to mix freely.[48]

In addition to providing legal protection the authorities also supervised development to ensure conformity with the norms. Two building inspectors (sing. *al-miʿmar al-sultani*, Turk. *mimar-i hassa* or *mimar başi*) issued building permits and inspected construction work in return for fees paid by builders and property owners. The judges dispatched them routinely to arrange the physical division of houses between co-owners, to survey the condition of buildings, and to assess rents.[49] These functionaries were actually local master builders who bought their official positions from the state. In typical fashion they continued to pursue their private business while in office. Muhammad ibn ʿAbd al-Qadir, who served as inspector during the middle years of the century, operated a quarry, handled the supply of building materials, and acted as contractor for major construction work.[50]

The builders of the day, who had the most direct hand in shaping the urban landscape, threw their weight on the side of conformity with the traditional norms. Their role was particularly important because they did the actual designing of buildings and in their work followed guild codes that were attentive to public concerns as well as professional standards. Without much training in architecture they were able to apply a technical expertise that had won their medieval colleagues regional renown, and continued to draw praise from visitors.[51] "Builders are not educated in any principle or rule; they learn by routine," noted the British consul in the city. Nevertheless, they "understand their trade and build securely and quickly."[52] Architectural novelty and originality were not among their concerns; in designing a structure they applied their skills to the arrangement of the rooms and facilities in the given lot to provide the optimum ventilation, lighting, privacy, and comfort.

Urban development in the course of the century conformed successfully to the vision inherited from previous generations. Residents were not prompted to reorder the existing arrangements by new economic and social needs, changes in the technology of construction and transportation, or imported urban models and designs. They continued to work with a stable and familiar set of choices. The potential for disorder lay not in conflicting values but rather in the harm that individuals pursuing their own ends could cause to the property rights of others or to the welfare of the wider public. Interests did collide; one person's improvement occasionally proved another's nuisance. Yet the overall level of harm and abuse was effectively limited by the public respect for established rights and standards as well as by official enforcement. Government, which contributed little to development by way of construction, financing, or planning, upheld the institutional framework that ordered the process. It played a similarly mixed role in the provision of public services.

PUBLIC SERVICES AND COMMUNAL INSTITUTIONS

D URING THE EIGHTEENTH century Aleppo maintained virtually no public museums, parks, libraries, orchestras, theaters, fire-fighting units, transportation system, orphanages, homes for the elderly, or hospitals. Those services and institutions financed or managed on some collective basis were limited essentially to sanitation, upkeep of public ways, schools and houses of worship, and water supply. On the face of it, this rudimentary setup appears a rather simple affair, confirming yet again the low level of corporate organization in municipal matters. The inner workings of the public services, however, were anything but simple: they were not organized under one authority, nor were they run according to a uniform set of institutional arrangements. Each displayed its particular modes of management, financing, and public input. Sanitation was handled largely by garbage collectors hired for a fee by the bath houses, although accountable to the public for the quality of their service; Aleppo's residents contributed no taxes to finance the service. The upkeep of streets, on the other hand, was their direct responsibility, with each of the neighborhoods paying for and hiring the necessary labor. The hundreds of schools, mosques, and other institutions were managed by autonomous foundations, which financed their public services from donations made by private individuals, with the waqf as their main instrument of operation. Finally, water supply depended on a peculiar mix of a public water system and private enterprise. The public system itself combined financing by means of taxes and donations, and management by officials, charitable foundations, and a guild of self-employed water technicians.

This diffuse and seemingly disorganized setup worked, even if imperfectly. It provided residents with a clean city, streets in good repair, a wide network of communal institutions and, with less success, access to water. The active part taken by the townspeople in this process rendered the services public in much more than the nominal sense that they were dedicated to the collective needs and interests of the community at large. Neighborhoods, trade guilds, religious communities, charitable foundations, and concerned residents all participated in the administrative and financial workings of the public services, and so helped to shape their quality and the distribution of their benefits. To observe the public decision-making process in full one must clearly look below the level of government. Yet here as in other areas the lackadaisical and uninvolved approach of the authorities in matters of social policy concealed the important play of official control and direction. The government imposed obligations, delegated responsibilities, supervised the adherence to rules, arbitrated disputes, and enforced legal rights.

Nothing intervened during the eighteenth century to alter the old premises on which this approach to public services rested. The community continued to define its ideals of comfort, health, education, and spiritual fulfillment in the same terms, and to pursue them with the same set of institutional arrangements. No technological innovations modified people's expectations, and the minimal role of government and the limited resources available—two constraints to which the traditional approach had adapted well—remained with the community throughout the century.

In public thought and daily behavior, urban issues tended to figure in narrow and specific terms rather than on a grand, citywide scale. Discussions, complaints, responsibilities, and expenditures in most matters involved limited groups of residents concerned about some local issue or specific facility. There was no point in residents from various parts of town organizing a campaign for an urban cause such as the increase in the number of water fountains, schools, or mosques in the city as a whole, or even in certain districts. The establishment and upkeep of these institutions depended on private charity, not collective pressure and government action. Grievances and donations also had to be directed toward specific facilities, since they ran their affairs independently with their own sources of funding rather than as units of an administratively connected network with a collective budget. Individual institutions and services, not the larger system and broad policy, dominated public attention.

Even mandatory tasks required of the population as a whole, such as the maintenance of streets and gates and the draining of sewage, were in practice highly localized. Each neighborhood was collectively responsible for such upkeep within its precincts only. The headman of the quarter, who was a resident of the locality rather than a government official, collected the necessary dues from the households in his district, hired repairmen, and oversaw the maintenance. Even here charity came into play. The neighborhood endowments for the support of the local poor helped to subsidize these expenses as also other financial obligations which ordinarily fell on the quarter, such as the wages of watchmen and water technicians, government taxes, and local contributions for the maintenance of the public water system.[53] Residents were accustomed to thinking of such matters in the narrow terms of their own specific quarters. Much of the politics surrounding urban issues played itself out at the neighborhood level, where concerned residents held discussions, applied pressures, bargained, and made decisions.

When the community allocated responsibilities and expenditures by neighborhood it was applying a practical principle which guided its general approach to urban upkeep: the direct users and beneficiaries bear the financial burden. For most purposes the neighborhood proved a natural unit for undertaking such responsibility. When a facility such as a sewage system served several quarters, the maintenance costs were spread among them.[54] In some situations, however, the level of responsibility was not so clear-cut; it had to be established by identifying individual beneficiaries, even cutting across neighborhood lines. In 1754, when two public latrines near the Great Mosque needed major repair after their plumbing had become clogged, the 550 piastres for the work were collected from the entire complex of the central market: all of the specialized markets, caravanserais, mosques, schools, commercial establishments, and neighboring houses in the area that benefited from the latrines and shared the same plumbing system were required to contribute. The court supervised the business of assessing the damage, dividing the cost, and collecting payments.[55] Such problems did not arise when a public latrine, usually the product of private philanthropy, was supported by funds from endowed property. When endowments had ceased to exist, the community addressed emergencies as they came up, working without a preallocated budget but with certain established procedures to guide the distribution of the financial burden.

The politics and economics of urban services are illustrated best by the issue of water supply. No public service occasioned as much strife, inconvenience, or expenditure. The key problem was the limited and unpredictable supply of the public water system (Qanat Halab), the city's chief source of drinking water. The flow, which drew on springs north of the city as well as the river, weakened considerably during the hot summer months. In years of poor rainfall the supply fell to the point of causing widespread thirst and misery. An appreciable portion of the source water never reached the city; the fields and orchards on the way drew on it for irrigation, often in excess of their allotted shares. Within the urban area an elaborate system of pipes distributed the water to public fountains, mosques, bath houses, and a small proportion of private homes.[56] Both the urban and agricultural users held defined legal rights entitling them to a limited amount of water supplied during certain specified hours of the day. The neighborhoods outside the western walls were not connected to the public system; they obtained their water from the nearby Quwayq, by an arrangement that entitled them to a limited share of the river's water. The landowners in the surrounding area also had legal claims on this water.[57] In the summers the river's flow dropped to a trickle, leaving both residents and farmers in dire straits.

While the water system was intended to supply primarily public facilities serving the general population, a portion of the water flowed to some private homes. Only several hundred of them enjoyed this luxury; as is evident from thousands of recorded sales deeds, most dwellings transferred on the market came without any legal right to public water. In the course of time a few residences joined the public network, some by purchasing rights from their neighbors or from public fountains, others by connecting to the system illegally.[58] Only the better-off could afford the regular water fees charged on domestic supply or the price of dwellings equipped with water rights, which were substantially more expensive than other homes. One Hasan Agha ibn ʿAbdallah, upset at discovering that a house he had bought did not come with the promised right to water, wanted to abrogate the contract, but finally settled for a substantial compensation from the seller of 175 piastres, a sum equivalent to the price of two or three lower-class houses.[59]

The majority of families were left to fend for themselves in other ways. How they fared depended on their level of wealth, their residential location, and the season of year. Every house was equipped with a draw well (*jubb maʾ*) which provided free water of varying quality. In the northern parts of the city the underground water was generally drinkable; in the southern neighborhoods, on the other hand, mostly brackish water was drawn up which was usable only for washing the floors and for other household purposes.[60] During the summer months even this source often dried up entirely. The better-off had recourse to a surer supply. They bought drinking water, storing it in large domestic tanks which, like their food stocks, insured them against shortages. The water carriers *(saqqaʾin)* who made this water available for purchase on the market belonged to a trade guild which divided among its members monopoly rights in the different neighborhoods.[61] During the wet season the townspeople also collected rain water from the house roofs into domestic cisterns.[62] The poor families, who could ill afford to pay for their water or to maintain large domestic reservoirs, depended almost entirely on the public fountains in their quarters, from which they carried water to their homes in pails. The fountains were unevenly distributed in the city: the older and better-off neighborhoods, which included the intramural city and the districts to its north, benefited far more frequently from the largesse of wealthy residents, and boasted a more elaborate network of public facilities.

The resourcefulness of the residents in exploiting all possible water sources relieved only in part the pressures on the public system. The demand on it was heavy, and often exceeded the available supply. In periods of severe drought there were acute shortages and mass suffering. Water, like bread, became a luxury, and public fountains the scenes of fist fights just like the bakeries. "The river has dried up completely, and the supply from the public water system is down to less than a fifth," commented al-Halabi during the severe water shortage in 1786. "The people are suffering greatly from thirst. Those living in the inner city can barely find any water." The supply to the public fountains was rationed, and those accustomed to buying water found the prices exorbitant. Even al-Halabi, who was comfortably off, felt the pinch. "During some days we had no choice but to drink from the draw well. But most people saw even their brackish wells dry up."[63] The owners of the orchards along the river, most of them wealthy urbanites, exacerbated the public's plight by illegally diverting water to their properties in amounts far in excess of their allotted shares. Such "theft," as al-Halabi termed their behavior, often accompanied water shortages; the powerful did not shirk from exercising their muscle when their interests were threatened. In 1738 residents brought suit against a group of landowners who diverted to their private properties water intended for the general public; the court proceedings established their responsibility for serious water scarcities.[64]

Water shortages, like scarcities of food, occasioned some manipulation of the weak by the strong, and exacerbated social tensions between them. More commonly, though, they gave rise to vehement conflicts between neighborhoods. Qastal ʿAli Bey, a large fountain that served several poor quarters in the southeastern part of the city, suffered periodically from insufficient supply because neighborhoods to the north tampered with the pipes and diverted the flow toward their own facilities. The deprived residents brought several suits against the usurpers, and even sent a collective petition to the sultan in Istanbul listing their grievances. At least on one occasion they retaliated in kind by cutting off the supply of water to their northern neighbors.[65] This bickering over water spilled over occasionally into conflicts with other localities. Many miles to the north of the city, in the area of ʿAyntab, villages tended to irrigate their fields and orchards with the source waters of the Quwayq despite an official ruling in favor of Aleppo's rights to them. In 1723, 1746, and 1758 the townspeople brought suit against them for theft of water.[66]

Occasionally confrontational, water supply politics remained on the whole bound by a set of institutional constraints. In litigation, arguments revolved ultimately around the issue of rights, as established by law or custom. The authorities not only enforced the rights when violations came to their attention, but also maintained a rudimentary machinery to oversee the orderly management of the public system. They appointed a water inspector *(nazir al-maʾ* or *nazir al-qanah)* to supervise the maintenance of the network and the distribution of water among entitled users; he also certified arrangements regarding water supply and heard related grievances. This public office, which was held in the middle years of the century by the wealthy merchant ʿAbd al-Qadir Agha Amir Zadeh, became the focus of popular complaints in times of crisis. In 1767 the residents of several quarters in the southern part of the city, upset by the shortage of water in their areas, accused the inspector of incompetence and went so far as to demand his removal from office.[67] Through the inspector the administration allotted 400 piastres a year to the subsidizing of the annual cleanup and repair of the aqueducts.[68] Much of the cost of this operation, however, was financed directly by the residents, each neighborhood contributing a lump sum. Part of this revenue went customarily into the pockets of the qadi, who formally supervised the cleanup. The judge in office in 1757 took uncharacteristic exception to this venal practice for its harm to the public and especially the poor; in a document couched in pious language he expressed the hope that his successors would follow his example of restraint and compassion.[69]

Most directly involved in running the public system were the water technicians *(qanawis)*, who roamed the city day and night, turning the water on and off to the multitude of facilities and homes according to their prescribed shares. Members of a trade guild rather than public employees, they were hired by homeowners, mosques, water fountains, and other public facilities with water rights to monitor their shares and to maintain the local plumbing in working condition. Much depended on the commitment of the technicians to an honest supply to the users. Some did betray their trust by short-changing customers or diverting water to individuals without title to it, presumably for private gain. Residents and institutions victimized by these manipulations fired such technicians or took them to court. The guild reprimanded dishonest members and periodically pledged before the authorities to uphold the rules of distribution.[70]

The running of the public water system depended in a still more fundamental way on nongovernmental skills and contributions. Since government did not contribute to the support of the two hundred or so public fountains run by the waqf foundations (although occasionally a governor or qadi volunteered to found or repair a fountain at his expense),[71] generous men and women donated to this public cause. A few built new fountains and endowed real estate for their continued support; others volunteered to repair old fountains that lacked any surviving endowments. More commonly, people dedicated property, usually a house or shop, for the support of their neighborhood facility.[72]

Although some parts of town tended to benefit more from such private largesse than others, the city as a whole does not appear to have lacked a sufficient number of fountains as much as a sufficient amount of water. Every new fountain required water rights, which were not always readily obtainable. When Muhammad Chalabi ibn Mahmud bequeathed money for a new neighborhood fountain the water had to be secured from the voluntary donations of forty-seven local residents who agreed to surrender a portion of their entitlements.[73] The 2,500 piastres which one As'ad ibn Nasir earmarked in his will for the construction of a new fountain were spent instead on the repair of the public water system. A group of residents argued in court that another fountain would prove less beneficial to the public good.[74]

Through the combined efforts, expenditures, and sacrifices of individuals and groups the community kept the public system working, but without overcoming its underlying weakness: insufficient water. New water sources were not readily available in this dry land, nor did the community possess the financial resources to undertake a major water project. Poor supply, in fact, continued to plague the city into recent times.[75] The only serious attempts to increase the supply focused on the maintenance of a long aqueduct which diverted water from the Sajur, a tributary of the Euphrates in northern Syria, into the Quwayq. The addition to the river's flow benefited the owners of the field and orchards on its banks more than it did the consumers within the city. Originally built in the fourteenth century, the aqueduct lay in a state of disrepair during good parts of the subsequent period. Around 1530 an earthquake damaged the system, cutting off the flow to the Quwayq. A hundred years later a wealthy Aleppine, Na'san Agha, restored the aqueduct at his expense, and endowed considerable property for its maintenance. By the early eighteenth century the aqueduct was again out of order, with all the endowment dissipated. The authorities organized its repair around 1737, after levying massive sums of money from the city's population and recruiting all of the city's builders for three months. Sometime in the second part of the eighteenth century the Quwayq again ceased to receive water from the Sajur.[76] Khurshid Pasha sought in 1819 to repair the aqueduct; his enormous tax demands to finance the project, coming in a period of great hardship in the city, helped to touch off a violent popular uprising.[77]

In comparison with water supply, the institutions of education and worship posed few formidable difficulties to the community. The network was hardly of insignificant size. Over 250 mosques and dozens of Sufi lodges, religious colleges, and Koranic schools dotted the landscape, the majority of them concentrated in the intramural districts and those north of them. Like water fountains, they too were established by private philanthropists and maintained from the revenue of endowed properties administered by waqf foundations. The origins of most of them predated the eighteenth century, but the townspeople continued to donate income-producing real estate to keep these communal heirlooms alive.[78] The authorities provided little financial support for the religious institutions short of some small stipends to subsidize certain positions. But the government upheld the public character of the services and their responsibility to the larger community. It appointed the foundation administrators and the staff of preachers, leaders of prayer, teachers, and other functionaries all the way down to the janitors.[79]

The public had some input too: many of the appointees obtained their positions by the recommendation of local residents. Residents were often present in the court to give their approval when the qadi made appointments to their neighborhood mosque or fountain. They also felt free to complain about incompetent administrators and to seek their replacement. Among the objects of such complaints were an administrator who kept a mosque closed for ten years while pocketing the revenues, and the administrator of a religious lodge who turned the rituals into sexual orgies, in addition to acting as a pimp for his wife and other women.[80]

Such occasional input by residents was one facet of a public spirit whose most powerful expression lay in the charitable basis of so many local institutions: the citizens who spent considerable sums to establish services dedicated to the larger public, and the many others who donated valuable income-producing real estate to help finance the ongoing costs of these services. The waqf, which mediated this transfer of private wealth to public uses and regulated the financial management of this wealth in the general interest, was central to the system of services.

The acts of charity were fed by several possible motivations, which were not mutually exclusive. Many were driven by a genuine desire to help their neighborhoods and communities. The chains of successive beneficiaries listed in the deeds of endowment were usually confined to institutions within the same neighborhood, indicating the strength of local attachments. Some probably hoped to win divine favor and improve their fate in the hereafter. And at least some had their eyes on the earthly rewards of philanthropy, seeking consciously to exchange wealth for honor. The upper-class families routinely made large donations as part of their claim to social recognition; inscriptions on public buildings and institutions named after them immortalized their generosity. Ahmad Effendi Taha Zadeh established the Ahmadiyya College, ʿUthman Pasha the ʿUthmaniyya College, and Bahram Pasha the Bahramiyya Mosque. Musa Agha Amir Zadeh named the mosque which he built in 1763 Jamiʿ al-Khayr (the Mosque of Beneficence), but it soon became popularly known as the mosque of Hajj Musa.

Whatever their motivations, sacrifices of private property for the support of public services and communal institutions were not daily events. They appear more impressive for their cumulative effect than their frequency. The most comprehensive list of waqf deeds for the period, compiled from the city's court archives, shows 687 endowments for the years 1718–1800.[81] Of these only 348 (51 percent) were genuinely charitable endowments; 270 (39 percent) were family trusts, and the remaining 69 were a combination of both. The donors, who included a high proportion of women (36 percent), were clearly a limited group, of which almost half dedicated property for private causes that made no contribution to the welfare of the general public. Only a few came to court every year to draw up deeds of endowment, and they usually contributed only one or two properties to existing institutions. In a few cases the donated assets were modest indeed: Husayn ibn Abu Bakr dedicated a one-twelfth share of a house, ʿAʾisha bint Ismaʿil donated one room in a dwelling along with half the courtyard, and Ahmad ibn Hijazi endowed a ruined house.[82]

The donors who contributed to charitable causes showed some clear preferences: half of the endowments went to places of worship and devotion (130 to mosques, 72 to religious lodges, and 13 to the four churches and the synagogue). Of the other half, 50 went to the support of public water fountains, 25 to religious schools and colleges, and the remainder to a miscellany of causes with no direct bearing on public services in the city (including donations to the holy cities of Mecca and Medina and the hiring of men to read portions of the Koran for the soul of the donor and his family). The Christians and Jews used the waqf, but far less than the Muslims. They relied heavily on other means, such as customary contributions, taxes, and fund raisers, to meet the needs of their communal institutions, which were in any case quite limited in comparison with the Muslim network.[83]

For better or worse, the terms of an endowment were at the discretion of the donor, not the public. In his deed he was free to determine how much property to donate, how its proceeds would be spent, and who would manage it. The broad initiative left to donors allowed charitable whims to find unrestricted outlet, but also fostered certain inequalities. The absence of a public mechanism for directing donations to needy institutions or to parts of town lacking in particular facilities resulted in a highly uneven distribution of services. In the old intramural city and in the better-off northern districts many more water fountains, mosques, and schools served the residents than in the other parts. Nor was there any central office to coordinate the activities of the waqf foundations that financed and managed the network of institutions. Each foundation operated independently under its own administrator, who rented out the assets and used the proceeds to finance the needs of the institution in his trust. The court supervised some of the operations of the foundations and audited their annual accounts, but beyond that each was left to fend for itself according to its resources and the skills of its administrators.

Some foundations fared better than others. Many institutions supported by endowments enjoyed a remarkable longevity. The residents drew water from fountains, prayed in mosques, and studied in schools established well before their time, many indeed before the Ottoman conquest. Maristan al-Nuri, the hospital established in the twelfth century, was still treating patients in the eighteenth century. Assets donated by successive generations of philanthropists helped these institutions to survive and fulfill their services. At the same time, not a few facilities met with financial difficulties and ceased to serve the public. Some were ultimately restored by well-to-do residents and caring officials; others fell into permanent ruin.

Overall, the level of endowment was not quite sufficient to finance the ongoing needs of the city's public services; many institutions operated on tight budgets and with chronic deficits. The fortunes of the foundations were also affected by the quality of their administrators and by market trends. Neglect of property, embezzlement of funds, falling rents, and long-term vacancies could spell financial doom for such facilities. The foundations operated on the market as economic enterprises, but a variety of constraints peculiar to the waqf institution set limits on their options. As a mode of financing and managing public services the waqf had its shortcomings as well as strengths. The rich body of waqf records in the court archives tell a story of mixed performance.

Aleppo's foundations drew their income from properties that formed

TABLE 8.1. Properties and Annual Income of 98 Charitable Foundations, 1751–1753

	Properties		Income	
Sources of Income	Number	Percent	Amount (in piastres)	Percent
Urban properties				
Commercial	448	32.6	6,122	49.3
Residential	180	13.0	2,356	19.0
Plots of land	620	45.1	1,097	8.8
Nonurban properties				
Agricultural	91	6.6	2,613	21.0
Plots of land	37	2.7	133	1.1
Interest on loans			106	
Total	1,376	100.0	12,427	100.0

SOURCE: Aleppo court records.

in their aggregate an impressive economic base. The annual financial accounts of ninety-eight mosques, schools, and water fountains audited by the court between November 1751 and October 1753 show combined assets of 1,376 properties (see table 8.1).[84] These included shares as well as whole properties. Half of the total income of the foundations came from commercial real estate—stores, workshops, bath houses, coffee houses, oil presses, and caravanserais—located in neighborhood markets and the central bazaar area. Endowed houses were far less numerous and yielded a smaller share of the income. Fields and orchards on the outskirts and in the countryside contributed almost a quarter of the revenues; they were twice as productive as urban properties. At the other end of the scale stood the least lucrative properties—plots of urban land. These were the sites of former waqf buildings that had fallen into ruin. Lacking the funds to rebuild them, the foundations were reduced to leasing them to prospective builders in return for a small annual ground rent *(hikr)*. Some endowments were totally dependent on these minimal payments while others drew the bulk of their income from them.[85] The waqf lands included Christian burial grounds and the synagogue. The Halawiyya College owned the land of an entire street (Zuqaq al-Muballat).[86]

The total expenditures of the institutions—14,762 piastres—ate up their entire income of 12,427 piastres as well as most of the 3,746 piastres that they had held in surplus at the beginning. Half of the expenditures went toward the routine operation of the foundations (see table 8.2). The managing staff collected wages for their labors; some foundations employed just one administrator *(mutawalli)*, while others provided for additional officers such as inspectors *(nazirs)*, revenue collectors *(jabis)*, and clerks *(katibs)*. About one-quarter of the outlays went to wages for other employees of the institutions—398 persons ranging from janitors and water technicians to preachers and professors. The routine operating expenses also covered various provisions such as oil, lamps, and mats; taxes on property; fees to the court for notarial services; and ground rent to landlords.

These were predictable and stable expenditures which varied little from year to year. The wages of both administrators and employees often remained fixed at low levels (usually 5 to 10 piastres a year) by stipulations of donors made decades earlier, providing some remuneration for the part-time service of men who were expected to have additional sources of livelihood. The unpredictable and financially burdensome pressures came from repairs and repayment of debts, which together accounted for half the total expenditures. The institutions invested routinely in painting, plastering, plumbing, tiling, and other repair work in their buildings. When buildings required major reconstruction work the administrators could often finance the necessary work only by borrowing the funds, thus throwing their foundations into indebtedness, at least temporarily. Most of the foundations had limited or no funds set aside for emergencies. Of the ninety-eight institutions, as many as forty-five ended their audited year with a deficit, and thirteen had a zero balance. Of the forty institutions that had a surplus at the end of the year, twenty four had less than 50 piastres in their coffers. Only one of the foundations purchased additional real estate to increase its sources of income.

The single most pervasive threat to the self-sufficiency of endowed public services was the failure to keep up with the deterioration of buildings. The foundations spent considerable funds on repair and maintenance, but often lacked the resources to keep their properties in optimum condition. They relied heavily on outside capital to carry them through emergencies. The administrators had to contend with constantly changing levels of expenditure: because of repair work and debts incurred in the process outlays could double or triple from one year to the next, surpassing the available income (see table 8.3). Revenues also tended to fluctuate, although to a lesser degree. Rents rose and declined,

TABLE 8.2. Annual Expenditures of 98 Charitable Foundations, 1751–1753

Expenditures	Amount (in piastres)	Percent
Wages of management	1,076	7.3
Wages of employees	3,998	27.1
Provisions	1,512	10.2
Taxes and fees	535	3.6
Rents	79	0.5
Repairs and maintenance	3,953	26.8
Repayment of debts	3,537	24.0
Investment in real estate	24	0.2
Unspecified expenses	48	0.3
Total expenditures	14,762	100.0

SOURCE: Aleppo court records.

depending on the physical condition of the properties and the general economic situation in the city. When foundations were able to charge higher rents or to attract new donations they saw a certain increase in their incomes; when they settled for reduced rents or failed to find tenants for some properties their incomes declined. All institutions experienced these ups and downs.

The kinds of financial pressures that bore on the foundations colored

TABLE 8.3. Income and Expenditure of Charitable Foundations in
Three Selected Years, 1746–1756
(amounts in piastres)

	1746–47	*1751–52*	*1755–56*
Husayn al-Fattal Mosque			
Income	94	94	118
Expenditure	34	106	136
Arghuniyya College			
Income	103	86	89
Expenditure	91	303	521
Bakraji Mosque			
Income	111	106	121
Expenditure	72	120	149
Dabbagha 'Atiqa Mosque			
Income	85	99	109
Expenditure	95	247	242
Qawanisa Mosque			
Income	92	78	67
Expenditure	63	223	225
Sa'd Allah Fountain			
Income	93	89	85
Expenditure	91	42	40
Zaynabiyya Mosque			
Income	672	678	677
Expenditure	685	404	327
Mushatiyya Mosque			
Income	80	98	142
Expenditure	148	165	207
Aghajik Mosque			
Income	131	145	145
Expenditure	156	147	162

SOURCE: Aleppo court records.

their daily activities in the market. With an eye to bringing in needed cash and outside investment they struck all sorts of deals, and even replaced deteriorated properties with others in better condition. These adaptations allowed them to survive hardships and maintain their public services. A practical spirit pervaded their economic operations, and with the blessing of the court. The qadis used their discretionary powers as overseers of the foundations in a pragmatic and responsive fashion. Openly conscious of the demands of economic life and the constraints faced by troubled foundations, they applied the law in a flexible and realistic fashion. They authorized deviations from the terms set down by the donors when this appeared to serve the interests of the foundation and the community. This approach did not extend into a preferential treatment of foundations. Waqfs lost legal suits over property rights, rent arrears, and taxes to Muslims, non-Muslims, and even resident Europeans.[87]

The search for relief from financial difficulties led foundations into leasing arrangements that proved beneficial, at least in the short term. One common method of raising cash was to collect the rent in advance for the entire period of the lease. Foundations justified this practice by the urgent need for funds to finance repairs or repay debts. They usually left in the tenants' hands small sums to cover taxes and routine maintenance.[88] To obtain larger immediate advances foundations turned to long-term leases extending over a decade or more. The court readily relaxed the stipulation in many endowment deeds that urban properties not be leased for more than one year at a time, accepting the claims of administrators that their institutions were in urgent need of the cash for repair work. Some foundations paid back their debts by way of long leases. In order to repay 1,200 piastres owed to its former administrator one foundation leased to him a house free of charge for thirty-six years.[89] In the case of raw land that they could not themselves redevelop, foundations obtained the court's permission to offer the plots in perpetual leases. In return for the payment of an annual ground rent the tenant enjoyed in perpetuity the right to use the land as he pleased, including full ownership of all the buildings and improvements that he added. The foundations usually collected less than one piastre a year for each lot.[90] Leasing parcels on such terms was often the best course available to foundations lacking the funds to redevelop their land, although by so doing they surrendered for good the use of these sites.

Foundation administrators tended to rely on their tenants, especially those with long-term leases, to invest in necessary repairs. Rather than reimburse tenants directly they usually repaid them with extended leases at reduced rates or free of charge.[91] In the case of major commercial facilities such as bath houses and caravanserais the foundations did not even refund the tenants for their outlays on repairs. They conveniently turned the invested sums into security deposits *(raqaba)* which the tenants obtained only at the end of their leases, and then from the new tenants rather than the foundations. A tenant who left before his lease was over forfeited his deposit.[92]

For the major renovation and reconstruction of mosques, schools, fountains, and endowed real estate many foundations had to rely on outside capital. Administrators appeared frequently in court to request authorization to debt-finance large-scale rebuilding. The building inspector and court officials assessed the necessary work, and upon its completion visited the site again to verify the reported outlays, which usually amounted to several hundred piastres. Administrators usually raised the necessary money by borrowing or putting up the needed sums from their own pockets by way of a loan to the foundation.[93] They also resorted to more creative methods of financing renovation work, by offering investors a variety of rewards, including long-term leases on easy terms, and even shares of annual rents from waqf properties that they rebuilt. One water fountain foundation struck a deal with a local resident by which he would repair the facility in return for the right to transfer the surplus water to his home.[94]

Rather than repair deteriorated properties foundations at times traded them for more productive private real estate. This exchange *(istibdal)*, carried out under court supervision, was designed to replace endowed properties that the foundations could not repair with private properties of higher rental yield. Sometimes the foundations exchanged shops and houses for cash, which was to be used for purchasing other property or to be lent out at interest, usually at the specified rate of 10 percent.[95] The exchange provided the waqfs with a means of reviving their sources of income, but at a cost. The private entrepreneurs who made these dealings with the foundations, usually members of wealthy families, acted not out of sheer altruism. They acquired properties with lower current rental values, but with potentially higher capital values. They invested in their repair and occasionally sold them at prices that suggest a good profit.[96]

The business activities of many public institutions showed the unhealthy effects of financial plight. Long-term and perpetual leases at constant rental rates were symptoms of certain economic weaknesses intrinsic to the waqf institution. The foundations proved imperfect as economic enterprises, often failing to maintain self-sufficiency; private capital, obtained at times on compromising terms, was essential to their survival. Their mode of operation, based as it was on the collection of rents from perpetually endowed properties, closed off to them the avenues of profit and capital gains available to the private businessman. The foundations possessed bath houses, coffee houses, oil presses, water mills, and other highly valuable properties in prime locations, but they did not involve themselves in operating them, either with hired labor or through partnerships that would provide for profit sharing. This activity and the ensuing profits were left to private entrepreneurs. Nor were the foundations free to respond fully to changing market conditions. If rents were falling, or a better investment opportunity appeared, or a chance for capital gain presented itself, only the private investor was in a position to dispose of his property and redirect his investment. But the conservative premises of the waqf had their merits too. Setups more enterprising and flexible would have required special business skills and entailed high economic risks. The remarkable even if troubled longevity of many public institutions rested in good part on the manageable nature of their funding.

The economic plight of the endowments worked to the benefit of people in the private sector. Craftsmen and merchants were able to acquire business premises at favorable and stable rents for extended periods. Many houses and shops were built at much reduced cost on waqf land made available at minimal rents. Virtually useless plots were recirculated and exposed to the benefits of outside capital. Through the exchange transactions many endowed properties rejoined the mainstream of market activity, and benefited from input by private capital. Clearly, the distributive effects of the waqf included not only the intended transfers of benefits to the larger public, but also transfers of material advantages to some of the tenants, builders, lenders, borrowers, entrepreneurs, and others who did business with financially troubled institutions. These advantages, which tended to benefit mostly people of means, reversed to some degree the progressive redistributive effects of the endowments.

The line between public service and personal benefit was not very distinct in the case of many institutions. Mosques, fountains, and schools were often managed exclusively by their founders' families, who also drew a good share of the income by way of an annual stipend. They thus functioned at once as public services and family trusts. Following the provisions made for them by the founders the relatives who served as administrators usually collected far higher salaries than the usual 5 to 10 piastres. The administrator of one mosque collected for herself as much as 560 piastres from the annual income of 800 piastres.[97] Relatives designated as beneficiaries also drew on the revenue of the institutions. In 1751–1752 the Koranic school of Shihab al-Din Ahmad paid one-third of its income to relatives of the founder, while as much as two-thirds of the revenue of the fountain of Isma'il Agha went to the pockets of three of his descendants.[98] Several hundred people, women as well as men, enjoyed such annual stipends. Women, who often administered family endowments, managed the foundations of public institutions only in those instances in which the founder had designated them for the position.[99]

The blurred boundary between private and public was only natural in a system of public services dependent on private charity. The widespread poverty and the lack of official responsibility for public needs rendered every private donation a welcome act, even when tempered by residual personal benefits. Under the circumstances there was nothing morally irregular about the blend of interests; it represented, after all, the incomplete transfer of private property to public use rather than the privatization of public property.

CHAPTER 9

The Urban Experience: Neighborhood Life and Personal Privacy

O N A SUMMER day in 1757 Mustafa ibn Khalil and his wife
Maryam bint Nasir walked out of the shariʿa courthouse under orders to move out of their residential quarter. Fifteen of
their neighbors filed out of the crowded session satisfied, having successfully engineered their expulsion. The man and his wife, they had explained to the judge, were immoral people and an offensive presence in
their district. Mustafa drank, neglected his prayers, and used foul language, while Maryam sold sexual favors with her husband's encouragement. The residents did not want persons of this sort in their midst,
and the qadi agreed.[1]

For the hapless couple, and for the townspeople in general, the
neighborhood was not merely a neutral area of residence. A neighborhood could affect the lives of its residents in a variety of ways, of which
the expulsion of undesirables was but one dramatic instance. The eighty-
odd quarters, which gave the city its distinctive cellular structure, were
relevant to the welfare of their members on two levels. Each was an
officially designated administrative unit responsible as a collectivity for
the taxes, security, physical upkeep, and public morals of its precinct.
And, in a less structured way, each was composed of a group of people
living in close proximity and involved in frequent and often intense
relations with each other.

What precise meaning this neighborhood setting had for the townspeople cannot be established accurately from the general features often
ascribed to the residential quarters in premodern Middle Eastern cities:
that they were socially homogeneous, each incorporating members of a

particular religious, ethnic, occupational or income group; that at least partly due to this social affinity they formed parochial solidarities that defended themselves collectively against other groups; and that they served as instruments of administrative management and government control, with the neighborhood headmen acting as intermediaries between the residents of their respective districts and the authorities. In Aleppo many of the quarters contained a social mix, and the rich texture of their inner life, with its squabbles, scandals, civic action, familiarity, warmth, social control and limited privacy, cannot be explained entirely in terms of local solidarity or official control.

The processes which shaped neighborhood life and gave it importance in the city's history can be located on several levels. The quarter was a major forum in which residents took part in the city's public life; on its limited stage they confronted some of the issues of the day. Although the records provide only faint glimpses of local activism, politics thrived at the neighborhood level, its issues revolving around internal management, nonconformity, the distribution of services and tax demands, and in the late eighteenth century, participation in the factional competition for power. The social makeup of the neighborhoods exposes the complex relation between social distance and physical distance in Aleppo, and the importance of factors other than affinity with a group in determining where one lived. The sociability which marked ties in various contexts was perhaps most vividly displayed in the quarter; for the meaning of company, conversation, and leisure one needs to visit not only the more institutionalized forms of social intercourse, such as the coffeehouses, baths, picnics and private parties, but also the casual yet often intense scene of the neighborhood streets. The intricate boundaries between self and society as they were drawn in Aleppo are also illustrated well at the level of the quarter; the give-and-take of neighborhood relations tested and defined the rights and duties of the individual vis-à-vis the group, and the limits on personal privacy give one indication of the weight exercised by the collective. In all these respects, a picture of the makeup and inner life of the neighborhoods based on empirical evidence rather than assumptions opens up essential aspects of the urban experience in Aleppo.

THE COMPOSITION OF THE QUARTERS

FOR A CITY with only one and a half square miles of built-up area Aleppo abounded with neighborhoods. A composite picture of the residential divisions in the middle years of the century, drawn from thousands of addresses listed in the court records, yields eighty-two quarters (sing. *mahalla*), including the residential area within the citadel (see figure 8.1).[2] About one-third of them (twenty-eight) were located in the intramural city, while the remaining two-thirds made up the extensive areas outside the old walls (twenty-nine in the east, sixteen in the north, and nine in the south and west). The fragmentation was actually even more pronounced because the large district of Kharij Bab al-Nasr in the northwestern area outside the walls corralled into one administrative precinct a group of small neighborhoods each with a distinct identity of its own. Although known usually as *zuqaqs* (literally, streets), many of them were composed of networks of streets rather than one single road.[3] The administrative unit that held them together since the early development of the area in the first part of the sixteenth century began to separate into its component elements in the second part of the eighteenth century.[4] From 1762 the authorities assessed most of the "streets" as separate tax collectivities endowed with fiscal autonomy and the makings of full-fledged quarters; the rest were combined in groups to form new neighborhoods or were appended to existing districts.[5]

While the city did not experience the outward physical expansion of the sixteenth and seventeenth centuries that added many new neighborhoods to the landscape, the number of quarters did increase somewhat through the subdivision of existing neighborhoods. Even the intramural city, fully built already several centuries earlier, added some new quarters, like Shahin Bey and Mustadam Bey, by the separation (*ifraz*) of residential districts from established neighborhoods. The process of fission, fueled usually by fiscal and administrative considerations, was part of the normal dynamic of the neighborhood system. It introduced minor modifications into the residential divisions rather than any new conception of urban organization. In the long term the arrangements were more striking for their stability than their changes. Most of the city's quarters in the eighteenth century had already existed by the late sixteenth century.[6]

The size of neighborhoods, like their number, tended also to fluctuate over time, but proved more responsive to demographic and social changes. Years of catastrophic mortality reduced the number of residents without affecting the number of quarters. Neighborhoods shrank or expanded as families moved or changed in composition, and as the number of houses underwent modification through division or change of land uses. On the whole they remained small, housing on the average some 1,200 to 1,500 individuals in an area of 4 or 5 hectares (10 to 12 acres). A few neighborhoods, like Bahsita, al-Jallum al-Kubra, Sahat Biza, and al-Shari'atli, boasted populations more than twice the average, while many residential quarters counted only a few hundred persons among their inhabitants.[7] The size affected the tasks of administration and tax collection, but not to any large degree social relations. In the smaller quarters people were likely to know a larger proportion of the local residents, but not necessarily a larger or smaller number of neighbors than the inhabitants of the more populated neighborhoods. In this respect the social composition of the quarter mattered much more than its size.

Aleppo's residential quarters were by no means homogeneous units or neat spatial embodiments of social groups. The makeup of each locality reflected the workings of several choices and constraints which tended to pull in different directions. The desire to live close to members of one's religious or immigrant group affected the choice of neighborhood, but so also did the practical need to live in proximity to one's place of work and the availability of affordable housing. The overall effect was a spatial distribution of the population in which the tendency of groups to concentrate in particular parts of town rather than to occupy exclusive quarters was the most distinct feature.

Neighborhoods varied in their level of wealth and social atmosphere. But there was no neighborhood inhabited exclusively by a single group, whether Jews or carpenters or upper-class families or ashraf or Turkman tribesmen. Even in quarters named after social groups the composition was inconsistent with the labels; these names tended to identify only one element in the locality, and were even at times anachronistic. The Jewish Quarter housed only a portion of the Jewish community and was also inhabited by many Muslims. The Kurdish Quarter in the northern part of the city had no remnant of the Kurdish population that had settled there in the Mamluk period; its eighteenth-century inhabitants were Christian and Muslim. The name survived even into the early twentieth century when a census found 93 percent of the residents to be Christian.[8] The Persians who once lived in the quarter of al-Aʿjam and the people from the Hawran who gave their name to al-Hawarina several centuries earlier had by the eighteenth century lost their distinct identity or were dispersed, while the old neighborhood names remained in common usage.

If some quarters began originally as homogeneous settlements of particular groups the dynamics of daily life gradually introduced variety into their midst and eroded their original character. Even the religious minorities, bound by a parochial communal life, did not enclose themselves in exclusive ghettos. They lived among their own kind, but in a number of mixed neighborhoods with large Muslim populations. The Jews were concentrated in three contiguous quarters (Bahsita, al-Bandara, and al-Masabin) in the northwestern section of the intramural city. Their immediate neighbors were often Muslim.[9] Jewish families lived in houses contiguous to the mosque of Bahsita, while a Muslim inhabited a dwelling adjoining the synagogue.[10]

Like the Jews the numerous Christians also lived in the midst of a substantial Muslim population. Their homes were scattered throughout the northern part of the city in an array of religiously mixed neighborhoods and streets. Even the quarter of al-Saliba, seat of the churches, religious hierarchies, and Christian elite, counted some Muslims among its residents. Although a few Christians gave addresses in the intramural city and the district of Banqusa outside the eastern walls,[11] the northern district remained throughout the century the natural habitat of the Christian population. A region of fine homes and thriving industrial enterprise, this part of the city attracted Muslim artisans and businessmen who settled alongside the Christians.

The Kurds, Turkman, bedouin, and poor rural folk who immigrated to Aleppo usually made their homes in the neighborhoods outside the eastern walls of the city; some, but not all, settled alongside members of their tribes or places of origin. Again, this depended on their place of employment and the availability of housing; many bedouin actually lived in residential *qaysariyyas* in the intramural city where they worked.[12] At the same time many poor urbanites employed in agriculture, weaving, and the servicing of the caravans also inhabited the eastern neighborhoods alongside the rural immigrants.

Markets, artisanal workshops, baths, mosques, schools, and other places of work were scattered in all parts of the city, and so also the men and women employed in them. Different parts of the city had their particular economic specializations, and the occupational makeup of their populations varied accordingly, without, however, resulting in neighborhoods organized neatly by profession. The Furriers (al-Farra'in), Caravan Guides (al-Dallalin), and the Messengers (Tatarlar) quarters near the Banqusa market were probably named during their early devel-

FIGURE 9.1. *Price levels of houses in Aleppo in the mid-eighteenth century. The numbers refer to the residential neighborhoods, listed in fig. 8.1.*

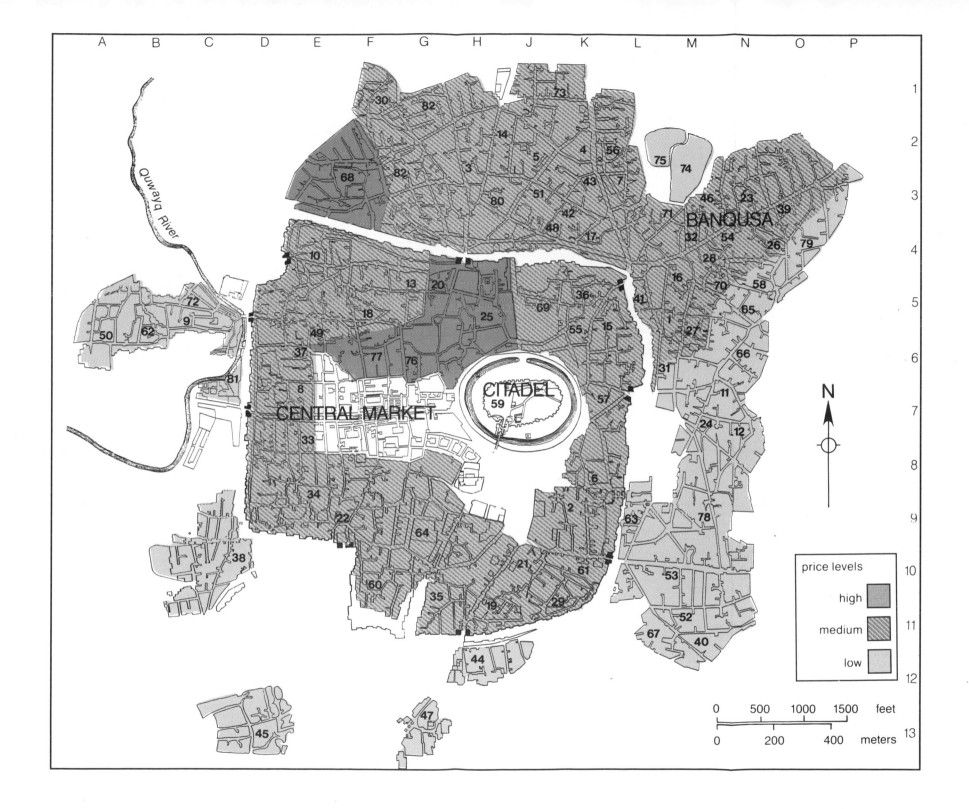

A B C D E F G H J K L M N O P

1
2
3
4
5
6
7
8
9
10
11
12
13

Quwayq River

30
82
73
14
5
4 56
75 74
68
82 82
3
43 7
23 39
51
80
46
71 BANQUSA
42
48 17
32 54 26 79
28
10
16 70 58
13 20
36
65
69 41
18 25
1 27
55 15
66
49 77 76
31
37
CITADEL
11
8 59 57 24 12
CENTRAL MARKET
6
33
34
2
63 78
22 64
21 61 53
38 60 35 19 29
67 52
40
44
47
45

price levels
high
medium
low

N

0   500   1000 1500 feet
0   200   400   meters

opment in the sixteenth century, and while the labels survived into the eighteenth century and after, their social makeup has not remained bound by the original pattern of settlement. Only al-Kallasa and al-Magha'ir, both isolated from the main centers of residence, may have had a measure of professional concentration not found in the other quarters. The first, located near the quarries, specialized in stonecutting and the production of lime; the second produced rope and may in fact have been the home of Aleppo's rope makers. The residents of most quarters, however, proved more homogeneous in social and economic status than in occupation.

The well-paved streets, abundant services, and handsome homes of some neighborhoods posed a marked contrast to the slumlike appearance of other districts. Yet the differentiation between neighborhoods on the basis of wealth defies simple generalizations. Some of the wealthiest families lived around the city center, while many of the poor inhabited neighborhoods in the outlying areas, but the distribution of classes did not fall into a neat concentric pattern, and many quarters actually housed a mix of income levels. Data on housing prices drawn from sales deeds make it possible to establish with more precision the residential distribution of the population by level of wealth, and more specifically the economic differentiation between and within the quarters.

Many neighborhoods were composed entirely or overwhelmingly of the smallest and least expensive dwellings. Housing prices in those parts seldom exceeded 200 piastres, and the average annual price of sales rarely rose above 150 piastres. In the twelve-month period between June 1750 and May 1751, twenty-one houses in al-'Aynayn sold for an average of 87 piastres, forty houses in al-Kallasa averaged 132 piastres, and fifteen in Sajlikhan al-Tahtani averaged 84 piastres. At the other extreme were a few neighborhoods lined with expensive residences ranging in price from 700 to several thousand piastres. In 1750–1751, eleven houses sold in al-Farafira averaged 1,242 piastres, ten in Su-wayqat Hatim averaged 854 piastres, and twenty-seven in al-Saliba averaged 977 piastres. Between the top and bottom ranges were many neighborhoods of different levels of wealth; the average prices of homes sold in them annually ranged between 200 and 700 piastres.

The distinction between neighborhoods of high, intermediate, and low housing price levels captures in rough form the main lines of economic differentiation. The quarters in each price level tended to be distributed in particular parts of town (see figure 9.1). The most expensive homes of the day were most highly concentrated in a few neighborhoods surrounding the central market and citadel, and, outside the intramural city, primarily in the quarter of al-Saliba in the northwest. The elite Muslim families favored the established neighborhoods in the inner city. The quarters of al-Farafira, Suwayqat ʿAli, Suwayqat Hatim, and Dakhil Bab al-Nasr in particular boasted some of the most expensive residences within the walls. Comparable to them was al-Saliba, home of the Christian elite, where houses in the thousands of piastres were standard. The predominantly poor neighborhoods were scattered outside the walls, forming an arc of poverty surrounding the city on the west, south, and east, with the exception of the Banqusa area in the northeast. The neighborhoods north of the walls, the Banqusa district, and the intramural quarters removed from the city center made up the areas of intermediate wealth. Of these three regions the mixed Christian-Muslim quarters in the north included the highest concentration of well-to-do and the Banqusa area the most modest population. In the intramural city houses were generally more expensive in the northern segment than in the area south of the market and citadel.

If wealth in the city decreased with distance from the center it was only in certain directions and in an uneven fashion. The regions to the east, south, and west of the walled city were predominantly poor, but the area to the north boasted an even higher proportion of expensive

TABLE 9.1. Prices of Houses Traded in Various Districts of Aleppo in Three Selected Years, 1750–1759

Price	Intramural		North	
(in piastres)	Number	Percent	Number	Percent
1–100	287	25.1	122	13.3
101–200	324	28.4	214	23.3
201–400	253	22.2	310	33.7
401–600	143	12.5	124	13.4
601–800	28	2.5	60	6.5
801–1,000	31	2.7	21	2.3
1,001–1,500	31	2.7	32	3.5
1,501–	44	3.9	37	4.0
Total	1,141	100.0	920	100.0

residences than the center (see table 9.1). Prices of houses in al-Hazzaza and al-Shariʿatli on the far northern edges of town were generally higher than in Dakhil Bab al-Nayrab or al-Qasila within the walls. Proximity to the center weighed with some more than others; many of the city's wealthy families chose to live in the generally attractive northern district away from the center. At the same time multitudes of modest households made their home in the neighborhoods within the walls, and poorer people inhabited even the generally better-off quarters, including the most prestigious. In al-Farafira, the home of many Muslim elite families, Asʿad Pasha al-ʿAzm purchased a large mansion for 11,500 piastres while one Asiya bint ʿAbdallah paid 35 piastres for a half-share in a two-room house.[13] Between these two extremes were houses in a wide range of prices.[14] In Suwayqat ʿAli, the residence of the wealthy merchant Musa Agha Amir Zadeh, some houses sold for as little as 100 piastres while others went for twenty-five times that price.[15] The powerful Chalabi Effendi lived in al-Jubayla, a neighborhood of many fine homes—but in which twenty-one out of thirty-seven houses sold in 1750–1751 were valued at less than 200 piastres each. In al-Jallum al-Sughra the wealthy Ahmad Effendi al-Kawakibi was also surrounded by many inexpensive homes; thirteen houses sold there for less than 100 piastres in 1750–1751, along with sixteen others valued at prices of up

TABLE 9.1. Prices of Houses Traded in Aleppo
(continued)

Price (in piastres)	East		South and West	
	Number	*Percent*	*Number*	*Percent*
1–100	450	48.7	233	72.2
101–200	241	26.1	52	16.1
201–400	148	16.0	34	10.5
401–600	57	6.2	4	1.2
601–800	13	1.4	0	0.0
801–1,000	4	0.4	0	0.0
1,001–1,500	7	0.8	0	0.0
1,501–	4	0.4	0	0.0
Total	924	100.0	323	100.0

SOURCE: Aleppo court records.
NOTE: The table analyzes the combined sales during three twelve-month periods (in 1750–1751, 1755–1756, and 1758–1759).

to a thousand piastres. Some differentiation in levels of wealth occurred even in the poor neighborhoods on the outskirts of town, where some houses sold for three or four times the value of others around them.

Many of the city's neighborhoods, in short, contained a mix of income groups rather than a homogeneous population of one single class. The distinction between quarters remained real: some neighborhoods were associated with high status and refinement while others had rather unsavory reputations.[16] But real too was the differentiation *within* quarters, which helps to refine the picture of neighborhood composition. The well-to-do did not segregate themselves in exclusive residential districts, and not for lack of concern with social distance. They could live amid a generally poorer population without having their status compromised precisely because so many social arrangements safeguarded that distance even in conditions of physical proximity.

The mix of social backgrounds, occupations, and faiths in many of the neighborhoods created some familiarity among groups whose members might have been drawn farther apart by residential segregation. While the boundaries of the neighborhood did not set limits on the social associations of people, and ties of friendship, patronage, kinship, and business cut across quarter lines, the quarter did foster local relationships of a distinct sort. It thrust residents into a milieu of familiarity, shared interests, and collective obligations which, for better or worse, involved them with neighbors.

LIVING WITH NEIGHBORS

R IGHT OUTSIDE ONE's front door thrived the neighborhood scene, with its companies of noisy children, vendors advertising their wares, and residents huddling for a casual chat. In the local markets, streets, fountains, mosques, and coffeehouses people came into frequent contact with neighbors, stopping to greet each other and to share news and gossip. The dense physical environment made for a lively climate of familiarity and high exposure; the narrow streets, attached houses, and open courtyards placed people very much in the public eye. Their comings and goings, their visitors, even their domestic quarrels became matters of public knowledge. Activities and conversations in the courtyards, especially in the multitude of small houses, could be overheard by neighbors and passersby. Many among the poor shared their dwellings and indoor facilities with other households, and the common use of draw wells, courtyards, and entranceways that accompanied multiple occupancy entailed routine exposure to neighbors.

The townspeople took for granted this intense familiarity and limited personal privacy. "No one knows you better than God and your neighbor," acknowledged a local saying.[17] Neighbors were familiar with details of each other's identity, origins, occupation, economic circumstances, and familial events. Hearsay, observation, and personal acquaintance kept them informed about local events and scandals. Much about themselves and their families they felt no particular need to conceal, and even advertised locally for the sake of social recognition. School graduations, circumcisions, weddings, and deaths were public events, celebrated with outdoor processions of relatives and friends. Even more intimate details such as the defloration of brides and the contents of their trousseaus were made public in displays to which the community attached social importance.[18] Such was the familiarity among neighbors that when questions arose in court about the marital status of women deserted by their husbands or the financial circumstances of imprisoned debtors or the character of an individual the testimony of their neighbors was routinely called to resolve the matter.[19]

Privacy did matter, but primarily in its physical form: while keenly protective of the body and home against unwelcome exposure, a relatively low priority was allocated to the privacy of information. This was largely a matter of cultural preference, in the sense that the community opted for a dense physical environment and for group life despite the fact that these choices inevitably limited personal privacy. In the scale of local priorities the advantages to be gained outweighed the sacrifice of privacy, which was essentially traded off.[20] The intimacy of neighborhood life radiated a warmth, security, and communal feeling that was much appreciated. People visited with neighbors, borrowed from them household utensils for parties, and helped them in time of need. Their familiarity tended to be especially close with residents of the same street.

This familiarity inevitably also had its darker side. Personal stories and rumors circulated uncontrollably, and almost everything was open to public scrutiny and censure. Scandalous gossip threatened the personal reputation of its defenseless subjects—to such a degree that people harassed by false information damaging to their honor even turned to the courts for protection. One woman filed suit against a man who spread untrue rumors that he had had sexual relations with her. Public reports that his unmarried daughter was no longer a virgin so disturbed one resident that he had the girl's innocence verified by four midwives and duly recorded in an official court document. An anxious mother told the judge how her four-year-old daughter had accidentally fallen off a stairwell, landed on one of her wooden clogs, and lost her virginity. She requested an official document certifying the facts of the incident, and had a group of neighbors ready on hand to confirm the story from hearsay. Other parents faced with the prospects of adverse publicity following similar mishaps publicized their version of events among their neighbors and obtained notarized records from the courts.[21]

Local lore, heavy with the lessons of experience, dwelt extensively on the mixed blessings of neighborly relations. For better or worse, neighbors were an inseparable part of one's life. Good neighbors could prove more forthcoming and supportive than relatives; bad ones threatened one's peace and well-being. "[Check] the neighbor before the house"— such was one piece of advice to people searching for a home.[22] Neighbors could inflict immeasurable damage if provoked; antagonizing them was highly unwise. "Offend even your pasha but not the people of your quarter," warned a local saying.[23] The popular lore also recognized the feelings of resentment that occasionally brewed among neighbors. One anecdote told how the folk wit Juha, upon becoming sultan, ordered that his neighbors be the first to be sent to the gallows.[24]

On the whole, however, the neighborly familiarity was appreciated, and it was accepted as natural and commendable that one feel a certain sense of identity with one's quarter. Generous residents endowed valuable private property specifically for the support of institutions and the needy in their own localities. The chain of alternative charitable causes that they listed in their deeds of endowment, to become operative should the original beneficiary cease to exist, were usually confined to the same neighborhood. During the revolts and political unrest of the late eighteenth century residents erected barricades within their neighborhoods, donated arms and money for local defense, and volunteered for patrol and fighting duties; together they went through unforgettable sieges and harrowing times. Like their counterparts of later periods children of the eighteenth century probably combined under neighborhood banners to engage in slingshot and fist fights with rival quarters.[25] Residents also joined to protect their local interests against those of other neighborhoods, especially in matters of water distribution, although the fierce hostilities that erupted between certain quarters during the Mamluk period had no equal in the eighteenth century.[26]

The collective responsibilities imposed on neighborhoods by the authorities added to the dense web of local relations and sentiments. The routine tasks of maintaining local facilities, collecting taxes, preventing crime, and upholding public morals occasioned much politicking, bargaining, prying, and social control, and generally helped to shape the texture of neighborhood life. Neighborhood headmen, or imams, handled many of the collective tasks of each quarter.[27] Local residents invested with official recognition rather than government officials, they received their remuneration from their district, which paid them a wage and exempted their homes from taxes.[28] While most of them were Muslim, the predominantly Christian neighborhoods in the north were often headed by Christian imams. In the religiously mixed neighborhood of Kharij Bab al-Nasr an Armenian served as deputy for the Muslim headman in 1757.[29] Through these men government orders were transmitted to the wider public and matters of local concern were brought to official attention. The authorities were not shy to recruit the headmen to serve their administrative needs. After the armed revolt of 1819 the governor entrusted the heads of the quarters with the collection of guns from the residents.[30]

The office of imam was of limited importance—one finds no distinguished names among those who held it. Many matters of collective concern reached the courts by the joint action of residents and not through the agency of the headmen. The inhabitants of a quarter or street occasionally appointed spokesmen (*mutakallimun*) to represent their case before the authorities.[31] In some cases a local resident other than the headman handled the collection of taxes due from the quarter.[32] Nonetheless, the headmen had to be figures of some means and local influence to perform their tasks. The financial contingencies often required them to put up their own funds to cover immediate expenses. Upon retiring from office they usually recovered what debts were owed to them.[33] The position afforded useful contacts with government officials and the capacity to dispense favors and cultivate clients, and the rewards were sufficiently attractive for some headmen to insist on holding on to their office in the face of local protests. Mikha'il ibn Nasur, a headman dismissed in 1757 at the request of the residents for corruption and the embezzlement of local funds, agreed to withdraw from the management of neighborhood affairs only after he was taken to court by a large group of residents.[34]

Some headmen, like Muhammad ʿAli ibn ʿAbdallah who retired in 1758, held office for as many as nine years.[35] Others withdrew after a year or two in the wake of a storm of local protest. The behavior of the headmen figured prominently in neighborhood talk and politics. Keenly aware of the opportunities for misappropriation of public funds, residents were apt to rise in protest once suspicions about the honesty of their headman worked their way into local opinion and gossip. In keeping with the normal pattern of political action, residents took their grievances before the leading men of the neighborhood to seek their weighty intervention as the representatives of respected opinion. Once an imam lost local trust and support his days in office were numbered. Some stepped down quietly after settling their accounts, while others stayed to face the consequences, which could be severe. In 1757 a large body of Muslims and Christians, among them men of standing, appeared in court to accuse the headman of their neighborhood, the Armenian Krikor ibn Nerses, of corruption and extortion. Supported by a legal opinion from the mufti, they requested that he be executed for his crimes. The judge found the headman guilty and sentenced him to death.[36]

When a group of ten or twenty residents appeared before the qadi to lodge a complaint or arrange some neighborhood business it was but the culmination of deliberations and maneuverings whose story had no chronicler. Popular involvement in local affairs extended into a variety of matters other than the conduct of headmen. Inadequate public services and facilities tested the patience of residents, driving them into joint action to redress the situation. When dissatisfied with the state of water supply they combined to press suit against the water inspector, water technicians, and other neighborhoods, to organize collective petitions to the sultan, and to divert the supply to their districts. Groups of residents also came to court to nominate men of their choice for the administration of local mosques and fountains, and to seek the removal of negligent or immoral administrators.[37]

Matters of taxation, although formally in the hands of neighborhood representatives, also tended to excite public involvement. How much taxes one's neighbors paid was a matter of great interest. Every household was assessed at a certain rate and paid its share of the collective sum imposed on each quarter. Tax evasion or exemption by some automatically increased the burden on the rest of the group and tended to provoke dissatisfaction and resentment. Ulama, ashraf, resident European merchants, and certain other social categories enjoyed exemption by virtue of their special status. There were in addition some who managed to obtain an official release from taxes on their homes, which was legally transferable along with the title to the property. One Ibrahim ibn Ahmad lived in 1754 in a house for which his grandfather had received a tax exemption seventy-five years earlier; both he and his father before him enjoyed the same privilege.[38] Still others arranged to have their houses counted as part of an adjacent quarter, apparently in the expectation of a lighter tax burden. And from year to year a few residents inadvertantly escaped mention in the tax registers and hence the obligation to pay until the mistake was corrected in subsequent books.

The tax exempt were the source of envy and resentment, and suspicious neighbors and quarter representatives did not neglect to take them to court when their fiscal status was in some doubt.[39] While they could do nothing to remove the legal exemptions of these neighbors, residents could succeed through joint action in thwarting unfair increases of their collective tax burden by outsiders. The residents of Sahat Biza were up in arms in 1752 after an adjacent district had arranged to pay its taxes as if it were part of their neighborhood. The headman and eight representatives went to court to protest against the arrangement because it unfairly increased their tax burden and benefited the neighboring district. The judge accepted their complaint and ordered that the two districts pay their taxes separately.[40] The inhabitants of Kharij Bab al-Nasr may have lobbied for the breakup of their conglomerate of districts into separate fiscal units. Groups of leading residents from each district welcomed the new arrangement, much preferring, they asserted, to pay their taxes separately.[41]

Of the collective tasks that fell on the neighborhoods none involved issues quite as sensitive and explosive as the maintenance of local security and morals. The police responsibilities and collective fines imposed by the authorities on entire quarters encouraged prying into the personal conduct of neighbors, fueled local resentment against troublemakers, and prompted joint action by residents to monitor and expel undesirables. The premise of the official policy of collective responsibility— that people ought to be familiar with their neighbors' conduct and be accountable for it—set a threshold of group intrusiveness which illustrates well the considerable weight of collective power vis-à-vis the individual. Through the force of public opinion, group pressure, intrusion, censure, and expulsion, the neighborhood policed and regulated the behavior of the members, its mechanisms of social control setting substantial limits on their personal autonomy and privacy.

Yet collective power worked only within limits, even in a milieu which promoted communalism rather than individualism. Group controls and penalties failed to stamp out vice from the quarters. Prostitutes and pimps, highest on the list of local offenders, provided services too much in demand to be eliminated. Pushed out of one district they reappeared in another. Residents concerned with the reputation and standards of their area had to wage constant battle against immoral neighbors. Their actions deterred some and drove others into less visible modes of conduct. That violations of social and religious norms persisted says something about the limits not only of group discipline, but of socialization as well. Aleppo's was clearly not a community sufficiently oppressive and ruthless to crush all nonconformist behavior. Its investments in moral guidance and supervision, heavy though they were, failed to mold a perfect society.

Conclusion

O UR TOUR OF eighteenth-century Aleppo, which began in the city's imperial setting and ended in its neighborhoods, took us back in time into a distant and now obscured world. We tried to observe its ways at close range, to pierce through its innocent facades, and to peak into its nooks and crannies. Many individuals, groups, institutions, ideas, pursuits, and changes drew our attention. In keeping with our set purpose, we worked to make sense of their meaning and to weave them into a historical portrait which explains the nature and workings of the community. The picture is rough in some parts and dotted with blank spots in others. Yet its breadth and level of detail allow us to draw some larger conclusions about the dynamics of this society, the forces which shaped its conditions and history, and the meaning of its story for our understanding of the Middle East and its past.

Did Aleppo change in the course of the eighteenth century? Did it develop in new directions? The city's historical experiences show both change and stability. When the evidence on the dynamics is pulled together from the different areas of life observed, the level and meaning of the changes becomes clearer. People of the period clearly witnessed all kinds of changes in the course of their lives: in government authority, political stability, public order, crime, trade, employment, market regulations, the availability of food, the cost of living, the quality of services, health conditions, population, mortality, migration, fashions, tastes, and attitudes. Some of these changes were cyclical while others were of a more prolonged duration; some touched small segments of the population while others affected the community as a whole. In addition to the known shifts and fluctuations there were surely others—perhaps in the rate of literacy, or the ages at marriage, or the treatment of certain diseases, or the artisanal techniques, or even the level of religious observance—which had no chronicler or which we failed to detect.

Yet society was not radically transformed by these changes. Aleppo in 1800 resembled in essential ways the community of one hundred years earlier—not a mere replica of it, yet fully continuous with its basic premises and arrangements. The social structure, the world of thought and belief, the system of rule, the main social and economic institutions, the demographic regime, and the general way of life maintained a striking continuity. They began to change in dramatic ways in the nineteenth century, when the process of undoing the past was set in motion by external pressures. Aleppo of the eighteenth century was clearly not a society in a state of transition toward Western-inspired modernity.

This underlying continuity must figure among the principal features of Aleppo's history in the eighteenth century. The chief conditions that promoted it, observed time and again in various contexts, help to explain the particular dynamics of this community and others like it. Islam sanctified many arrangements and institutions, placing them beyond debate and challenge. The culture stressed the virtues of obedience, conformity, deference to hierarchy, and respect for past wisdom; individualism and innovation were not among its cherished ideals. The townspeople were secure in their values, and bound by a consensus on essentials. There were no major scientific and technological innovations in the areas of medicine, transportation, communications, or production to set in motion great changes in society. The culturally stable Middle Eastern region with which the city was associated reinforced these continuities. The state followed a conservative policy which upheld the existing order, and various groups, not least of them the influential local elite, had a vested interest in its perpetuation.

Those aspects of Aleppo's society which were inherited from the past and were successfully perpetuated in the course of the eighteenth century formed an impressively wide sphere. A community which maintained this level of continuity in its structures and ways deserves to be considered "traditional," although the historical realities of the period indicate that the label ought not to be understood to mean static, or culturally monolithic, or blindly conformist, or socially harmonious.

Not everything was universally accepted as just and good, or followed loyally by everyone, or obeyed without external pressure. People violated laws and moral prescriptions; various types of social control, supervision, and enforcement were needed to ensure conformity, and even these proved not entirely successful. The notion of conformity, however, was not defined as adherence to one formula of conduct; in many areas the community accommodated variant customs and practices, tolerating popular pleasures despite the misgivings of moralists and allowing some personal latitude in religious observance. Some arrangements were accepted from lack of choice rather than satisfaction; there was no point in challenging rules that had withstood assault time and again. People displayed open discontent with certain conditions considered unjust, such as high food prices and heavy taxes, and took action to redress their grievances. Yet there was no large-scale organized movement to reshape any of the basic structures of society; even the factional revolts and encroachments on government authority, which figure as the most far-reaching attempts by local groups to alter their place in the scheme of things, were limited in their ends.

The stability in Aleppo's society, like the changes it experienced, reflected the work of complex processes. What the community considered desirable, required, and attainable, what it knew and understood, certainly helps to explain them. Without this cultural setting it would be difficult to make sense of local conditions and the behavior of people. And yet the differences between what people sought and what they had, and between required and actual behavior, point to the play of other factors. The city's history illustrates how much facts of power, economics, demography, and social structure were relevant as well to the course of events and the realities of the community. Our knowledge of the historical role of these factors and of the culture is incomplete and, in some areas, rudimentary. The body of available evidence, however, is sufficiently rich to help us identify those aspects which deserve particular attention in our search of a better understanding of Aleppo and Middle Eastern society in general.

The cultural setting, so indispensable to an informed sense of the historical realities, presents a mix of ideas, values, beliefs, customs, and attitudes which derived from various sources, took different subcultural forms, and were not all compatible with each other. What we know of this scene is still highly inadequate, but it seems essential to start with an approach broad enough to do justice to the richness and diversity of the culture. Islam loomed large in local life—as the dominant system of

religious belief, the principal moral and legal code governing behavior
in many areas, and the central component of personal and collective
identity for the majority of the population. Aleppo illustrates, however,
how false it would be to ascribe all thought and behavior to Islam. The
popular culture, the social prejudices and attitudes, the corpus of state
and customary laws, the regulation of the marketplace, the material
culture, and the physical layout of the city display the influence of rules,
ideas, and values which had little or nothing to do with Islam, and in
some cases were even at odds with its moral outlook. The question of
Islam's role is a thorny one, especially since in the course of history
Islam shaped and was itself shaped by various Middle Eastern ideas and
institutions. It is worthwhile considering that many aspects of the culture can be traced back to the pre-Islamic period, that local Muslims
and non-Muslims shared so much in common, and that some of Aleppo's features can be found in non-Muslim societies, notably in the
Mediterranean area.

The city's social structure and the particular pattern of relations
between self and society which prevailed in it are also essential for
understanding the conditions and workings of the community. The
marked differences in wealth, life-styles, rights, opportunities, interests,
customs, influence, and social standing throw light on a diversity which
warns against generalizing too freely as if there existed a single set of
circumstances applying uniformly to all residents. Patterns of thought
and behavior took variant forms which correlated most often with differences in religious affiliation, sex, and class. Group life added its distinct
mark to the experiences of people in this society. Guilds, quarters, and
religious communities—together about 250 known entities in the middle
years of the century—made demands on their members, imposed controls on their behavior, provided supports, and excited a certain corporate identity. Government, for its administrative convenience and political control, had a major part in strengthening the collective powers of
the groups. But while the limits the groups set on personal autonomy
and privacy appear to be considerable indeed, they ought not to be
exaggerated to the point of reducing individuals to passive agents of
collective wills. Even in a society in which communalism seemed to
thrive at the expense of individualism groups left room for personal
initiative in many areas and succeeded only imperfectly in imposing
their will on their members. Tensions between self-interest and obligations to the group were a normal part of the social scene.

The limits of group power bear some emphasis because of the excessive stress on the corporative structure of premodern Middle Eastern society, which is often described as a "mosaic," a cellular collection of communities organized along various lines and linked by the overarching authority of government. Such a view not only conveys the misleading impression that the main actors in society were groups, but may also be partly responsible for the tendency to belittle the importance of class differences, and even to speak of society as classless. While groups did include people of different social and economic circumstances and fostered some contacts between them, they certainly did not cancel out the relevance of hierarchy. People were not automatically eligible in marriage, or even acceptable as friends, just by virtue of being neighbors, coreligionists or professional colleagues. The deference and formality in the relations among unequals was intended precisely to affirm the importance of hierarchy and protect against possible social compromise in situations of physical proximity. Group life and stratification need not be seen as mutually exclusive; they describe different aspects of the same social scene. The actual social relations, not neat models and ideal schemata, offer the best clues to the meaning of class and group, and also help to obtain a more realistic picture of the status of women and non-Muslims. The texture of ties, fairly clear in most areas, turns especially dim when one enters the family, a unit of unquestioned importance whose personal and emotional aspects, unlike the economic, have left few written traces.

The forms and workings of power also explain much about the world in which Aleppines lived. The Ottoman state figured as a central influence in the community, both by what it did and what it did not do. Even in a period of limited government involvement in society the behavior and effective authority of the state were variables which affected the stability and fortunes of the city and region. Official corruption, abuse, and weakness certainly left their marks on the city's history, but while the bad press enjoyed by the Ottomans in Arab historiography is not entirely undeserved it seems simplistic to blame everything that went wrong on the Ottoman Empire and its state of "decline." If local leaders were more responsible and caring than Ottoman officials they certainly did not show it when they assumed control of local affairs in the late eighteenth and early nineteenth centuries. Government and the local elite dominated the structure of authority in the city, and their interaction was essential to the course of events. But the processes by which rules and policies were made need to be followed also to lower levels: a host of parochial issues were handled by guilds, neighborhoods, and religious communities. Much civic action and politics found expression in the context of small groups rather than on a citywide scale, and are indications of a public life which may have been quite more vibrant than is commonly associated with premodern Middle Eastern cities.

Many aspects of Aleppo's society—its politics, social structure, and general living conditions—were also profoundly shaped by economic pursuits and constraints. The realities of food, clothing, housing, services, health, and technology reveal the vulnerabilities as well as the practical sophistication of premodern material life. Access to the various material comforts of the day depended on one's means. The forms which wealth took and the ways in which it was acquired, used, and distributed in Aleppo indicate a complex economic system which is understood most fully when we take into account all its main components: external associations as well as domestic business; investment as well as work; and nonmarket transfers as well as market activities. The nonmarket transfers of wealth, by way of charity, appropriation, patronage, and intrafamily transactions, involved vast sums and deserve to be integrated more fully than they have been into the economic history of the city and the wider region.

Aleppo's society was also profoundly shaped by the particular conditions and events imposed by the demographic regime of the period. In the absence of figures it seems impossible to reconstruct with any measure of precision the local rates of birth and death, or the fluctuations in population size, or the relative roles of fertility, mortality, and migration in shaping these changes, or the correlation between population trends and economic prosperity. Much more can be established about the important personal, social, and cultural implications of the demographic conditions, which tend to be ignored in favor of quantitative issues relating to population. What it meant to live in a society in which death was so frequent and familiar, how people sought to defend themselves against death, and how they coped with the death of others are questions which shed important light on society and deserve more attention than they have received in Middle Eastern history.

When seen against the complexity of its structures and conditions, Aleppo of the eighteenth century must be reckoned a highly civilized society. Its technological level and capacity to manipulate nature— criteria which all too often shape our evaluation of the level of advancement of societies—were rudimentary by present-day standards, but its institutions and social arrangements were anything but simple. The ways in which people thought and did things may appear alien, but they were not necessarily less complex than more familiar patterns associated with modernity. The community, for instance, lacked specialized institutions such as a municipality, vocational schools, hospitals, parliaments, theaters, orphanages, banks, nursing homes, and public playgrounds; yet it had its own ways, some of them intricate and elusive, of handling education, medical and social care, banking, recreation, and urban management. And many of the arrangements worked fairly efficiently. The local record in such areas as keeping the urban streets clean or providing a prompt hearing to litigation in the courts actually appears to compare well with the conditions current in many modern societies. The physical environment of the premodern Middle Eastern city, viewed for a time as disorderly and backward, is now winning appreciation for its functional qualities as well as its aesthetic charm. "Traditional" and "premodern" ought not to be understood to mean primitive, simple, or irrational, but neither should they lead to idyllic images of a paradise lost, a wholesome and happy society brutally violated by imperialism. Premodern life had its share of suffering, want, corruption, violence, exploitation, and uncertainty.

The features of eighteenth-century Aleppo were hardly unique to this single community, which formed but a fragment of a larger world sharing much in common. They capture, in a general way, the nature of urban society in the contemporary Middle East, and more specifically in the Arab lands. Of course, on a more specific level experiences varied even among Arab cities of comparable stature such as Aleppo, Damascus, Cairo, and Baghdad. The precise social makeup of the elites, the alignment of political forces, and the relations with the central government took different forms and shaped different political histories despite the participation in a common state and political culture. Economic histories also varied, each city experiencing particular circumstances depending on its specific hinterland, its place in the currents of trade, and its distinct domestic conditions. Larger developments of social and economic consequence such as wars, plague epidemics, crop failures, political instability, and shifts in trade patterns did not affect all places simultaneously or uniformly. More local histories would be needed before we can make informed comparisons between places on a broad scale and build a regional synthesis grounded in empirical evidence rather than assumptions.

How much Aleppo tells us about the rural society in the region is far less clear. Village life in Syria and other parts of the region is so obscure that virtually no basis for comparison exists. Given the serious inadequacy of the sources it is unlikely that the history and features of the rural population will ever be known with anything resembling the level of depth possible for the larger cities. Our understanding of the region's past will of necessity be shaped largely by the knowledge drawn from the urban milieu. Under the circumstances it is worthwhile to bear in mind that observations about the structures and workings of urban society, such as those presented in this study, may or may not be valid for the countryside; they certainly cannot be assumed to apply without the backing of supporting evidence.

The type of premodern Middle Eastern society which Aleppo represents was transformed in some radical ways in the course of the last two centuries. It is artificial, however, to change mental lenses every time we cross the conventional historical divide at the turn of the nineteenth century, as if a new society was somehow in existence after 1800. Both the transformations and the continuities of the last two hundred years can be appreciated more fully when the eighteenth century is integrated into the study of the modern period instead of being set apart from it as the terminal point of a different and irrelevant era.

By the same token it appears unhelpful to think of eighteenth-century Aleppo as a precise model of the city's premodern history in general, as if a timeless continuity prevailed before modernization. Eighteenth-century Aleppo inherited many old institutions and arrangements, but under the facade of sameness there may have occurred marked shifts in social realities. The ulama of seventeenth-century Aleppo, for instance, may have differed from their eighteenth-century counterparts in their social and geographical origins, their level of learning, their involvement in the economy, and their political influence. The charitable foundations may have been in better or worse financial condition, and the rate of endowment may have been higher or lower than that of the eighteenth century. The research has not yet been done to answer these and many other questions about earlier periods in local history. Informed comparisons must await the emergence of a broader base of empirical knowledge. The story of eighteenth-century Aleppo is in a sense one piece in this larger puzzle of the city's and region's past.

APPENDIX

A Note on Population

N O RELIABLE POPULATION figures are available for Aleppo in the eighteenth century, or for that matter for the entire period before the turn of the twentieth century. Regular population censuses and the keeping of comprehensive vital statistics were not part of administrative practice in the premodern period. Some types of official records, particularly the Ottoman fiscal surveys, provide data from which general population levels and trends can be gauged; problems of accuracy and interpretation render the figures drawn from them less than precise. Citywide statistics on births, deaths, marriages, divorces, and migration simply do not exist. What can be reconstructed of Aleppo's demographic history in the premodern period must perforce be quite crude. Even the general level of population in the city has yet to be established.

Eighteenth-century travelers, European consuls, and local residents hazarded guesses of the city's population. Their estimates are too wide apart to suggest even rough orders of magnitude. Two Europeans who visited Aleppo in the 1720s assessed its population at 300,000 and 500,000 respectively.[1] Russell, an observer who knew the city well from long residence, estimated the population at 235,000 at midcentury.[2] A rough calculation by a local Maronite, based on bread consumption, household size, and other indicators, arrived at the figure of 334,000 for the same time.[3] Estimates for the late eighteenth century, which are generally lower, range between 50,000 and 150,000 people,[4] although the Venetian consul at the time could pronounce the population 320,000 strong.[5]

It would be fruitless to attempt to reconcile these figures. Most of them are implausible, reflecting above all a tendency (which has found its way into present-day writings) to exaggerate the city's size. The residents themselves harbored inflated notions of the population levels, and passed them on to visitors. Ignorance and eagerness to impress helped to manufacture fantastic figures. When he visited the city in 1783, the Frenchman Volney was told that it contained 200,000 people; on a closer look he concluded that 100,000 was a more realistic estimate.[6] By contemporary standards Aleppo appeared impressively large, which encouraged high estimates of its population. The Venetian consul Navagero estimated the population at 400,000 in 1578.[7] Five years later an Ottoman fiscal survey (which probably counted most of the population) came up with a total of only 9,361 housing units.[8] A Catholic missionary reported in 1657 that Aleppo's population was 110,000, while just at the same time a colleague of his came up with a figure of 250,000 and a European merchant 200,000.[9] Estimates of mortality from plague and famine were often equally impressive, ranging even in the hundreds of thousands.[10]

While Aleppo was certainly a major metropolis second only to Istanbul and Cairo, the population that has often been attributed to it by scholars—around 200,000 in the sixteenth and seventeenth centuries,[11] and 200,000[12] or even 250,000[13] in the late eighteenth century—seems excessive. The study of Aleppo's history during the Ottoman period suggests two general propositions about the city's population: that it probably did not exceed 130,000 before the twentieth century, certainly not in the eighteenth century; and that it declined in the course of the eighteenth and first part of the nineteenth centuries, following a substantial expansion in the previous two centuries. On the basis of Ottoman fiscal records for the city Raymond has arrived at more acceptable population levels: around 80,000 in the late sixteenth century and 115,000 in the late seventeenth century.[14] These are compatible with the long-term demographic trends as well as with reasonable population densities.

In the eighteenth century Aleppo's built-up area reached about 365 hectares (about 1.5 square miles). With a surface area of this order the average density would have been around 550 persons per hectare for a population of 200,000, and 685 persons per hectare for a population of 250,000. These are unrealistic figures for a city in which houses did not exceed two stories. Conditions in other cities in the region with a similar layout and urban tradition suggest far lower densities. Cairo, with its many taller buildings and apartment complexes, is estimated to have had an average density of 398 persons per hectare in 1798. Its population of 263,000 was settled on a net built-up area of 660 hectares, far larger than that of Aleppo. Tunis, with a layout quite similar to Aleppo's, had a population density of 380 persons per hectare in 1881.[15] The case of modern Tripoli in Lebanon is also instructive. In the early 1960s it had an estimated population of 180,000 living in an area the same as that of Aleppo in the eighteenth century. Its density (460 persons per hectare gross), however, was certainly higher because of the predominance of modern multistoried apartment buildings.[16]

If the average densities in Aleppo were on the order of 350–380 persons per hectare, the population levels revolved around 130,000. This would describe the order reached in the periods of peak growth. The eighteenth century was not one of them. Especially in its second part and the early decades of the nineteenth century the city experienced a steady decline in population. In the 1830s and 1840s almost all observers were unanimous in ascribing to the city a population in the 70,000–85,000 range.[17] The population began to show real and steady growth only in the second half of the nineteenth century. New neighborhoods emerged on the outskirts for the first time in many years, and by the turn of the century censuses were showing a population in excess of 100,000. It was only after World War I, however, that the city reached 150,000, having received a massive influx of Armenian war refugees.[18]

With this general picture in mind it seems reasonable to think of Aleppo's population as standing at around 110,000–120,000 at the beginning of the eighteenth century and declining toward its end to about 100,000. These figures provide no more than crude orders of magnitude, especially for a population that experienced numerous short-term fluctuations. The recurrent epidemics, famines, and economic slumps produced catastrophic mortality as well as substantial movements of people in and out of the city. The plague epidemics alone, of which twelve struck the city between 1700 and 1830, each carried off as much as 10–15 percent of the population in the course of a year or so. How this order of mortality affected fertility and migration, and how soon the community replenished the heavy human losses, are among the many unanswerable questions about the population dynamics of the period.

Like the overall population, the number and average size of households in the city can also be estimated only in rough fashion. The

evidence indicates that in the eighteenth century the number of households ranged between 14,000 and 16,000. Ottoman fiscal surveys in the
sixteenth century recorded figures revolving around nine and ten thousand "housing units" *(hanes)*.[19] By the late seventeenth century the
number of houses or households ("portes ou maisons") had risen to some
14,000.[20] For the year 1752, Russell reported the number of houses in
the city to be 10,742, using as a source an Arabic listing of households
obtained evidently from the office of the *muhassil*, or farmer general of
taxes.[21] That this figure was far lower than that from the late seventeenth century does not actually indicate that the overall number of
households had fallen by a quarter in the interval. Given its origin,
Russell's listing may very well have included only the tax-paying households, omitting the many others that had by then escaped from the tax
rolls.

Contemporary household numbers tend often to be inconsistent with
each other because they actually count different units. Unless specified,
figures for "houses" or "families" could refer either to physical houses,
or to taxed households, or to total households. These were by no means
identical categories. Because of multiple occupancy and extended family
arrangements the stock of houses was always considerably smaller than
the number of households. And because of tax exemptions, which were
especially widespread during the eighteenth century, the number of
taxable households was substantially smaller than the total number of
households in the city. A figure of 14,000 given by one source in 1734
was preceded just a few years earlier by a figure of 12,000 offered by
another.[22] In 1836, when the city's population had declined from its
mid-eighteenth century levels, the British consul in the city reported
that the number of local families stood at 15,497.[23] At the turn of the
twentieth century, when the population was on the rise, a census of the
houses *(buyut)* in the premodern parts of the city came up with a figure
of 11,761 for a population of about 100,000.[24] This figure was not
identical with the number of households, which was certainly larger
than the number of houses.

Clearly, some distinction ought to be drawn between the various
categories of reference. A rough estimate would suggest that in the
middle decades of the eighteenth century Aleppo had some 11,000–
12,000 houses, 10,000–11,000 taxed households, and a total of 14,000–
16,000 households. These indicate orders of magnitude that are in
accord with the general historical and demographic scene of the time.
With an overall population of 100,000–120,000 in the eighteenth cen-

tury, the average household size in Aleppo would have revolved therefore around 7. This relatively high figure is quite in keeping with the observed features of local families: the extended form of many households; the common tendency of single adults to reside with relatives; the absorption of orphaned relatives and aged parents into existing units; the presence of live-in domestics and, among the wealthy, of slaves, concubines, and a plurality of wives; and, above all, the relatively large number of children, of which there were on the average between four and five per household.

While the average household size in the city must have fluctuated in response to economic and demographic developments, a figure of around 7 appears to represent a realistic order of magnitude that can substitute for unconfirmed assumptions. It provides a sound household multiplier, one useful for demographic computations from Ottoman tax records, which often employed household heads or units as the standard categories of registration. To compute the overall population from the household numbers available scholars have been applying widely varying multipliers, usually hypothetical rather than empirical ones. Barkan used a multiplier of 5 to compute the population of Aleppo (as well as other Ottoman localities) in the sixteenth century, while more recently Raymond chose the much higher multiplier of 8, which he considered more realistic. These two multipliers produce widely different demographic results. Based on the same household data for the early decades of the sixteenth century one multiplier yields a population of around 50,000 while the other yields one of about 80,000.[25]

The population characteristics of Aleppo, like those of almost all premodern settlements in the region, will never be known with any firm precision. The data needed for an exact demographic reconstruction simply do not exist. Yet the situation is clearly not a hopeless one. A critical evaluation of contemporary figures, and the reconstruction of different bits and pieces of the demographic puzzle from judicial and other records, can go a certain way toward placing our grasp of the demographic scene on a more sound basis.

Notes

Throughout the notes, Sijill is used as the abbreviated reference to the archival records of the city's shari'a court.

I. THE PLACE: SETTING AND LOCAL CONSCIOUSNESS

1. See appendix for a discussion of Aleppo's population during the period.

2. The following brief analysis of conditions in the Ottoman Empire draws in a general way on the following works: Naff and Owen, eds., *Studies in Eighteenth Century Islamic History*; Shaw, *History of the Ottoman Empire*, vol. 1; Itzkowitz, *Ottoman Empire and Islamic Tradition*; Inalcik, *The Ottoman Empire: The Classical Age 1300–1600* and *The Ottoman Empire: Conquest, Organization and Economy*; Hourani, "The Ottoman Background of the Modern Middle East" and "Ottoman Reform"; Holt, *Egypt and the Fertile Crescent*; Owen, *The Middle East in the World Economy*; Lewis, *The Emergence of Modern Turkey*; and Issawi, "Europe, the Middle East and the Shift in Power."

3. For collections of local inscriptions see Herzfeld, *Inscriptions*; Gaube, *Arabische Inschriften*; and al-Athar al-kitabiyya, Bibliothèque Orientale MS. 143. For a review of the city's history see Sauvaget, *Alep*, and the brief summary in his article "Ḥalab."

4. The provincial boundaries did not remain entirely fixed throughout the century. From time to time the government transferred a peripheral district from one province to the jurisdiction of another for political or fiscal reasons. For a survey of Ottoman provincial boundaries, see Birken, *Provinzen*.

5. Tabbakh, *I'lam*, 6:528–530.

6. Charles-Roux, *Échelles*, pp. 201–202.

7. Majmu', folio 51a; Asadi, *Mawsu'at Halab*, 1:204.

8. Commonly cited estimates of Istanbul's population run as high as 800,000. Such an order of magnitude appears quite unlikely. Inalcik has argued, on the basis of valid premises, that the city's population did not exceed half a million before the nineteenth century. See his article "İstanbul," pp. 238–245.

9. For example, Thevenot, *Travels*, part 2, pp. 31–32; d'Arvieux, *Mémoires*, 6:411–428; Hasselquist, *Voyages*, p. 398; Perry, *A View*, p. 141; Olivier, *Voyage*, 4:173; Aimé-Martin, *Lettres*, 1:198, 214; Pococke, *Description*, vol. 2, part 1, p. 150; Russell, *Aleppo*, 1:14–15; Drummond, *Travels*, p. 184; Griffiths, *Travels*, p. 334.

10. On these population trends see Raymond, "Population of Aleppo," and the appendix, this volume.

11. Sijill, 90:7; 97:37, 40, 61, 72; 102:187, 230.

12. For reports on emigration in response to local hardships see Archives Nationales, Paris, Ministère des Affaires Étrangères, B¹ 87, folio 391 (December 29, 1757), and B¹ 90, folio 56a (July 8, 1766); Public Record Office, London, State Papers, Foreign, Archives of the Levant Company, Aleppo, 110/29, folio 185 (September 7, 1775); Fahd, *Taʾrikh al-rahbaniyya*, 1:251; and Bodman, *Political Factions*, p. 128.

13. Russell, *Aleppo*, 1:235.

14. Raymond, *Artisans et commerçants*, 2:477–492; Qaraʾli, *al-Suriyyun*, 1:83–94, 100–134; Hourani, "The Syrians in Egypt," pp. 222–223.

15. Ben Yaʿakov, "Yomano," pp. 363–382; Sassoon, *Jews in Baghdad*, pp. 209–210.

16. For many examples see Tabbakh, *Iʿlam*, vols. 6 and 7, *passim*. In the course of the eighteenth century only one grand vizier, two provincial governors, and two qadis appear to have been natives of Aleppo. See Uzunçarşılı, *Osmanlı Tarihi*, vol. 4, part 2, pp. 343–347. See also Tabbakh, *Iʿlam*, 3:318–320; 6:447–454, 524; 7:67–78. No Aleppine appears among the holders of the high office of Shaykh al-Islam: Uzunçarşılı, *Osmanlı Tarihi*, vol. 4, part 2, pp. 455–512.

17. Tabbakh, *Iʿlam*, 6:483.

18. Ghazzi, *Nahr*, 1:385, 436–437, 498–499, 516, 527–529.

19. Sijill, 77:383; 78:262; 79:2, 64; 83:184; 85:304, 313, 333, 338; 89:112, 686; 91:365; 92:106; 103:128.

20. Sijill, 77:452, 459; 78:228, 366; 79:217, 219; 87:222; 91:225; 95:55, 341; 101:263.

21. See Raymond, *Great Arab Cities*, for a comparative survey of urban forms in the region.

22. Jundi, *Taʾrikh Maʿarrat al-Nuʿman*, 1:250.

23. Qushaqji, *al-Adab al-shaʿbi*, p. 47; also Asadi, *Mawsuʿat Halab*, 1:225.

24. Asadi, *Mawsuʿat Halab*, 1:168; also 1:225.

25. Hamida, *Muhafazat Halab*, p. 377; Asadi, *Mawsuʿat Halab*, 1:225. For another saying expressing local refinement see Kitab al-amthal, Rylands Arabic MS. 775, folio 42b.

26. Majmuʿ, Leeds Arabic MS. 147, folio 54a; Hamida, *Muhafazat Halab*, p. 380.

27. Ghazzi, *Nahr*, 1:67–81; Tabbakh, *Iʿlam*, 3:546–560; Qushaqji, *al-Adab al-shaʿbi*, *passim*.

28. Sijill, 83:67.

29. Fahd, *Taʾrikh al-rahbaniyya*, 3:12–13, quoting from a manuscript church history of Agustin Zanduh.

30. Contemporary Hebrew writings by Jews from the region did use the

term *Suria*. See, for example, Sassoon, *Ohel David*, 2:1026, 1027, 1030. The term *Bilad al-Sham* was usually applied to central and southern Syria, excluding Aleppo. In common usage *Shami* meant Damascene.

31. Tabbakh, *Iᶜlam*, 7:98.

32. See the comments in Hourani, "Introduction: Aspects of Islamic Culture," p. 269.

2. THE PEOPLE: GROUPS, CLASSES, AND SOCIAL CONTRASTS

1. Majmuᶜ, Leeds Arabic MS. 147, folio 49a. The author of the handbook is not known, but the contents indicate that he was a local Christian who lived in the first half of the century.

2. Arrangements made periodically among the Christian communities usually allocated about half of the tax load to the Melkites. The rest fell on the other three communities in proportions that tended to vary over the century. See Sijill, 87:130–131 and 91:185–186, 205; Taoutel, "Wathaᵓiq al-qarn al-thamin ᶜashar," pp. 252–253; and Devezin, *Nachrichten*, p. 54.

3. *Al-kufr kulluhu milla wahida*: Sijill, 83:179. The term *milla* (or *millet*) was rarely used at the time. I came across only two other references to it in the court records, both applied to Muslims: Sijill, 87:320, 397. Christians used it occasionally in formal writings as a synonym of *taᵓifa* (community), referring to the Christian, Maronite, or Orthodox *milla*. See Majmuᵓ, folios 79a, 87, 88b. On the infrequent use of the term in other parts of the Ottoman Empire before the nineteenth century see Braude, "Foundation Myths," pp. 69–83.

4. Most notably, the word *walad* substituted for *ibn* in non-Muslim names. The documents used a special orthography for non-Muslim names, most commonly replacing the Arabic letter *sin* with a *sad*. This usage applied to names that Muslims also used, such as Musa and Sulayman, and to names specific to non-Muslims.

5. See Sijill, 73:1–2, 7–8, for balance sheets of charitable foundations dedicated to the payment of the poll tax, and Sijill, 87:263, for charity in the Jewish community.

6. Rabbath, *Documents*, 2:95–97, 100–106, 110.

7. Sijill, 83:147; 90:24–25, 78. In the early 1560s the authorities ordered the demolition of a synagogue established by the Jews in a private house. See Ibn al-Hanbali, *Durr al-habab*, 1:444–445.

8. Russell, *Aleppo*, 1:223.

9. Russell, *Aleppo*, 1:104; 2:42–43, 45, 59, 62.

10. See, for example, Halabi, Murtad, Baghdad MS. 6299, pp. 16–19, 30, 39–40, 47, 62–63, 247; Public Record Office, London, State Papers, Foreign, Archives of the Levant Company, Aleppo, 110/29, folio 185b (September 7, 1775); Taoutel, "Wathaᵓiq al-akhawiyyat," pp. 382–383; and Rabbath, *Documents*, 2:54, 83.

11. Sijill, 97:52; also Sijill, 81:29; 101:265.

12. Taoutel, *Wathaᵓiq*, 1:109–111, 135–138; Qasin, *Mahaneh*, part 1, folios 1b–2a and part 2, folios 9a, 39b.

13. The large collections of Christian documents in Rabbath's *Documents* and Taoutel's works illustrate the routine communications between Christians in Aleppo and the outside.

14. Fahd, *Ta'rikh al-rahbaniyya*, 1:123–125; 2:488–489; 4:141–143; 5:122–123, 182–183, 216–219. See also Ghazzi, *Nahr*, 2:542, 546, 559, 564, 566, 570, 608.

15. Qasin, *Mahaneh*, part 2, folio 17a.

16. Sijill, 75:24.

17. Ettinger, *Toldot*, pp. 38, 42, 46–47.

18. Sijill, 87:130–131; 90:216–217; 91:166, 185–186, 205. See also Taoutel, "Watha'iq al-qarn al-thamin ʿashar," pp. 252–253.

19. Sijill, 74:138; 79:204, 212, 219; 83:190; 90:153; 91:4, 263; 103:126.

20. Sijill, 83:62.

21. Budayri, *Hawadith Dimashq*, p. 95.

22. Sijill, 75:20; 76:40; 79:226; 83:89, 168; 85:362, 409, 554; 91:131; 98:240, 249, 263, 413; 101:143, 145, 290; 102:41, 93, 180; 103:444.

23. Sijill, 76:128; 83:168; 101:166, 276, 412; 102:93, 180, 186, 257; 103:249.

24. On interconfessional transfers of real estate see Marcus, "Men, Women and Property," pp. 156–158. For the joint ownership of houses and other property by Muslims and non-Muslims, see Sijill, 76:481; 78:71, 89, 123, 301; 86:290; 89:736; 91:432; 92:162. For intercommunal business and credit transactions, see Sijill, 74:231, 279; 76:117, 130; 78:289; 82:475–476; 87:182, 202, 203, 231, 281, 351–353, 362, 373; 89:756, 762; 90:91, 186; 91:1, 234; 97:207; 101:61; 102:44, 76–77, 236, 257, 276; 103:283, 377, 608, 614. See also Laniado, *Bet dino*, folios 62b–69a, 121b, 189b. For business partnerships between Muslims and non-Muslims, see Sijill, 74:231, 279; 76:30, 130; 77:293; 78:289; 82:475–476; 83:82; 87:72; 93:149; 97:69; 98:301; 101:166, 231, 261, 276; 102:41, 93, 257; 103:53.

25. Majmuʿ, folio 60a (saying 592); Kitab al-amthal, Rylands Arabic MS. 775, folio 8b. For sayings on the subject from various Arab localities, see Tikriti, *al-Amthal al-baghdadiyya*, 4:409–411.

26. Sijill, 87:2, 19, 26, 33, 34, 59, 69, 77, 81, 94, 101, 120, 143, 146, 162, 164, 174, 175, 241, 250, 260, 265, 268, 284, 290, 292, 303, 308, 318, 320, 323, 329, 334, 336, 365, 384, 387, 394; 102:6, 38, 43, 50, 52, 78, 79, 81, 93, 95, 103, 135, 136.

27. Sijill, 83:30, 125; 88:145; 90:188; 91:243; 93:192; 97:72, 120; 102:136, 137, 227.

28. For instances of conversion to Islam, see Sijill, 76:515; 78:123, 226; 79:1, 2; 87:73, 158; 88:20; 90:121; 91:145, 243; 92:208, 214; 101:276; 102:12, 227, 237.

29. Sijill, 78:226.

30. Shaykhu, *Shuʿara' al-nasraniyya*, pp. 397–408, 474–484, 499–507; Maʿluf, "Nukhba."

31. Shaykhu, *Shuʿara' al-nasraniyya*, pp. 455–464, 474–484, 497–507. On the literary revival see Haddad, *Syrian Christians*, pp. 14–22, 52–53. For a biography of Sulayman al-Nahawi (d. 1728), see Tabbakh, *Iʿlam*, 6:478–480. The biography makes no mention of his Christian students.

32. Both the English Levant Company and the Chamber of Commerce in

Marseille discouraged resident merchants from marrying locally. The few Europeans who did take local Christian wives obtained assurances that they would not be reduced to the legal status of dhimmis. For examples see Sijill, 87:32; 91:42.

33. On the social life of resident Europeans in Aleppo and other commercial stations in the Middle East see Russell, *Aleppo*, 2:1–27; Ambrose, "English Traders"; Davis, *Aleppo and Devonshire Square*, ch. 1; Charles-Roux, *Échelles*, pp. 32–38; and Paris, *Le Levant*, pp. 263–293.

34. Haddad, *Syrian Christians;* Paris, *Le Levant*, pp. 254–255; Rey, *Protection*, p. 298, n. 2.

35. On the Italian Jews and the consular service of Raphael Picciotto, see Haus-, Hof- und Staatsarchiv, Vienna, Türkei II, K. 128 (April 1802) and K. 129 (September 1802); Halabi, Murtad, pp. 119–121; Lutzky, "Ha-Francos be-Haleb"; Weyl, "Les juifs protégés"; Paris, *Le Levant*, pp. 256–260; and Rey, *Protection*, pp. 229–243.

36. Bağış, *Osmanlı ticaretinde*, p. 44; Ghazzi, *Nahr*, 3:311.

37. Sijill, 102:88; 83:257; 87:44; 91:17.

38. Taoutel, "Watha'iq al-qarn al-thamin 'ashar," pp. 267–270; Taoutel, *Watha'iq*, 1:69.

39. Laniado, *Bet dino*, folios 199a–208b; Lutzky, "Ha-Francos be-Haleb," p. 58.

40. See Bağış, *Osmanlı ticaretinde;* and Taoutel, "Watha'iq al-akhawiyyat," p. 393.

41. Rich documentary evidence can be found in the French consular archives and in the works of Rabbath and Taoutel. For an account of the schisms and their impact, see Haddad, *Syrian Christians*, and Frazee, *Catholics and Sultans.*

42. Taoutel, "Watha'iq al-qarn al-thamin 'ashar," pp. 252–253; Sijill, 87:130–131; Devezin, *Nachrichten*, p. 54. More than half of the decline was among the Melkites.

43. Sijill, 83:218; 87:129, 154; 89:769; 91:134, 474; 95:10; 101:412; 102:47. Incomes are discussed in greater detail in chapter 5, this volume. The piastre (*ghirsh*) was a silver coin equivalent at the time to 120 'uthmanis or akçes.

44. Sijill, 83:81.

45. Sijill, 101:124–125, 409–413; 102:30, 34.

46. See Marcus, "Privacy," pp. 170–171, and the discussion of housing in chapter 5, this volume.

47. References to the poor and to institutions for their support abound. Many neighborhoods maintained endowments designated for the support of the local poor: Sijill, 73:17, 33, 49, 50, 56, 89, 126, 134; 76:429, 526; 78:61, 370; 80:39, 194, 197–198, 234; 85:319; 87:366; 89:674, 683, 695; 91:325; 93:117; 101:74. For references to the Jewish poor, see Qasin, *Mahaneh*, part 1, folio 24b; Laniado, *Bet dino*, folios 49b, 53a; and Sijill, 75:24 and 87:263. For endowments for the Christian poor see Sijill, 73:1, 7–8; and Taoutel, *Watha'iq*, 1:50, 67, 134. For transactions relating to the poor members of trade guilds see Sijill, 76:146; 79:135; 98:147, 309, 361; 103:194.

48. Sijill, 87:138; 101:51, 71; 104:56, 120, 145, 167, 179.

49. Majmu', folio 55a.

50. Kitab al-amthal, folio 73b; Ayyub, "Amthal Halab," p. 829.

51. Ayyub, "Amthal Halab," p. 829; Hamida, *Muhafazat Halab*, p. 384.

52. Sijill, 77:11, 28, 49, 60, 73, 79, 151, 154, 157, 174, 237; 78:69, 77, 99, 215; 79:6, 63, 83, 90, 131, 159, 224; 83:4, 23, 110, 120; 86:327; 101:41, 97, 131, 134, 145, 263, 278, 311, 351, 363, 375, 379, 383, 413; 102:5, 14, 23, 28, 56, 66, 77, 79, 82, 153, 169, 177, 190, 251, 295.

53. Sijill, 77:22; 83:61, 110, 141, 142, 148, 211, 242, 251; 87:44, 159, 194, 196, 278, 396; 90:58, 99, 248; 101:7, 16; 102:26.

54. Sijill, 78:42, 46, 63, 126, 195, 203, 280; 79:106, 151, 153, 186; 80:70; 83:70; 87:2, 324, 377; 88:13, 27, 32, 38, 42, 54, 61, 70, 75, 88, 114, 140, 148, 159, 164, 178; 89:15, 859; 90:48; 91:248, 249; 92:10, 91, 166; 101:287; 102:26, 182, 288.

55. Russell, *Aleppo*, 1:161.

56. Sijill, 77:6, 37, 90, 127, 383, 396, 407; 79:159, 216; 80:30; 97:68; 102:56, 134.

57. Sijill, 83:78; 87:231; 95:108; 97:219; 98:39, 115, 163, 369, 413; 101:219; 103:194, 221, 287, 295, 611.

58. Sijill, 85:311; 87:268; 95:127; 97:178; 98:54, 147; 101:105, 110; 102:93; 103:7, 344, 358, 519.

59. For cases of equal distribution among members, see Sijill, 76:146, 578, 583; 85:76; 90:117; 98:344; 101:248; 103:358, 569. For cases of unequal distribution, see Sijill, 76:362; 79:190; 81:54–55, 63; 83:116, 129, 168; 85:333; 87:72, 262, 268, 291; 91:149, 384; 95:122, 286, 380; 98:54, 147, 263, 309, 362; 103:7, 238, 329, 634. The guilds and their role in society are discussed in detail in chapter 5, this volume.

60. Sijill, 75:105; 76:321; 78:151; 89:805; 91:27, 38, 39, 211; 93:143; 101:3.

61. Russell, *Aleppo*, 1:217–220.

62. Sijill, 76:394; 77:439; 78:254; 79:200–203; 80:148; 82:535; 83:214–215; 85:144–145, 326–327; 95:271–274; 98:393–394, 396–397; 101:353–363; 102:110–134; 103:109–110, 402–403. See also Tabbakh, *Iʿlam*, 7:24.

63. Sijill, 79:8; 83:241; 87:78, 84, 311; 99:90; 101:54, 98; 102:181; 103:268.

64. Sijill, 99:90–93; 86:328–339; 89:4, 6, 7.

65. Tabbakh, *Iʿlam*, 7:24–25.

66. Qushaqji, *al-Amthal al-shaʿbiyya al-halabiyya*, 2:536.

67. Taoutel, *Wathaʾiq*, 1:109–111, 135–138; 2:88–89; 3:57–58, 135. See also Qasin, *Mahaneh*.

68. Sijill, 79:169, 206; 83:8, 42, 62, 247; 87:335; 89:791; 90:2, 5, 7, 23, 42, 67, 149; 91:13, 154, 165, 186, 216, 276, 278, 286; 97:36, 40, 61, 72, 78, 81, 82, 87, 94, 121, 149, 177; 101:13, 113, 153, 205, 311, 378; 102:32, 57, 187, 230. See also Archives Nationales, Paris, Ministère des Affaires Étrangères, B¹ 85, folio 13 (January 15, 1746).

69. For details see Marcus, "Men, Women and Property."

70. Ghazzi, *Nahr*, 3:291, 299–300; Tabbakh, *Iʿlam*, 3:349; Russell, *Aleppo*, 1:294–295.

71. Paton, *Modern Syrians*, p. 245.

72. Russell, *Aleppo*, 1:98–99, 162–165.

73. Boucheman, *Suhné*, pp. 19–20, 112–113.

2. The People: Classes and Social Contrasts

74. During this century residents referred to the semiurbanized inhabitants of the eastern districts as "outsiders" *(ahl barra)*, differentiating them from the "insiders" *(ahl juwwa)*. See Hamida, *Muhafazat Halab*, pp. 195–196. Residents of the inner city actually feared to venture into the quarters to the east. See Sauvaget, *Alep*, p. 231.

75. The data are drawn from the collection of biographical notices in Tab-bakh, *I'lam*, 6:422–547; 7:3–151.

76. See, for example, Qushaqji, *al-Amthal al-sha'biyya al-halabiyya*, 2:534–537, and *passim;* Ayyub, "Amthal Halab," pp. 878–879; and various sayings in Majmu' and Kitab al-amthal.

77. Sijill, 79:115; 83:4, 9, 14, 22, 40, 43, 45, 46, 51, 53, 63, 72, 85, 88, 97, 98, 111, 113, 135, 137, 142, 227, 251, 256; 87:8, 57, 118, 238, 265, 288, 311, 322, 330; 90:17, 30, 77; 91:141, 146; 101:7, 102.

78. The term *a'yan*, which was also used commonly in a general sense to mean "notables," appears in official documents only in reference to tax farmers, and not as a general label for all prominent figures. See Sijill, 77:78; 83:51, 106, 111, 151, 201; 87:148, 234, 261, 291, 380; 90:30, 77, 202, 209; 91:250; 97:168; 101:57, 102, 293, 343; 102:16.

79. Bodman, *Political Factions*, pp. 61–62.

80. Hamud, *al-'Askar*, pp. 107–115, 191–196; Bakhit, "Aleppo and the Ottoman Military," pp. 27–38; Rafeq, "Local Forces," pp. 302–304.

81. Sijill, 76:610; 79:208; 83:163; 85:2, 56; 90:205; 101:277.

82. For a detailed description of the Janissaries see Bodman, *Political Factions*, ch. 3.

83. Muradi, *'Arf al-basham*, pp. 5–24.

84. For example, Tabbakh, *I'lam*, 6:416; 7:20–21, 133, 183, 196.

85. Sijill, 96:223; 101:136. See also Tabbakh, *I'lam*, 6:483, 532; 7:83, 105.

86. For the activities of Kawakibi, see Sijill, 75:245, 376, 377; 76:428, 586, 640; 77:6, 50, 51, 95, 114, 123, 124, 131, 386; 78:1, 20, 39, 40, 86, 87, 110, 119, 266, 323, 324, 331; 85:344, 348, 351; 87:40, 376; 89:791; 90:82, 89, 142, 312, 469; 91:32, 48; 92:37; 95:37, 80, 349; 98:104, 332; 100:89; 102:166. For Tara-bulsi, see Sijill, 74:262, 263; 77:159, 230; 78:159; 79:198–199; 87:28, 69, 116; 90:80, 86; 94:32–33; 97:64, 132, 143, 183, 247–248; 101:25, 48, 72, 73, 81; 102:24, 25, 145. For Taha's activities, see Sijill, 74:309; 75:38, 244; 76:389, 586; 77:79, 87; 79:77, 78, 220, 222, 229; 80:206; 83:144–145, 185–186, 241, 242; 87:36, 37, 38, 147, 208–209, 211, 222, 223, 229, 230, 233, 235, 238–240, 243, 245, 247, 285, 393; 88:44; 90:85, 86, 95, 199; 91:303–304; 95:39, 56–57, 81, 88–89, 93, 98, 101, 112–115, 158–161, 211, 279, 314; 97:28, 29, 81, 90, 190; 98:19, 30, 74, 81, 84–85, 141, 293, 294, 303–304, 404–406; 100:184–185; 101:6, 17, 380, 409–411, 412, 413; 102:30, 34, 59, 68, 94, 152, 153, 171, 184, 208, 213, 281; 104:164–166. For the activities of 'Imadi, see Sijill, 75:173, 212, 248; 77:26, 103, 125, 390–391; 78:65, 68; 83:201; 87:41, 42, 98, 247, 264, 313; 88:54, 59; 89:747, 748; 90:55; 91:18, 28, 252; 95:356.

87. Russell, *Aleppo*, 2:91–92. See chapter 6, this volume, for details on the state of education and literacy.

88. For a copy of an appointment letter (dated 1755) see Sijill, 87:338.

89. Rafeq, *al-ʿArab wa ʾl-ʿuthmaniyyun*, pp. 53–54, 318–320; Rafeq, "Changes in the Relationship," pp. 65–66.

90. Bodman, *Political Factions*, pp. 96–99. See also Sijill, 76:610; 87:9, 236, 360; 91:223; 101:271.

91. Tabbakh, *Iʿlam*, 7:148. See also Sijill, 83:18; 87:75; 102:223.

92. For example, Tabbakh, *Iʿlam*, 6:446–447, 461–462; 7:40–41, 57–58, 120, 172–173.

93. Sijill, 77:54, 78, 96, 110, 140; 78:20, 21, 321; 79:8, 97, 204; 83:40, 241; 87:45, 78, 84, 142, 311; 89:748, 749; 101:54, 98, 380; 102:3, 9, 38, 85, 181, 182, 205, 215; 103:268.

94. For an extensive contemporary sample of preambles, see Majmuʿ, folios 67b–90a. Russell's tableau of Aleppo's society illustrates amply the local preoccupation with politeness and ceremony.

95. Sijill, 79:171; 81:16–17; 83:139, 224, 242; 95:108; 101:83, 271; 103:287. See also Majmuʿ, folios 67b, 82b, 83b, 85a, 86b, 88b; Taoutel, *Wathaʾiq*, 1:50–51, 58, 71, 72; and Taoutel, "Wathaʾiq al-akhawiyyat," pp. 236, 237, 238.

96. Majmuʿ, folio 55a; Kitab al-amthal, folio 39b; Ayyub, "Amthal Halab," p. 832.

97. Sijill, 74:37; 77:52; 78:98; 79:73; 82:505; 89:747, 748, 749, 750; 92:88; 97:4, 201; 98:47; 101:64; 102:95, 176, 205. See also Tabbakh, *Iʿlam*, 7:14.

98. Christian writings made reference to the communal *aʿyan* (notables) and *kahana* (priests), who were distinguished from the commoners (*ʿawamm*): Taoutel, *Wathaʾiq*, 1:50–51, 58, 71, 72; Taoutel, "Wathaʾiq al-akhawiyyat," pp. 236–238; Halabi, Murtad, pp. 52, 195, 197, 198. Hebrew writings spoke of *tovey ha-ʿir* (notables) and the *rabbanim ve hakhamim* (religious leaders), distinguishing them from the rank and file *(rov ha-tzibur):* Qasin, *Mahaneh*, part 2, folio 39b; Dwek, *Birkat Eliyahu*, folio 88a; Laniado, *Degel*, folio 12b.

99. Ayyub, "Amthal Halab," p. 831.

100. Sijill, 74:622; 98:287; 101:105; 103:345, 359, 379, 404, 408, 444, 580, 613.

101. Sijill, 83:48; 101:256.

102. Sijill, 87:26, 77, 330, 357; 90:166; 91:221; 97:2, 203; 101:147; 102:144. The monopolies and restrictive practices in the marketplace are discussed in greater detail in chapter 5, this volume.

103. Sijill, 76:315; 77:83; 78:164; 83:218; 85:328; 97:104, 107, 135; 101:59, 81.

104. Sijill, 79:160; 83:17, 115, 185, 231; 87:31, 202, 218, 365, 366; 90:21, 109; 91:126; 101:5, 8, 9, 59, 145, 161, 178, 280, 370; 102:53, 62, 64, 209.

105. Sijill, 79:215; for a similar case see Sijill, 101:327.

106. Sijill, 87:365, 366.

107. Sijill, 87:103.

108. See the biographical sketches in Tabbakh, *Iʿlam*, vols. 6 and 7.

109. Sijill, 101:24, 403; 102:72, 178.

110. For illustrations of the continuity of the title of effendi, see Sijill, 76:440, 516; 78:69, 77, 88, 251, 329, 339, 357; 79:52, 115, 132, 183; 80:32, 66, 110, 178, 274; 85:308, 318; 88:13, 46, 54, 64, 97, 99, 109; 92:30, 94; 102:35. For aghas, see Sijill, 76:493, 505, 510; 78:46, 81, 92, 131, 152, 156, 209, 236; 80:67,

205; 82:182; 85:337; 87:324, 386–387; 88:20, 59, 64, 75, 81, 101, 102, 113, 151, 162, 181, 186, 188; 89:772; 92:68; 102:155. For chalabis, see Sijill, 78:126, 128, 196, 201, 240, 243, 270, 280, 326, 336, 412; 80:54, 222, 292; 86:290, 341; 88:1, 8, 12, 13, 18, 27, 29, 32, 38, 41, 42, 45, 49, 50, 54, 55, 61, 68, 70, 71, 72, 79, 88, 90, 91, 106, 112, 115, 121, 140, 152, 175, 179; 91:248, 334, 418; 101:47; 102:188, 192, 237.

111. Sijill, 88:75; 101:224–230.

112. For illustrations, see Sijill, 76:441, 499, 516, 538; 78:54, 93, 95, 135, 136, 169, 181, 190, 210, 224, 237, 247, 307; 79:111, 157, 186, 188, 224; 80:29, 66, 109, 202, 208; 86:306; 87:376; 88:1, 2, 11, 12, 15, 20, 32, 34, 38, 46, 72, 75, 93, 94, 97, 99, 109, 143, 146, 162, 168, 180, 185, 197; 89:859; 91:403; 92:1, 14, 19, 50, 87, 89, 150, 151; 102:3, 72, 185, 275.

3. ORDER AND DISORDER: POWER, POLITICS, AND THE LAW

1. Halabi, Murtad, Baghdad MS. 6299, p. 123.

2. For a broad comparative examination of this regional pattern, see Hourani, "Ottoman Reform." I have avoided the term "notables" because of the ambiguities that have come to surround it in the literature. While Hourani uses it strictly to denote political leaders, the term is also often used in a more general way as a synonym for the socially distinguished and prominent, including those who did not necessarily play a leading role in politics. When employed loosely the category of "notables" can confuse important social and political distinctions. For instance, in a study of the politics of Damascus in the eighteenth century, the discussion of relations between government and the "notables" (whose precise makeup is not clearly defined) touches on the practice of state patronage, describing among others the payment of small government stipends to hundreds of local ulama and even students, many of whom were clearly not elite figures (Barbir, *Ottoman Rule in Damascus*, ch. 2). The implication that these individuals were "notables" broadens the composition of this social category well beyond the top men of prominence and power who enjoyed the key positions and resources, and so lumps together people who differed substantially in wealth, status, and influence. For the purposes of identifying the specific group of politically influential men in Aleppo I preferred less ambiguous terms such as "political elite," "local leaders," and "power figures."

3. There is no study of the city's legal system, nor of its political history in the first half of the eighteenth century. Bodman, *Political Factions*, examines local politics in the years 1760–1826. Halabi's manuscript chronicle adds much fresh information, unavailable in the known primary sources, to what we know about this turbulent period. The chronicle, which covers the years 1771–1805, has hitherto remained unconsulted. For more details on its contents see the comments on historical writing in Aleppo in chapter 6, this volume.

4. Sijill, 90:81. For a detailed description of the governor's staff see Devezin, *Nachrichten*, pp. 12–37.

5. Sijill, 103:458.

6. Archives Nationales, Paris, Ministère des Affaires Étrangères (hereafter Affaires Étrangères), B¹ 86, folio 227 (September 11, 1752); Majmuʿ, Leeds

Arabic MS. 147, folio 66a. The figures on the number and tenure of governors are based on a complete list compiled from the partial contemporary lists of governors in Majmuᶜ, folio 66 and in Mingana, "List of the Turkish Governors," pp. 518–519, and also from the references in Halabi, Murtad; Tabbakh, *Iᶜlam*, vol. 3; Ghazzi, *Nahr*, vol. 3; Bodman, *Political Factions;* and in the shariᶜa court records. For a complete list of the qadis see Ghazzi, *Nahr*, 1:307–309.

7. Halabi, Murtad, p. 86; also pp. 61, 78.

8. Affaires Étrangères, B¹ 90, folio 72 (October 25, 1766).

9. Sijill, 101:277, 306.

10. For more details on Chalabi Effendi, see Halabi, Murtad, pp. 77–78, 82, 86–90; and Bodman, *Political Factions*, pp. 100–101.

11. Halabi, Murtad, pp. 42, 47–48, 61; Tabbakh, *Iᶜlam*, 3:345, 354–357; Ghazzi, *Nahr*, 3:305; Bodman, *Political Factions*, p. 101.

12. Halabi, Murtad, p. 61.

13. Bodman, *Political Factions*, pp. 111–113; Halabi, Murtad, pp. 30–37.

14. Halabi, Murtad, pp. 39–43; Bodman, *Political Factions*, p. 114.

15. For a detailed description see Halabi, Murtad, pp. 48–49, 62–78. Halabi's account sheds light on the hitherto obscure circumstances of the revolt. See Bodman, *Political Factions*, p. 115.

16. Halabi, Murtad, pp. 84–107. Bodman's account makes no mention of this revolt.

17. Halabi, Murtad, pp. 121–123.

18. Halabi, Murtad, pp. 129–138; Haus-, Hof- und Staatsarchiv, Vienna (hereafter Staatsarchiv, Vienna), Türkei II, K. 97, no. 11 (December 12, 1791) and no. 12 (December 24, 1791).

19. Bodman, *Political Factions*, pp. 118–119; Halabi, Murtad, pp. 237–239; Staatsarchiv, Vienna, Türkei II, K. 116, no. 32 (October 25, 1797) and K. 117, no. 15 (May 10, 1798) and no. 17 (May 25, 1798); Taoutel, "Wathaᵓiq al-akhawiyyat," pp. 376, 392–393.

20. Halabi, Murtad, pp. 265–266. This account clarifies the confusion about the episode, discussed in Bodman, *Political Factions*, pp. 120–121.

21. Bodman, *Political Factions*, pp. 122–125; Halabi, Murtad, pp. 266–270.

22. Bodman, *Political Factions*, pp. 57–59, 128.

23. Halabi, Murtad, pp. 4–5, 13–14, 122–123, 255–256, 264; Bodman, *Political Factions*, pp. 106, 107, 111, 116, 127; Taoutel, "Wathaᵓiq al-akhawiyyat," pp. 375–376, 377, 396; Laniado, *Bet dino*, folios 73b–74a.

24. See Tabakoğlu, *Osmanlı maliyesi*, for a detailed survey of the taxes current in the empire during the eighteenth century.

25. On the income of the governors see Bodman, *Political Factions*, pp. 42–46; Devezin, *Nachrichten*, pp. 12–13; and Russell, *Aleppo*, 1:315–316. Bodman (p. 44) reproduces a breakdown of the pasha's income, with a stated total of 327,300 piastres, drawn from a report by the French consul. The amounts in the list actually add up to 199,000 piastres, of which 70,000 or 80,000 piastres came from *avanias* and exactions rather than established taxes.

26. For a copy of the register of payments see Taoutel, "Wathaᵓiq al-qarn al-thamin ᶜashar," pp. 258–266.

27. A detailed record of the taxes and exactions is given in Sijill, 83:122–124.

28. Bodman, *Political Factions*, pp. 22, 43–44.

29. Taoutel, *Wathaʾiq*, 1:69; Burayk, *Taʾrikh al-Sham*, p. 149.

30. Taoutel, "Wathaʾiq al-akhawiyyat," p. 374.

31. Halabi, Murtad, pp. 38–43.

32. Halabi, Murtad, pp. 49–50. For a detailed description of the oppression see Halabi, Murtad, pp. 44–54; and Tabbakh, *Iʿlam*, 3:357–359.

33. Halabi, Murtad, p. 59.

34. Halabi, Murtad, p. 61.

35. For more details on taxation in those years see Halabi, Murtad, pp. 54–62.

36. Halabi, Murtad, pp. 62–64, 83 (the quotation is from p. 83).

37. For other examples of popular pashas see Affaires Étrangères, B¹ 88, folio 313 (March 13, 1761) and B¹ 89, folio 227b (October 22, 1764); and Tabbakh, *Iʿlam*, 3:338–339.

38. Ghazzi, *Nahr*, 3:300; for other petitions see Halabi, Murtad, p. 21; Budayri, *Hawadith Dimashq*, p. 160; and Ghazzi, *Nahr*, 3:299–300.

39. Taoutel, "Wathaʾiq al-akhawiyyat," pp. 374, 391, 393, 395.

40. For these and similar cases see Halabi, Murtad, pp. 16–19, 30, 47, 62–63, 247.

41. Taoutel, "Wathaʾiq al-qarn al-thamin ʿashar," p. 267; Laniado, *Bet dino*, folio 27a. For reference to a similar sale by the Jews sometime in the early nineteenth century see ʿAntebi, *Mor*, folio 21b.

42. Halabi, Murtad, pp. 265–266.

43. Ghazzi, *Nahr*, 3:297, 300; Affaires Étrangères, B¹ 86, folios 72b–73a (July 3, 1751); Tabbakh, *Iʿlam*, 3:351–352; Halabi, Murtad, pp. 96, 98–99. See also chapter 4, this volume, for a general discussion of food and subsistence crises.

44. Sijill, 79:92, 119, 193; 83:172, 209, 216, 221; 87:116, 215, 239, 284, 328; 90:184; 91:19, 221; 101:95, 210, 244, 363; 102:285. Russell observed that theft was an uncommon crime: *Aleppo*, 1:22, 333.

45. Sijill, 87:117.

46. Sijill, 76:444, 479; 78:99, 120, 151, 167, 173, 345; 83:2, 11, 38, 39, 64, 66, 67, 79, 98, 106, 110, 130, 131, 133, 133, 168, 186, 186, 304, 330, 87:114, 13, 33, 34, 60, 104, 114, 136, 164, 167, 191, 242, 256, 260, 267, 280, 289, 389, 392; 88:45; 89:3, 79, 701, 710, 727, 738, 822, 836; 90:71, 81, 83, 102, 112, 158, 169, 241, 257; 91:123, 182, 193, 203, 214, 275, 279, 400, 414, 448; 92:161; 93:6, 64, 88, 96, 126, 176, 177; 97:76, 82, 114, 180; 102:3, 8, 14, 252.

47. Sijill, 79:163, 165, 208; 83:1, 15, 49, 95, 163; 87:7, 360; 97:201; 101:71.

48. See Heyd, *Old Ottoman Criminal Law*, for a discussion of the *qanun* and other aspects of Ottoman law.

49. Sijill, 103:287.

50. "Yutraku al-qadim ʿala qidamihi": Sijill, 76:580; 83:27, 247; 87:9, 134; 90:218.

51. For example, Sijill, 76:40, 214, 362, 414; 79:190; 81:54–55, 63; 83:102, 116, 129, 168, 173; 87:182, 262, 268; 91:384; 97:178; 98:46, 147, 208, 309, 344, 362; 101:28, 105, 110; 102:93; 103:221, 238, 577–578, 603, 634. Guild rules and practices are discussed in detail in chapter 5, this volume.

52. Sijill, 78:80; 85:403; 86:349; 88:45; 91:401; 92:106; 93:122; 103:465. See

also Devezin, *Nachrichten*, pp. 42–52; Russell, *Aleppo*, 1:318–319; and Bodman, *Political Factions*, p. 49.

53. For example, Sijill, 73:319; Burayk, *Taʾrikh al-Sham*, pp. 151–152.

54. Bodman, *Political Factions*, pp. 49, 108–109.

55. Sijill, 78:164; 79:76; 85:328; 97:104, 107, 135; 101:59, 81, 202.

56. Sijill, 101:203–240.

57. Sijill, 102:76, 86; 104:34.

58. Sijill, 79:131, 136, 138, 140, 148, 154, 156; 83:23, 54, 76, 88, 171; 87:97, 192, 309; 90:129, 133, 134, 152, 159, 212, 219, 225; 91:137, 138, 189, 236; 93:185, 190; 101:29, 39, 150, 154, 193, 223, 330; 102:76, 85, 86, 139; 104:34, 61.

59. On the *naqib al-ashraf*, see Sijill, 87:173; Halabi, Murtad, p. 49; Russell, *Aleppo*, 1:321–322; and Bodman, *Political Factions*, pp. 92–93. On the Janissary *serdar*, see Halabi, Murtad, p. 49; Devezin, *Nachrichten*, p. 38; and Bodman, *Political Factions*, p. 66. On the *muhassil*, see Russell, *Aleppo*, 1:322; and Tabbakh, *Iʿlam*, 7:65. The *shahbandar's* judicial functions in the late seventeenth century are described in d'Arvieux, *Mémoires*, 6:432, 451–452. The post was still in existence in the mid-eighteenth century, presumably with the same functions: Sijill, 79:154; 103:203.

60. Dwek, *Birkat Eliyahu*, folios 91a–92a, 98b–101a, 103a–105a; Laniado, *Kiseh Shlomo*, folios 1a–9a; Dwek, *Reyah sadeh*, folios 64a–67b; Laniado, *Bet dino*, folio 81a.

61. Laniado, *Degel*, folios 48a–49a.

62. Russell, *Aleppo*, 1:318–319. On arbitration, see Russell, *Aleppo*, 1:233.

63. Bodman, *Political Factions*, p. 108.

64. For example, Sijill, 76:435; 79:136, 154; 80:182, 207; 87:106, 153, 199, 215, 239; 101:35, 37, 39, 60, 174, 243, 250, 283, 294, 334, 352; 102:36, 107, 142, 165, 192, 211, 264, 278.

65. Halabi, Murtad, pp. 39–40; Sijill, 83:157, 90:218, and 103:134–135. See also Sijill, 76:9, 17, 280, 512; 77:33, 354; 83:26, 70; 85:63, 94; 87:309; 94:106; 103:311.

66. For example, Sijill, 79:203; 83:215, 241; 90:175, 214; 91:216; 101:363; 102:30, 130, 293.

67. Sijill, 74:516; 76:639; 79:136; 80:436; 82:46, 326, 609, 610; 83:179; 87:32, 45, 72, 105, 117, 140, 141; 89:867; 90:239; 91:260, 274; 94:85, 135; 95:20, 250, 342, 382; 96:361; 97:52, 181; 98:62, 148; 101:47, 110, 116, 136, 138, 148, 154, 172, 197, 201, 210, 245, 253, 259; 102:76, 86, 102, 137, 160, 198, 214, 252; 103:24, 100; 104:34, 78, 252.

68. For example, Sijill, 79:47; 83:8, 143, 157; 101:41, 303, 341, 344, 384, 387; 103:134–135; 104:61.

69. Russell, *Aleppo*, 1:319.

70. Russell, *Aleppo*, 1:319–320.

71. Halabi, Murtad, p. 12.

72. Sijill, 79:131, 136, 138, 140, 148, 154, 156; 83:23, 54, 76, 88, 171; 87:97, 192, 309; 90:129, 133, 134, 152, 159, 212, 219, 225; 91:137, 138, 189, 236; 93:185, 190; 101:29, 39, 150, 154, 193, 223, 330; 102:76, 85, 86, 139; 104:34, 61.

73. Sijill, 97:101; 101:105, 166; see also Sijill, 79:154; 101:29, 220, 330; 102:204; 104:61.

74. Sijill, 83:23. See also Sijill, 79:136.

75. Sijill, 79:169.

76. Halabi, Murtad, p. 63.

77. Halabi, Murtad, pp. 30, 49, 62; Russell, Aleppo, 1:22, 315–317; Sauvaget, Alep, p. 237.

78. Sijill, 85:198.

79. Sijill, 79:119; 83:21.

80. Sijill, 82:553; 97:252; 101:219, 262, 370; 102:267, 290, 291.

81. Ghazzi, Nahr, 3:297; Tabbakh, Iᶜlam, 6:488.

82. Sijill, 83:62. See also Affaires Étrangères, Bᵉ 85, folio 13 (January 15, 1746); and Russell, Aleppo, 2:55–56.

83. Russell, Aleppo, 2:84.

84. Sijill, 79:36, 37, 74, 133, 155; 80:535; 81:53; 83:44, 60, 80, 126, 206, 212; 87:78, 92, 146, 197, 293; 90:27, 50, 71, 103, 104, 105, 107, 108, 117, 126, 129, 132, 140, 154, 167, 228, 233; 91:128, 245, 295; 93:72, 125; 97:123, 139; 101:192, 285; 102:12.

85. Sijill, 97:123.

86. Sijill, 97:68; 90:105; 74:264.

87. Sijill, 79:53; 90:227.

88. Sijill, 87:117.

89. Sijill, 79:67, 86, 89, 97, 107, 108, 116, 117, 129, 180, 205, 212, 217; 83:31, 42, 52, 73, 77, 129, 149, 153, 207, 231; 87:60, 79, 90, 109, 144, 147, 152, 160, 209, 218, 234, 312, 371; 89:753, 761, 766, 773, 776, 777, 781, 782, 861, 864, 867, 870; 90:5, 13, 29, 43, 79, 98, 103, 110, 171, 202, 207, 209, 235, 238; 91:21, 44, 130, 131, 133, 141, 152, 178, 184, 216, 218, 228, 232, 237, 264, 265, 279, 294, 296; 97:56, 58, 115, 146; 101:9, 94, 150, 155; 102:38, 57, 80, 91, 101, 106, 138, 147, 206, 207, 292.

90. Sijill, 79:154, 156; Taoutel, Wathaᵓiq, 1:57–58, 69; Burayk, Taᵓrikh al-Sham, pp. 143, 150–151.

91. See Heyd, Old Ottoman Criminal Law, pp. 252–254.

92. Sijill, 83:216; 87:215, 397; 90:220, 239; 101:210, 214; 102:163, 172, 285.

93. Affaires Étrangères, Bᵉ 89, folio 362a (July 20, 1765); Bodman, Political Factions, pp. 21–22, 112; Russell, Aleppo, 1:325; 2:407.

94. Tabbakh, Iᶜlam, 3:359–360.

4. ECONOMIC WELFARE: THE EXTERNAL SOURCES OF WEALTH AND SUBSISTENCE

1. Dayyan, Holekh tamim, part 1, folio 69b.

2. Tabbakh, Iᶜlam, 3:337; Ghazzi, Nahr, 3:300–302; Archives Nationales, Paris, Ministère des Affaires Étrangères (hereafter Affaires Étrangères), Bᵉ 87, folios 376a–391 (August 30–December 24, 1757), passim, and Bᵉ 88, folio 32a (May 1, 1758); Public Record Office, London, State Papers, Foreign, Archives of the Levant Company, Aleppo (hereafter Public Record Office, S.P.), 110/35, folios 3a, 4b (April 27, 1759); Sijill, 90:160; Russell, Treatise, p. 9.

3. Affaires Étrangères, B¹ 88, folio 35 (May 31, 1758).

4. Ghazzi, *Nahr*, 3:301–302, citing a contemporary chronicle of Qustantin al-Tarabulsi.

5. Tabbakh, *Iᶜlam*, 3:338; Ghazzi, *Nahr*, 3:301–302. The governor of Diyarbakr at the time confirmed these reports to the French consul in Aleppo: Affaires Étrangères, B¹ 87, folio 376a (August 30, 1757), B¹ 88, folios 37b–38a (June 13, 1758), and folio 48 (August 20, 1758). The same accounts reached Damascus: Burayk, *Taᵓrikh al-Sham*, p. 70.

6. Sijill, 91:261.

7. Affaires Étrangères, B¹ 88, folios 43b–82 (August 8, 1758–March 20, 1759), *passim;* Public Record Office, S.P. 110/35, folios 3a, 4b (April 27, 1759).

8. Affaires Étrangères, B¹ 88, folio 110a (July 27, 1759), folio 131 (September 17, 1759), and folio 138 (October 25, 1759); Sijill, 91:125.

9. Public Record Office, S.P. 110/36, folios 46b–47a (December 22, 1759); Affaires Étrangères, B¹ 88, folios 153, 157, 163, 212, 219 (December 1759–April 1760); Russell, "Account," pp. 529–534; Russell, *Aleppo,* 1:72–73.

10. Russell, *Treatise,* pp. 1–70; Affaires Étrangères, B¹ 88, folios 221–469 (May 1760–December 1762), *passim;* Public Record Office, S. P. 110/35, folios 67–224 (July 1760–August 1761), *passim,* and S.P. 110/37, folios 18ff (December 1761–September 1762).

11. Sijill, 97:46, 47–50, 54, 70.

12. Affaires Étrangères, B¹ 89, folios 173–384 (May 2, 1764–October 10, 1765), and B¹ 90, folios 3–72 (January 30–October 25, 1766), *passim;* Tabbakh, *Iᶜlam,* 3:345; Ghazzi, *Nahr,* 3:305; Sijill, 102:282.

13. Sijill, 101:83, 84.

14. These crises occurred in 1696–1697, 1714–1716, 1727–1730, 1734–1735, 1751, 1757–1759, 1761, 1764–1768, 1771, 1773, 1775, 1777–1779, 1783, 1786–1787, 1792–1793, 1804–1805. For descriptions of them see Ghazzi, *Nahr,* 3:294–310, *passim;* Tabbakh, *Iᶜlam,* 3:337–368, *passim;* Halabi, Murtad, Baghdad MS. 6299, *passim;* Affaires Étrangères, *passim;* Taoutel, *Wathaᵓiq,* 1:59, 83–85, 89, 105–106; and Fahd, *Taᵓrikh al-rahbaniyya,* 1:251–252, 334.

15. This observation is based on the study of contemporary price lists which are cited with references in the course of this section.

16. Halabi, Murtad, p. 96.

17. For 1729, see Taoutel, *Wathaᵓiq,* 1:59; for 1765, see Affaires Étrangères, B¹ 89, folios 358b–359a (July 5, 1765) and folio 384 (October 10, 1765); for 1771, see Tabbakh, *Iᶜlam,* 3:352; for 1775 and 1783, see Halabi, Murtad, pp. 20, 108.

18. Halabi, Murtad, p. 85, as well as pp. 11, 12, 96, 98, 137; Tabbakh, *Iᶜlam,* 3:305.

19. Tabbakh, *Iᶜlam,* 3:368; Bodman, *Political Factions,* pp. 124–125.

20. Halabi, Murtad, pp. 97–98; Taoutel, "Wathaᵓiq al-akhawiyyat," p. 387.

21. Halabi, Murtad, pp. 41, 118; Fahd, *Taᵓrikh al-rahbaniyya,* 1:251–252.

22. For example, Affaires Étrangères, B¹ 87, folio 391 (December 24, 1757).

23. Halabi, Murtad, p. 96.

24. Halabi, Murtad, p. 96.

25. Halabi, Murtad, pp. 88, 98.

26. Halabi, Murtad, pp. 88, 96–98.

27. For the 1762 price, see Sijill, 97:47; for the others, see Halabi, Murtad, pp. 11–12, 100, 136–137.

28. Tabbakh, *I'lam*, 3:305; Ghazzi, *Nahr*, 3:301; Halabi, Murtad, pp. 137–138, 267.

29. Taoutel, *Watha'iq*, 1:59; Bodman, *Political Factions*, p. 28. See also Sijill, 74:91, 151; 76:3, 4, 100, 112, 135, 136, 141–142, 236, 238, 388, 429, 485, 550, 552, 563–564; 79:113, 122, 123; 85:10, 32, 35, 37, 38–39, 41, 44, 51, 161–162, 165, 166, 170, 185, 190, 203, 265, 268, 269, 270, 276, 287, 290, 297–298, 309, 353, 375, 377, 380; 87:41; 89:832, 852; 90:55, 95; 91:18, 51, 52, 59, 117, 118, 199; 101:113; 102:25, 42, 47, 48, 56, 58, 61, 62, 265, 269; 103:371, 380–381.

30. Taoutel, *Watha'iq*, 1:59 (for 1729); Ghazzi, *Nahr*, 3:301 and Tabbakh, *I'lam*, 3:337 (for 1758); Halabi, Murtad, p. 100 (for 1787); Bodman, *Political Factions*, p. 28 (for 1811); and Qara'li, *Ahamm*, p. 59 (for 1820). Those prices given for a *shunbul* of wheat were multiplied by 16 to give the price per *makkuk*.

31. Taoutel, *Watha'iq*, 1:85.

32. Halabi, Murtad, p. 267.

33. Halabi, Murtad, p. 103.

34. Halabi, Murtad, p. 12.

35. Sijill, 74:667; 76:430, 489, 490, 526; 78:64, 124, 149, 210, 232, 282, 285, 343, 352; 79:76, 96, 126; 80:38, 68, 75, 84, 154, 193. See also Russell, *Aleppo*, 1:44–48, 74, 78–94; Corancez, *Itinéraire*, pp. 25–28, 36–37; and Bowring, *Report*, pp. 16, 20, 34, 78–80.

36. Halabi, Murtad, pp. 14, 42, 62, 82, 84, 87, 110, 112–114, 124, 232. Abdel Nour refers to a long-term climatic shift in Syria during the eighteenth century. See his *Introduction*, pp. 250–251, 303–304.

37. For instances of damage to the crops by locusts, see Ghazzi, *Nahr*, 3:294, 296–297; and Halabi, Murtad, pp. 128, 129, 252, 260.

38. Affaires Étrangères, B¹ 90, folios 3, 20, 67, 72b, 159a, 167, 250b–251a (January 30, 1766–June 16, 1768). See also Bodman, *Political Factions*, pp. 60–61.

39. Burayk, *Ta'rikh al-Sham*, pp. 24, 61, 64, 70, 86, 108, 110, 111, 118; Budayri, *Hawadith Dimashq, passim*; Rafeq, *Province of Damascus*, pp. 95, 113, 222–233.

40. Halabi, Murtad, pp. 85, 98–99.

41. Tabbakh, *I'lam*, 3:352.

42. Bodman, *Political Factions*, pp. 28–29, 39; Russell, *Aleppo*, 2:326.

43. Halabi, Murtad, pp. 11–12, 136–138.

44. Tabbakh, *I'lam*, 3:352; Halabi, Murtad, pp. 11, 102.

45. Halabi, Murtad, pp. 88, 99, 102, 135–138. See also chapter 3, this volume, for more details on the factional competition over food.

46. Halabi, Murtad, pp. 20, 93.

47. Bodman, *Political Factions*, p. 28.

48. Sijill, 77:51, 95, 230; 79:91, 97, 121, 149, 163; 83:10, 108–109, 227; 87:6, 10–11, 175, 293, 387; 95:211, 314; 98:141, 275, 277, 402–405; 101:25, 48, 72; 102:213.

49. The data are compiled from Sijill, 73:19–67, 88–160. For more on these figures see chapter 8 and table 8.1, this volume.

50. Sijill, 79:18, 77, 78, 111, 113, 122, 123, 126, 159–160; 83:37–40, 51,

106, 107, 135, 151, 180, 185, 186, 201, 228, 249–251; 87:129, 209, 261, 285, 310, 361; 89:770, 780, 866, 870; 90:17, 30–32, 43, 104, 115, 194, 202, 209, 253–256; 91:9, 24, 25, 36, 155, 174, 180, 190–191, 218, 238, 240, 250; 97:16, 74, 90, 142, 168, 213–214, 228, 256; 101:153; 102:25, 33, 42, 45, 63, 167, 215, 229, 253.

51. Sijill, 76:98–99; 78:168, 260, 265; 79:229; 80:206; 83:144, 145, 241, 242, 255–256; 87:40–42, 161, 208, 209, 223, 229–233, 235, 238–240, 243, 245, 247, 313; 88:28, 44; 91:18, 28, 252; 97:28–29, 31; 102:11. For more on the economic relations of Syrian cities with their regions in the Ottoman period, see Abdel Nour, *Introduction*, ch. 12.

52. Sijill, 101:409–413; 102:30, 34.

53. Halabi, Murtad, p. 11.

54. Sijill, 102:205; 101:164. He was a tax farmer of the same village as early as 1746: Sijill, 74:37.

55. Wirth, *Syrien*, pp. 162–166; Wirth, "Die Ackerebenen Nordostsyriens"; Wirth, "Damaskus–Aleppo–Beirut," pp. 110–111; Lewis, *Nomads and Settlers*, ch. 3; Lewis, "Frontier of Settlement," pp. 51–59.

56. Affaires Étrangères, B¹ 87, folio 376a (August 30, 1757).

57. See Sijill, register 73, *passim*.

58. Lewis, *Nomads and Settlers*, ch. 1; Lewis, "Frontier of Settlement," pp. 48–51; Wirth, *Syrien*, pp. 159–161.

59. Russell, *Aleppo*, 1:338–339; Drummond, *Travels*, p. 182; Volney, *Voyage*, 2:135; Burckhardt, *Travels in Nubia*, pp. xxv, xxxviii; Olivier, *Voyage*, 2:312; Corancez, *Itinéraire*, p. 22; Eton, *Survey*, p. 267; Sauvaget, *Alep*, p. 194, n. 712; Bodman, *Political Factions*, pp. 15–17, 28.

60. Sijill, 78:168, 260; 79:196; 83:56–58, 74–75, 90, 164, 249–251; 87:40, 41, 42, 313; 101:112–113; 102:25, 45, 47, 61, 259. In the mid-eighteenth century the regular taxes on villages included the *miri, salyan, avariz, kharaj, qishlaq, dhakhira, imdad al-hidriyya, kasr al-jabbul, ramiyyat al-ʿarab, qudumiyya*, and *kasr al-baqar*.

61. Sijill, 76:127, 136, 308; 77:92, 248, 286; 80:52; 84:1; 86:1, 128; 93:2, 3; 98:1; 103:1. See also the inside front covers of Sijill, registers 74, 77, 95, and 99.

62. Sijill, 83:6, 80, 104, 218; 87:5, 15, 63, 64, 67, 70, 76, 79, 103, 109, 227, 237, 240, 266; 90:178; 91:260; 93:97; 97:40, 53, 76, 96, 98; 101:286; 102:9, 29, 40, 75, 159, 163, 191, 209.

63. Sijill, 83:216.

64. Affaires Étrangères, B¹ 89, folios 12–13 (March 1, 1763) and B¹ 88, folio 110a (July 22, 1759), folio 219b (April 19, 1760), folio 221 (May 20, 1760), folio 313b (March 13, 1761); Bodman, *Political Factions*, pp. 13–14.

65. Halabi, Murtad, pp. 45–46, 50, 54; Tabbakh, *Iʿlam*, 3:358–359; Bodman, *Political Factions*, p. 115. For similar occurrences see also Tabbakh, *Iʿlam*, 3:348, 367.

66. Gräf, "ʿAnaza," p. 483; Lewis, "Frontier of Settlement," p. 50; Boucheman, "Note," pp. 23, 36–37; Bodman, *Political Factions*, p. 13; Barbir, *Ottoman Rule in Damascus*, pp. 103–104; Grant, *Syrian Desert*, pp. 21–22. For maps of the tribal migration areas in Syria see Wirth, *Syrien*, map 11; and Raswan, "Tribal Areas," pp. 494–502.

67. Ghazzi, *Nahr*, 3:322; Bodman, *Political Factions*, pp. 12–13, 131–132, 136; Shamir, "Effects of the *Hacc*," p. 213; Dayyan, *Holekh tamim*, part 1, folio 70a; Polk, "Rural Syria," p. 509; Taoutel, *Watha³iq*, 3:108, 121, 122; Corancez, *Itinéraire*, pp. 108, 114, 216; Rousseau, *Pachalik de Bagdad*, p. 95; Rousseau, *Voyage*, p. 3; Buckingham, *Travels in Mesopotamia*, pp. 1–2, 125–126, 130–156; Buckingham, *Travels Among the Arab Tribes*, pp. 501, 563–564; Taylor, *Lands of the Saracens*, p. 201; Benjamin, *Acht Jahre*, p. 43.

68. Maʿoz, *Ottoman Reform*, pp. 129–148; Lewis, *Nomads and Settlers*, chs. 2 and 3; Lewis, "Frontier of Settlement," pp. 52–55; Polk, "Rural Syria," p. 509.

69. Gould, "Lords or Bandits," pp. 496–501.

70. Kitab al-amthal, Rylands Arabic MS. 775, folio 18b.

71. De Tott, *Memoirs*, vol. 2, part 4, pp. 130–132.

72. Grant, *Syrian Desert*, pp. 29, 141–142, 153–156, 172–173.

73. Sijill, 79:19, 39; 83:47, 101; 87:28, 267; 89:872; 90:27; 91:19, 289; 97:86; 101:18, 19, 122, 235, 272; 102:4, 15; Boucheman, "Note," pp. 23–24.

74. Affaires Étrangères, B¹ 89, folio 281 (February 7, 1765), folios 293b–294a (February 19, 1765), and folio 398b (November 19, 1765).

75. Bodman, *Political Factions*, p. 11.

76. Sijill, 83:133.

77. Sijill, 102:18–19; Affaires Étrangères, B¹ 89, folio 227b (October 22, 1764), folio 246 (January 6, 1765), folio 281a (February 7, 1765), folio 355b (June 20, 1765), folio 358 (July 5, 1765).

78. Halabi, Murtad, pp. 15, 83, 133–134, 299.

79. Affaires Étrangères, B¹ 89, folio 398b (November 19, 1765).

80. For accounts of expeditions against tribes see Bodman, *Political Factions*, pp. 7–8, 12–13, 52, 104–105, 112–115, 118, 123, 127, 129–131; Ghazzi, *Nahr*, 3:295, 296, 299, 322; Sijill, 102:18–19; Halabi, Murtad, p. 58; Affaires Étrangères, B¹ 86, folio 72b (July 3, 1751), folios 94b–95a (September 20, 1751), folios 179b–180a (May 5, 1752), B¹ 88, folio 110a (July 22, 1759), folio 219b (April 19, 1760), folio 221 (May 20, 1760), folio 313b (March 13, 1761), folio 472 (December 17, 1762), and B¹ 89, folios 12–13 (March 1, 1763), folio 227b (October 22, 1764), folio 246 (January 8, 1765), folio 281a (February 7, 1765), folio 397 (November 19, 1765); Charles-Roux, *Échelles*, pp. 70–71; and Masson, *Commerce français au XVIIIe siècle*, p. 285.

81. See Halabi, Murtad, pp. 78–81.

82. Grant, *Syrian Desert*, chs. 4–6; Carruthers, *Desert Route to India, passim*; Parsons, *Travels*, p. 76; Howel, *Journal*, pp. 77, 86; Capper, *Observations*, pp. 130–133, 144–145, 179–185; Browne, *Travels*, p. 410; Pococke, *Description of the East*, vol. 2, part 1, pp. 170–171; Rousseau, *Voyage*, p. 3; de Tott, *Memoirs*, vol. 2, part 4, pp. 129–131; Russell, *Aleppo*, 2:24–25; Masson, *Commerce français au XVIIIe siècle*, p. 286; Affaires Étrangères, B¹ 86, folios 179b–180a (May 5, 1752).

83. Sijill, 87:71 and 91:125; Affaires Étrangères, B¹ 86, folios 212a–213b (August 1, 1752) and B¹ 89, folio 246 (January 8, 1765), folio 281a (February 7, 1765), folio 341 (May 30, 1765), folio 355b (June 20, 1765); Masson, *Commerce français au XVIIIe siècle*, p. 286; Ambrose, "English Traders," p. 264, n. 2.

84. Charles-Roux, *Échelles*, pp. 70–71.

85. Sim, *Desert Traveller*, p. 102. See also Grant, *Syrian Desert*, pp. 29, 213.

86. Sijill, 79:190; 81:63; 83:116, 144; 87:48, 72, 262; 91:149.

87. Sijill, 76:146, 578; 83:129; 85:175; 90:117; 91:384; 95:108, 380; 98:54, 147, 153, 300, 334, 362; 103:7, 238, 329, 334–335, 352, 358, 506, 627, 634. For more details on these guild practices see chapter 5, this volume.

88. In the 1930s the peasantry in the northern Syrian countryside was found to possess only a few processed goods, most of them produced locally rather than in the towns. See Weulersse, "La primauté des cités," p. 238.

89. Sijill, 79:3, 34, 109, 110, 205; 83:84, 85; 87:112, 217, 289, 307; 90:104, 119, 178; 97:79; 102:67, 71, 89, 178, 183, 255, 267, 281.

90. Sijill, 83:23; 93:176; Dayyan, Imrei no'am, part 1, folio 9.

91. Aleppo's trade with Mecca and Arabia is reported to have declined in the late eighteenth century. See Russell, Aleppo, 1:199, and Burckhardt, Travels in Nubia, p. xxvi.

92. For a detailed analysis of these developments see Steensgaard, The Asian Trade Revolution, especially ch. 4.

93. Davis, Aleppo and Devonshire Square, ch. 8; Charles-Roux, Échelles, pp. 74–77.

94. Paris, Le Levant, pp. 414–415; Masson, Commerce français au XVIIIe siècle, pp. 522–523. Paris (p. 415, n. 1) quotes figures that place Aleppo's trade in 1785 at over 10 million livres.

95. For figures tracing the sharp decline in Aleppo's trade, see Sauvaget, Alep, p. 203.

96. Paris, Le Levant, pp. 414–418.

97. For the places of origin of cloth exported through Aleppo, see Sauvaget, Alep, p. 202, n. 750; and Masson, Commerce français au XVIIIe siècle, p. 457.

98. Davis, Aleppo and Devonshire Square, pp. 159–160.

99. Davis, Aleppo and Devonshire Square, ch. 7; Sauvaget, Alep, p. 202, n. 750.

100. Paris, Le Levant, pp. 417, 574–581, 600–601.

101. On the competition among the Europeans, see Charles-Roux, Échelles, pp. 37–38, 197–199; Paris, Le Levant, pp. 325–326; and Davis, Aleppo and Devonshire Square, ch. 9.

102. Public Record Office, S.P. 110/35, folio 202b (June 12, 1761) and 110/37, folio 18 (December 31, 1761). The French correspondence contained similar comments: see Affaires Étrangères, B¹ 88, folio 339b (June 30, 1761) and folio 402 (April 27, 1762).

103. Charles-Roux, Échelles, p. 107. The records of the English Levant Company and of the French consulate contain the most vivid documentation on the vagaries of this trade. Davis, Aleppo and Devonshire Square, gives many illustrations.

104. Paris, Le Levant, p. 415, n. 2 and p. 447, n. 1.

105. Steensgaard, The Asian Trade Revolution, pp. 34–35, 185–187; Masson, Commerce français au XVIIIe siècle, pp. 372–373.

106. On the relative share of Aleppo in total French trade, see Paris, Le Levant, pp. 504–566.

107. Davis, "English Imports," pp. 196–206. On the general patterns of European trade in the Middle East in the eighteenth century, see Owen, "Introduction," pp. 148–150.

108. Paris, *Le Levant*, pp. 557–561; Sauvaget, *Alep*, p. 191, n. 703.
109. See Issawi, "Transformation," for some of these changes.
110. Sauvaget, *Alep*, p. 204.
111. Sauvaget, *Alep*, p. 239.

5. ECONOMIC WELFARE: THE MARKET, FAMILY, AND CHARITY

1. Sijill, 83:55; 87:268; 95:174; 97:166; 101:379. See also Russell, *Aleppo*, 1:301. On the widespread child labor in the 1830s, see Bowring, *Report*, p. 84.

2. For examples of female employment, see Sijill, 76:194; 82:358; 83:42, 91, 204; 87:32, 58–59, 183, 299; 90:18; 91:276, 278; 95:342; 97:88; 98:393, 413; 101:136; 102:193; 103:287; and Russell, *Aleppo*, 1:138, 142, 157, 161–162, 242, 282, 286, 299, 302–303, 307, 308, 439–440; 2:55–56, 65, 80, 83, 140–141.

3. For these and other examples, see Sijill, 76:414; 80:380; 85:186; 91:131; 95:45, 127; 98:243, 301, 327, 365; 101:28; 103:264.

4. Sijill, 97:88.

5. The large-scale expenditures on construction and repair are evident from numerous court documents, especially the detailed accounts of work on waqf properties. Aspects of construction are discussed in chapter 8, this volume.

6. See the numerous references to the uses of servants in Russell, *Aleppo*, 1:121, 137–138, 145, 166, 167–170, 254–256, 259, 377; 2:10, 65.

7. The figures are computed from the financial accounts of the institutions, found in Sijill, 73:19–67, 88–160. They are analyzed in detail in chapter 8 and table 8.2, this volume.

8. For example, Sijill, 74:231; 75:346; 76:128, 580; 79:53; 85:311, 362; 87:58–59, 129, 154, 225, 258, 268; 89:850; 95:127, 130–131, 139, 391; 91:22; 97:178; 98:46, 249, 369; 101:105, 166, 379, 412; 102:47, 180, 186, 212; 103:249, 460, 519, 603.

9. Sijill, 74:495; 75:346; 76:264, 611; 82:160; 83:81, 218; 87:154; 89:769; 91:134, 207, 278, 474; 95:10; 101:412; 102:47, 212; 103:246.

10. Sijill, 79:34, 38, 65, 72, 74, 77, 94, 107, 109, 110.

11. For references to equipment for cloth production see Sijill, 74:622; 76:115, 450; 77:91, 314; 78:50, 29, 98, 125, 194; 80:277, 394; 83:55, 82; 87:129; 88:175, 394; 89:4, 811; 91:223; 101:274; 102:160. The traditional techniques in the textile industry, which have not entirely disappeared, are described, with photographs and illustrations, in Moser, *Die Ikattechnik in Aleppo;* and Chevallier, "Techniques et société" and "Les tissus ikatés."

12. Russell, *Aleppo*, 1:161.

13. For examples of observations by Europeans, see Gaube and Wirth, *Aleppo*, p. 313.

14. For the state of industrial technology in contemporary Cairo, see Raymond, *Artisans et commerçants*, 1:218–220.

15. Sijill, 77:91, 314; 78:50, 98, 125; 80:277; 83:82; 89:4, 811; 91:223, 332; 101:274, 339; 103:345, 419.

16. Sijill, 85:414.

17. Sijill, 76:146, 578, 610; 83:129; 85:76, 333; 87:72, 268; 90:117; 91:384;

95:122, 286, 380; 97:62; 98:54, 147, 334, 344, 362, 634; 103:7, 238, 329, 352, 358, 506.

18. Sijill, 76:362, 583; 81:54–55; 83:144; 85:409; 98:309; 101:110; 103:345.

19. Sijill, 103:500–501; see also Sijill, 103:379, 404, 408, 444, 559, 580, 613, 653.

20. Sijill, 76: 414; 83:144; 87:48; 101:28.

21. Sijill, 76:40; 98:265; 103:194.

22. Sijill, 76:414; 87:48; 101:28.

23. Sijill, 87:72, 103. The number of tanners is derived from a list of guild members who appeared in court to settle a collective matter.

24. Sijill, 76:115, 450, 583; 77:91, 314; 78:50, 98, 125; 85:414; 87:129; 89:811; 91:223, 332; 98:369; 101:105, 274; 103:500–501.

25. Russell, *Aleppo*, 1:161. Large manufacturing establishments existed in other Middle Eastern cities, where they may have been organized along similar lines. General references to them without clarifying their organization can create anachronistic and misleading impressions about the nature of industry in the premodern period. See, for example, the brief comments in Owen, *The Middle East in the World Economy*, p. 46.

26. Sijill, 75:251; 76:30, 572–573, 653.

27. Sijill, 97:108–110.

28. Sijill, 87:305.

29. Sijill, 76:604, 647; 80:304, 329; 85:263, 331; 95:283–284, 391; 97:69; 98:226; 101:97; 103:213–214, 221, 287, 455, 457.

30. Sijill, 76:7; 89:792–793; 98:243; 101:410; 103:565, 569, 622.

31. Sijill, 98:266; see also Sijill, 103:611.

32. Sijill, 85:322.

33. Sijill, 87:357. On the weighers, see Sijill, 76:122; 77:445; 79:21; 85:379; 87:26, 330, 340; 90:166; 97:2, 203, 249; 101:24, 122, 144, 147, 409. On the brokers, see Sijill, 85:175, 552; 87:139, 140, 357; 90:66; 97:138, 170, 184, 211; 101:54, 63; 102:144.

34. See Sijill, 97:47–50.

35. Sijill, 98:243; 103:194; see also Sijill, 98:111, 115.

36. See Sijill, 97:108–110; Bodman, *Political Factions*, pp. 64–65; Tabbakh, *Iˤlam*, 3:341–342; and Ghazzi, *Nahr*, 3:303–304.

37. Sijill, 83:132; 97:62.

38. Sijill, 79:173; 90:219; 91:227; 101:167.

39. Owen, for example, notes in remarks on the guild system in the Middle East around 1800 that "competition was made virtually impossible by the practice of fixing uniform prices." See *The Middle East in the World Economy*, p. 47. Conclusions drawn from Istanbul's guilds, which are better known than many others, do not necessarily hold for Aleppo. Guild practices in the capital were definitely more restrictive and official controls more pronounced than they were in Aleppo, and possibly in other provincial cities as well. The literature on Middle Eastern guilds is still too limited in its coverage of different places, periods and themes to allow a regional profile sensitive to the local variations and historical changes. For examples of studies devoted to guilds, see Raymond, *Artisans et commerçants*, ch. 12; Rafeq, "The Law Court Registers of Damascus"

and "Mazahir"; Gerber, "Guilds"; and the series of studies by Baer listed in the bibliography.

40. Rafeq, "Mazahir," which presents the only study of Aleppo's guilds published so far, provides some details on their organization and practices in the late sixteenth and early seventeenth centuries which show that the main features of the system were already in place then.

41. Cases of successful defiance of the *muhtasib* by guilds in the early seventeenth century appear to lend support to this explanation. See Rafeq, "Mazahir," pp. 43 and 44, where two such cases, dated 1608 and 1617, are cited.

42. Sijill, 75:220; 76:387, 597, 623, 627; 79:72, 181; 83:253; 85:234, 262; 87:103, 185, 291; 91:131, 175, 414; 95:94–95, 304; 97:38, 183; 101:11, 27, 31, 62, 165, 175, 291; 102:204, 207; 103:143, 239.

43. For example, Sijill, 76:567, 584; 87:231, 305; 91:384; 95:86; 97:88, 91, 219; 98:147, 153, 163, 226, 278, 282, 295, 361; 102:41; 103:7, 42, 238, 334–335, 577–578, 643.

44. For example, Sijill, 85:362; 91:317, 462; 95:122; 97:47; 98:54; 103:238, 344, 358, 500.

45. For examples of hereditary rights, see Sijill, 83:48; 95:387; 101:219, 223, 256; 103:247, 548.

46. See Sijill, 76:2, 30, 57, 89, 139, 147, 179, 219, 527, 619; 79:139; 83:65; 85:186, 253, 420, 442; 91:61, 328; 95:45, 77, 127, 139, 280, 365, 393, 401, 405, 407; 98:57, 86, 102, 115, 159, 327, 405, 427; 101:24, 26, 43, 145, 159, 245; 103:56, 197, 238, 263, 264, 270, 344, 360, 431, 442, 443, 455, 559, 611, 622–623, 651, 652.

47. Sijill, 76:302, 494, 522, 577, 639, 648; 78:151; 85:185, 372, 377, 437; 87:304; 95:372, 409; 97:102; 98:74; 101:233; 103:357, 502.

48. Sijill, 76:214; 85:56; 95:25; 98:389; 101:271, 328; 102:223.

49. Sijill, 76:454, 610, 621; 79:38, 208; 83:61, 89; 85:17–18, 74–75, 222; 91:223, 319; 95:28, 354–355; 98:153, 280; 101:32, 83, 84; 102:282; 103:460.

50. Sijill, 76:561; 83:132–133; 85:17–18; 87:377; 90:148, 235; 101:53; 103:285, 318.

51. Sijill, 76:214, 610; 79:208; 83:163; 85:2, 56, 378; 87:360; 91:223; 94:404; 95:130, 131, 177, 399; 101:136, 271, 328, 103:346, 460, 569.

52. Bodman, *Political Factions*, pp. 98–99.

53. For examples, see Halabi, Murtad, Baghdad MS. 6299, pp. 44–54, 62–64; Tabbakh, *Iʿlam*, 3:357–359; and the instances of fiscal exploitation discussed in chapter 3, this volume.

54. Sijill, 74:622, 627; 89:802; 91:317; 101:194, 339; 103:404, 408, 444. The term *khulw* or *khilw*, found in some cities in the region as a synonym for *gedik* or as a reference to a form of tenancy in a shop, was not used in those senses in Aleppo during the middle decades of the century. Sales deeds do speak often of *al-khulw al-ʿurfi* in shops, but the reference is to a form of property unrelated to the *gedik*. The term indicated those ownership rights in a shop which applied to the structure but not to the land. This type of ownership existed in cases in which private property was built on endowed waqf land with the permission of the charitable foundation. The use of the land was leased to the owner of the building in return for an annual ground rent *(hikr)*. In this sense, the owner was

a tenant. The shop itself, however, was considered the private property (*mulk*) of the owner, who was free to sell, rent and even endow it. In 1750, for example, a woman bought the *khulw* in a shop, and then had it endowed with the provision that the income from renting the property would be dedicated to a charitable cause (Sijill, 80:31, 34).

The references to the institutions of the *gedik* and the *khulw* in the literature, usually brief and general, reveal some confusing inconsistencies born of the current diversity of terms and usages. Terms were occasionally used in more than one sense in the same locality; the usages varied somewhat between places during the same period; and the meaning of terms, as well as the institutions themselves, changed over time. For a sample of such references covering different periods and places, see Raymond, *Artisans et commerçants*, 1:271; Baer, "Monopolies," pp. 159–164; Rafeq, "The Impact of Europe," p. 428; Gerber, "Enterprise," pp. 42–43; Pakalın, *Osmanlı tarih deyimleri*, 1:656–659; and Abu-Lughod, *Cairo*, p. 155. References to the *gedik* and *khulw* in works on the Islamic laws of property and waqf also illustrate the usages. See, for example, Ibn ʿAbidin, *Radd al-muhtar*, 4:391, 521–524; and Qadri Pasha, *Qanun al-ʿadl*, pp. 95, 97.

55. Sijill, 101:105; also 79:226; 85:362; 97:178; 102:93.

56. Sijill, 74:622; 76:354; 89:802; 98:386; 103:379, 404, 408, 444, 559, 580, 613, 653.

57. Sijill, 74:627; 76:117, 354, 408, 533; 83:96; 91:317, 462; 98:386; 101:47, 194, 338; 103:57, 95, 101, 237, 282, 283, 326, 377, 379, 404, 408, 500–501, 559, 580, 613.

58. Sijill, 74:627; 76:115, 235, 450; 77:415; 78:194; 80:394; 83:82; 87:129, 372; 91:223, 425; 101:274; 103:95, 419.

59. For the prices of asses, see Sijill, 74:627; 76:479; 78:345; 80:44, 55, 59, 76, 268, 286, 356; 82:13, 368; 83:64, 151; 85:4, 58–59, 413; 86:286; 91:278; 92:221; 95:150; 99:112; 103:53. For the prices of mules, see Sijill, 78:99; 79:2, 9; 83:67, 106; 85:115, 123, 147; 92:273; 94:22, 428; 95:301; 101:60, 135; 103:202, 306.

60. For example, Sijill, 77:229; 78:69, 209; 79:186; 80:154; 82:575; 86:322, 332; 87:31, 49, 142, 202; 88:38, 48; 89:59; 91:130, 266; 92:79, 150; 95:88–89; 98:30, 303–304; 102:208, 273. Where a sale involved only a share of the property, the value of the whole was computed on the basis of that share.

61. For the prices of barber shops, see Sijill, 76:440; 78:98, 288; 85:331; 89:61. For the prices of dyeing shops, see Sijill, 80:13; 87:116; 89:25, 806, 847. For the prices of shops for the sale of coal, see Sijill, 78:216, 270, 300; 80:74; 85:308; 91:427.

62. For example, Sijill, 87:334, 372; 91:425; 93:41, 44. On the structure and uses of the *qaysariyyas* see Sauvaget, *Alep*, pp. 222–223.

63. Sijill, 79:53; 98:249; 101:379; 102:180, 186.

64. For a detailed discussion of this type of partnership see Udovitch, *Partnership and Profit*, ch. 4.

65. For examples of intercommunal partnerships, see Sijill, 77:293; 87:72; 89:834–835; 97:69; 98:301; 101:231, 261, 390; 103:53. For examples of partnerships between kin see Sijill, 77:183; 80:329; 101:349; 103:340.

66. For other references to partnerships and their terms, see Sijill, 75:237, 243; 76:43, 123, 292; 79:146; 82:475–476; 83:21, 120–122; 85:343; 87:64, 172, 193, 294; 89:836; 90:4; 91:416, 437; 92:92; 93:83, 93, 100; 95:135, 174 319, 322, 334; 97:5; 98:154–156, 330–331; 101:231, 317; 102:284; 103:102–105, 112, 144.

67. For examples, see Sijill, 74:194, 225; 76:74, 335; 77:422; 78:176–177, 330; 79:75, 92, 129; 80:40, 192, 271; 87:100, 158, 216, 300, 303, 332; 90:234; 91:383; 101:251; 102:32, 34, 38, 48, 108, 239.

68. Public Record Office, London, State Papers Foreign, Archives of the Levant Company, Aleppo (hereafter Public Record Office, S.P.), 110/29, folios 184b, 186a (September 7, 1775). On the financial activities of the moneychangers, see also Sijill, 74:115; 75:246, 247; 76:115, 142, 156, 221, 321, 574; 77:3, 112; 87:155; 89:872; 90:65; 91:9; 97:207; 101:250, 371; 102:44; 103:614; Laniado, *Kiseh Shlomo*, folio 29a; Laniado, *Bet dino*, folio 121b; and Dwek, *Birkat Eliyahu*, folios 92a–93b.

69. For example, Sijill, 73:17, 22, 33, 49, 50, 71–78, 103, 130, 160, 188, 195, 207, 228, 244, 252, 254, 258, 288, 290, 307, 326, 345; 76:320; 78:381; 79:2, 82; 80:273; 83:35; 87:110; 95:392; 101:6; 102:152, 153, 266. On the controversy over the cash waqfs, see Mandaville, "Usurious Piety."

70. Sijill, 95:354–355.

71. See, for example, Jennings, "Loans and Credit," pp. 184, 188–191; Inalcik, "Capital Formation," p. 139; and Çağatay, "Riba," pp. 64–65. In Europe, where usury also aroused moral objections, a similar distinction between usurious rates and the fair cost of money evolved by the eighteenth century. See Braudel, *The Wheels of Commerce*, pp. 559–566; and Homer, *History of Interest Rates*, pp. 70–81.

72. For example, Archives Nationales, Paris, Ministère des Affaires Étrangères (hereafter Affaires Étrangères), B¹ 84, folios 247a, 249a (1743), which refers to a current rate of 15 percent; B¹ 91, folios 178b–179a (June 6, 1770), which refers to a rate of 10 percent; Public Record Office, S.P. 110/35, folio 75b (July 31, 1760), which refers to interest rates of 9–12 percent; and Davis, *Aleppo and Devonshire Square*, ch. 12. Rates similar to Aleppo's prevailed in contemporary Cairo. Raymond, *Artisans et commerçants*, 1.281.

73. Sijill, 76:82; 77:54, 443–444; 83:55; 102:233.

74. Davis, *Aleppo and Devonshire Square*, ch. 12; Davis, *Rise of the Atlantic Economies*, pp. 240–241; Homer, *History of Interest Rates*, pp. 136–143, 163–178; Braudel, *The Wheels of Commerce*, p. 386.

75. Public Record Office, S.P. 110/29, folio 71a (June 18, 1756).

76. Public Record Office, S.P. 110/35, folio 75b (July 31, 1760). For examples of large-scale defaults on loans see Davis, *Aleppo and Devonshire Square*, ch. 12; and Ambrose, "English Traders at Aleppo," pp. 259–260.

77. Sijill, 101:9, 67; 87:147; 102:91. For other examples, see Sijill, 79:67, 89, 97, 107, 108, 116, 117, 129, 180, 205, 212, 217; 83:31, 45, 52, 72, 73, 77, 184, 231; 85:485; 87:60, 79, 90, 109; 91:228; 101:57, 94, 99, 131, 282, 295, 411; 102:57, 101, 104, 138, 147, 206, 230, 292.

78. Sijill, 76:534, 653. For other examples, see Sijill, 74:269; 75:212, 371; 76:534, 653; 77:31; 83:3; 87:144; 90:39, 89, 100, 130, 146; 91:146, 242, 244, 275; 95:8; 101:151; 103:608.

79. For examples, see Sijill, 75:173; 76:212, 309–310; 77:262, 263, 311; 78:46; 80:257; 82:609; 87:2; 89:764; 90:89, 100, 118, 201; 92:89; 94:234; 101:35; 102:78, 83, 103, 138, 233; 103:487.

80. Sijill, 74:388, 462, 472; 75:112; 77:279, 332, 367, 471; 78:216; 79:5, 208; 80:74, 92, 146, 160, 219, 231, 287, 290, 494; 83:94, 158–159; 87:32, 206; 89:757–758; 90:115; 91:43, 137, 165; 92:119; 93:103; 95:281–282; 97:121; 101:237; 102:143; 103:318; 104:51.

81. Sijill, 101:124–125.

82. Sijill, 77:311; 90:118; 102:78, 83.

83. Sijill, 83:187–188. For similar cases, see Sijill, 74:253; 76:660; 79:35; 90:234.

84. For examples, see Sijill, 74:260; 75:371; 76:212, 446; 77:219, 262, 451, 471; 78:330; 79:92; 80:40, 190, 192, 221, 271; 82:118; 83:55; 87:126, 158, 216, 281, 300; 90:89, 118; 91:5, 142, 245; 102:108, 138, 239; 103:75.

85. Affaires Étrangères, B¹ 84, folios 125–126 (February 14, 1743); folios 202–203 (September 16, 1743); folios 254–255 (April 30, 1744); and folios 334–335 (July 27, 1745).

86. Sijill, 77:276, 360; 79:7, 9; 80:284; 83:134–135; 87:46, 244; 89:23, 868, 872; 90:2; 101:104, 215; 102:77. This aspect of the market, and real property in general, are discussed in greater detail in my "Real Property and Society" and "Men, Women and Property."

87. Sijill, 76:558, 476, 513; 78:58, 103, 198, 199, 239, 299, 308, 328, 350, 351; 79:84, 157; 80:44, 58, 96, 115, 141, 162; 85:306, 314, 324, 331; 86:292, 305, 312; 87:356; 88:10, 145, 173; 89:24, 49, 68, 107, 109, 111, 238, 287, 686, 728, 817, 828; 91:329, 330, 361, 387, 443, 449; 92:9, 25, 67, 81, 99, 129, 130, 146, 160; 93:29, 41, 108, 167, 170, 182.

88. Sijill, 75:290, 305; 76:225, 482, 614; 78:101, 287, 295, 312, 324; 79:169, 482; 82:77, 157, 354; 85:286; 89:770; 91:225; 92:34, 134; 94:233, 258, 359; 98:198, 221; 101:40; 103:200, 360.

89. For more details, see Marcus, "Men, Women and Property."

90. Sijill, 74:224; 76:260, 344–345, 611; 77:336, 366, 462; 78:115; 79:79, 111, 165, 222; 80:124; 83:86; 85:48, 239–240; 87:19, 174; 92:94; 95:204; 96:368; 102:103; 103:160–161. Credit arrangements were actually much more common than the sales deeds indicate. The parties made them in separate agreements, while registering in the deeds the fiction that full price had been paid. The veiled credit arrangements usually surfaced when sellers died before collecting the balance still due to them, or when a dispute arose over failure to meet the payment schedule.

91. For additional details and figures, see Marcus, "Men, Women and Property."

92. Marcus, "Men, Women and Property," pp. 147–150; Marcus, "Real Property and Society," p. 115. The most prominent Christian investor in the 1750s and 1760s was Shukri ʿAʾida, the interpreter of the English consulate. For some of his numerous real estate transactions, see Sijill, 75:22; 76:511, 523, 556; 77:249; 85:306; 87:85, 307; 88:89, 124, 150; 89:764, 847, 860, 861; 90:48, 74; 91:333, 344, 397; 95:93, 191–192; 97:170–173, 221; 98:261–262, 337; 100:89, 91, 230; 102:179, 190, 193, 201, 202; 103:45.

93. For examples of his dealings, see Sijill, 75:245, 376–377; 76:428, 586, 640; 77:6, 51, 95, 386; 78:1, 20, 86, 87, 110, 119, 141, 266, 281, 323, 331, 430; 82:312, 469; 85:344, 348, 351; 87:376; 89:786, 791; 90:82, 89, 142; 91:32, 48; 92:37; 95:37, 80, 349; 98:104, 332; 100:89. See also Marcus, "Real Property and Society," p. 121.

94. Sijill, 75:52; 76:632; 77:109, 432; 78:32, 46, 112, 162, 347; 82:430, 458, 464, 553, 554, 575, 585, 592, 632; 85:257, 308, 359; 87:78, 155; 88:20; 90:101, 121; 91:1, 109, 299, 457; 95:215; 97:27, 73, 145, 179, 182, 270; 98:104–105; 102:12, 26, 63, 162.

95. Sijill, 75:80, 81, 157; 77:20–22, 229, 245, 314, 321, 328, 361, 464; 78:63, 64, 67, 77, 210, 264, 288, 290, 314, 326, 352, 370, 371, 372, 395; 79:8, 45, 46, 171, 187; 82:521; 87:44, 151, 196; 88:3, 4, 38, 48, 121, 149; 89:810, 818; 92:113; 95:23. For his biography and deed of endowment, see Ghazzi, *Nahr*, 2:178–189; and Tabbakh, *I'lam*, 7:23–28.

96. For example, Sijill, 76:389, 516, 538, 586; 80:178–179; 87:196; 89:774; 90:85, 86, 199; 91:258, 303, 304, 381, 394, 422, 451; 95:56–57, 81, 88–89, 93, 96, 101, 158, 159–161, 211, 279, 314; 98:19, 30, 74, 81, 84–85, 141, 293, 299, 303–304, 404–406; 100:184–185; 101:17, 412; 102:59, 68, 94, 208, 213, 281; 103:164, 166.

97. Sijill, 74:667; 76:441, 458, 487, 492, 542; 78:67, 124, 129, 143, 195, 209, 232, 239, 260, 282, 284, 285, 286, 343, 347, 352; 79:151; 80:4, 16, 29, 38, 40, 68, 75, 84, 91, 106, 173, 177, 193, 250, 266, 272, 287, 301; 85:299, 308, 361, 362, 371; 86:305, 323, 335, 347, 349; 88:6, 25, 83, 149, 188; 89:100, 108. See also Marcus, "Men, Women and Property," p. 146.

98. For example, Sijill, 74:504; 78:65, 83, 192, 246; 79:46, 118, 186; 80:38, 105, 266; 86:332; 87:142; 88:140; 91:143, 195; 101:330; 102:6, 206.

99. Sijill, 74:237; 77:107, 154; 85:19; 95:211.

100. Sijill, 80:185; 73:72; 78:342, 352; 97:247–248, 253; 102:24–25, 26.

101. See, for example, Sijill, 79:124, 198–199; 83:237; 87:5; 90:6; 91:158; 97:11, 143; 101:108, 254–255, 395–396, 404; 102:166, 289.

102. Sijill, 90:17.

103. Sijill, 87:333; 101:220. For other references to *'a'ila*, see Sijill, 79:92; 87:140; 93:119, 261; 103:99, 613. For observations on the term, see Lecerf, "'A'ila," pp. 305–306, and "Note," pp. 31–40.

104. For examples of marriage by minors and adolescents, see Sijill, 76:603; 82:2; 85:95, 312, 554; 98:398. See also Russell, *Aleppo*, 1:281–282, 296; 2:79. In the early twentieth century Ghazzi deplored the widespread practice of early marriage: *Nahr*, 1:283. Legal majority (*bulugh*) was usually determined by the physical signs of puberty rather than by arbitrary age. Judging from actual cases recorded in court documents, boys reached majority between ages 13 and 16, and girls between 12 and 15. See Sijill, 86:121, 180; 87:140; 93:141, 151, 172, 196, 213, 220, 234, 258, 261, 272, 310, 361, 373.

105. Sijill, 87:25.

106. Russell, *Aleppo*, 1:280–281.

107. For examples, see Sijill, 79:104, 174; 80:94, 224; 82:25, 37, 284; 83:150; 84:29, 45, 62, 278, 315, 317, 321, 325, 332, 348, 402, 427; 86:219, 313, 340; 87:46; 88:17; 93:17, 23, 40, 50, 194, 240; 101:5, 23, 88; 102:36, 68; 103:84, 145,

271, 272, 450, 536. The causes and consequences of high mortality are discussed in detail in chapter 7, this volume.

108. For examples, see Sijill, 74:56, 455; 76:305, 478, 479, 483, 508, 509; 79:104, 121, 129, 145; 80:280, 307; 83:98, 150; 85:313; 86:343; 88:117; 91:135, 328, 368; 101:148, 329, 333; 102:252; 103:88, 345.

109. Sijill, 93:261.

110. Taoutel, "al-Shaykh Muhammad Abu ʾl-Wafaʾ," p. 165.

111. For example, Sijill, 74:17, 126, 323, 499; 79:132, 155; 80:13, 128, 203, 302; 84:64, 107, 356, 381, 461, 471; 86:195, 213, 291, 309; 87:286, 320; 93:80, 286; 97:5, 7, 37; 101:215, 234, 322, 325; 102:155, 168; 103:110, 114, 526, 583. Laniado, *Kiseh Shlomo*, folio 18 discusses a wealthy Jew who maintained three wives and fell into debt due to expenditures on them. See also the observations on polygamy in Russell, *Aleppo*, 1:277–278, 292; 2:82–83.

112. Sijill, 102:155; and Tabbakh, *Iʿlam*, 7:24.

113. Estimates of the number and size of households are discussed in the appendix.

114. See Russell, *Aleppo*, 1:299, 303, 439–440.

115. Sijill, 76:583; 82:415, 472, 498; 85:305; 89:795; 90:219; 91:165, 208; 92:8; 93:71, 119; 96:140; 102:8, 86, 180; 104:176.

116. Russell, *Aleppo*, 1:289.

117. For a detailed description of the marriage customs see Russell, *Aleppo*, 1:281–290; 2:47–54, 79–82. The customs were virtually the same in the early twentieth century: Ghazzi, *Nahr*, 1:249–255.

118. For examples, see Sijill, 76:603; 77:481; 78:12, 318, 364; 79:213; 80:299; 83:81, 126; 85:312; 86:320; 89:715; 90:131, 242; 91:8, 256; 92:136; 93:254; 95:235; 97:39; 98:147; 101:156, 203.

119. Taoutel, *Wathaʾiq*, 1:109–111, 135–138; ʿAntebi, *Mor*, folio 78a; Qasin, *Mahaneh*, part 2, folio 32b.

120. Sijill, 76:461; 78:238, 333; 79:229; 80:317; 82:122, 131, 459, 487, 538, 545, 552; 83:114, 236; 85:322, 338, 352, 364; 87:163, 282, 320; 88:10, 15, 132, 135, 167; 89:52; 91:139, 194, 266; 93:160; 97:208; 101:289, 336, 393; 102:223, 271; 104:152.

121. Sijill, 80:33, 36, 39, 52, 57, 69, 81, 84, 104, 137, 139, 147, 188, 200; 89:235, 261, 271; 101:2, 4, 27, 56; 102:9, 13, 41, 109, 198, 199, 224, 263.

122. For example, Sijill, 80:202; 87:209; 93:383; 101:137; 102:14, 15, 16, 32, 34, 38, 40, 48, 108, 292.

123. Sijill, 77:165, 166; 79:143; 80:33, 40, 77, 129, 192, 200; 82:283, 543; 83:130; 87:143; 90:126; 91:265; 98:101, 137, 281, 441; 101:154, 171, 257; 102:55, 61, 108; 103:84, 186.

124. See Russell, *Aleppo*, 1:278–279.

125. For non-Muslim divorces, see Sijill, 76:250, 306, 347, 381, 453, 603, 618; 77:86, 231, 372, 457; 80:10, 17, 40, 582; 82:74, 125, 160, 239, 321, 322, 463; 85:9, 38, 103, 168, 257, 490; 87:31; 90:83; 91:308; 92:225; 94:36, 152, 285, 366; 95:86; 98:30, 88, 277, 422; 101:155; 103:493; 104:174.

126. For examples, see Sijill, 74:459; 79:174; 80:7; 82:18, 230; 84:54, 57, 60, 80, 117, 130, 145, 151, 192, 243, 244, 247, 255, 261, 350, 381, 408, 413, 442, 462; 86:4, 8, 25, 171, 217, 312; 93:16, 36, 93, 116, 181, 253, 396, 399; 101:5,

23, 88, 164, 330, 373; 102:21; 103:4, 5, 15, 19, 20, 62, 67, 91, 128, 155, 230, 262, 369, 413, 453, 465, 467, 490, 649.

127. The higher frequency of remarriage by men appears to be in keeping with a pattern common in many past societies. See the historical case studies in Dupâquier et al., eds., *Marriage and Remarriage.*

128. Tabbakh, *I^clam,* 6:513.

129. Sijill, 74:455; 76:305, 320, 478, 479, 483, 503, 509, 515; 77:271, 276, 440; 79:145, 147, 207; 80:213, 222, 239, 252, 280, 307; 84:286, 335; 85:21, 310, 313; 86:121, 315; 87:107; 88:117; 89:678, 739, 791, 832, 844; 91:368; 92:92; 93:18, 33, 36, 42, 66, 71; 94:363; 97:211; 101:23, 42, 104, 117, 171, 205, 217, 232, 237, 292, 351; 102:21, 26, 32, 72, 75, 139, 177, 226, 239, 272; 103:613; 104:1.

130. For examples, see Sijill, 76:460, 473; 79:97, 121; 80:523; 83:81; 84:56; 85:358, 362; 87:197; 88:19, 69, 147; 90:59; 91:150; 93:138; 101:10; 102:30, 171, 207, 279.

131. For example, Sijill, 74:469; 78:40, 141, 192; 79:113; 82:588, 590; 85:356; 87:60; 90:119; 93:41; 97:57; 101:255.

132. For a detailed survey of the Muslim laws of inheritance see Coulson, *Succession in the Muslim Family.*

133. Sijill, 87:46; 74:459; 102:36; 101:304, 325; 103:3; 74:433; 86:246; 77:90; 98:13. For other examples see Sijill, 74:144, 429, 461, 608; 77:115; 79:174; 82:17; 83:7, 150, 233; 84:44, 52, 76, 217, 285, 321, 325, 352, 360; 86:25, 41, 222, 285, 346; 87:16; 93:8, 10, 22, 40; 101:23, 164, 330, 373, 376, 393; 102:179; 103:54, 67, 145, 536, 602, 613.

134. Sijill, 101:164; 102:155.

135. The case of the Jews is somewhat ambiguous. From references in the court records, inheritance by Jews appears to conform to Islamic rather than Jewish laws. Thus wives, excluded under Jewish law, inherited from their husbands, while daughters, including married ones, took a share of a parent's estate even when the presence of brothers should have excluded them. For examples of such cases, see Sijill, 76:447; 78:47, 80, 161, 228; 81:61; 82:475; 85:296; 88:157; 91:96, 388, 92:28, 181, 208, 282; 98:67, 401; 101:69; 103:210, 387, 640, 645. At the same time Jewish writings from the eighteenth and nineteenth centuries discuss the application of Jewish law in the handling of specific cases of inheritance, wills and the fate of dowries after the death of a spouse. See, for example, Laniado, *Degel,* folio 33b; Laniado, *Kiseh Shlomo,* folios 18a–20b, 25a–37a; Dwek, *Birkat Eliyahu,* folio 98; ^cAntebi, *Mor,* folios 35b–40a, 51a–58a, 122a, 123b–124b; Dwek, *Emet,* folios 61a–63b; and Laniado, *Laqedoshim,* pp. 170–173.

136. Sijill, 91:34–35, 37–38. For similar cases see Sijill, 77:429–430; 88:107–109; 95:191.

137. For cases of equal distribution, see Sijill, 76:79–80, 413–414, 500; 78:70, 148; 82:513; 83:214–215, 243–246; 86:159; 91:72–73, 203; 93:112–114; 94:232–233; 95:48–49; 96:62, 327–328, 713; 98:250–251; 103:359; 104:46–47, 292.

138. Sijill, 74:390; 76:79–80, 394; 79:200–203; 80:152–153, 510–511; 83:243–246; 84:213–214; 87:252–253; 89:231–232, 629–630; 91:72–73; 93:112–114; 95:48–49; 96:90–91; 98:407; 99:90–93.

139. See Sijill, register 73, *passim*.

140. For example, Sijill, 87:154, 190; 101:27, 29, 58, 108, 263, 392; 102:99, 146, 220.

141. Sijill, 79:157, 204, 208, 209, 228; 87:376; 90:49, 149; 91:157; 101:200; 104:275.

142. The words of Aldous Huxley, quoted in Johnson, "The Charity Market," p. 92.

143. Ghazzi, *Nahr*, 1:257–258, 263, 267; Russell, *Aleppo*, 1:191–192, 204, 206, 311; 2:82. See also Taoutel, *Watha'iq*, 3:58, 100, 118.

144. Sijill, 91:426; 98:286; 103:170.

145. Sijill, 87:263; 90:61; 103:18. See also Sijill, 103:25.

146. Sijill, 101:74. For other transactions by neighborhood waqfs, see Sijill, 80:197–198; 87:151, 366; 93:180; 97:118. For the annual financial statements of these foundations, see Sijill, 73:17, 33, 49, 50, 89, 103, 126, 130, 134, 151, 160, 188, 195, 204, 213, 220, 223, 228, 240, 244, 251, 254, 258, 277, 288, 289, 295, 307, 325, 345.

147. For endowments in favor of the neighborhood poor, see Sijill, 76:526; 78:376; 80:248; 84:27; 89:148; 91:389; 94:104. See also Ghazzi, *Nahr*, 2:546, 551, 552, 553, 607. Chapter 8 in this volume provides a breakdown of endowments made during the eighteenth century.

148. See, for example, the deeds of endowment recorded in Sijill, 74:628; 75:332; 76:14, 340–341, 571; 82:44; 84:446; 85:272–273; 86:61; 89:97, 158, 460, 604; 92:22–23, 168, 179; 93:270–271; 95:194; 98:110, 411; 102:274; 103:127, 183–184, 358, 401–402; 104:149, 151, 183, 184, 189, 288.

149. The annual financial statements of the foundations are recorded in Sijill, 73:1–2, 7–8, 9–10, 85–86, 97–99, 155–156, 211–212, 225, 262. In 1793, the Christians paid a total of 30,800 piastres, distributed among 5,200 registered taxpayers by level of wealth. Members of the poorest category were assessed at 2.75 piastres each. For the details and figures, see Devezin, *Nachrichten*, pp. 54–55. In 1754 the number of registered payers of the poll tax stood at 7,213: Sijill, 87:130–131.

150. Sijill, 83:199; 101:212, 217. See also Taoutel, *Watha'iq*, 1:50–51, 134; and Russell, *Aleppo*, 2:46.

151. Laniado, *Bet dino*, folios 49b, 53a; Qasin, *Mahaneh*, part 1, folios 3a, 24b and part 2, folios 16b, 37b; Laniado, *Kiseh Shlomo*, folios 9a–11a; Laniado, *Degel*, folio 12b; and Lutzky, "Ha-Francos be-Haleb," pp. 66, 70–72.

152. Russell, *Aleppo*, 2:61. In the sixteenth century the Jewish community added a surcharge to the price of meat sold by its butchers, using the tax revenue to finance poor relief (Rafeq, "Mazahir," p. 43). For arrangements regarding the sale of meat by the Jews, see Sijill, 95:372; 101:118, 265, 312, 374; 103:578.

153. Sijill, 79:135; 103:312.

6. THE MIND: RELIGION, LEARNING, AND POPULAR CULTURE

1. Fahd, *Ta'rikh al-rahbaniyya*, 3:225–226; 6:299–302.
2. Taoutel, *Watha'iq*, 1:44–45.

3. "Al-ziyadeh baradeh hatta fi ʾl-ʿibadeh": Qushaqji, al-Amthal al-shaʿbiyya al-halabiyya, 1:229.

4. Russell, Aleppo, 2:66.

5. See, for example, the biographies in Tabbakh, Iʿlam, 6:416; 7:153, 183, 196.

6. See Tabbakh, Iʿlam, 6:428–429, 462–463, 513–514, 519–520; 7:71–72, 136–137, 139, 144–146, 147, 153, 161, 163, 178, 186, 196. See also Sijill, 91:203; 102:63, 262.

7. Sijill, 101:147.

8. Taoutel, "Wathaʾiq al-akhawiyyat," p. 377. For cases of outdoor transgressions see pp. 227–228, 234, 374, 376, 379, 381, 383–384, 388–389, 391–392.

9. Ghazzi, Nahr, 1:285; Russell, Aleppo, 2:100–105; Niebuhr, Travels, 2:285. For various superstitious practices connected with healing see chapter 7, this volume.

10. Sijill, 90:96.

11. Ghazzi, Nahr, 2:348.

12. Tabbakh, Iʿlam, 6:530–531.

13. Qushaqji, al-Amthal al-shaʿbiyya al-halabiyya, 2:561.

14. The poem on food, which was written sometime in the nineteenth century, is published in Qushaqji, al-Adab al-shaʿbi, pp. 10–46, along with a detailed commentary and much local lore about culinary matters. For additional popular material on food, see Asadi, Mawsuʿat Halab, 1:198–201 and passim; and Qushaqji, al-Amthal al-shaʿbiyya al-halabiyya, 1:31–36 and passim.

15. Sijill, 97:47–50.

16. Russell, Aleppo, 1:173; for detailed descriptions of local foods and eating see also 1:73–94, 115–119, 172–177.

17. For a detailed description of local dress see Russell, Aleppo, 1:100–115.

18. Russell, Aleppo, 1:286.

19. Taoutel, Wathaʾiq, 1:109–111, 135–138; 3:135.

20. Russell, Aleppo, 1:108, 365.

21. Russell, Aleppo, 1:140, 142 143, 251.

22. Majmuʿ, Leeds Arabic MS. 147, folios 61a–63a.

23. Laniado, Degel, folio 42; Taoutel, Wathaʾiq, 1:135–138, 2:88–89, 93, and 3:135; Ghazzi, Nahr, 1:279–280; Russell, Aleppo, 1:144.

24. Russell, Aleppo, 1:141–142, 156–157, 286–289.

25. See Ghazzi, Nahr, 1:243–285 for a detailed description of local customs and of the variations among groups.

26. Qasin, Mahaneh, part 1, folios 1b–2a and part 2, folio 37a; Laniado, Degel, folio 13a; Qushaqji, al-Adab al-shaʿbi, pp. 129–144; Ghazzi, Nahr, 1:274–276; Archives Nationales, Paris, Ministère des Affaires Étrangères, Bʾ 90, folio 140a (April 22, 1767) and folio 154 (May 26, 1767); Rabbath, Documents, 2:55; Russell, Aleppo, 1:49–51, 254–257; Pococke, Description, vol. 2, part 1, p. 151.

27. See Kawakibi, "al-Hammamat fi Halab," pp. 169–181; and Asadi, Mawsuʿat Halab, 3:254–256.

28. Taoutel, Wathaʾiq, 1:109–114, 135–138; Russell, Aleppo, 1:136–137, 188, 254.

29. Ghazzi, Nahr, 1:279.

30. Russell, *Aleppo*, 1:23, 146–147; Griffiths, *Travels*, pp. 336–337.
31. For a detailed study of the debate, see Hattox, *Coffee and Coffeehouses*.
32. Tabbakh, *Iᶜlam*, 3:249–251.
33. Bodman, *Political Factions*, pp. 26–27, 103; Tabbakh, *Iᶜlam*, 3:341; Ghazzi, *Nahr*, 3:303.
34. Sijill, 95:130–131; Russell, *Aleppo*, 1:119–126, 166, 168–169, 176–177, 185.
35. Russell, *Aleppo*, 1:126–130, 161, 182–185, 233.
36. Sijill, 97:127; 96:514. See also Russell, *Aleppo*, 1:125–126.
37. Russell, *Aleppo*, 1:145.
38. D'Erlanger, *La musique arabe*, 5:xiv, 380–381; Kurd ʿAli, *Khitat al-Sham*, 4:98, 100–101.
39. Tabbakh, *Iᶜlam*, 7:101, 284; Russell, *Aleppo*, 1:150–155.
40. The literature on the musical aspects of the Christian liturgy is extensive. For an overview of the Arab influences and a good bibliography see Husmann, "Syrian Church Music." For examples of the Arab modal system in Jewish liturgical music in Aleppo see Idelsohn, *Hebräisch-orientalischer Melodienschatz*, 4:38, 254–274; and Katz, "The Singing of Baqqashôt by Aleppo Jews." Local collections of Hebrew liturgical songs were often organized by *maqams*. See Sassoon, *Ohel David*, 1:207–215 and 2:801–815, 817.
41. Tabbakh, *Iᶜlam*, 7:47.
42. Russell, *Aleppo*, 1:148–150.
43. Russell, *Aleppo*, 1:147–148; and Qataya, *Nusus*, a study of the local shadow play which includes the texts of thirteen sketches from the early twentieth century. For a general discussion of the shadow play in the Middle East see Landau, *Studies*, ch. 3.
44. For example, Ghazzi, *Nahr*, 1:277.
45. Russell, *Aleppo*, 1:145, 157, 251, 267.
46. Majmuᶜ, folio 55b, sayings 343 and 365, and folio 59b, saying 565. For other sayings of a similar tone see Majmuᶜ, folios 48b–59b, sayings 37, 93, 106, 107, 343, 365, 407, 414, 442, 551, 564, 565, 666, 667, and 682; and Kitab al-amthal, Rylands Arabic MS. 775, folios 5b, 27b, 45b, 51b, 59b, 63b, 64b, 76b, 79b, 107b.
47. An encyclopedic compilation of local lore, still being published, is Asadi's *Mawsuᶜat Halab*. For local sayings see also the contemporary manuscript collections in Majmuᶜ and Kitab al-amthal; and Qushaqji, *al-Amthal al-shaᶜbiyya al-halabiyya;* Ayyub, "Amthal Halab"; and Hamida, *Muhafazat Halab*, pp. 374–388.
48. See Majmuᶜ.
49. Russell, *Aleppo*, 2:95. Russell bought numerous manuscripts and had them shipped to scholars in Europe.
50. On the Ahmadiyya library see Tabbakh, *Iᶜlam*, 7:68–69, 71, 76. Ahmad Effendi added more books to the library in 1765. The titles are listed in Sijill, 102:130–134. On the state of local libraries and their manuscript holdings see also Ghazzi, *Nahr*, 1:174–176; Qataya, "al-Maktabat fi Halab" and *Makhtutat;* Talas, "al-Makhtutat"; and Kayyali, "Makhtutat Halab."
51. On Ottoman printing during the eighteenth century see Shaw, *History of*

the Ottoman Empire, 1:236–238. On the first printing press in Aleppo see Sabat, *Taʾrikh al-tibaʿa*, pp. 101–103; and ʿAnuti, *al-Haraka al-adabiyya*, pp. 45–47.

52. For the financial accounts of colleges see Sijill, 73:90, 91, 100, 112, 133, 140, 148, 176, 177, 195, 196, 217, 228, 234, 240, 250, 259, 260, 264, 283, 311, 314, 327, 331, 339. The number of colleges is based on references compiled from the court records and from other contemporary accounts.

53. See the biographies in Tabbakh, *Iʿlam*, vols. 6 and 7 for a mass of information on the educational careers of the distinguished ulama of the day.

54. For these and other examples see Tabbakh, *Iʿlam*, 6:482, 487, 488–502; 7:53–55, 105–107, 241. See also Sijill, 87:365, 366.

55. Tabbakh, *Iʿlam*, 6:543–544; 7:8, 178–181.

56. Tabbakh, *Iʿlam*, 7:171–172.

57. Tabbakh used such collections as a source for his historical and biographical accounts. In his bibliography he lists twenty-four handbooks to which he had access: *Iʿlam*, 7:707–708.

58. For details on the literary output in Aleppo and other parts of Syria during the eighteenth century see ʿAnuti, *al-Haraka al-adabiyya*, and the numerous references included in the biographies in Tabbakh, *Iʿlam*, vols. 6 and 7. For a description of the contemporary religious literature see ʿAnuti, *al-Haraka al-adabiyya*, chs. 5 and 6.

59. See Yaʿari, *Ha-dfus ha-ʿivri*, 1:31–52; and Rofeh, "Toldot." Most of the published Hebrew works from the period appear in the bibliography.

60. For many examples of contemporary poetry see Tabbakh, *Iʿlam*, vols. 6 and 7, *passim;* Shaykhu, *Shuʿaraʾ al-nasraniyya*, pp. 455–507; Shaykhu, "al-Shaʿir Nasrallah al-Tarabulsi al-Halabi"; and Maʿluf, "Nukhba." For a discussion of the contemporary prose and poetry see ʿAnuti, *al-Haraka al-adabiyya*, chs. 2–4.

61. See Halabi, Murtad, Baghdad MS. 6299. The manuscript has not been used before in histories of the city. The other important chronicles from the period are quoted extensively in the histories of al-Tabbakh and al-Ghazzi. For an example of historical information collected in a resident's notebook, see Majmuʿ, folios 46a and 65a–66b. Dayyan, *Holekh tamim*, folios 66–70, gives another resident's compilation of local events.

62. For medical writings of the period, see ʿAnuti, *al-Haraka al-adabiyya*, pp. 247–249. On Ibrahim al-Hakim see Shaykhu, *Shuʿaraʾ al-nasraniyya*, pp. 474–484. Medical knowledge and practice are described in greater detail in chapter 7, this volume.

63. Davis, *Aleppo and Devonshire Square*, p. 150.

64. Volney, *Voyage*, 2:386. See also Russell, *Aleppo*, 1:160, 235.

65. Tabbakh, *Iʿlam*, 7:23, 64; 6:416–417.

66. Muradi noted his personal encounters with Aleppo's ulama in an untitled collection of biographies. For a copy of the manuscript, written in his own hand, see MS. 4630 (650), Yahuda Arabic Collection, Princeton University Library, Princeton, N.J.

67. Tabbakh, *Iʿlam*, 7:154.

68. For example, Tabbakh, *Iʿlam*, 6:452–453, 470, 471–473, 506; 7:187–188, 195.

69. Roads in Syria remained in a state of disrepair until the second part of

the nineteenth century, when the Ottoman authorities launched a systematic effort at road construction and maintenance. See Bowring, *Report*, pp. 46, 124, 136; Ma'oz, *Ottoman Reform*, pp. 168–169; and Wirth, *Syrien*, pp. 346–347.

70. Europeans became more frequent visitors in the city and the Middle East as a whole as the century progressed. Of forty-nine Englishmen who traveled in the Arab lands in the eighteenth century and had their experiences published, twenty-three visited Aleppo. See Hachicho, "English Travel Books," pp. 1–206.

71. Raymond, *Great Arab Cities*, pp. 93–103, 108–109, 121–122; Carswell, "From the Tulip," pp. 328–334; Sauvaget, *Alep*, p. 235.

7. THE BODY: HEALTH, DISEASE, AND DEATH

1. Majmu', Leeds Arabic MS. 147, folio 49b.

2. Majmu', folio 53b.

3. Sijill, 79:174, 103; 102:179; 79:155.

4. For example, Sijill, 82:25, 37, 284; 84:29, 62, 215, 278, 315, 317, 321, 325, 332, 348, 402, 427; 86:54, 219, 313, 346; 93:23, 40, 50, 194, 240; 103:84, 145, 271, 272, 450, 536.

5. Qushaqji, *al-Amthal al-sha'biyya al-halabiyya*, 2:550.

6. The sample was drawn from Tabbakh, *I'lam*, vols. 6 and 7. The ages are given here in Gregorian rather than Muslim years.

7. Shaykhu, *Shu'ara' al-nasraniyya*, p. 476.

8. Sijill, 75:159; 76:455; 78:206; 79:101; 83:55, 99; 87:15, 215, 331, 354; 89:768, 861; 90:111; 91:36, 374; 93:91, 101; 97:63, 166, 239; 101:42, 88, 91, 210, 242, 283, 332, 334, 363, 379, 393; 102:54, 181, 191.

9. Only a few major fires are recorded for the Ottoman period, none of which occurred in the eighteenth century. See Tabbakh, *I'lam*, 3:200, 216, 303, 461; and Ghazzi, *Nahr*, 3:258, 265, 291. On a major flooding see Tabbakh, *I'lam*, 3:349–350.

10. See Ghazzi, *Nahr*, 3:295, 302, 315; Archives Nationales, Paris, Ministère des Affaires Étrangères (hereafter Affaires Étrangères), B¹ 88, folios 153 (December 11, 1759), 157 (December 24, 1759), 163 (January 14, 1760), 219 (April 19, 1760), 329 (May 11, 1761), 332 (June 2, 1761), B¹ 89, folio 144a (January 7, 1764), and B¹ 90, folios 126b–127a (February 6, 1767); and Russell, "An Account of the Late Earthquakes in Syria," pp. 529–534.

11. Qushaqji, *al-Adab al-sha'bi*, pp. 221–234; Qara'li, *Ahamm*, pp. 77–78; Tabbakh, *I'lam*, 3:400–411; Ghazzi, *Nahr*, 3:329–334; Galles, "Un document contemporain"; Taoutel, *Watha'iq*, 1:133–134; Dayyan, *Holekh tamim*, part 1, folio 70a.

12. Sijill, 87:173.

13. For a detailed description of local diseases and a medical journal of the epidemics in the years 1742–1753, see Russell, *Aleppo*, 2:298–333. The "Aleppo boil" (Ar. *hibbat Halab* or *hibbat sana*, Turk. *Halep çıbanı*, Fr. *mal d'Alep*) was endemic in areas around the Mediterranean as well as in parts of Africa and Asia. People in the city attributed it at the time, and indeed well into this century, to the water. It has now been traced to the flagellate *leishmania tropica*, and is known as Leishmaniasis, or the Oriental sore. See Russell, *Aleppo*, 2:308–

314; Ghazzi, *Nahr*, 3:239–242; Asadi, *Mawsu'at Halab*, 3:167–168; *Türk Ansiklopedisi*, s.v. "Haleb"; and *New Encyclopaedia Britannica*, 15th ed., s.v. "Oriental sore."

14. Russell, *Aleppo*, 2:79, 83.

15. Ghazzi, *Nahr*, 1:283.

16. For references to these plagues, occasionally accompanied by mortality estimates and descriptions of public responses, see Tabbakh, *I'lam*, 3:328, 367–368, 379–380; Ghazzi, *Nahr*, 3:295, 297, 298, 302, 303, 309; Halabi, Murtad, Baghdad MS. 6299, pp. 80–83, 109–117, 140–141; Russell, *Aleppo*, 2:336–338, 344–345; Russell, *Treatise*, pp. 1–70, 280, 337; Taoutel, *Watha'iq*, 1:44, 50, 83, 89–90; Taoutel, "Watha'iq al-akhawiyyat," pp. 371–373, 385–388; Devezin, *Nachrichten*, p. 7; Public Record Office, London, State Papers, Foreign, Archives of the Levant Company, Aleppo (hereafter Public Record Office, S.P.), 110/35, folios 67b–244b (July 2, 1760–August 10, 1761), *passim*, and 110/37, folios 18ff; Affaires Étrangères, B¹ 88, folios 221b–469 (May 20, 1760–December 11, 1762), *passim;* Rabbath, *Documents*, 2:33, 52–54; and Aimé-Martin, *Lettres*, 1:224–225. Panzac, *La peste*, pp. 30–34, presents a list of plagues in Syria that includes two additional eruptions for Aleppo, in 1712 and 1721. Unlike the other eight epidemics, for which evidence from multiple sources exists, these two appear rather suspect. I have found no reference to a plague epidemic in 1712, and only one brief mention of a "violent plague" in 1721 (Ghazzi, *Nahr*, 3:295) for which I have not located corroborating evidence. Faulty dates appear in the sources frequently enough to call for some caution. Panzac's detailed table is not accompanied by sources.

17. Taoutel, "Watha'iq al-akhawiyyat," pp. 391, 394, 397, 403; Dayyan, *Holekh tamim*, part 1, folio 70a; Ghazzi, *Nahr*, 3:320, 351; Tabbakh, *I'lam*, 3:380–381, 411–412; Barker, *Syria*, 1:164–168.

18. Ghazzi, *Nahr*, 3:255, 257, 258, 261, 287, 291, 292; Tabbakh, *I'lam*, 3:244, 379–380; Taoutel, *Watha'iq*, 1:11–14, 44; Rabbath, *Documents*, 2:4–6, 8, 10–11. For the trends in the wider Middle Eastern region see Dols, "Second Plague Pandemic," pp. 176, 183.

19. Aimé Martin, *Lettres*, 1:224–225 (estimate by a French missionary for 1719); Rabbath, *Documents*, 2:54 (estimate by a Carmelite missionary for 1733); Affaires Étrangères, B¹ 88, folio 339b (June 30, 1761) (estimate by the French consul for 1761); Tabbakh, *I'lam*, 3:367–368 (estimate by a local resident for 1787). For additional estimates see Devezin, *Nachrichten*, p. 7; and Taoutel, *Watha'iq*, 1:89.

20. Halabi, Murtad, p. 115.

21. Rabbath, *Documents*, 2:52–54.

22. A detailed breakdown of the mortality figures as well as a mass of medical observations are included in Russell, *Treatise*.

23. Russell, *Aleppo*, 2:344–345. These figures and those of Patrick Russell are analyzed in Panzac, *La peste*, pp. 353–357.

24. For the daily journal, see Halabi, Murtad, pp. 112–115. Halabi's figures are similar to those available for 1761–1762, when Russell counted 3,050 non-Muslim victims, and another English physician arrived at a figure of 3,500. See Panzac, *La peste*, p. 356.

25. Laniado, *Degel*, folio 12b.

26. For a detailed description of the plague see Russell, *Aleppo*, 2:335–387.

27. Russell, *Treatise*, p. 49.

28. Dols, "Second Plague Pandemic," pp. 163–164. For a general discussion of Muslim attitudes and responses, see Panzac, *La peste*, pp. 279–295.

29. Halabi, Murtad, pp. 111–112, 141.

30. For descriptions of confinement and other precautions, see Halabi, Murtad, pp. 81, 83, 110; Taoutel, *Watha'iq*, 1:89–90; Taoutel, "Watha'iq al-akhawiyyat," pp. 387–388, 391, 394; Russell, *Treatise*, pp. 34–36, 51, 55; and Russell, *Aleppo*, 2:376, 383–384. See also the comments on Aleppo and other parts of the empire in Panzac, *La peste*, pp. 333–338.

31. Halabi, Murtad, pp. 116–117.

32. There is evidence for acts of precaution in other localities. In the plague of 1760 in Damascus, Christians withdrew to their homes and Muslims confined themselves in secret: Burayk, *Ta'rikh al-Sham*, p. 81. In 1785 villagers near Beirut deserted infected people and left the dead unburied for fear of contagion. A year later many residents of the coastal area fled to Aleppo to escape the plague. In 1787 some residents of Antioch left the city to avoid the plague there. See Halabi, Murtad, pp. 80, 92, 104, 109, 110. These responses call into question Dols' statement ("Second Plague Pandemic," pp. 181–182) that for the period 1347–1894 "there is no evidence for any significant change in the traditional methods of plague prevention and treatment except for the European importation of quarantine, which appears to have been largely confined to the European communities."

33. Taoutel, "Watha'iq al-akhawiyyat," p. 394.

34. For descriptions of business conditions during periods of plague see Public Record Office, S.P. 110/37, folio 18 (December 31, 1761); Affaires Étrangères, B¹ 88, folio 339b (June 30, 1761), folio 402 (April 27, 1762); Russell, *Treatise*, p. 34; Russell, *Aleppo*, 2:383; and Ambrose, "English Traders," p. 265.

35. Halabi, Murtad, p. 81.

36. Russell, *Treatise*, p. 49.

37. Russell, *Treatise*, pp. 34, 49, 61–64.

38. In the cholera epidemic of 1848 Muslims died in higher proportions than their Christian and Jewish neighbors. See Chevallier, "Non-Muslim Communities," p. 160.

39. Russell, *Aleppo*, 2:305.

40. Russell, *Aleppo*, 1:35, 39; 2:181, 223–226.

41. De Tott, *Memoirs*, vol. 2, part 2, p. 122; Evliya Çelebi, *Seyahatname*, 9:377; Griffiths, *Travels*, p. 334; Parsons, *Travels*, p. 60.

42. Sijill, 80:304; 85:263; 95:283–284; 101:97; 103:213–214.

43. Sijill, 103:577–578.

44. Halabi, Murtad, p. 98.

45. Sijill, 101:221.

46. Sijill, 76:452.

47. Ghazzi, *Nahr*, 1:282.

48. Affaires Étrangères, B¹ 88, folios 115b, 131b (1759) and B¹ 89, folios 358b–359a, 361a, 364, 371, 384 (1765); Halabi, Murtad, pp. 82, 93, 95. See also Sijill, 89:779–780; 101:85; 102:144. For more details on water shortages and their effects see chapter 8, this volume.

49. Sijill, 103:287.

50. Sijill, 103:603.

51. Sijill, 79:3, 34, 38, 65, 72, 74, 77, 94, 107, 109, 110, 177, 205; 102:57, 67, 71, 73, 82, 89, 158, 163, 172, 178, 182, 206, 281. See also Russell, *Aleppo*, 2:114–143.

52. For details on the hospitals see Ghazzi, *Nahr*, 2:64–66, 103–104; Duwaydari, "al-Bimaristanat fi Halab"; and Kurd ᶜAli, *Khitat al-Sham*, 6:160–161. See also Sijill, 87:365; 102:171. For the floor plans of the hospitals see Sauvaget, *Alep*, plan LXI in the album; and Sauvaget, "Inventaire," fig. 3, plan 17.

53. Sijill, 90:27. For comments on the treatment of the mentally ill see Russell, *Aleppo*, 1:211; and Duwaydari, "al-Bimaristanat fi Halab."

54. Laniado, *Degel*, folio 12b; Laniado, *Bet dino*, folio 49b; Lutzky, "Ha-Francos be-Haleb," pp. 70–72.

55. Sijill, 79:3, 34, 38, 65, 72, 74, 77, 94, 107, 109, 110, 205; 83:29, 54, 69, 82, 84, 105, 117, 124; 87:87, 108, 112, 200, 217, 222, 227, 267, 289, 306, 307, 315; 90:104, 119, 132, 138, 178, 215; 91:4; 97:68, 79, 95, 149, 156, 183, 245; 101:92, 172, 177, 184, 245; 102:57, 67, 71, 73, 82, 89, 158, 163, 172, 178, 182, 206, 281.

56. Russell, *Aleppo*, 2:117–121.

57. Ghazzi, *Nahr*, 1:275, 282; Asadi, *Mawsuᶜat Halab*, 6:197.

58. Russell, *Aleppo*, 1:211–213; 2:84, 86.

59. Russell, *Aleppo*, 1:211–213; 2:84, 86.

60. Muradi, *ᶜArf al-basham*, p. 22.

61. Tabbakh, *Iᶜlam*, 6:478.

62. Taoutel, *Wathaᵓiq*, 3:126–127; Taoutel, "Wathaᵓiq al-akhawiyyat," pp. 411–412, 541, 557, 564, 574; Ghazzi, *Nahr*, 3:392, 403, 425, 460; Tabbakh, *Iᶜlam*, 3:481. See also Barker, *Syria*, 1:331 and 2:276–279; and Bowring, *Report*, p. 68. For a discussion of cholera epidemics in the Ottoman Empire see Panzac, *La peste*, ch. 15.

63. Ghazzi, *Nahr*, 1:176–177.

64. Kitab al-amthal, Rylands Arabic MS. 775, folio 38b. The details on the death rituals and customs of the three religious communities are drawn from Ghazzi, *Nahr*, 1:255–258, 262–264, 266–267, 272; and Russell, *Aleppo*, 1:305–312 and 2:56–57, 86–87.

65. Two published collections of local epitaphs are Laniado, *La-qedoshim*, which covers Hebrew inscriptions, and Siwrmeian, *Histoire*, which lists Armenian inscriptions. Some Arabic tomb inscriptions are scattered in Ghazzi, *Nahr*, vol. 2; Tabbakh, *Iᶜlam*, vols. 6 and 7; and Taoutel, "Awliyaᵓ Halab."

66. Russell, *Aleppo*, 1:311–312.

67. For example, Ghazzi, *Nahr*, 1:256. See Albani, *Ahkam al-janaᵓiz wa bidaᶜiha*, for a treatise on Muslim death rites which lists numerous popular practices not sanctioned by religion.

68. Taoutel, *Wathaᵓiq*, 1:110–111.

69. Russell, *Aleppo*, 1:254. See also Rabbath, *Documents*, 2:55.

70. Sijill, 81:14.

71. Laniado, *Bet dino*, folio 49b; Laniado, *Degel*, folio 12b.

72. Ghazzi, *Nahr*, 2:383.

73. Tabbakh, *Iᶜlam*, 6:383, 447, 466, 474, 484–485; 7:60, 72, 114, 190. See

also Ghazzi, *Nahr*, 2:45–46, 53, 59, 71–72; Taoutel, "Awliya' Halab," p. 392; and Halabi, Murtad, p. 89.

74. Taoutel, "Awliya' Halab," pp. 387–406; Tabbakh, *I'lam*, 6:429, 463, 484, 533 and 7:21, 42, 129, 153, 231, 292; Ghazzi, *Nahr, passim*.

75. Tabbakh, *I'lam*, 6:480; 7:63, 147, 181, 192, 236, 243, 268, 275, 295. See also Taoutel, "Awliya' Halab," pp. 347–348, 352, 354, 355, 356, 363–365, 366–367, 375, 378, 379, 380, 385, 391, 393.

76. Taoutel, "Awliya' Halab," p. 329; Ghazzi, *Nahr*, 2:368.

77. For an annotated edition of al-Rifa'i's work see Taoutel, "Awliya' Halab."

78. Sijill, 103:626–627. For similar acts of endowment, see Sijill, 74:53–54, 346, 584, 587; 75:332; 76:66–67, 392; 77:390; 78:311; 80:34; 82:577; 85:79–80, 174–175; 87:344–348; 88:226; 93:111–112; 95:408; 97:193–195; 102:194–195, 274; 103:86, 401–402, 626–627.

79. Sijill, 75:30–31; 76:202–203; 78:104–107, 176; 81:136–140; 82:148, 535; 84:27; 85:73–74, 144–145, 171–172; 87:269–279; 88:404–405; 89:267, 604; 93:264, 270–271; 95:47–50; 96:90–91, 118, 520; 98:238–239; 101:353–363; 103:109–110, 127.

80. Asadi, *Mawsu'at Halab*, 1:211; Ayyub, "Amthal Halab," p. 927.

81. Majmu', folio 4a.

82. Majmu', folio 50b.

83. Ayyub, "Amthal Halab," p. 927; Hamida, *Muhafazat Halab*, p. 383. For this and other popular notions about death see Qushaqji, *al-Amthal al-sha'biyya al-halabiyya*, 2:389, 550–553.

84. Sijill, 76:455; Russell, *Aleppo*, 1:310–311.

85. Qushaqji, *al-Adab al-sha'bi*, pp. 142–145.

8. THE URBAN EXPERIENCE: SPACE, SERVICES, AND PUBLIC SPIRIT

1. Sijill, 76:514; 78:50; 80:208; 85:367; 87:376; 88:171; 89:68, 89, 92, 99, 683, 691, 696, 737; 91:331, 340, 408, 415, 421; 92:55, 89; 93:13, 41; 102:108.

2. See Qara'li, *Ahamm*, pp. 37–61, for a detailed contemporary description of the siege and the points of attack on the outskirts.

3. The figure is computed from my reconstructed map of the city. It does not include some 30 hectares of unbuilt space. Raymond, *Great Arab Cities*, p. 57, gives a surface area of 367 hectares.

4. See Sijill, 76:645, 678; 80:209; 89:324, 799; 91:448; 97:133, 166; 103:12.

5. Sijill, 77:1, 3, 262; 78:50, 74, 137, 186; 82:189; 87:376; 89:108, 193, 599, 694; 91:341; 92:77, 92; 93:11; 96:237. See also Russell, *Aleppo*, 1:6–7.

6. David, "Alep," pp. 32, 47.

7. Raymond, *Great Arab Cities*, p. 15.

8. Sijill, 79:119; 83:21. For similar sentiments, see also Sijill, 87:22.

9. The twenty caravanserais in the center are listed in Sijill, 87:4. Five of them were not in use in 1754. For those in other parts of the intramural city, see Sijill, 75:30; 76:46, 130, 140, 193, 208, 229, 533, 562, 597, 610; 78:53, 59, 348; 80:380; 86:344; 87:378; 88:42, 133; 89:805; 91:327; 92:139; 101:309. See also Ghazzi, *Nahr*, 2:178. For the caravanserais of Banqusa, see Sijill, 74:211;

79:118, 80:425; 89:716; 95:365; 102:101. For the other caravanserais, see Sijill, 73:54; 77:445; 78:246; 83:129; 89:101; 91:394; 92:147; 97:110.

10. For the thirty-seven markets in the central bazaar, see the list drawn up by the court in Sijill, 87:4. Many of these markets were also known by other names, usually denoting their economic specialization. For examples of these multiple usages, see Sijill, 75:210; 76:229, 345; 77:5, 34, 162, 300; 78:128, 386, 395; 85:326; 87:271, 344; 89:629; 90:3; 101:357; 102:230; 103:346, 626. For the markets in the area of al-Qasila, see Sijill, 74:576; 76:51; 77:11, 425; 85:497. For the markets in the Banqusa area, see Sijill, 74:29, 346, 410, 659; 86:347; 89:716.

11. Sijill, 76:502; 78:69, 182; 80:70, 82; 89:670, 683, 694; 91:330, 382, 397; 93:47, 102, 137.

12. For examples of individual shops in neighborhoods, see Sijill, 74:104, 232, 385; 76:38, 163, 209, 262; 78:152, 284; 79:45; 80:109, 230, 233; 85:299, 351; 89:67; 91:404; 92:7; 93:18; 101:358. For references to the forty-four local neighborhood markets, see Sijill, 73:63; 74:10, 183, 399; 75:211; 76:143, 271, 431, 436, 458, 487; 77:1, 6; 78:53, 65, 229, 260, 381; 79:137; 80:34, 137, 144, 222, 410; 81:9; 82:517; 83:231; 85:350; 86:291; 87:370; 88:4, 13; 89:23, 34; 91:220, 331, 381; 92:14; 94:40, 72; 97:110; 101:14; 103:558.

13. The list of butcher shops, drawn up by the court, appears in Sijill, 97:108–110.

14. Sijill, 87:146.

15. Sijill, 74:140, 543; 76:262, 287, 400, 450, 585, 656; 78:233; 80:74, 306; 83:9; 91:404; 93:44; 101:276.

16. For references to *qaysariyyas* in the intramural city, see Sijill, 76:110, 430, 450; 78:81, 89, 153, 244, 367; 79:85; 88:149, 153; 89:21, 847; 91:399, 439. In the northern districts: Sijill, 78:54, 114, 126, 248, 361; 80:157; 85:330; 86:295, 306; 88:24, 39, 147, 153; 89:53, 96, 698, 718, 784; 91:323, 327, 391; 92:8, 43, 52, 69, 97, 122, 150; 93:14, 31, 41, 51, 151. In the eastern districts: Sijill, 78:535; 80:94, 120; 88:38; 89:36, 665, 692, 722; 91:374, 422; 93:9, 150.

17. Sijill, 85:76; 87:333; 95:118. At some earlier period the slaughterhouse was located near the quarter of al-Magha'ir on the outskirts of town. The records make reference to the "old slaughterhouse" there: Sijill, 82:259; 88:93; 91:445.

18. See Raymond, "Le déplacement des tanneries."

19. Russell, *Aleppo*, 1:40.

20. The figures for mosques and lodges were compiled from references in the court records, and are probably incomplete. D'Arvieux, *Mémoires*, 6:437, gives a figure of 272 mosques for 1683; Tabbakh, *Iʿlam*, 3:539, records 300 mosques and 34 lodges for the early twentieth century.

21. For his comments, written in 1850, see Taoutel, *Wathaʾiq*, 2:79–80.

22. Sijill, 81:29. The figure for the number of baths is compiled from references in the court records. D'Arvieux, *Mémoires*, 6:438, gives a figure of sixty-four for 1683, while Tabbakh, *Iʿlam*, gives forty-two for the early twentieth century.

23. Taoutel, "Awliyaʾ Halab," p. 333.

24. For studies of spatial perception see Downs and Stea, *Maps in Minds*, and Downs and Stea, eds., *Image and Environment*. For studies of perceptions of

space in Arab cities, see Boughali, *La représentation de l'espace*, especially ch. 6, and Gulick, "Images of an Arab City."

25. Premodern descriptions of the city as well as official documents testify to the remarkable continuity of names. See, for example, Sourdel, *La description d'Alep d'Ibn Šaddād;* Sourdel, "Esquisse topographique d'Alep"; Sauvaget, *Les perles choisies* and *Les trésors d'or;* and Ottoman fiscal registers and court documents. Many of the same names have survived up to the present day. For a comprehensive dictionary of local place names see Asadi, *Aḥyaʾ Ḥalab.*

26. Sijill, 80:149.

27. Sijill, 79:190; 83:21, 116; 91:149.

28. For quarters named after religious institutions in the locality, see Sijill, 83:105; 86:300; 88:152; 97:8, 62, 109, 110; 101:88. After water fountains: Sijill, 85:360; 91:179, 422; 97:177; 101:112, 354; 102:271. After squares: Sijill, 80:209; 89:96, 799; 97:133, 175, 199. After gates: Sijill, 97:109; 102:104; 104:59. After markets: Sijill, 81:114; 87:50; and 104:34.

29. Sijill, 97:108–110. The observations about the street names are based on a list of 191 names compiled from the court records. The breakdown was as follows: 79 streets named after individuals and families; 61 streets named after local institutions and landmarks; 18 streets named after their physical and spatial features; 7 streets named after social groups; and the remaining 26 streets with names of unclear origins.

30. Taoutel, *Wathāʾiq,* 4:103.

31. Sijill, 76:443; 78:44, 108, 322, 324, 343, 346, 354; 80:63, 65, 131; 85:324, 367, 376; 86:285, 288; 87:287, 370; 88:191, 334; 89:794; 91:344, 387; 92:18, 169.

32. Public Record Office, London, Foreign Office, General Correspondence: Turkey (hereafter Public Record Office, F.O.), 78/1418, Barker to Redcliffe, Aleppo, May 19, 1856; Tabbakh, *Iʿlam,* 3:349–350; Ghazzi, *Nahr,* 3:287; Russell, *Aleppo,* 1:5, 11, 35, 71; Taoutel, *Wathāʾiq,* 3:35, 77; Qushaqji, *al-Adab al-shaʿbi,* pp. 58, 199.

33. Halabi, Murtad, Baghdad MS. 6299, pp. 37–38.

34. Sijill, 87:84; 90:198; 101:57.

35. For descriptions, floor plans, and photographs of contemporary houses see Sinjab, "Das arabische Wohnhaus"; David, "Alep"; Twair, "Die Malereien des Aleppo-Zimmers"; Himsi, *Halab al-qadima;* Qataya, "Tasawir"; Witmer-Ferri, "La maison bourgeoise arabe"; Sarre, "Bemalte Wandverkleidung aus Aleppo"; and Reuther, "Die Qāʿa."

36. Ghazzi, *Nahr,* 2:52–62, 159–171, 178–189, 542, 543; Tabbakh, *Iʿlam,* 3:318–325 and 7:23–28; Sijill, 102:110–134. Musa Agha al-Amiri accumulated the properties he donated over many years. For some of his transactions, see Sijill, 75:80, 81, 157; 77:20–22, 229, 245, 314, 321, 464; 78:63, 64, 67, 77, 210, 264, 288, 290, 314, 326, 340, 341, 342, 352, 395; 79:8, 45, 46, 187; 82:521; 87:44, 196; 88:3, 4, 38, 48, 121, 139; 89:810, 818; 92:113.

37. See Sauvaget, *Alep,* pp. 214, 216; and Raymond, *Great Arab Cities,* pp. 28–30.

38. For documents containing financial and technical details on particular construction projects, see Sijill, 79:40–44, 59, 141–142; 87:58–59, 198, 225, 246, 249, 251, 380–381; 90:158; 91:490, 491; 97:179, 181; 102:225; and 103:608.

39. For the repair of the citadel sometime in the mid-eighteenth century, see Erdoğan, "Osmanlı mimarisi," p. 128. For construction work in the pasha's palace, see Sijill, 79:25, 59; 87:249.

40. Cezar, *Typical Commercial Buildings*, pp. 254–255.

41. Erdoğan, "Osmanlı mimarisi," notes these priorities from the study of Ottoman construction registers *(tamirat defterleri)*.

42. Russell, *Aleppo*, 1:6, 38; Volney, *Voyage*, 2:137; Egmont and Heyman, *Travels*, 2:335; Drummond, *Travels*, p. 183; Teonge, *Diary*, p. 158; d'Arvieux, *Mémoires*, 6:420; Thevenot, *Travels*, 2:30.

43. Sijill, 101:283.

44. Sijill, 76:276.

45. Sijill, 103:256.

46. Sijill, 82:553; 97:252; 101:219, 246, 262, 370; 102:267, 290, 291.

47. Marcus, "Privacy," pp. 169–170.

48. Sijill, 87:32.

49. Sijill, 79:40–44, 59, 67, 141–142; 87:52, 75, 84, 101, 102, 113, 114, 134, 144, 151, 161, 168, 172, 220, 225, 306, 339, 373, 374, 378; 90:29, 181, 189, 190; 91:4, 278; 97:93; 102:96–99, 106, 135, 139, 148, 152–153, 155, 156, 170, 175, 223.

50. Sijill, 75:166; 79:25; 103:608.

51. Sauvaget, *Alep*, p. 11, n. 28; Ghazzi, *Nahr*, 1:109.

52. Public Record Office, F.O. 78/1418, Barker to Redcliffe, Aleppo, May 19, 1856.

53. Sijill, 73:17, 33, 126, 195, 244, 277, 295.

54. Sijill, 91:257.

55. Sijill, 87:4.

56. For a study of the technical aspects of the public water system, see Mazloum, *L'ancienne canalisation*.

57. Sijill, 101:221; 102:144.

58. Sijill, 78:310; 79:36, 194; 85:5; 87:111; 97:64, 224, 253; 101:213.

59. Sijill, 79:81.

60. On the quality of the underground water in the different neighborhoods see Ghazzi, *Nahr*, 1:39, and vol. 2, *passim*.

61. Sijill, 97:69.

62. Ghazzi, *Nahr*, 1:38–39; Russell, *Aleppo*, 1:41–45.

63. Halabi, Murtad, pp. 82, 95. For other instances of severe water shortages, see Sijill, 89:779–780; 101:85; 102:144. See also Archives Nationales, Paris, Ministère des Affaires Étrangères, B¹ 88, folios 115b, 131b (1759) and B¹ 89, folios 358b–359a, 361a, 364, 371, 384 (1765).

64. Halabi, Murtad, pp. 93, 95; Mazloum, *L'ancienne canalisation*, pp. 90–93.

65. Mazloum, *L'ancienne canalisation*.

66. Sijill, 89:779–780.

67. Sijill, 101:85.

68. Sijill, 89:864; 101:78, 83, 192; 102:151.

69. Sijill, 90:198.

70. Sijill, 83:219; 94:9, 10, 12; 97:116, 122, 217; 101:41; 103:211; 104:124.

71. Ghazzi, *Nahr*, 2:505; Tabbakh, *Iʿlam*, 3:311 and 7:129; al-Athar al-

kitabiyya, Bibliothèque Orientale MS. 143, p. 19. The number of fountains in the early twentieth century was 258: Tabbakh, *I'lam*, 3:539.

72. For endowments, see Sijill, 78:176, 377; 79:194, 218; 80:148; 81:2, 136–139; 82:148; 83:242; 85:272–273; 94:169; 95:47–48, 138; 96:520; 103:558. References to the founding and restoration of fountains can be found in al-Athar al-kitabiyya, *passim;* and Ghazzi, *Nahr*, vol. 2, *passim*.

73. Sijill, 79:185.

74. Sijill, 81:16–17. A copy of the court document is reproduced in Tabbakh, *I'lam*, 3:312–314.

75. See Jabiri, *Bayan*, a report by Aleppo's mayor on the city's water problems (published in the late 1940s).

76. Ghazzi, *Nahr*, 1:55–57; Sauvaget, *Alep*, p. 233. In the 1750s bath houses in the city and water mills on the Quwayq paid a tax for use of the Sajur's water *(ma' al-nahr wa 'l-Sajur):* Sijill, 73:12, 14, 19, 23, 26, 36, 43, 46, 55, 62, 68.

77. Bodman, *Political Factions*, pp. 29, 133.

78. For example, Sijill, 74:349, 628; 75:331; 76:14, 340–341, 571, 618, 624–625; 80:64, 577; 82:44, 134; 83:28–29; 84:446; 86:61, 182; 89:97, 158, 604; 90:215; 92:26, 168, 179; 93:270–271; 94:44; 95:39, 194; 98:110, 280, 411; 103:183–184; and 104:151.

79. Sijill, 79:160, 215; 83:17, 115, 231; 87:188, 202, 207, 218, 365, 366; 101:5, 9, 24, 59, 85, 280, 370; 102:5.

80. Sijill, 76:2; 81:60; 83:51; 87:235; 95:146; 97:138; 101:137, 147, 183, 207, 273, 407.

81. See Ghazzi, *Nahr*, 2:538–569, 605–630, for abstracts of the deeds.

82. Sijill, 89:158; 92:168; 103:183–184.

83. Sijill, 74:138; 83:139, 147, 199; 101:236–237, 301. See also Taoutel, *Watha'iq*, 1:9, 35–37, 134; Siwrmeian, *Patmowt'iwn*, 3:357, 666, 699–700; Sanjian, *Armenian Communities*, pp. 153, 260; Qasin, *Mahaneh*, part 1, folios 3a, 24b and part 2, folios 16b, 37b; and Lutzky, "Ha-Francos be-Haleb," pp. 65–66, 70–72. My thanks to Mr. Hagop Barsoumian for translating the Armenian materials from Siwrmeian's book.

84. The financial accounts are found in Sijill, 73:19–67, 88–160. The money amounts in tables 8.1, 8.2, and 8.3 have been rounded to the nearest piastre. Not included in the income in table 8.1 are 61.5 *ratls* (about 300 pounds) of lighting oil paid by tenants in lieu of rent.

85. Sijill, 73:14, 19, 33, 40, 44, 45, 48, 50, 52, 65, 91, 125.

86. Sijill, 73:49, 94; 78:282; 102:196.

87. Sijill, 76:310; 79:116, 164–165; 80:436–437; 81:29, 30, 31; 83:71; 87:106, 112, 154, 264; 88:143; 93:149; 97:245; 102:185.

88. Sijill, 76:365, 615; 78:227, 273; 80:269; 83:10–11; 87:189, 288; 89:775, 833; 90:30, 65, 113, 156; 91:7, 359; 101:160, 401; 102:54, 101.

89. Sijill, 76:169; 80:269; 83:10–11; 85:333–334; 87:288; 89:823, 833; 90:204; 91:2, 359; 101:389, 401; 102:54.

90. Sijill, 76:222; 86:333; 87:166; 90:145, 227; 102:224, 267, 290, 291.

91. Sijill, 76:442; 79:69; 82:48; 83:16; 85:346; 87:77, 80; 91:259, 261.

92. Sijill, 76:632; 78:9; 83:44; 91:317, 462; 95:92, 172, 173; 100:176; 103:79–80, 89.

93. Sijill, 79:4, 40–44, 141–142; 85:333–334; 87:75, 84, 113, 114, 161, 172, 220, 225, 243; 89:763; 90:194; 91:273; 97:232; 102:106, 146, 149, 276.

94. Sijill, 76:169, 591; 79:128, 134, 194; 80:477; 87:77, 80, 124; 90:213; 97:94, 254; 101:280, 323; 102:260.

95. Sijill, 87:52, 134, 151, 373, 378; 101:6, 394–398; 102:96–99, 135, 152–153, 266, 289.

96. Sijill, 87:65; 90:187, 199; 97:247–248, 253; 101:7, 254–255, 257; 102:21, 24–25, 26, 286, 289.

97. Sijill, 73:18. For similar cases, see Sijill, 73:115–116, 127, 143–144.

98. Sijill, 73:34, 46. For similar cases, see Sijill, 73:14, 59, 61, 67.

99. Sijill, 87:52, 154, 188, 190; 101:9, 27, 29, 58, 108, 263, 392; 102:99, 146, 185, 220, 230.

9. THE URBAN EXPERIENCE: NEIGHBORHOOD LIFE AND PERSONAL PRIVACY

1. Sijill, 90:228.

2. Although not usually identified as a quarter the area of houses within the citadel was for all intents and purposes a residential neighborhood. One sales deed for a house actually referred to it as a *mahalla*: Sijill, 103:403.

3. See, for example, Sijill, 77:161; 95:101; 102:114, 196; 103:33.

4. For descriptions of this administrative setup in the sixteenth century, see Başbakanlık Arşivi, Istanbul, Mufassal register no. 493, pp. 87–94; and Raymond, "Population of Aleppo," pp. 453, 455. In 1537 the area was known as Daqashir, a name replaced later by Kharij Bab al-Nasr.

5. Sijill, 95:190; 97:199, 202, 210, 216, 226, 249.

6. See the list of quarters for 1570 in Mufassal register no. 493.

7. Official fiscal censuses, which computed neighborhood populations by housing units *(hanes)*, show wide interquarter discrepancies. In 1570 the quarter of Qadi ʿAsker had 29 housing units compared with 439 in Jubb Asad Allah: Mufassal register no. 493, pp. 33, 48–51. In 1683 the reported sizes ranged from 69 to 542 housing units, with 100–200 being the most common: d'Arvieux, *Mémoires*, 6:434–437. See also the detailed census data for the early twentieth century in Ghazzi, *Nahr*, vol. 2, *passim*, which have been tabulated in Gaube and Wirth, *Aleppo*, pp. 427–434.

8. Ghazzi, *Nahr*, 2:449–450.

9. Sijill, 76:437, 440; 78:91, 127, 230, 268, 354; 81:112; 88:9, 29, 46, 75, 76, 103, 122; 92:148, 159, 161.

10. Sijill, 76:437; 88:52; 80:100.

11. Sijill, 80:535; 85:248; 87:31; 92:278, 101:5, 155, 301, 302; 103:493.

12. Sijill, 75:290, 305; 76:225, 482, 614; 78:101, 287, 295, 312, 324; 79:169; 82:77, 157, 354; 85:286; 89:770; 91:225; 94:233, 258, 359; 98:198, 221; 101:40; 103:200, 360.

13. Sijill, 90:174–175; 78:112.

14. Sijill, 76:490; 78:43–44, 68, 126, 198, 295; 79:8, 90; 85:317, 324, 335, 344; 87:386–387; 88:154, 188; 89:784, 798, 813, 854; 91:327, 336, 358, 374; 92:16, 53, 140.

15. Sijill, 78:207, 283; 87:228; 88:38, 146, 173.

16. The reputations of some quarters found their way into popular lore. See, for example, Asadi, *Mawsuʿat Halab*, 1:182; 2:22, 203.

17. Asadi, *Mawsuʿat Halab*, 1:216.

18. Marcus, "Privacy," p. 176.

19. Sijill, 75:11; 78:49, 61, 83, 160, 162, 164, 306; 83:45, 72, 231; 101:9, 90, 94, 96, 116, 150, 155; 102:101, 138, 147, 230, 292.

20. See Marcus, "Privacy," for a detailed discussion of the local notions of privacy.

21. Sijill, 97:177; 87:183, 299; 90:18, 35; 91:276.

22. "Al-jar qablu ʾl-dar": Kitab al-amthal, Rylands Arabic MS. 775, folio 13b.

23. Majmuʿ, Leeds Arabic MS. 147, folio 55a.

24. Asadi, *Mawsuʿat Halab*, 1:316. For other sayings on neighbors see Majmuʿ, folios 49b, 52a, 52b, 53b, 59b; Kitab al-amthal, folios 33b, 55b, 116b; Qushaqji, *al-Amthal al-shaʿbiyya al-halabiyya*, 1:100–103 and 2:408; and Asadi, *Mawsuʿat Halab*, 3:11–12.

25. For references to hostilities between quarters in the early twentieth century see Mardini, *Qissat hayah*, ch. 2; Godard, *Alep*, p. 16; and Qushaqji, *al-Adab al-shaʿbi*, p. 147.

26. On the interneighborhood hostilities of the Mamluk period see Lapidus, "Muslim Urban Society," p. 198, and *Muslim Cities*, pp. 88–90. On the hostilities over water see chapter 8, this volume.

27. This was a rather unusual usage of the term *imam*, which was commonly employed for positions of religious leadership. Neighborhood headmen in contemporary Damascus were also known by this term. See Budayri, *Hawadith Dimashq*, p. 216.

28. Sijill, 83:219; 85:365; 87:13.

29. Sijill, 83:66; 90:61, 105, 168, 205; 91:257.

30. Qaraʾli, *Ahamm*, p. 57.

31. Sijill, 74:264; 75:348; 98:277.

32. Sijill, 95:95, 190.

33. Sijill, 83:66; 90:105, 205.

34. Sijill, 90:61; also 90:205.

35. Sijill, 91:222.

36. Sijill, 90:220, 239.

37. Sijill, 76:678; 81:60; 83:51; 95:146; 97:118, 138; 101:147.

38. Sijill, 87:7.

39. Sijill, 76:210; 79:163, 165; 81:45; 83:1, 49, 71, 95, 165, 217; 87:7, 9; 91:256; 94:94; 95:305; 97:201; 101:71.

40. Sijill, 83:27.

41. Sijill, 97:199, 202, 210, 216, 226, 249.

APPENDIX

1. Egmont and Heyman, *Travels*, 2:338; Myller, *Peregrinus*, pp. 653–654.

2. Russell, *Aleppo*, 1:97–98.

3. Taoutel, "Watha'iq al-qarn al-thamin ʿashar," pp. 249–254.

4. De Tott, *Memoirs*, vol. 2, part 2, p. 120 (150,000); Olivier, *Voyage*, 4:170 (150,000); Coote, "Diary," p. 211 (120,000); Volney, *Voyage*, 2:139 (100,000); Eton, *Survey*, p. 267 (50,000).

5. Morana, *Saggio*, p. 62.

6. Volney, *Voyage*, 2:139.

7. Berchet, *Relazioni*, p. 59.

8. Raymond, "Population of Aleppo," p. 455.

9. Rabbath, *Documents*, 2:63, 189; Aigen, *Sieben Jahre*, p. 39.

10. For example, Archives Nationales, Paris, Ministère des Affaires Étrangères, B¹ 88, folio 469 (December 11, 1762): a French consul reports that 250,000 are said to have died in the plague and famine of recent years; Devezin, *Nachrichten*, p. 7: a British consul reports that 170,000 died in the plague of 1786–1787; Halabi, Murtad, Baghdad MS. 6299, p. 115: a local resident relates local speculations that some 100,000 died in the plague of 1787; d'Arvieux, *Mémoires*, 6:414: a French consul reports that 100,000 died in the plague of 1669–1670; Tucci, *Lettres*, p. 7: a Venetian merchant estimates the deaths from a plague in 1555 at 170,000; Chesneau, *Voyage*, p. 251: another Venetian estimates the victims from the same plague at 120,000; Ghazzi, *Nahr*, 3:301–302: a local resident estimates the victims of the famine of 1757–1758 at 87,000; Aimé-Martin, *Lettres*, 1:224–225: a French missionary cites public reports in Aleppo that 120,000 died in the plague of 1719.

11. Issawi, *The Economic History*, p. 205.

12. Baer, "Village and City," p. 79.

13. David, "Quartiers anciens," p. 135.

14. Raymond, "Population of Aleppo," p. 458.

15. Raymond, "Population du Caire," pp. 207–208.

16. Gulick, *Tripoli*, pp. 32, 189–190.

17. Guys, *Statistique*, pp. 50–51; Issawi, *The Economic History*, p. 244; Bowring, *Report*, pp. 7, 87, 112; Barker, *Syria*, 2:297; Russeger, *Reisen*, 1:377; Poujoulat, *Voyage*, 2:18; Robinson, *Three Years*, 2:307; Houry, "Commerce," p. 178.

18. Ghazzi, *Nahr*, 1:333, 334 and vol. 2 *passim*; Tabbakh, *Iʿlam*, 3:170, 199, 541; *Salname Vilayet-i Halep, 1326*, p. 224.

19. Raymond, "Population of Aleppo"; Barkan, "Research," p. 168.

20. D'Arvieux's detailed listing of houses or households by neighborhoods for 1683 adds up to 14,146: d'Arvieux, *Mémoires*, 6:434–437. A decade or two earlier Evliya Çelebi attributed to the city 14,000 houses: Barbié du Bocage, "Notice," p. 230.

21. Russell, *Aleppo*, 1:97–98, 352.

22. Otter, *Voyage*, 1:91; Myller, *Peregrinus*, p. 653.

23. Bowring, *Report*, pp. 3–4.

24. Computed from the detailed figures in Ghazzi, *Nahr*, vol. 2. For two neighborhoods (Suwayqat Hatim and al-Ballat al-Fawqani) Ghazzi provides the number of residents but not of houses. Using the population density in neighboring quarters as a guide, I estimated the number of houses in each of these at 100.

25. Barkan, "Research"; Raymond, "Population of Aleppo."

Glossary

agha   an official title, usually held by army officers, administrators, tax farmers, and merchants.

alim   a member of the Muslim religious establishment; see *ulama*.

ashraf (sing. *sharif*)   lineal descendants of the Prophet Muhammad.

a'yan   in official usage, the provincial tax-farming class in the service of the Ottoman administration; in more general usage, the elite.

chalabi   a title of honor, held commonly by merchants, craftsmen, scribes in government service, and lower-level members of the Muslim religious establishment.

dhimmi   a Christian or Jew subject to the special taxes and legal arrangements applying to non-Muslims in a Muslim state.

effendi   an official title, held by the higher members of the Muslim religious establishment and by ranking scribes in government service.

gedik   a license to run a commercial or artisanal business, usually in a designated shop or establishment.

imam   Muslim leader of prayer; also neighborhood headman.

mufti   Muslim jurisconsult, a high-ranking member of the religious establishment authorized by official appointment to issue legal opinions in disputed matters.

naqib al-ashraf   officially appointed head of the lineal descendants of the Prophet Muhammad.

pasha   a high official title commonly held by provincial governors, and hence a synonym for governor.

piastre (ghirsh)   a silver coin, equivalent to 120 'uthmanis or akçes.

qadi   Muslim judge.

qanun   the body of laws and regulations issued by the state, primarily in matters of administration.

qaysariyya   a building in the form of a compound, the rooms serving as workshops or dwellings.

qirat   A fraction equivalent to one twenty-fourth of a whole, used commonly to compute shares in property.

ratl   a unit of weight equivalent in Aleppo to 4.8 pounds.

shariᶜa   Islamic law.

shaykh   head of a guild, village, or tribe; also title of respect for religious leaders, especially in the Sufi orders.

suq   market.

tujjar (sing. *tajir*)   merchants in the export-import trade.

ulama (sing. *alim*)   members of the Muslim religious establishment, including legal experts, teachers, scholars, and mosque functionaries.

waqf   endowment, created by the dedication of property for a charitable public cause or for the support of the donor's family.

watan   the place one considers home.

Bibliography

ARCHIVAL SOURCES

Archives Nationales, Damascus. Sijill al-mahkama al-shar'iyya, Halab (Shari'a Court Records, Aleppo). Vols. 73–102, 1159–1184 A.H./1746–1771 A.D.
Archives Nationales, Paris. Ministère des Affaires Étrangères, Correspondance Consulaire, Alep. B¹ 84–92, 1743–1774.
Başbakanlık Arşivi (Office of the Prime Minister's Archives), Istanbul. Mufassal register no. 493 of Liwa of Aleppo, 978 A.H./1570–1571 A.D.
Haus-, Hof- und Staatsarchiv, Vienna. Türkei II, K. 28–K. 129, 1755–1802 (selected dispatches).
Public Record Office, London. Foreign Office, General Correspondence: Turkey. F.O. 78/1418, 1856.
Public Record Office, London. State Papers, Foreign, Archives of the Levant Company, Aleppo. S.P. 110/29–40, 1747–1784.

MANUSCRIPTS

al-Athar al-kitabiyya al-'arabiyya 'ala 'l-abniya al-halabiyya. MS. 143, Bibliothèque Orientale, St. Joseph University, Beirut.
al-Halabi, Yusuf ibn Dimitri. al-Murtad fi ta'rikh Halab wa Baghdad. MS. 6299, Baghdad Museum, Baghdad.
Kitab al-amthal. MS. 775 (47), John Rylands University Library, Manchester, England.
Majmu'. MS. 147, Department of Modern Arabic Studies, University of Leeds, England.
al-Muradi, Muhammad Khalil. Untitled MS. no. 4630 (650), Yahuda Arabic Collection, Princeton University Library, Princeton, N.J.

PUBLISHED WORKS

Abdel Nour, Antoine. *Introduction à l'histoire urbaine de la Syrie ottomane (XVIe–XVIIIe siècle)*. Beirut, 1982.

Abu-Lughod, Janet. *Cairo*. Princeton, 1971.

Adler, E. N. "Aleppo." In M. Brann and F. Rosenthal, eds., *Gedenkbuch zur Erinnerung an David Kaufmann*, pp. 128–137. Breslau, 1900.

Aigen, Wolffgang. *Sieben Jahre in Aleppo (1656–1663)*. Ed. Andreas Tietze. Vienna, 1980.

Aimé-Martin, L., ed. *Lettres édifiantes et curieuses concernant l'Asie, l'Afrique et l'Amérique*. Vol. 1. Paris, 1838.

al-Albani, Muhammad. *Ahkam al-jana'iz wa bida'iha*. Beirut, 1969.

Ambrose, Gwilyn. "English Traders at Aleppo (1658–1756)." *The Economic History Review* (1931–1932), 3:246–267.

ʿAntebi, Abraham. *Mor va-ahalot*. Livorno, 1843.

ʿAnuti, Usama. *al-Haraka al-adabiyya fi Bilad al-Sham khilal al-qarn al-thamin ʿashar*. Beirut, 1971.

Arvieux, Laurent d'. *Mémoires du Chevalier d'Arvieux*. 6 vols. Ed. Jean-Baptiste Labat. Paris, 1735.

al-Asadi, Muhammad Khayr al-Din. *Ahya' Halab wa aswaqiha*. Damascus, 1984.

—— *Mawsuʿat Halab al-muqarana*. 6 vols. Aleppo, 1981–1987.

Ayyub, Tuma. "al-Muntakhab min amthal Halab." *al-Mashriq* (1907), 10:827–832, 874–879, 925–929.

Baer, Gabriel. "The Administrative, Economic and Social Functions of Turkish Guilds." *International Journal of Middle East Studies* (1970), 1:28–50.

—— *Egyptian Guilds in Modern Times*. Jerusalem, 1964.

—— "Guilds in Middle Eastern History." In M. A. Cook, ed., *Studies in the Economic History of the Middle East*, pp. 11–30. London, 1970.

—— "The Structure of Turkish Guilds and Its Significance for Ottoman Social History." *Proceedings of the Israel Academy of Sciences and Humanities* (1970), 4:176–196.

—— "Village and City in Egypt and Syria: 1500–1914." In A. L. Udovitch, ed., *The Islamic Middle East, 700–1900: Studies in Economic and Social History*, pp. 595–652. Princeton, 1982.

Bağış, Ali İhsan. *Osmanlı ticaretinde gayri müslimler*. Ankara, 1983.

Bakhit, Muhammad Adnan. "Aleppo and the Ottoman Military in the Sixteenth Century (Two Case Studies)." *al-Abhath* (1978–1979), 27:27–38.

Barbié du Bocage, J. G. "Notice sur la carte générale des paschaliks de Baghdad, Orfa et Hhaleb, et sur le plan d'Hhaleb de M. Rousseau." *Recueil de voyages et mémoires publiés par la Société de Géographie* (1825), 2:194–244.

Barbir, Karl. *Ottoman Rule in Damascus, 1708–1758*. Princeton, 1980.

Barkan, Ömer Lûtfi. "Research on the Ottoman Fiscal Surveys." In M. A. Cook, ed., *Studies in the Economic History of the Middle East*, pp. 163–171. London, 1970.

Barker, Edward B. B. *Syria and Egypt Under the Last Five Sultans of Turkey*. 2 vols. London, 1876.

al-Basha, Qustantin. *Muhadara fi ta'rikh ta'ifat al-rum al-kathulik fi Misr*. Beirut, 1930.

Benjamin, J. J. *Acht Jahre in Asien und Afrika von 1846 bis 1855.* 2d ed. Hanover, 1858.

Ben-Yaʿakov, Abraham. "Yomano shel ha-mityashev ha-yehudi ha-rishon be-Calcutta." In Meir Benayahu, ed., *Sefer Zikaron le-Itzhak Ben-Zvi,* pp. 363–382. Jerusalem, 1965.

Berchet, G., ed. *Relazioni dei consoli veneti nella Siria.* Turin, 1866.

Birken, Andreas. *Die Provinzen des Osmanischen Reiches.* Wiesbaden, 1976.

Bodman, Herbert L., Jr. *Political Factions in Aleppo, 1760–1826.* Chapel Hill, N.C., 1963.

Boucheman, Albert de. "Note sur la rivalité de deux tribus moutonnières de Syrie, les 'Mawali' et les 'Hadidiyn.' " *Revue des études islamiques* (1934), 8:11–58.

——— *Une petite cité caravanière: Suḫné.* Beirut, n.d.

Boughali, Mohamed. *La représentation de l'espace chez le marocain illettré: Mythes et tradition orale.* Paris, 1974.

Bowring, John. *Report on the Commercial Statistics of Syria.* London, 1840.

Braude, Benjamin. "Foundation Myths of the *Millet* System." In Benjamin Braude and Bernard Lewis, eds., *Christians and Jews in the Ottoman Empire,* 1:69–88. New York, 1982.

Braudel, Fernand. *Civilization and Capitalism, Fifteenth–Eighteenth Century.* Vol. 2: *The Wheels of Commerce.* Tr. Siân Reynolds. New York, 1982.

Browne, William G. *Travels in Africa, Egypt, and Syria, from the Year 1792 to 1798.* London, 1799.

Buckingham, J. S. *Travels Among the Arab Tribes Inhabiting the Countries East of Syria and Palestine.* London, 1825.

——— *Travels in Mesopotamia.* London, 1827.

al-Budayri, Ahmad. *Hawadith Dimashq al-yawmiyya 1154–1175.* Ed. Muhammad Saʿid al-Qasimi. n.p., 1959.

Burayk, Mikhaʾil. *Taʾrikh al-Sham.* Ed. Ahmad Ghassan Sabbanu. Damascus, 1982.

Burckhardt, John Lewis. *Travels in Nubia.* 2d ed. London, 1822.

Çağatay, Neşʾet. "Riba and Interest Concept and Banking in the Ottoman Empire." *Studia Islamica* (1970), 32:53–68.

Capper, James. *Observations on the Passage to India Through Egypt.* 3d ed. London, 1785.

Carruthers, Douglas, ed. *The Desert Route to India.* London, 1929.

Carswell, John. "From the Tulip to the Rose." In Thomas Naff and Roger Owen, eds., *Studies in Eighteenth Century Islamic History,* pp. 328–355. Carbondale, Ill., 1977.

Cezar, Mustafa. *Typical Commercial Buildings of the Ottoman Classical Period and the Ottoman Construction System.* Istanbul, 1983.

Charles-Roux, François. *Les échelles de Syrie et de Palestine au XVIIIe siècle.* Paris, 1928.

Chesneau, Jean. *Le voyage de Monsieur d'Aramon, ambassadeur pour le roy en Levant.* Paris, 1887.

Chevallier, Dominique. "Non-Muslim Communities in Arab Cities." In Benjamin Braude and Bernard Lewis, eds., *Christians and Jews in the Ottoman Empire,* 2:159–166. New York, 1982.

Chevallier, Dominique. "Techniques et société en Syrie: Le filage de la soie et du coton à Alep et à Damas." *Bulletin d'études orientales* (1963–1964), 18:85–93.

—— "Les tissus ikatés d'Alep et de Damas." *Syria* (1962), 39:300–324.

Coote, Sir Eyre. "Diary of a Journey with Sir Eyre Coote from Bussora to Aleppo in 1780 (?)." *Journal of the Royal Geographical Society* (1860), 30:198–211.

Corancez, Louis Alexandre Olivier de. *Itinéraire d'une partie peu connue de l'Asie Mineure.* Paris, 1816.

Coulson, N. J. *Succession in the Muslim Family.* Cambridge, 1971.

Cuisenier, Jean and André Miquel. "La terminologie arabe de la parenté: Analyse semantique et analyse componentielle." *L'Homme* (July–December 1965), 5:17–59.

David, Jean-Claude. "Alep, dégradation et tentatives actuelles de réadaptation des structures urbaines traditionelles." *Bulletin d'études orientales* (1975), 28:19–49.

—— "Les quartiers anciens dans la croissance moderne de la ville d'Alep." In Dominique Chevallier et al., eds., *L'espace social de la ville arabe*, pp. 135–144. Paris, 1979.

Davis, Ralph. *Aleppo and Devonshire Square: English Merchants in the Levant in the Eighteenth Century.* London, 1967.

—— "English Imports from the Middle East, 1580–1780." In M. A. Cook, ed., *Studies in the Economic History of the Middle East*, pp. 193–206. London, 1970.

—— *The Rise of the Atlantic Economies.* Ithaca, 1973.

Dayyan, Abraham. *Holekh tamim u-foʿel tzedeq.* Livorno, 1850.

Dayyan, Yeshaʿya. *Imrei noʿam.* Aleppo, 1903.

Devezin, Michael. *Nachrichten über Aleppo und Cypern.* Tr. Dr. Harles. Weimar, 1804.

Dols, Michael W. "The Second Plague Pandemic and Its Recurrences in the Middle East: 1347–1894." *Journal of the Economic and Social History of the Orient* (1979), 22:162–189.

Dotan, Alexander. "Le-toldot bet ha-kneset ha-qadmon be-Haleb." *Sefunot* (1965), 1:25–61.

Downs, Roger M. and David Stea, eds. *Image and Environment: Cognitive Mapping and Spatial Behavior.* Chicago, 1973.

—— *Maps in Minds: Reflections on Cognitive Mapping.* New York, 1977.

Drummond, Alexander. *Travels Through Different Cities of Germany, Italy, Greece, and Several Parts of Asia as Far as the Banks of the Euphrates.* London, 1754.

Duda, Dorothea. *Innenarchitektur syrischer Stadthäuser des 16. bis 18. Jahrhunderts.* Beirut, 1971.

Dupâquier, Jacques, et al., eds. *Marriage and Remarriage in Populations of the Past.* London, 1981.

Duwaydari, Anwar. "al-Bimaristanat fi Halab." *ʿAdiyyat Halab* (1975), 1:129–145.

Dwek, Eliyahu. *Birkat Eliyahu.* Livorno, 1793.

Dwek, Shaʾul. *Emet me-Eretz.* Jerusalem, 1909.

Dwek, Shimʿon. *Reyah sadeh.* Istanbul, 1738.

Egmont, J. A. van and John Heyman. *Travels Through Parts of Europe, Asia Minor . . . Syria, Palestine, Egypt.* 2 vols. Translated from the Dutch. London, 1759.

Erdoğan, Muzaffer. "Osmanlı mimarisi tarihinin otantik yazma kaynakları." *Vakıflar Dergisi* (1965), 6:111–136.

Erlanger, Baron Rodolphe d'. *La musique arabe.* Vol. 5. Paris, 1949.

Eton, W. *A Survey of the Turkish Empire.* London, 1798.

Ettinger, Shmuel, ed. *Toldot ha-yehudim be-artzot ha-islam.* Jerusalem, 1981.

Evliya Çelebi. *Seyahatname.* Vol. 9: *Anadolu, Suriye, Hicaz (1671–1672).* Istanbul, 1935.

Fahd, Butrus. *Taʾrikh al-rahbaniyya al-lubnaniyya.* 6 vols. Junya, 1963–1968.

Frazee, Charles A. *Catholics and Sultans: The Church and the Ottoman Empire 1453–1923.* Cambridge, 1983.

Galles, R. "Un document contemporain et inédit sur le treblement de terre d'Alep, en 1822." *Bulletin de Société Polymathique du Morbihan* (1885), 10:3–10.

Gaube, Heinz. *Arabische Inschriften aus Syrien.* Beirut and Wiesbaden, 1978.

Gaube, Heinz and Eugen Wirth. *Aleppo.* Wiesbaden, 1984.

Gerber, Haim. "Enterprise and International Commerce in the Economic Activity of the Jews of the Ottoman Empire in the Sixteenth–Seventeenth Centuries." *Zion* (1978), 43:38–67. (Hebrew).

—— "Guilds in Seventeenth Century Anatolian Bursa." *Asian and African Studies* (1976), 11:59–86.

al-Ghazzi, Kamil. *Nahr al-dhahab fi taʾrikh Halab.* 3 vols. Aleppo, 1923–1926.

Gibb, H. A. R. and Harold Bowen. *Islamic Society and the West.* Vol. 1, 2 parts. London, 1950–1957.

Godard, Charles. *Alep: Essai de géographie urbaine et d'économie politique et sociale.* Aleppo, 1938.

Gould, Andrew G. "Lords or Bandits? The Derebeys of Cilicia." *International Journal of Middle East Studies* (1976), 7:485–506.

Gräf, E. "ʿAnaza." *Encyclopaedia of Islam.* 2d ed., 1:482–483.

Grant, Christina Phelps. *The Syrian Desert: Caravans, Travel and Exploration.* London, 1937.

Griffiths, J. *Travels in Europe, Asia Minor, and Arabia.* London, 1805.

Gulick, John. "Images of an Arab City." *Journal of the American Institute of Planners* (1963), 29:179–198.

—— *Tripoli: A Modern Arab City.* Cambridge, Mass., 1967.

Guys, Henri. *Statistique du pachalik d'Alep.* Marseille, 1853.

Hachicho, Mohamad Ali. "English Travel Books about the Arab Near East in the Eighteenth Century." *Die Welt des Islams* (1964), N.S. 9:1–206.

Haddad, Robert M. *Syrian Christians in Muslim Society: An Interpretation.* Princeton, 1970.

Hamida, ʿAbd al-Rahman. *Muhafazat Halab.* Damascus, n.d.

—— *La ville d'Alep: Étude de géographie urbaine.* Paris, 1959.

al-Hamud, Nawfan Raja. *al-ʿAskar fi Bilad al-Sham fi ʾl-qarnayn al-sadis ʿashar wa ʾl-sabiʿ ʿashar al-miladiyayn.* Beirut, 1981.

Hasselquist, Frederick. *Voyages and Travels in the Levant in the years 1749, 50, 51, 52.* London, 1766.

Hattox, Ralph S. *Coffee and Coffeehouses: The Origins of a Social Beverage in the Medieval Near East.* Seattle, 1985.

Herzfeld, Ernst. *Inscriptions et monuments d'Alep.* 2 vols. Cairo, 1954–1956.

Heyd, Uriel. *Studies in Old Ottoman Criminal Law.* Ed. V. L. Ménage. Oxford, 1973.

al-Himsi, Fayiz. *Halab al-qadima.* Damascus, 1983.

Hinz, Walther. *Islamische Masse und Gewichte.* Leiden, 1955.

Holt, P. M. *Egypt and the Fertile Crescent 1516–1922: A Political History.* Ithaca, 1966.

Homer, S. *A History of Interest Rates.* 2d ed. New Brunswick, N.J., 1977.

Hourani, Albert. "Introduction: Aspects of Islamic Culture." In Thomas Naff and Roger Owen, eds., *Studies in Eighteenth Century Islamic History,* pp. 253–276. Carbondale, Ill., 1977.

—— "Ottoman Reform and the Politics of Notables." In W. R. Polk and R. L. Chambers, eds., *The Beginnings of Modernization in the Middle East: The Nineteenth Century,* pp. 41–68. Chicago, 1968.

—— "The Changing Face of the Fertile Crescent in the Eighteenth Century." *Studia Islamica* (1957), 8:89–122.

—— "The Ottoman Background of the Modern Middle East." In Albert Hourani, *The Emergence of the Modern Middle East,* pp. 1–18. London, 1981.

—— "The Syrians in Egypt in the Eighteenth and Nineteenth Centuries." In *Colloque internationale sur l'histoire du Caire,* pp. 221–233. Leipzig, 1969.

Houry, C. B. "Commerce de la Syrie: Alep et Damas." *Revue de l'Orient* (1843), 2:177–186.

Howel, Thomas. *A Journal of the Passage from India.* 2d ed. London, 1791.

Husmann, Heinrich. "Syrian Church Music." *The New Grove Dictionary of Music and Musicians,* 18:472–481.

Ibn ʿAbidin, Muhammad Amin. *Radd al-muhtar ʿala ʾl-Durr al-mukhtar.* 8 vols. Cairo, 1966–1969.

Ibn al-Hanbali, Radi al-Din Muhammad. *Durr al-habab fi taʾrikh aʿyan Halab.* 2 vols. Ed. Mahmud al-Fakhuri and Yahya ʿAbarra. Damascus, 1972.

Idelsohn, A. Z. *Hebräisch-orientalischer Melodienschatz.* Vol. 4: *Gesänge der orientalischen Sefardim.* Jerusalem, Berlin, and Vienna, 1923.

Idlibi, Naufitus. "al-Ayqunat al-halabiyya." ʿ*Adiyyat Halab* (1975), 1:182–219.

Inalcik, Halil. "Capital Formation in the Ottoman Empire." *The Journal of Economic History* (1969), 29:97–140.

—— "İstanbul." *Encyclopaedia of Islam.* 2d ed., 4:224–248.

—— *The Ottoman Empire: Conquest, Organization and Economy.* London, 1978.

—— *The Ottoman Empire: The Classical Age 1300–1600.* Tr. Norman Itzkowitz and Colin Imber. New York, 1973.

Issawi, Charles. "Europe, the Middle East and the Shift in Power: Reflections on a Theme by Marshall Hodgson." *Comparative Studies in Society and History* (1980), 22:487–504.

—— "The Transformation of the Economic Position of the *Millets* in the Nineteenth Century." In Benjamin Braude and Bernard Lewis, eds., *Christians and Jews in the Ottoman Empire,* 1:161–185. New York, 1982.

Issawi, Charles, ed. *The Economic History of the Middle East 1800–1914: A Book of Readings.* Chicago, 1966.

Itzkowitz, Norman. *Ottoman Empire and Islamic Tradition.* Chicago, 1980.

al-Jabiri, Majd al-Din. *Bayan li ᵓl-raᵓy al-ᶜamm al-karim ᶜan qadiyyat miyah Halab wa tatawwuratiha.* Aleppo, n.d.

Jennings, Ronald C. "Loans and Credit in Early Seventeenth Century Ottoman Judicial Records." *Journal of the Economic and Social History of the Orient* (1973), 16:168–216.

Johnson, David B. "The Charity Market: Theory and Practice." In *The Economics of Charity,* pp. 81–106. London, 1973.

al-Jundi, Muhammad Salim. *Taᵓrikh Maᶜarrat al-Nuᶜman.* 3 vols. Damascus, 1963–1967.

Katz, Ruth. "The Singing of Baqqashôt by Aleppo Jews: A Study in Musical Acculturation." *Acta Musicologica* (1968), 40:65–86.

al-Kawakibi, Saᶜd Zaghlul. "al-Hammamat fi Halab ᶜibra ᵓl-taᵓrikh wa ᵓl-adab." *ᶜAdiyyat Halab* (1975), 1:146–181.

al-Kayyali, Sami. "Makhtutat Halab." *Majallat maᶜhad al-makhtutat al-ᶜarabiyya* (1967), 13:211–223.

Khoury, Philip. *Urban Notables and Arab Nationalism.* Cambridge, 1983.

Kurd ᶜAli, Muhammad. *Khitat al-Sham.* 6 vols. Beirut, 1969–1972.

Landau, Jacob M. *Studies in the Arab Theater and Cinema.* Philadelphia, 1958.

Laniado, David. *La-qedoshim asher be-Aram Soba.* Jerusalem, 1951.

Laniado, Ephraim. *Degel mahaneh Ephraim.* Jerusalem, 1901.

Laniado, Raphael Shlomo. *Bet dino shel Shlomo.* Istanbul, 1774.

—— *Kiseh Shlomo.* Jerusalem, 1899.

Lapidus, Ira Marvin. *Muslim Cities in the Later Middle Ages.* Cambridge, Mass., 1967.

—— "Muslim Urban Society in Mamluk Syria." In A. H. Hourani and S. M. Stern, eds., *The Islamic City,* pp. 195–205. Oxford, 1970.

Lecerf, Jean. "ᵓÄᵓila." *Encyclopaedia of Islam.* 2d ed., 1:305–306.

—— "Note sur la famille dans le monde arabe et islamique." *Arabica* (1956), 3:31–60.

Lewis, Bernard. *The Emergence of Modern Turkey.* 2d ed. London, 1968.

Lewis, Norman N. "The Frontier of Settlement in Syria." *International Affairs* (1955), 31:48–60.

—— *Nomads and Settlers in Syria and Jordan, 1800–1980.* Cambridge, 1987.

Lutzky, Alexander. "Ha-Francos be Haleb ve hashpaᶜat ha-capitulatziot ᶜal toshaveiha ha-yehudim." *Zion* (1940), 6:46–79.

al-Maᶜluf, ᶜIsa Effendi Iskandar. "Nukhba min diwan Ibrahim al-Hakim al-Halabi." *al-Mashriq* (1907), 10:833–844, 890–897, 1017–1026, 1110–1120.

Mandaville, Jon E. "Usurious Piety: The Cash Waqf Controversy in the Ottoman Empire." *International Journal of Middle East Studies* (1979), 10:289–308.

Maᶜoz, Moshe. *Ottoman Reform in Syria and Palestine, 1840–1861.* Oxford, 1968.

Marcus, Abraham. "Men, Women and Property: Dealers in Real Estate in Eighteenth-Century Aleppo." *Journal of the Economic and Social History of the Orient* (1983), 26:137–163.

Marcus, Abraham. "Privacy in Eighteenth-Century Aleppo: The Limits of Cultural Ideals." *International Journal of Middle East Studies* (1986), 18:165–183.
—— "Real Property and Society in the Premodern Middle East: A Case Study." In Ann Elizabeth Mayer, ed., *Property, Social Structure and Law in the Modern Middle East*, pp. 109–128. Albany, 1985.
al-Mardini, Jirjis. *Qissat hayah: ayyam min al-hadatha.* Beirut, 1972.
Masson, Paul. *Histoire du commerce français dans le Levant au XVIIe siècle.* Paris, 1896.
—— *Histoire du commerce français dans le Levant au XVIIIe siècle.* Paris, 1911.
Maundrell, Henry. *A Journey from Aleppo to Jerusalem, at Easter 1697.* 7th ed. Oxford, 1749.
Mazloum, S. *L'ancienne canalisation d'eau d'Alep (le qanāyé de Ḥailān).* Beirut, n.d.
Mingana, A. "List of the Turkish Governors and High Judges of Aleppo from the Ottoman Conquest to A.D. 1747." *Bulletin of the John Rylands Library* (1926), 10:515–523.
Monro, Vere. *A Summer Ramble in Syria, with a Tartar Trip from Aleppo to Stamboul.* 2 vols. London, 1835.
Morana, Giovanni Antonio M. *Saggio delli commerciali rapporti dei Veneziani colle ottomane scale di Durazzo ed Albania e con quelle d'Aleppo, Siria e Palestina.* Venice, 1816.
Moser, Reinhard-Johannes. *Die Ikattechnik in Aleppo.* Basel, 1974.
al-Muradi, Muhammad Khalil. ʿArf al-basham fiman waliya fatwa Dimashq al-Sham. Ed. Muhammad Mutiʿ al-Hafiz and ʿAbd al-Hamid Murad. Damascus, 1979.
Myller, Angelicus Maria. *Peregrinus in Jerusalem.* Vienna and Nürnberg, 1735.
Naff, Thomas and Roger Owen, eds., *Studies in Eighteenth Century Islamic History.* Carbondale, Ill., 1977.
New Encyclopaedia Britannica. 15th ed., 1985, s.v. "Oriental sore."
Niebuhr, Carsten. *Travels Through Arabia and Other Countries in the East.* 2 vols. Tr. Robert Heron. Edinburgh, 1792.
Olivier, G. A. *Voyage dans l'Empire Othoman, l'Égypte et la Perse.* Vol. 4. Paris, 1804.
Otter, Jean. *Voyage en Turquie et en Perse.* 2 vols. Paris, 1748.
Owen, Roger. "Introduction: Resources, Population and Wealth." In Thomas Naff and Roger Owen, eds., *Studies in Eighteenth Century Islamic History*, pp. 133–151. Carbondale, Ill., 1977.
—— *The Middle East in the World Economy 1800–1914.* London, 1981.
Pakalın, Mehmet Zeki. *Osmanlı tarih deyimleri ve terimleri sözlüğü.* 2 vols. Istanbul, 1971–1972.
Panzac, Daniel. *La peste dans l'Empire Ottoman 1700–1850.* Leuven, 1985.
Paris, Robert. *Le Levant.* Vol. 5 of Gaston Rambert, ed., *Histoire du commerce de Marseille.* Paris, 1957.
Parsons, Abraham. *Travels in Asia and Africa, Including a Journey from Scanderoon to Aleppo, and Over the Desert to Bagdad and Bussora.* London, 1808.
Paton, A. A. *The Modern Syrians.* London, 1844.
Perry, Charles. *A View of the Levant.* London, 1743.
Pococke, Richard. *Description of the East.* 2 vols. London, 1743–1745.

Polk, William R. "Rural Syria in 1845." *Middle East Journal* (1962), 16:508–514.

Poujoulat, Baptistin. *Voyage dans l'Asie Mineure, en Mésopotamie, à Palmyre, en Syrie, en Palestine et en Égypte.* 2 vols. Paris, 1840–1841.

Qadri Pasha, Muhammad. *Qanun al-ʿadl wa ʾl-insaf li ʾl-qadaʾ ʿala mushkilat al-awqaf.* Cairo, 1902.

Qaraʾli, Bulus. *Ahamm hawadith Halab fi ʾl-nisf al-awwal min al-qarn al-tasiʿ ʿashar.* Cairo, n.d.

—— *al-Suriyyun fi Misr.* Cairo, n.d.

Qasin, Yehuda. *Mahaneh Yehuda.* Livorno, 1803.

Qataya, Salman. *Makhtutat al-tibb wa ʾl-saydala fi ʾl maktabat al-ʿamma bi-Halab.* Aleppo, 1976.

—— "al-Maktabat fi Halab." *ʿAdiyyat Halab* (1976), 2:170–218.

—— *Nusus min khayal al-zill fi Halab.* Damascus, 1977.

—— "al-Tasawir al-zaytiyya fi ʾl-dur al-halabiyya al-qadima." *ʿAdiyyat Halab* (1978–1979), 4–5:103–117.

Qushaqji, Yusuf. *al-Adab al-shaʿbi al-halabi.* Aleppo, 1976.

—— *al-Amthal al-shaʿbiyya al-halabiyya.* 2 vols. Aleppo, 1978–1984.

Rabbath, Antoine, ed. *Documents inédits pour servir à l'histoire du Christianisme en Orient (XVI–XIX siècle).* 2 vols. Paris and Beirut, 1905–1910.

Rafeq, Abdul-Karim. *al-ʿArab wa ʾl-ʿuthmaniyyun 1516–1916.* Damascus, 1974.

—— "Changes in the Relationship Between the Ottoman Central Administration and the Syrian Provinces from the Sixteenth to the Eighteenth Centuries." In Thomas Naff and Roger Owen, eds., *Studies in Eighteenth Century Islamic History,* pp. 53–73. Carbondale, Ill., 1977.

—— "The Impact of Europe on a Traditional Economy: The Case of Damascus, 1840–1870." In Jean-Louis Bacqué-Grammont and Paul Dumont, eds., *Économie et sociétés dans l'Empire Ottoman,* pp. 419–432. Paris, 1983.

—— "The Local Forces in Syria in the Seventeenth and Eighteenth Centuries." In V. J. Parry and M. E. Yapp, eds., *War, Technology and Society in the Middle East,* pp. 277–307. London, 1975.

—— "Mazahir min al-tanzim al-hirafi fi Bilad al-Sham fi ʾl-ʿahd al-ʿuthmani." *Dirasat taʾrikhiyya* (1981), 4:30–62.

—— "The Law-Court Registers of Damascus, with Special Reference to Craft-Corporations During the First Half of the Eighteenth Century." In J. Berque and D. Chevallier, eds., *Les Arabes par leurs archives (XVIe–XXe siècles),* pp. 141–159. Paris, 1976.

—— *The Province of Damascus 1723–1783.* Beirut, 1966.

Raswan, Carl R. "Tribal Areas and Migration Lines of the North Arabian Bedouins." *The Geographical Review* (1930), 20:494–502.

Raymond, André. *Artisans et commerçants au Caire au XVIIIe siècle.* 2 vols. Damascus, 1973–1974.

—— "Le déplacement des tanneries à Alep, au Caire et à Tunis à l'époque ottomane: un 'indicateur' de croissance urbaine." *Revue d'histoire maghrebine* (1977), 7–8:192–200.

—— *The Great Arab Cities in the Sixteenth–Eighteenth Centuries: An Introduction.* New York, 1984.

—— "The Population of Aleppo in the Sixteenth and Seventeenth Centuries

According to Ottoman Census Documents." *International Journal of Middle East Studies* (1984), 16:447–460.

—— "La population du Caire, de Maqrīzī à la *Description de l'Égypte.*" *Bulletin d'études orientales* (1975), 28:201–215.

Reuther, Oscar. "Die Qāᶜa." *Jahrbuch der asiatische Kunst* (1925), 2:205–216.

Rey, Francis. *La protection diplomatique et consulaire dans les échelles du Levant et de Barbarie.* Paris, 1899.

Robinson, George. *Three Years in the East.* 2 vols. London, 1837.

Rodinson, Maxime. *The Arabs.* Chicago, 1981.

—— *Islam and Capitalism.* Tr. Brian Pearce. New York, 1973.

Rofeh, Yosef. "Toldot batey ha-dfus ha-ᶜivriyim be-Livorno." *Tagim* (1971), 2:123–134; (1972), 3–4:132–140.

Rousseau, Jean-Baptiste. *Description du pachalik de Bagdad.* Paris, 1809.

—— *Voyage de Bagdad à Alep (1808).* Ed. Louis Poinssot. Paris, 1899.

Russegger, Joseph. *Reisen in Europa, Asien und Afrika.* 6 vols. Stuttgart, 1841.

Russell, Alexander. *The Natural History of Aleppo.* 2d rev. ed. 2 vols. London, 1794.

Russell, Patrick. "An Account of the Late Earthquakes in Syria." *Philosophical Transactions of the Royal Society of London* (1759–1760), 51:529–534.

—— *A Treatise of the Plague.* London, 1791.

Sabat, Khalil. *Taʾrikh al-tibāᶜa fi ʾl-sharq al-ᶜarabi.* Cairo, 1966.

Sahillioğlu, Halil. "Taghayyur turuq al-tijara wa ʾl-tanafus bayna minaʾay Tarabulus wa ʾl-Iskandarun fi ʾl-qarn al-sabiᶜ ᶜashar." *Majallat al-muʾarrikh al-ᶜarabi* (1979), 11:255–276.

Salname-i Vilayet-i Halep, 1326 A.H.

Sanjian, Avedis K. *The Armenian Communities of Syria Under Ottoman Dominion.* Cambridge, Mass., 1965.

Sarre, Friedrich. "Bemalte Wandverkleidung aus Aleppo." *Berliner Museen* (1920), 41:145–158.

Sassoon, David Solomon. *A History of the Jews in Baghdad.* Letchworth, England, 1949.

—— *Ohel David.* 2 vols. Oxford, 1932.

Sauvaget, Jean. *Alep.* Paris, 1941.

—— "Halab." *Encyclopaedia of Islam.* 2d ed., 3:85–90.

—— "Inventaire des monuments musulmans de la ville d'Alep." *Revue des études islamiques* (1931), 5:59–114.

—— *Les perles choisies d'Ibn ach-Chihna.* Beirut, 1933.

—— *Les trésors d'or de Sibt Ibn al-ᶜAjami.* Beirut, 1950.

Seetzen, U. J. "Mémoire pour servir à la connaissance des tribus arabes en Syrie et dans l'Arabie déserte et Pétrée." *Annales des voyages, de la géographie et de l'histoire* (1809), 8:281–324.

Segur Dupeyron, P. de. "La Syrie et les bédouins sous l'administration turque." *Revue des Deux Mondes* (1855), 9:1270–1301.

Shamir, Shimon. "The Effects of the *Hacc* on the Socio-Economic and Political Structure of Syria in the Eighteenth Century." In *Proceedings of the 27th International Congress of Orientalists, Ann Arbor, Michigan, 1967,* pp. 216–217. Wiesbaden, 1971.

Shamma͑, Eliyahu. *Qorban isheh.* Livorno, 1820.

Shaw, Stanford J. *History of the Ottoman Empire and Modern Turkey.* Vol 1. Cambridge, 1976.

Shaykhu, Louis. "al-Sha͑ir Nasrallah al-Tarabulsi al-Halabi." *al-Mashriq* (1900), 3:397–408.

—— *Shu͑ara͐ al-nasraniyya ba͑d al-islam.* 2d ed. Beirut, 1967.

Sim, Katharine. *Desert Traveller: The Life of Jean Louis Burckhardt.* London, 1969.

Sinjab, Kamil. "Das arabische Wohnhaus des 17. bis 19. Jahrhunderts in Syrien." Dissertation, Technischen Hochschule, Aachen, 1965.

Siwrmeian, Artawazd. *Histoire des cimetières arméniens d'Alep et épitaphes arméniennes.* Aleppo, 1935. (Armenian).

—— *Patmowt͑iwn Halepi Hayots͑ (Histoire des Arméniens d'Alep).* Vol. 3: *1355–1908.* Paris, 1950.

Sobernheim, M. "Ḥalab." *Encyclopaedia of Islam.* 1st ed., 2:227–237.

Sobernheim, M. and E. Mittwoch. "Hebräische Inschriften in der Synagoge von Aleppo." In *Festschrift zum siebzigsten Geburtstage Jakob Guttmanns,* pp. 273–283. Leipzig, 1915.

Sourdel, Dominique. *La description d'Alep d'Ibn Šaddād.* Damascus, 1953.

—— "Esquisse topographique d'Alep intra-muros à l'époque ayyoubide." *Annales archéologiques de Syrie* (1952), 2:109–133.

Steensgaard, Niels. *The Asian Trade Revolution of the Seventeenth Century.* Chicago, 1974.

Tabakoğlu, Ahmet. *Gerileme dönemine girerken osmanlı maliyesi.* Istanbul, 1985.

al-Tabbakh, Muhammad Raghib. *I͑lam al-nubala͐ bi-ta͐rikh Halab al-Shahba͐.* 7 vols. Aleppo, 1923–1926.

Talas, Muhammad As͑ad. *al-Athar al-islamiyya wa ͐l-ta͐rikhiyya fi Halab.* Damascus, 1956.

—— "al-Makhtutat wa-khaza͐iniha fi Halab." *Majallat ma͑had al-makhtutat al-͑arabiyya* (1955), 1:8–36; (1956), 2:246–263.

Taoutel, Ferdinand. "Awliya͐ Halab fi manzumat al-Shaykh Wafa͐." *al-Mashriq* (1940), 38:321–422.

—— "al-Shaykh Muhammad Abu ͐l-Wafa͐ al-Rifa͑i," *al-Mashriq* (1941), 39:164–184.

—— *Watha͐iq ta͐rikhiyya ͑an Halab.* 4 vols. Beirut, 1958–1964.

—— "Watha͐iq ta͐rikhiyya ͑an Halab akhdhan ͑an dafatir al-akhawiyyat wa ghayriha." *al-Mashriq* (1948), 42:215–241, 371–412; (1949), 43:140–160, 297–320, 537–603.

—— "Watha͐iq ta͐rikhiyya ͑an Halab fi ͐l-qarn al-thamin ͑ashar." *al-Mashriq* (1947), 41:249–270.

Tavernier, Jean-Baptiste. *The Six Voyages of John Baptista Tavernier, Baron of Auboune.* London, 1684.

Taylor, Bayard. *The Lands of the Saracens.* New York, 1886.

Teonge, Henry. *The Diary of Henry Teonge.* London, 1927.

Thevenot, Jean de. *The Travels of Monsieur de Thevenot Into the Levant.* London, 1687.

al-Tikriti, ͑Abd al-Rahman. *al-Amthal al-baghdadiyya al-muqarana.* Vol. 4. Baghdad, 1969.

Tott, Baron F. de. *Memoirs of Baron de Tott.* 2 vols. London, 1785.

Tucci, Ugo. *Lettres d'un marchand vénitien Andrea Berengo (1553–1556).* Paris, 1957.

Türk Ansiklopedisi. Ankara, 1970, s.v. "Haleb."

Twair, Kassem. "Die Malereien des Aleppo-Zimmers im Islamischen Museum zu Berlin." *Kunst des Orients* (1969), 6:1–42.

Uzunçarşılı, İsmail Hakkı. *Osmanlı Tarihi.* 2d ed. Vol. 4, part 2. Ankara, 1983.

Volney, C. F. *Voyage en Syrie et en Égypte, pendant les années 1783, 1784 et 1785.* 2 vols. Paris, 1787.

Weulersse, J. "La primauté des cités dans l'économie syrienne." In *Congrès international de géographie, Amsterdam, 1938,* 2:233–239. Leiden, 1938.

Weyl, Jonas. "Les juifs protégés français aux échelles du Levant et en Barbarie." *Revue des études juives* (1886), 12:267–282; (1886), 13:277–294.

Wirth, Eugen. "Damaskus–Aleppo–Beirut: Ein geographischer Vergleich dreier nahöstlicher Städte im Spiegel ihrer sozial und wirtschaftlich tonangebenden Schichten." *Die Erde* (1966), 97:96–137.

—— "Die Ackerebenen Nordostsyriens." *Geographische Zeitschrift* (1964), 52:7–42.

—— *Syrien: Eine geographische Landeskunde.* Darmstadt, 1971.

Witmer-Ferri, H. "La maison bourgeoise arabe du 17e et 18e siècles en Syrie." *Les annales archéologiques de Syrie* (1958–1959), 8–9:101–106.

Wood, Alfred C. *A History of the Levant Company.* New York, 1964.

Ya'ari, Abraham. *Ha-dfus ha-'ivri be-artzot ha-mizrah.* Vol. 1. Jerusalem, 1947.

Index

Arabic personal names are entered by family name where that is known, and otherwise by first name.

Sephardim, 40
serdar, 58
Servants, 48, 51, 54, 55, 66, 117,
158, 159, 160, 161, 204; income
of, 162; live-in, 199; slaves as, 52
Services, *see* Merchants (retail) and
servicemen
Sewage, 298
Shadow play, 235
Shafi'is, 103
al-Shahba', 13
shahbandar, 108
Shahbandar Zadeh, Mustafa Agha,
85
shahhatin, 215
Shahin Bey quarter, 316
Shami, 35, 344*n*30
Shari'a court: and administrative
judges, 108, 114-15; and charitable foundations, 80, 305, 310,
311; as clearinghouse for public
appointments, 70, 80, 173, 303;
deputy judges in, 57, 82, 106,
112; and employees' rights, 178-
79, 182; and fair market price,
172, 189; functions and organization, 10-11, 80, 103, 106-7; and
guild matters, 166, 167, 173-74;
Jews and, 108-9, 184; judicial procedures and performance, 107,
111-14, 118-19, 335; and lending
at interest, 184-85; location of offices, 284, 288; posts in, 60, 70,
106, 241; responsibility for legal
expenses in, 109; and urban development, 294; *see also* Qadi
Shari'a court records: as a historical
source, 10-11; protective function,
107, 111; religious distinctions
made in, 40, 345*n*4
Shari'a (Islamic) law: characteristics
and scope, 102-3, 105; and economic matters, 156; and family
matters, 202, 203, 204, 207, 208,
209-10; and real property, 188-89;
and revolts, 73, 88-89; and social
inequalities, 38, 53; as source of

institutional stability, 86; and state
legislation, 103, 110; study of,
103, 238, 241, 242, 243; and uses
of space, 282-83, 294-95
al-Shari'atli quarter, 317, 321
Shaykh, *see* Guild headman (shaykh)
Shaykh al-Islam, 344*n*16
shirkat 'inan, 183
Shops, 170, 181, 281, 285-86, 307,
312, 363*n*54; *see also* Markets
shuhud al-hal, 112
shunbul, 128, 357*n*30
Shurayyif, 'Abd al-Wahhab Agha,
68, 72, 137, 209, 358*n*54
Sidon, 124
Sijill, *see* Shari'a court records
Silk, 23, 147, 148-50, 153
Singers, 54, 158, 159
Slaughterers, 171
Slaughterhouse, 171, 262, 281, 286,
379*n*17
Slaves, 48, 52-53, 69, 160, 199, 200;
see also Concubines
Smoking, 221, 224, 227, 230, 232-
33, 235, 264, 268
Snuff, 225, 232
sofer, 108
Songs, *see* Music and musicians
Spices, 148-49, 228
Spinners, 159, 164, 165, 168, 286
Spinning wheel, 163, 180
State law, 103-4, 105, 110, 156
Stone (in building), 13, 33, 291,
292-93
Storytellers, 227, 234, 235
Streets, 32, 33, 282-83, 294; clean-
ing and upkeep, 262-63, 296-98,
335; names, 289, 290, 380*n*29
Subsistence crises: and charity, 123,
129, 218; climatic causes, 123,
124, 131-32, 357*n*36; and crime,
73, 102, 129-30; and disease, 123,
124, 128, 255, 261; duration and
frequency, 125, 356*n*14; and economic conditions, 123, 129, 145,
152; and emigration, 124, 129;
government policies and controls,